ORACLE® *Oracle Press*™

OCP Introduction
to Oracle9*i*:
SQL Exam Guide

Jason Couchman

Tata McGraw-Hill Publishing Company Limited

NEW DELHI

McGraw-Hill Offices

New Delhi New York St Louis San Francisco Auckland Bogotá Caracas
Kuala Lumpur Lisbon London Madrid Mexico City Milan Montreal
San Juan Santiago Singapore Sydney Tokyo Toronto

Tata McGraw-Hill

OCP Introduction to Oracle 9i: SQL Exam Guide

Tata McGraw-Hill Edition 2002

Twelfth reprint 2006
RCZLCRQKRAZBA

Reprinted in India by arrangement with The McGraw-Hill Companies,
Inc., New York

Sales territories: India, Pakistan, Nepal, Bangladesh, Sri Lanka and Bhutan

ISBN 0-07-047420-6

Published by Tata McGraw-Hill Publishing Company Limited,
7 West Patel Nagar, New Delhi 110 008, and printed at
Gopaljee Enterprises, Delhi 110 053

The **McGraw-Hill** Companies

To the victims of the September 11, 2001 terrorist attack

About the Author

Jason S. Couchman is a database consultant and the author of *Oracle8i Certified Professional DBA Certification Exam Guide*, also from Oracle Press. He is a regular presenter on Oracle and OCP at international Oracle user conferences and meetings. His work has been published by *Oracle Magazine*, Harvard Business School Publishing, and Gannett newspapers, among others.

OracleCertified Professional

About the Oracle Certification Exams

The expertise of Oracle database administrators (DBAs) is integral to the success of today's increasingly complex system environments. The best DBAs operate primarily behind the scenes, looking for ways to fine-tune day-to-day performance to prevent unscheduled crises and hours of expensive downtime. They know they stand between optimal performance and a crisis that could bring a company to a standstill. The Oracle Certified Database Administrator Track provides DBAs with tangible evidence of their skills with the Oracle database.

The Oracle Certified Professional (OCP) Program was developed by Oracle to recognize technical professionals who can demonstrate the depth of knowledge and hands-on skills required to maximize Oracle's core products according to a rigorous standard established by Oracle. By earning professional certification, you can translate the impressive knowledge and skill you have worked so hard to accumulate into a tangible credential that can lead to greater job security or more challenging, better-paying opportunities.

Oracle Certified Professionals are eligible to receive use of the Oracle Certified Professional logo and a certificate for framing.

Requirements for Certification

To become an Oracle Certified Database Administrator for the Oracle9*i* track, you must pass four tests. These exams cover knowledge of the essential aspects of the SQL language, Oracle administration, backup and recovery, and performance tuning of systems. The certification process requires that you pass the following four exams:

- Exam 1: Introduction to Oracle9*i*: SQL (1Z0-007)

- Exam 2: Oracle9*i* Database: Fundamentals I (1Z0-031)

- Exam 3: Oracle9*i* Database: Fundamentals II (1Z0-032)

- Exam 4: Oracle9*i* Database: Performance Tuning (1Z0-033)

If you fail a test, you must wait at least 30 days before you retake that exam. You may attempt a particular test up to three times in a twelve-month period.

Recertification

Oracle announces the requirements for upgrading your certification based on the release of new products and upgrades. Oracle will give six months' notice announcing when an exam version is expiring.

Exam Format

The computer-based exams are multiple-choice tests, consisting of 50–65 questions that must be completed in 90–120 minutes.

Acknowledgments

There are many people I would like to thank for their help with writing this book. My first and most heartfelt thanks go to the dedicated readers of my other books who took time out of their busy schedules to send feedback on the book. I have listened to your praise and constructive criticism, and made every effort to correct and amplify my work based on the points you made. Please keep the email coming—it is by far the most effective way to make the book better!

Next, a note of gratitude to the folks at Oracle who made the book possible. Ulrike Schwinn has been a loyal associate, colleague, and friend during my ongoing effort to help 110,000-plus readers get Oracle certified. Thanks also to Oracle University for its feedback and assistance with the overall direction for the OCP DBA track. As always, thanks to the fine folks at Osborne—Scott Rogers, Lisa McClain, Jeremy Judson, and Athena Honore.

This book is dedicated to the memory of countless thousands of people who lost their lives in the tragic and senseless terrorist acts that took place on September 11, 2001. My heartfelt condolences go out to the families and friends of those victims, and my gratitude and thanks also to those hardworking firefighters, police, military, medical, and other personnel who provided relief for their suffering.

Contents

PART II
OCP Oracle9*i* DBA Practice Exams

Preface

y interest in Oracle certification began in 1996 when I read about the Oracle DBA certificate offered by the Chauncey Group. I found it difficult to prepare for that certification exam for two reasons. First, there was an absence of practice questions readily available. Second, preparation for the exam involved reviewing six or seven different manuals and Oracle Press books, none of which were particularly suited to the task. Judging from the response to the proliferation of titles now available in the OCP Exam Guide Series from Oracle Press, it would seem others have had similar experiences.

This book is divided into two units, the first containing preparatory material for the Oracle9i Introduction to SQL exam part of the Oracle9i DBA certification track. The first unit has eight chapters, each containing several discussions that focus on a particular topic or subtopic objective listed by the *Oracle Certified Professional Oracle9i DBA Track Candidate Guide* for the Introduction to SQL exam. (For a complete listing of all the topics tested for this exam, check Chapter 1.) These discussions are followed by a "For Review" section, each listing the three or four most important concepts for you to retain from the discussion. After the review, you'll see two to six exercise questions in exam-based multiple-choice or short-answer format. Following the questions you will find an answer key for those questions, which should help you master the material even more quickly. Thus, with this book you're never more than a few pages away from demonstrating what you've learned about Oracle SQL for the OCP exam.

At the end of each chapter, you will find a short summary of what was covered in the chapter, followed by a Two-Minute Drill. The Two-Minute Drill contains another bulleted list of fast facts to review, or crib notes for the days leading up to your OCP exam. The chapters conclude with 5 to 20 short-answer and exam-based multiple-choice questions designed to help you further test your understanding of the materials you learned in the chapter.

The second unit consists of one chapter containing three full-length practice exams. Each test contains exam-based multiple-choice and scenario-based questions that are designed to help you strengthen your test-taking skills for the OCP exams. You will also find answers and in-depth explanations for the questions in the back of the chapter, along with a reference back to the exam topic and subtopic objectives from the *OCP Candidate Guide*. This feature should help you determine with pinpoint accuracy the areas in which you need further improvement.

Finally, a note about updates and errata: Because OCP covers such vast ground in a short time, this has become a living text. If you feel you have encountered difficulties due to errors, you can either check out **www.exampilot.com** to find the latest errata, or send me an email directly at **jcouchman@mindspring.com**.

Good luck!

Introduction

he Oracle Certified Professional DBA certification exam series from Oracle Corporation is a great opportunity for you to demonstrate your expertise on the use of Oracle database software. Called OCP, the exam series represents the culmination of many peoples' requests for objective standards in Oracle database administration, one of the hottest markets in the software field. The presence of OCP on the market indicates an important reality about Oracle as a career path. Oracle is mature, robust, and stable for enterprise-wide information management. However, corporations facing a severe shortage of qualified Oracle professionals need a measurement for Oracle expertise.

The OCP certification core track for database administrators (DBAs) consists of four tests in the following areas of Oracle9i: Structured Query Language (SQL), database administration fundamentals I and II, and tuning, with the current content of those exams covering Oracle through Oracle9i. As of this printing, each test consists of about 60 multiple-choice questions pertaining to the recommended usage of Oracle databases. You have about 90 minutes to take each exam. Obtaining certification for Oracle9i through the core track is contingent on taking and passing *all* core examinations. This book will help you prepare for the first exam in the DBA track.

Why Get Certified?

If you are already an Oracle professional, you may wonder, "Why should I get certified?" Perhaps you have a successful career as an Oracle DBA or developer, enjoying the instant prestige your resume gets with that one magic word on it. With market forces currently in your favor, you're right to wonder. But, although no one is saying you don't know Oracle when you put the magic word on your resume, can you prove how well you *do* know Oracle without undergoing a technical interview? I started asking myself that question when Oracle certification began to emerge. I was surprised to find out that after years of using Oracle, developing Oracle applications, and administering Oracle databases for Fortune 500 companies, there were a lot of things about Oracle I *didn't* know. And the only reason I know them now is because I took the time and effort to become certified.

If you're looking for another reason to become certified in Oracle, consider the computer professionals with Novell NetWare experience in the late 1980s and early 1990s. Back then, it seemed that anyone with even a little experience in Novell could count on a fantastic job offer. Then Novell introduced its Certified NetWare Engineer/Certified NetWare Administrator (CNE/CNA) programs. At first, employers were okay with hiring Novell professionals whether they had a certificate or not. As time went on, however, employers no longer asked for computer professionals with Novell NetWare *experience*; they asked for CNEs and CNAs. A similar phenomenon can be seen in the arena of Microsoft Windows NT, where the Microsoft Certified Systems Engineer (MCSE) exam has already become the standard by which those professionals are measuring their skills. Furthermore, with the latest economic downturn in the technology-driven U.S. economy comes the possibility of involuntary IT job changes. If you want to stay competitive in the field of Oracle database administration or development through those changes, your real question shouldn't be *whether* you should become certified, but *when*.

If you are not in the field of Oracle development or database management, or if you want to advance your career using Oracle products, there has never been a better time to do so. OCP is already altering the playing field for DBAs and developers by changing the focus of the Oracle skill set from "How many years have you used it?" to "Do you know *how* to use it?" That shift benefits organizations using Oracle as much as it benefits the professionals who use Oracle because the emphasis is on *skills*, not attrition.

Managers who are faced with the task of hiring Oracle professionals can breathe a sigh of relief with the debut of OCP as well. By seeking professionals who are certified, managers can spend less time trying to determine if the candidate possesses the Oracle skills for the job, and more time assessing the candidate's work habits and compatibility with the team.

TIP
*You can find the exam objectives of the OCP exam
on SQL at the beginning of Chapter 1.*

How Should You
Prepare for the Exam?

If you spend your free time studying things like the maximum number of nested
subqueries permitted in SQL, you are probably ready to take the OCP Oracle9*i* SQL
exam now. For the rest of us, Oracle and other companies offer classroom- and
computer-based training options to learn Oracle. Now users have another option—
this book! By selecting this book, you demonstrate two excellent characteristics: that
you are committed to a superior career using Oracle products, and that you care
about preparing for the exam correctly and thoroughly. And by the way, the
maximum number of subqueries permitted in SQL is 255, and it is on the OCP
Oracle9*i* SQL exam. That fact, along with thousands of others, is covered
extensively in this book to help you prepare for, and pass, the OCP Oracle9*i* SQL
exam.

DBA Certification Past and Present

Oracle certification started in the mid-1990s with the involvement of the Chauncey
Group International, a division of the Educational Testing Service. With the help of
many Oracle DBAs, Chauncey put together an objective, fact-based, and scenario-
based examination on Oracle database administration. This test did an excellent job
of measuring knowledge of Oracle7, versions 7.0 to 7.2. Consisting of 60 questions,
Chauncey's exam covered several different topic areas, including backup and
recovery, security, administration, and performance tuning, all in one test.

Oracle Corporation has taken DBA certification ahead with the advent of OCP.
Their certification examination is actually five tests, each consisting of about 60
questions. By quintupling the number of questions you must answer, Oracle requires
that you have an unprecedented depth of knowledge in Oracle database
administration. Oracle has also committed to including scenario-based questions on
the OCP examinations, and preparation material for these new questions is included
in this book as well. Scenario-based questions require you to not only know the
facts about Oracle, but also understand how to apply those facts in real-life
situations.

Oracle's final contribution to the area of Oracle certification is a commitment to reviewing and updating the material presented in the certification exams. Oracle-certified DBAs will be required to maintain their certification by retaking the certification exams periodically—meaning that those who certify will stay on the cutting edge of the Oracle database better than those who do not.

The Next Steps

Next, we'll cover the test interface you will encounter on exam day. Figure I-1 contains a diagram of the actual test graphical user interface (GUI). Let's delve into an explanation of the interface. The top of the interface tells you how much time has elapsed and the number of questions you have answered. You can use the checkbox in the upper left-hand corner of the interface to mark questions you would like to review later. In the main window of the interface you'll find the actual exam question, along with the choices. Generally, the interface enables the user to select only one answer (unless the question specifically directs you to select more answers). In this case, the interface will enable you to select only as many answers as the question requests. After answering a question, or marking the question for later review, the candidate can move onto the next question by clicking the appropriate button in the lower left-hand corner. To return to the previous question on the OCP exam, hit the next button over to the left. You can exit your exam at any time by pressing the exit button on the bottom right-hand side. The final point feature to cover is the exhibit button. In some cases, you may require the use of an exhibit to answer a question. If the question does not require the use of an exhibit, the button will be grayed out. An exhibit can take the form of a graphic, table listing, or some other meaningful piece of information from the Oracle database you must use as the basis for answering the question.

When you've completed all questions on the exam, the Sylvan Prometric interface will display a listing of all the answers you selected, shown in Figure I-2. The questions you marked for later review will be highlighted, and the interface will guide you through a review of all those questions you marked. You can review individual questions or simply have Sylvan Prometric grade your exam.

The assessment test indicates your performance by means of a grade window, such as the one displayed in Figure I-3. It details the number of questions you answered correctly, along with your percentage score based on 100 percent. You will be shown a section-by-section breakdown of how you did according to the topics covered on the exam as published in the *OCP DBA Candidate Guide* from Oracle. Finally, a bar graph indicates where your performance falls in comparison to the maximum score possible on the exam. The OCP exam reports your score immediately after you exit the exam, so you will know right then whether you passed or not in a similar fashion as the assessment test. Both interfaces offer you the ability to print a report of your score.

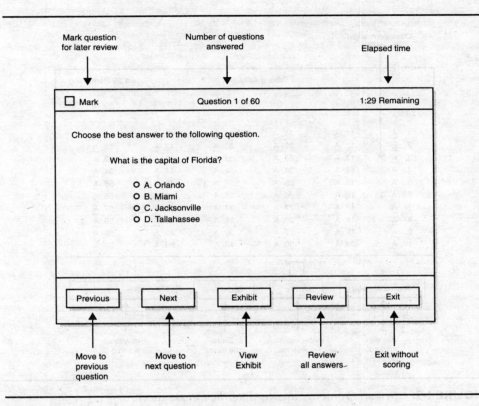

FIGURE I-1. *Sylvan Prometric exam interface illustration*

Strategies for Improving Your Score

When OCP exams were first released, the score range for each OCP exam was between 200 and 800. However, Oracle has vacillated on whether to scale the OCP exam score and has experimented lately with reporting only a raw score of the number of questions you answered correctly. However, the bottom line is still the same. Because an OCP exam typically contains 60 questions, you want to make sure you get at least 75 percent, or 45 of the questions right, in order to pass. Given the recent use of questions with two or even three correct answers on OCP exams, you need to be careful to select *all* correct answer choices on a question or you may not get full credit for a correct answer. *There is no penalty for wrong answers.*

The rest of this section covers some preliminary items for taking the OCP exams. The first tip is, *don't wait until you're the world's foremost authority on Oracle to take the OCP exam.* If your OCP exam is scaled as it was when the exams were first

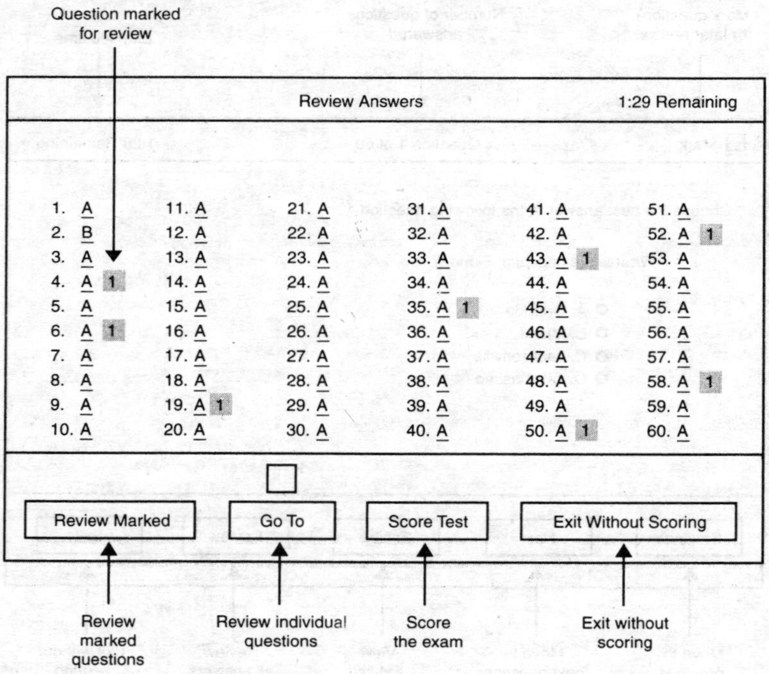

Question marked
for review

Review Answers					1:29 Remaining

1. A	11. A	21. A	31. A	41. A	51. A					
2. B	12. A	22. A	32. A	42. A	52. A 1					
3. A	13. A	23. A	33. A	43. A 1	53. A					
4. A 1	14. A	24. A	34. A	44. A	54. A					
5. A	15. A	25. A	35. A 1	45. A	55. A					
6. A 1	16. A	26. A	36. A	46. A	56. A					
7. A	17. A	27. A	37. A	47. A	57. A					
8. A	18. A	28. A	38. A	48. A 1	58. A 1					
9. A	19. A 1	29. A	39. A	49. A	59. A					
10. A	20. A	30. A	40. A	50. A 1	60. A					

Review Marked	Go To	Score Test	Exit Without Scoring

Review
marked
questions

Review individual
questions

Score
the exam

Exit without
scoring

FIGURE I-2. *Sylvan Prometric answer interface illustration*

released, the passing score for most exams is approximately 650. You have to get 45 to 50 questions right, or about 75 to 80 percent of the exam. So, if you are getting about four questions right out of five on the assessment test or in the chapters (more on chapter format in a minute), you should consider taking the OCP exam. Remember, you're certified if you pass with 77 or 96 percent of the correct answers.

The second tip is, *if you can't answer the question within 30 seconds, mark it with the checkbox in the upper left-hand corner of the OCP interface for review later.* The most significant difference between the OCP interface and the assessment test interface is a special screen appearing after you answer all the questions. This screen displays all your answers, along with a special indicator next to the questions you marked for review. This screen also offers a button for you to click in order to review the questions you marked. You should use this feature extensively. If you spend only 30 seconds answering each question in your first pass on the exam, you will have at least an hour to review the questions you're unsure of, with the added bonus of knowing you answered all the questions that were easiest to you first.

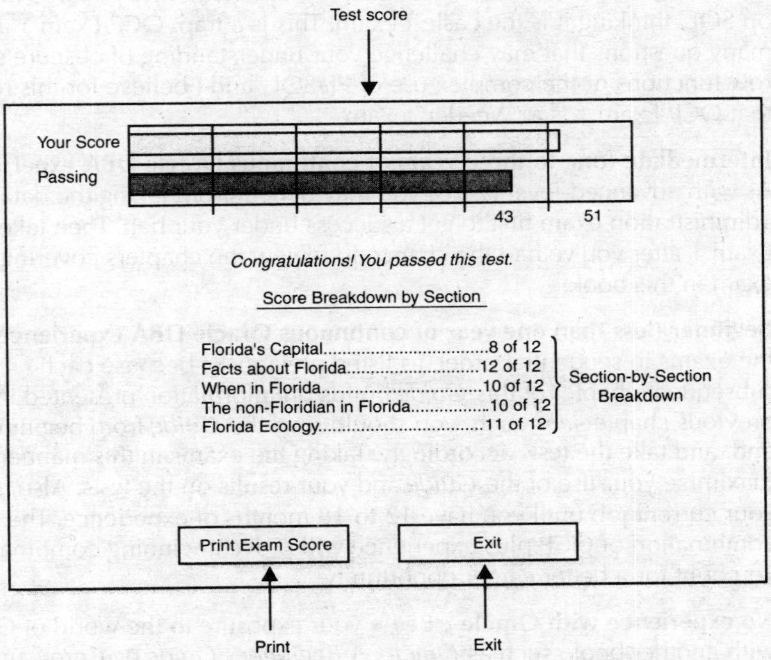

Test score

Your Score

Passing

43   51

Congratulations! You passed this test.

Score Breakdown by Section

Florida's Capital...................................8 of 12
Facts about Florida............................12 of 12
When in Florida..................................10 of 12
The non-Floridian in Florida.................10 of 12
Florida Ecology....................................11 of 12

Section-by-Section
Breakdown

Print Exam Score   Exit

Print   Exit

FIGURE I-3.   *Sylvan Prometric score interface illustration*

Third, as stated previously, *there is no penalty for guessing.* If you answer the question correctly, your score goes up; if not, your score does not change. If you can eliminate any choices on a question, you should take the chance in the interest of improving your score. In some questions, the OCP exam requires you to specify two or even three choices. This can work in your favor, meaning you need to eliminate fewer choices to get the question right.

OCP for the Experienced DBA

Here are some tailor-made notes on taking OCP exams for users with specific levels of expertise:

- **Advanced (three to five years of continuous Oracle DBA experience)**
  Take the database administration exam first, and then take the exams in any order you want. This is especially recommended for readers who are more experienced with database administration because chances are, you will do

well on the matters tested in that exam. Many test takers go for OCP Exam 1 on SQL, thinking it is the easiest exam. This is a trap. OCP Exam 1 asks many questions that may challenge your understanding of obscure single-row functions or the complex use of PL/SQL, and I believe for this reason that OCP Exam 1 is a "weeder" exam.

■ **Intermediate (one to three years of continuous Oracle DBA experience)** As with advanced-level DBAs, you may benefit from taking the database administration exam first to get a success under your belt. Then take OCP Exam 1 after you've had the chance to review the chapters covering that exam in this book.

■ **Beginner (less than one year of continuous Oracle DBA experience)** Take the exams in sequential order, as listed previously, because each subsequent chapter of this *Guide* builds on information presented in the previous chapters. As such, you should read the *Guide* from beginning to end, and take the tests accordingly. Taking the exams in this manner will maximize your use of the *Guide* and your results on the tests. Also, stay in your current job until you have 12 to 18 months of experience. The combination of OCP plus experience will prove a winning combination as you hunt for a better career opportunity.

■ **No experience with Oracle** Begin your exposure to the world of Oracle with another book, such as *Oracle: A Beginner's Guide* by Corey and Abbey, also from Oracle Press. Then use this book to prepare for taking the exams in sequential order as listed previously because each subsequent chapter of this *Guide* builds on information presented in the previous chapters. As such, you should read the *Guide* from beginning to end and take the tests accordingly. Taking the exams in this manner will maximize your use of the *Guide* and your results on the tests. However, don't be surprised if your job search still takes awhile. Most employers want to see at least six months of experience plus certification. If you're having trouble gaining experience, try sending me an email for some tailor-made advice.

A Note About Updates and Errata

If you have comments about the book or would like to contact me about it, please do so by email at **jcouchman@mindspring.com**. You can also find related information such as posted updates, corrections, and amplifications at **www.exampilot.com**. Check back on this site and email me often, as new issues arise all the time in the pursuit of OCP. Plus, I love hearing about OCP success stories—especially yours!

PART
I

Preparing for OCP
DBA Exam 1:
Introduction to SQL

Part I

Oracle9*i* Introduction to SQL Exam Objectives

The first exam in the OCP DBA and Developer tracks covers fundamental usage of the SQL programming language for interacting with the Oracle9*i* database. The following list identifies all OCP objectives for this exam as of this printing. This information comes from the OCP Candidate Guide published for this exam by Oracle Corporation. This candidate guide is online at www.oracle.com/education/certification:

1. Writing Basic SQL `Select` Statements
   1.1 List capabilities of SQL `select` statements
   1.2 Execute a basic `select` statement
   1.3 Differentiate between SQL and SQL*Plus commands

2. Restricting and Sorting Data
   2.1 Limit the rows retrieved by a query
   2.2 Sort the rows retrieved by a query

3. Single-Row Functions
   3.1 Describe various types of functions available in SQL
   3.2 Use character, number, and date functions in select statements
   3.3 Use conversion functions

4. Displaying Data from Multiple Tables
   4.1 Write `select` statements to access data from more than one table using equality and nonequality joins
   4.2 View data that generally does not meet a join condition by using outer joins
   4.3 Join a table to itself using a self-join

5. Aggregating Data Using Group Functions
   5.1 Identify the available group functions
   5.2 Use group functions
   5.3 Group data using the `group by` clause
   5.4 Include or exclude grouped rows using the `having` clause

6. Subqueries
   6.1 Describe the types of problems that subqueries can solve
   6.2 Define subqueries

CHAPTER
1

Overview of Oracle
Databases

n this chapter, you will learn about and demonstrate knowledge in the following areas:

- Overview of Oracle databases
- Selecting data from Oracle

The first exam in the OCP series covers your understanding of basic areas of database usage and design. Every Oracle user, developer, and DBA should have complete mastery in these areas before moving into other test areas. This unit assumes little or no prior knowledge of Oracle on your part in order to help you go from never having used Oracle to having enough expertise in the Oracle server product to maintain and enhance existing applications and develop small new ones. This chapter will introduce Oracle and cover the basic aspects of data retrieval from the Oracle database.

This chapter covers material comprising approximately 8 percent of the test content of OCP Exam 1.

Try Following along on Your Own Database!   As we move through the chapter, you will see examples of SQL statements issued on an Oracle database. For the most part, you can follow along with most of these examples on your own working database if you want. If the following instructions below look like a foreign language to you, show this page to your Oracle DBA and ask for his or her help:

1. On the command line of your machine hosting Oracle, change the directory to $ORACLE_HOME/rdbms/admin.

2. Log into Oracle as a privileged user, such as SYSTEM, who is allowed to create other users.

3. Issue the command @utlsampl.sql. This command runs the utlsampl.sql script, which creates objects owned by the user SCOTT/TIGER that we will use in the examples throughout the rest of the book.

4. If you're more experienced with Oracle and want to specify your own username and password instead of using SCOTT/TIGER, you can run the demobld.sql script found in $ORACLE_HOME/sqlplus/demo while logged into Oracle as a user other than SCOTT.

TIP
Some of the more trivial examples in the chapter may use tables not created by utlsampl.sql. These examples are noted in the text. No script is available for creating those examples. If you want to

*use these tables, you have to create them yourself.
Instructions for creating tables appear in Chapter 5.*

Overview of Oracle

This section covers the following topics as an overview of the Oracle database:

- Theoretical and physical aspects of relational databases
- Oracle's RDBMS and ORDBMS implementations
- Usage and benefits of PL/SQL

Welcome to the world of Oracle databases. Although this section is not associated with an official exam objective, it covers a great deal of the introductory material you may find helpful in order to get started with Oracle in preparation for using query operations to obtain data from the database. Many readers who have never used Oracle before find this material helpful in order to get the big picture of Oracle software before digging into the nitty-gritty. If you're one of those readers, then read on! Even if you're already a whiz at using Oracle SQL, you still might want to skim the material in this discussion before moving on, especially if you've never had an overview of Oracle software before. We'll first talk about several basic aspects regarding theoretical and physical aspects of relational databases, as well as Oracle's RDBMS and ORDBMS implementations. The use and benefits of PL/SQL— Oracle's own language for developing database applications that are stored and executed directly inside the Oracle database—will be explained as well.

Theoretical and Physical Aspects of Relational Databases

Oracle finds its roots in relational database theory, as conceived by E. F. Codd in the 1950s, and extends those theories into an infinite variety of directions, such as data warehousing, online transaction processing, and Web-enabled applications. Undoubtedly, the popularity of this software is part of the reason you are reading this book. This book has the answers to your questions about what an Oracle database is, how it works, and what you can do with it, all of which you'll need to know in order to pass the Introduction to SQL exam.

Software-development companies have taken many different approaches to information management. In years gone by, the more popular software packages for data storage and retrieval focused on flat-file systems as the storage means of choice while simultaneously requiring you to define how information is stored and retrieved, using a programming language such as COBOL. Some early breeds of flat-file systems included hierarchical storage systems, where data records were stored in a hierarchy similar to the hierarchical directory structure you might see on your PC's hard drive in Windows Explorer. These applications ran on mainframes, and brand names of these older data-management packages included IMS from IBM and IDMS from Computer Associates. The language most often used to develop mechanisms to add or manage data in those systems was COBOL.

Those older flat-file systems were great for certain tasks, such as defining parent/child relationships. A parent/child relationship might include the relationship of salespeople within a food service distribution company to the company's customers. Another parent/child relationship might be the tracking number for an invoice as it relates to product line items on the customer's order from that food service distribution company. However, one drawback to flat-file systems stems from the fact that a parent/child relationship cannot model every possible type of data relationship. Within the food service company example, a customer's order may list many different products. Each of those products themselves will probably appear on many different orders. In this case of a "many products to many orders" relationship, which way should the hierarchy be designed? What should be the parent and what should be the child? The usual solution was to create two separate hierarchies—one with product as parent, the other with order as parent. Unfortunately, this often meant maintaining much of the same information in two (or more) places, creating redundant data. Keeping data content consistent across multiple places where it is kept makes storage and retrieval complex. Another shortcoming of hierarchical databases using flat-file systems is that they are not easily adaptable to changing business needs. If the food service distributor creates a new sales system that calls for joint ownership of customer accounts by multiple salespeople, the hierarchical database needs to be redesigned.

Motivated by dissatisfaction with the cumbersome characteristics of hierarchical flat-file databases, E. F. Codd, a computer scientist working for IBM in the 1950s, developed an alternative: the *relational* model. Instead of storing data in hierarchies, Codd proposed storing related data items, such as control numbers and ordered products, in tables. If the tables were designed according to a few simple principles, they were both intuitive and extremely efficient in storing data, as Codd discovered. A single data item could be stored in only one place. Over time, many software makers recognized the significance of Codd's work and began developing products that adhered to Codd's model. Since the 1980s, virtually all database software products (including Oracle's) conform to the relational model.

Central to the success of the relational model is the use of a relational database management system, or *RDBMS*, for storing, retrieving, and manipulating data in a database. Earlier products required organizations to have many COBOL programmers on staff to code mechanisms for managing data-retrieval routines that interact directly with the files of the database. In contrast, the RDBMS handles these tasks automatically using a functional programming language called *SQL* (pronounced either *sequel* or as the letters spelled out). SQL stands for *structured query language,* and it allows users to request the data they want according to strict comparison criteria. For example, if we wanted to look at an employee ID number and salary information for an employee named SMITH, the following code block shows a SQL statement that would help us do so:

```
SQL> SELECT EMPNO, ENAME, SAL FROM EMP
  2  WHERE ENAME = 'SMITH';
```

TIP
The preceding block was taken directly from SQL*Plus, a tool Oracle provides for interacting with the Oracle database. The "2," which indicates that you are typing in the second line, is written automatically by SQL*Plus. As such, you do not actually need to type "2" yourself. For now, don't worry about what this SQL statement actually does or what the results would be, just understand that it is an example of a SQL statement.

Behind the scenes, an RDBMS translates this statement into a series of operations that retrieve the actual data from a file somewhere on the machine hosting your database. This step is called *parsing.* After parsing is complete, the RDBMS executes the series of operations to complete the requested action. That series of operations may involve some or all of the following tasks, listed below in no particular order:

- Implicit datatype conversion
- Index lookups (if appropriate) for faster response time
- Disk reads or disk writes
- Filtering table data according to search criteria
- Sorting and formatting data returned

TIP
An index is a special database object that can be used to enhance performance of certain RDBMS operations. A datatype is literally a definition of the type of data being stored in the table's column. You'll learn more about both these topics in later chapters.

RDBMS vs. Flat-File System Quick Reference

Table 1-1 shows a quick comparison of flat-file systems to relational database management systems.

For Review

1. Understand the tasks an RDBMS completes behind the scenes when users request certain pieces of data.

2. Be sure you can describe the features, advantages, and disadvantages of flat-file systems and relational database management systems.

Exercises

1. **You are exploring theoretical aspects of the Oracle RDBMS. Which of the following choices identifies an aspect of data management that the Oracle RDBMS does not handle on your behalf?**

   A. Datatype conversion

   B. Disk reads

   C. Sorting and formatting return data

   D. Defining required information via SQL

2. **You are evaluating the use of Oracle to replace legacy pre-relational systems in your organization. In comparison to the Oracle RDBMS, which of the following aspects of prerelational database systems did those systems handle as well as their relational counterpart?**

   A. Many-to-many data relationships

   B. Parent-child relationships

   C. Adaptability to changing business needs

   D. Data manipulation

3. **What is the name of the scientist who first conceptualized the use of relational database management systems?** _____

Answer Key

1. D 2. B 3. E. F. Codd

Task	FlatFile System	RDBMS
Handles parent/child data relationships?	Yes	Yes
Handles other types of data relationships?	Not well	Yes
Handles data manipulation easily?	No	Yes
Easily adaptable to changing business needs?	No	Yes
Handles data retrieval easily?	Sometimes	Yes
Handles data retrieval quickly?	Sometimes	Sometimes

TABLE 1-1.   *Comparing Relational Databases to Other Data Management Systems*

Oracle's RDBMS and ORDBMS Implementations

Although every relational database offers an RDBMS that accepts basically the same types of SQL statements, not all databases have the same components. An Oracle database is considerably more complicated than some other PC-based databases you may have seen, such as Microsoft Access or even SQL Server. The components of an Oracle database are broken into three basic areas, corresponding to the three basic areas of host machines that run Oracle databases. In this section, pay close attention to how each component in each part of the Oracle database interacts with a component in another part. Figure 1-1 illustrates the various elements of the Oracle database, which are tested thoroughly on OCP Database Administration Fundamentals I exam (1Z0-022). The components are as follows:

- **Memory**   The Oracle System Global Area (SGA), sometimes also called the Shared Global area because this allocation of memory is shared between all users of the Oracle database.

- **Disk**   Oracle datafiles, redo logs, control files, password files, and parameter files. These files contain the stored data of the Oracle database.

- **Processes**   Threads in the `oracle.exe` background process (Windows) or individual processes (UNIX) and the server process. These processes do all the behind-the-scenes work to keep the Oracle database functioning properly.

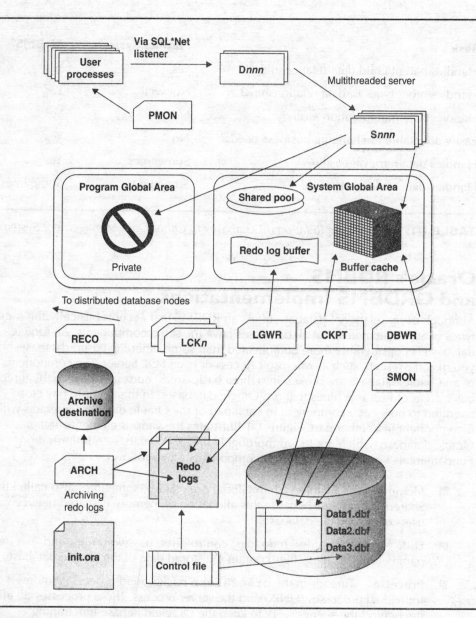

FIGURE 1-1. *Oracle server architecture*

Oracle SGA

Oracle's memory component, the SGA, consists of several elements, each of which is designed for a specific purpose.

Buffer Cache   The buffer cache stores Oracle data in memory for users to view or change. In this way, users never make changes directly to disk files. Instead, Oracle reads the appropriate data into memory for the user process to change, and it writes the changes back to disk at some point later. The buffer cache follows a modified least-recently used (LRU) algorithm to determine when data in this area can be eliminated when more space is needed in the buffer cache to make room for user data requested. The information in the buffer cache is shared among all concurrent users connected to the Oracle database.

Log Buffer   The log buffer stores special information called *redo*, which helps Oracle reconstruct data changes in the event of a system failure. Redo information is written to the log buffer by users making data changes and is stored in the log buffer until Oracle can write the redo information to disk.

Shared Pool   The shared pool stores many items that are "mission critical" to the operation of your Oracle database. Components of the shared pool include the library cache, for storing parsed SQL statements for reuse by other users; the dictionary or row cache, for storing Oracle data dictionary information in memory where it can be accessed quickly; and latches and other database-control mechanisms.

TIP

The Oracle data dictionary is a set of information stored in Oracle that tells you all kinds of important things about your database. The data dictionary is used frequently by users and Oracle processes alike, so it is important for overall database performance to store dictionary information in memory whenever possible. Hence, you can see the need for the dictionary cache in your shared pool.

Large Pool   The fourth and less frequently used component of Oracle's SGA is the large pool, which is a large memory allocation area used to support Oracle backup and restore operations, I/O server processes, and session memory for the shared server. Introduced in Oracle8, this component is optional for Oracle database operation.

Other Memory Areas There are other components to the SGA in Oracle8i and later versions, such as the Java pool and large pool, that are not shown in Figure 1-1. The items not included in this discussion and/or the figure are excluded because a detailed examination of these topics is not necessary for passing the OCP exam on SQL. This figure and the current discussion are merely meant to give you the larger picture of Oracle before digging into a meaningful discussion of SQL queries.

Oracle Disk Components

The Oracle disk components store all kinds of vital information in your Oracle database. You cannot run Oracle without having all your disk components (except password files) in their proper places.

Datafiles This mandatory disk component is used for storing Oracle dictionary and application database objects. These components often grow extremely large in size. Information in the buffer cache and the dictionary cache in memory comes from datafiles on disk. Every Oracle database has at least one datafile (but usually more). Datafiles store Oracle data. If you create a table in Oracle and populate it with rows, Oracle places the table and the rows in a datafile. Each datafile can be associated with only one database.

Redo Logs This mandatory disk component is used for storing redo information on disk. Information from the log buffer in memory eventually gets written here. This component is meant to record all changes made to data in your Oracle database. These logs are critical for recovery of data in the event of a database failure.

Control Files This mandatory disk component is used for storing vital information about the location of Oracle disk components on the host system. The physical locations of both datafiles and redo logs in the server's file system are stored in your control file. There can be one or many control files in an Oracle database. If there is more than one control file, each will be an identical copy. Oracle reads the control files every time you start the database and updates the control files when redo logs or datafiles are added or moved.

Password Files This optional disk component is used for securing privileged user connection information to allow the database to be managed remotely via Enterprise Manager, Oracle's database-management tool. It also controls the number of the privileged system-management connections that can be made to the database at the same time. Without a password file, you may only administer your database by connecting directly to the machine hosting the Oracle database and using management tools such as SQL*Plus directly from the host machine.

Parameter Files   This mandatory disk component is used for configuring how Oracle operates while it is running. To start the database instance, Oracle must read the parameter file to determine what the configuration parameters are for that instance. A parameter file contains many parameters and their set values. Oracle reads the parameter file when you start the database. Some Oracle professionals refer to the parameter file as the `init.ora` file. You may maintain one or many parameter files for a database, corresponding to different instance configurations you may want to implement at various times.

Oracle Server and Background Processes

The final component of Oracle to be covered is the set of elements that comprise Oracle on your host system's CPU. The Oracle server process reads data from datafiles into the buffer cache on behalf of user processes. It can either be shared between multiple users or be dedicated to one user. The Oracle database also has one background process in Windows environments—`oracle.exe`. If you hit CTRL-ALT-DELETE on your system hosting the Oracle database, click the Task Manager button to bring up the Task Manager, and then click on the Processes tab, you will see this process running on your Windows machine. In Windows, this process has many threads that handle other important activities your database is engaged in at all times in the background. If you want to find information in Windows about services setup for use with Oracle software, you can look in Start | Settings | Control Panel. For NT, the Services icon lists all the Windows services available on the machine. For Windows 2000, you can double-click the Administrative Tools icon to find the Services icon. On UNIX machines, Oracle consists of multiple background processes. If the database is running on a UNIX machine, you can usually see its background processes if you issue the command `ps -fu oracle` on your UNIX command line.

What an ORDBMS Is

As object-oriented programming has gained popularity, Oracle has adjusted its relational database-management paradigm to include support for object-relational database design. This methodology incorporates the best features of object programming with the best features of relational programming and allows the developer to draw from both when designing a system in Oracle. Two important features supported on the object side include:

- Permitting users to define the structure of the data they wish to store
- Allowing users to define programmatic methods for manipulating that data and associating those methods directly to the data stored

For Review

Know the three components of the Oracle database, and be able to name each of the elements in each component.

Exercises

1. **You are examining the components of an Oracle database. Which of the following choices identifies an aspect of Oracle that resides on the disk of the machine hosting the Oracle database?**

   A. SGA

   B. Datafile

   C. Background process

   D. Java pool

2. **You are interested in seeing Oracle running on your Windows-based host machine. In which of the following areas would you look?**

   A. Control Panel | Services Icon

   B. Desktop

   C. Windows Explorer

   D. Start Menu

3. **You are interested in seeing Oracle running on your UNIX machine. Which of the following commands might you use?**

   A. ls

   B. grep

   C. ps

   D. df

Answer Key

1. B. 2. A. 3. C.

Usage and Benefits of PL/SQL

How to write programs in PL/SQL is no longer a topic being tested on the OCP Introduction to SQL exam. Nevertheless, it is worth your time as an Oracle professional to know about the existence of PL/SQL and its usage and benefits. PL/SQL is Oracle's own language for developing database applications. In addition to supporting all SQL operations that Oracle SQL supports, PL/SQL adds programming language extensions such as conditional statement processing, loops, variables, cursor operations, abstract datatypes, modularization, encapsulation, overloading, and more. The following bullets list frequently cited reasons why PL/SQL developers use the language:

- *PL/SQL is easy to learn and use.* Professionals with even a modest programming background can usually pick up PL/SQL syntax before too long and develop programs of moderate complexity without much effort. Professionals without a programming background can learn PL/SQL with more effort spent learning basic constructs, such as variable declaration, conditional statement processing, and so on.

- *PL/SQL is stored in the Oracle database, dramatically improving performance.* This means that you only have to compile the code into the Oracle database to make that code available to every user on the system. There is no need for an extended deployment as with traditional client/server applications. The result is code that runs quickly and works natively with your Oracle data.

- *PL/SQL integrates well with the Oracle database.* No special command syntax is needed to perform SQL operations involving data in the Oracle database. No colons, question marks, or other odd characters are required to prefix variables as in other languages. One exception to this rule relates to trigger development, which is a hybrid between a database object and PL/SQL.

- *PL/SQL is especially adept at processing large blocks of data.* Oracle PL/SQL provides a special construct called a `cursor for` loop, which allows you to query several rows of table data and then process through each row of that data in an iterative fashion. This feature allows you to process large amounts of data in bulk.

- *PL/SQL comes with lots of Oracle-supplied code to assist in performing tasks.* Oracle distributes several packages of PL/SQL code with every database shipped. This code enables you to perform highly specialized operations, such as file input/output, or I/O, retrieving Web pages into your database, job scheduling, dynamic SQL, interprocess communication, resource management, and much more. You can refer to these Oracle-supplied packages just like any other PL/SQL program.

■ *PL/SQL supports named and anonymous programs.* There are many different types of named programs you can develop in PL/SQL, including stored procedures, functions, and packages. These code blocks are actually compiled and stored in the database and are available for later use. You can also write anonymous programs, which are compiled at the time you submit the code for execution, executed, but not stored in the database.

■ *PL/SQL can be integrated into database tables via triggers.* Oracle integrates PL/SQL programmatic activity into database tables via triggers. This feature allows you to develop applications that use complex business rules for regulating data inside the database, thus reducing the potential for corrupt or inappropriate data from users.

■ *PL/SQL supports encapsulation and modularization. Encapsulation* involves using one named PL/SQL program to call another named PL/SQL program. *Modularization* involves breaking down a large task into several smaller components and then writing named PL/SQL programs to handle those smaller tasks. The result is code that's easier to read and maintain.

■ *PL/SQL supports overloading. Overloading* occurs when you have a package containing procedures or functions with the same name that accept different variables of different datatypes. When you call the overloaded procedure, Oracle dynamically decides which version of the procedure to use based on the datatype of the variable you pass.

■ *PL/SQL allows programmers to package their Oracle code.* Oracle PL/SQL supports a construct called a *package.* This feature allows you to logically group several procedures or functions that work together into one single construct. Procedures grouped together using packages perform better than they would individually because all procedures in the package will be loaded into memory as soon as one of the procedures is referenced. In contrast, stand-alone procedures are only loaded into memory when called. This reduces the overhead Oracle requires for memory management, thus improving performance.

■ *PL/SQL supports advanced datatypes.* PL/SQL gives users the ability to define abstract datatypes, such as records, allowing you some object-oriented flexibility in your procedural code. PL/SQL also offers table constructs for variable definition and use, approximating the use of arrays. Finally, PL/SQL allows you to declare REF datatypes, which gives PL/SQL the ability to use datatypes similar to pointers in C and C++.

■ *PL/SQL code is portable.* You can write a PL/SQL program on an Oracle database running on Solaris and then move the program to Oracle running on Windows 2000 or some other operating system without rewriting the program.

For Review

Be sure you understand the benefits of PL/SQL programming at a conceptual level as part of the Oracle database. However, OCP Exam 1 no longer tests your knowledge of how to develop PL/SQL applications, so a conceptual level is sufficient at this point.

Exercises

1. **You develop a PL/SQL package for use with Oracle. Which of the following choices identifies where that code is stored?**

   A. As an executable file on the host system

   B. As uncompiled code in the database

   C. As compiled code in the database

   D. As a flat file, sent to the database when you want to run the program

2. **You want to develop a PL/SQL package containing different procedures with the same name but different variable datatypes. What is the name of the PL/SQL feature that allows this?**

   A. Packaging.

   B. Overloading.

   C. Encapsulation.

   D. This functionality is not possible in PL/SQL.

3. **What is the name of the special loop that makes PL/SQL especially adept at processing large numbers of data records?** _____

Answer Key

1. C. 2. B. 3. The cursor for loop.

Writing Basic SQL Statements

This section will cover the following areas related to selecting rows:

- Capabilities of SQL `select` statements
- Executing `select` statements
- Differentiating between SQL and SQL*Plus commands

Now, let's dig in and start your approach to Oracle systems. This section maps directly to objectives on the OCP exam, and in the section you will learn what SQL provides you in the Oracle working environment. You'll also cover how to develop the all-important `select` statement, used for obtaining data from Oracle. You will even learn how to distinguish SQL commands from SQL*Plus commands. This skill becomes increasingly important as you use SQL*Plus for developing and running queries and because there are certain SQL*Plus commands you must know for passing the OCP exam.

Capabilities of SQL `select` Statements

If you've already developed SQL code for other database applications, you're in for some good news. Oracle SQL complies with the industry-accepted standards, such as ANSI SQL92. But before exploring SQL `select` statements in detail, consider the following overview of all the statement categories available in SQL and their associated usage:

- **`select`** Used for data retrieval and query access. Many developers consider this statement to be part of data manipulation language (DML) operations against the database. However, Oracle does not. When OCP refers to DML statements, you should make a mental note that Oracle is not referring to the `select` command.

- **`insert`, `update`, `delete`** Used for DML operations against the Oracle database, including adding new records, changing existing records, and removing records, respectively.

- **`create`, `alter`, `drop`** Used for data definition language (DDL) operations against the Oracle database, including adding, modifying, and removing database objects such as tables, indexes, sequences, and so on, respectively.

- **`commit`, `rollback`, `savepoint`** Used for transaction-control activities inside a user's session, including saving changes, discarding changes, and marking logical breakpoints within the transaction, respectively.

■ **grant**, **revoke**   Used for data control language (DCL) operations against your Oracle database, where you might need to control user access to data.

Getting Started: SQL*Plus

Many developers, designers, DBAs, and power users begin their experience with Oracle using an existing Oracle application in an organization. The first tool many people see for selecting data directly from the Oracle relational database management system is SQL*Plus. When users first start SQL*Plus, in most cases, they must enter their Oracle username and password in order to begin a session with the Oracle database. There are some exceptions to this rule that use the password authentication provided with the operating system. The following example shows how you might begin a session with Oracle on the UNIX command line if the database is present on the UNIX machine you are connected to:

```
$/home/oracle> sqlplus scott/tiger
```

TIP
*From Windows, you can execute the above command at a DOS prompt to run the command-line version of SQL*Plus. Or, you can click on Start | Programs | Oracle ORACLE_HOME | Application Development | SQL*Plus to run the GUI version of SQL*Plus. On most systems, ORACLE_HOME will be replaced with the name of the Oracle software home location, such as OraHome1.*

Alternately, if you want to connect to an Oracle database not present on the machine you are currently connected to, you might issue the `sqlplus` command with a specified database name tacked onto the end of your username and password, as you'll see in the code block following this paragraph. That extra `@orcl` tacked onto the end of your username and password tells the operating system the name of the Oracle database you want to connect to. Here's the example:

```
$/home/oracle> sqlplus scott/tiger@orcl
```

TIP
*For our purposes in this book, we'll assume that the Oracle database you want to connect to is present on the same machine where you'll be running SQL*Plus.*

Whenever you log into Oracle via SQL*Plus, you create a session with the database. A *session* is an interactive runtime environment similar to a command-line environment, such as UNIX or DOS, in which you enter commands to retrieve data. Oracle performs a series of activities to obtain the data you ask for based on the SQL command you enter. The session starts as soon as you log into Oracle, and ends when you log out. Think of it as a conversation, which in turn implies *language*. Remember, you communicate with Oracle using the structured query language, SQL, to obtain the information you need.

TIP
To connect to the database, you must be granted permission to do so—simply having a user ID and password isn't enough. For more information on permissions, see Chapter 8.

SQL is a *functional* programming language, which means that you specify the types of things you want to see happen in terms of the results you want. You define the result you want, and Oracle determines how to get it for you. Take another look at the select statement I showed you earlier:

```
SQL> SELECT EMPNO, ENAME, SAL FROM EMP
  2  WHERE ENAME = 'SMITH';
```

The first point you should understand about SQL statements is that they can be entered across multiple lines. Our statement above contains two lines of keywords and text string expressions. However, notice also that we did not split any keywords across two lines—this is not permitted in Oracle. Finally, SQL statements are not case-sensitive. Thus, the following statement is logically equivalent to the one shown above:

```
SQL> select empno, ename, sal from emp
  2  where ename = 'SMITH';
```

NOTE
While column names, table names, and keywords (such as select, from, *and* where) *are not case-sensitive, text strings like SMITH, appearing in the code sample above in single-quotes, are case-sensitive. This is because Oracle stores the text exactly as you type it, so if you typed SMITH in uppercase when you stored that string in the EMP table, then that is exactly what Oracle stored.*

Sometimes text strings are called literals for this reason—they are literally what you entered.

Now let's look at the content of the SQL statement. This statement asks Oracle to provide data from the EMP table, where the value in a certain column called ENAME equals SMITH. We don't care how Oracle gets it, just as long as Oracle returns only the record from table EMP we asked for. Contrast this approach to other languages you may have heard about or programmed in, such as C++ and COBOL. These languages are often referred to as *procedural* or *iterative* programming languages because the code written in these languages implies an end result by explicitly defining the *process* for obtaining the result. The following block of code from an imaginary procedural programming language similar to C illustrates how the same function may be handled by explicitly defining the means to the end:

```
Include <stdio.h>
Include <string.h>
Include <rdbms.h>

Int *empno;
Char *statement;

Type emp_rec is record (
Int            empno;
Char[10]       emp_name;
Int            sal; )

Void main() {
  login_to_oracle(scott,tiger);
  Access_table(emp);
  Open(statement.memaddr);
  Strcpy("SELECT EMPNO, ENAME, SAL FROM EMP WHERE
        ENAME = 'SMITH'",statement.text);
  parse(statement);
  execute(statement);
  for (I=1,I=statement.results,I+1)
    fetch(statement.result[I],emp_rec);
    printf(emp_rec);

  close(statement.memaddr);
}
```

Of course, this C-like block of code will not compile anywhere but in your imagination, but the point of the example is clear—other languages make you define the process, whereas SQL lets you define the result.

For Review

What is SQL? What is SQL capable of? How does SQL compare to other programming languages you might use, such as Java and C?

Exercises

1. You are determining which type of SQL statement to use in your Oracle database. Which of the following choices identifies the type of statement you would use when trying to obtain data from the database?

   A. select

   B. update

   C. insert

   D. delete

2. Which of the following choices identifies a functional programming language?

   A. C

   B. Java

   C. COBOL

   D. SQL

3. Identify a command that is part of SQL's data control language (DCL).

   _____

4. Identify a command that is part of SQL's data manipulation language (DML). _____

5. Identify a command that is part of SQL's data definition language (DDL).

   _____

Answer Key

1. A. **2.** D. **3.** B. grant or revoke **4.** select, update, delete, or insert Oracle considers the select command to be part of data manipulation language even though it technically doesn't allow you to change the data being stored. **5.** create, alter, drop

Executing `select` Statements

The most common type of SQL statement executed in most database environments is the `select` statement, which queries a table in the database for requested data. Tables in Oracle are similar in concept to spreadsheets (but not necessarily similar to the table in your kitchen!). Examine the following code block, where you see a `select` statement in the context of a session with Oracle:

```
$/home/oracle> sqlplus scott/tiger
SQL*Plus: Release 8.1.7.0.0 - Production on Fri July 06 18:53:11 2001
Copyright (c) Oracle Corporation 1979, 2000.  All rights reserved.
Connected to: Oracle9i Release 9.0.1.0.0
With the partitioning option
JServer Release 9.0.1.0.0 Production
SQL> select * from emp;
```

EMPNO	ENAME	JOB	MGR	HIREDATE	SAL	COMM	DEPTNO
7369	SMITH	CLERK	7902	17-DEC-80	800		20
7499	ALLEN	SALESMAN	7698	20-FEB-81	1600	300	30
7521	WARD	SALESMAN	7698	22-FEB-81	1250	500	30
7566	JONES	MANAGER	7839	02-APR-81	2975		20
7654	MARTIN	SALESMAN	7698	28-SEP-81	1250	1400	30
7698	BLAKE	MANAGER	7839	01-MAY-81	2850		30
7782	CLARK	MANAGER	7839	09-JUN-81	2450		10
7788	SCOTT	ANALYST	7566	19-APR-87	3000		20
7839	KING	PRESIDENT		17-NOV-81	5000		10
7844	TURNER	SALESMAN	7698	08-SEP-81	1500	0	30
7876	ADAMS	CLERK	7788	23-MAY-87	1100		20
7900	JAMES	CLERK	7698	03-DEC-81	950		30
7902	FORD	ANALYST	7566	03-DEC-81	3000		20
7934	MILLER	CLERK	7782	23-JAN-82	1300		10

```
14 rows selected.
```

TIP

The last part of the code block is where Oracle tells you how many rows it obtained from the database table in response to your SQL command. Later code blocks in this book omit that part to conserve space. You can tell SQL*Plus not to display row count information as well using the `set feedback off` command. We'll talk more about SQL*Plus commands later in the chapter.

The first part, containing the copyright information, is a welcome message from SQL*Plus. If you wanted, you could suppress this information in your call to SQL*Plus from the operating system command line by entering `sqlplus -s` and pressing ENTER, where the `-s` extension indicates SQL*Plus should run in silent mode. This is sometimes useful for batch programs that write output to an automated feed file where you don't want a lot of extraneous junk in the feed because an error will result. We'll explore some other SQL*Plus commands that help you control the appearance of your output later in the chapter. The bold line in the block illustrates a simple SQL `select` statement. In essence, you're asking Oracle to return all data from all columns in the EMP table. Oracle replies with the contents of the EMP table. The main components of a `select` statement are listed next, and *both* are required in every `select` statement you issue on the database:

- **The `select`, or *column*, clause**   This clause contains columns or expressions containing data you want to see, separated by commas. The preceding query uses a *wildcard* (*) character, indicating we want data from every column in the table.

- **The `from`, or *table*, clause**   This clause tells Oracle what table to get the data from.

TIP
*Always use a semicolon (;) to end SQL statements when entering them directly into SQL*Plus. You can use a slash(/) in some situations, such as for SQL*Plus batch scripts, but be careful—a slash at the end of a SQL statement already ended with a semicolon makes the statement run twice!*

A Note about Columns and Datatypes

Tables in the Oracle database are comprised of columns, each storing a unit of information for the row. These units taken together across a single row comprise a record stored in the table. Review the first record in the preceding code block for EMPNO 7369, which is listed here:

```
EMPNO ENAME     JOB        MGR HIREDATE   SAL COMM DEPTNO
--------- -------- --------- ----- --------- ---- ---- ------
     7369 SMITH    CLERK     7902 17-DEC-80  800           20
```

Each column identifies an aspect of this unique employee. EMPNO identifies his employee number, ENAME identifies his name, and so on. The information stored in each column of the table for this fellow must correspond to the datatype defined for that column. For example, column EMPNO is defined as a NUMBER column, meaning that only numbers of a certain size can be stored for records in that column. No text, date, or nonnumerical information can be stored in EMPNO, because doing so would violate the column's stated datatype. I'll refer to a column's datatype frequently throughout the rest of the book, so it's worth your time to master this fundamental concept. The column datatypes permitted in Oracle tables that we'll work with most frequently are listed here:

- ■ **NUMBER**   A datatype used for storing numerical data. No dashes, text, or other nonnumerical information are allowed in columns of this datatype.

- ■ **DATE**   A datatype used for storing date information. Internally, Oracle stores dates as numbers, which it can then convert into any DATE format you want. By default, DATE information is displayed in DD-MON-YY format (for example, 25-DEC-79).

- ■ **VARCHAR2**   A datatype used for storing text data. Any text character (including special characters, numbers, dashes, and so on) can be stored in a VARCHAR2 column.

- ■ **CHAR**   A datatype used for storing text data. Any text character (including special characters, numbers, dashes, and so on) can be stored in a CHAR column, padded with spaces so that the text stored in the CHAR column fills the entire length available. Thus, the name SMITH would take up ten spaces in a column declared as CHAR(10), even though the name itself is only five characters long, with the other five characters occupied by blank spaces.

TIP
The main difference between VARCHAR2 and CHAR columns is the amount of space required for storing text data, which is greater for CHAR columns than for VARCHAR2 columns. This is because CHAR columns have a fixed length and always store the same number of bytes, whereas VARCHAR2 has a variable length and only contains the number of bytes you provide it.

Datatypes for storing other types of information exist in Oracle; however, there aren't as many of them as you might encounter in database products from other vendors. For example, Oracle has no currency datatype. Monetary values are treated simply as numbers, and as such they can be stored in a column defined as the NUMBER datatype.

TIP
Another datatype we'll observe from time to time in the book is the ROWID datatype. This is a special datatype used by Oracle to format the information used to display the physical location of the row on disk.

The "Schema" of Things

Take a look at the following code block:

```
SQL> select empno, ename, sal
  2  from scott.emp;
    EMPNO ENAME            SAL
--------- ---------- ---------
     7369 SMITH            800
     7499 ALLEN           1600
     7521 WARD            1250
     7566 JONES           2975
     7654 MARTIN          1250
     7698 BLAKE           2850
     7782 CLARK           2450
     7788 SCOTT           3000
     7839 KING            5000
     7844 TURNER          1500
     7876 ADAMS           1100
     7900 JAMES            950
     7902 FORD            3000
     7934 MILLER          1300
```

Notice anything different about the way table EMP is referenced in this table clause? It has the name of the owner, SCOTT, prefixed to it. Oracle developers and DBAs refer to the concept of referencing the table owner as well as the table itself as a *schema*. If you create a database object such as a table, this object belongs to you. It is part of your schema. The identity you use when you log into your database to run `demobld.sql` determines the schema that all those tables will belong to.

When the table you reference in a query isn't prefixed with the schema it belongs to, Oracle assumes the table exists in your schema and tries to query it. If the table doesn't exist in your schema, you must prefix the table name with the schema information, separating the schema owner from the table name with a period.

TIP
A schema is a logical grouping of database objects based on the user who owns the objects.

Prefixing Columns with Table Names

The same aliasing concept works in the column clause, too—you can prefix the column name with the table name separated by a dot (.) in the table clause for your query. Make sure you understand how to specify a schema owner, the table name, and the column name in a `select` statement in SQL*Plus. The following code block demonstrates the most formal usage for prefixing with appropriate schema and table information:

```
SELECT table_name.column_name, table_name.column_name
FROM schema.table_name;
```

Arithmetic and Table Data

Oracle lets you perform arithmetic operations on your numeric table data as well. The operators used in Oracle are the same as in daily use (+ for addition, − for subtraction, * for multiplication, and / for division). Say, for example, you are performing a simple annual review that involves giving each user a cost-of-living increase in the amount of 8 percent of his or her salary. The process involves multiplying each person's salary by 1.08. Oracle makes the work easy if you use arithmetic expressions, as shown here:

```
SQL> select empno, ename, sal, sal*1.08
  2  from emp;
    EMPNO ENAME           SAL  SAL*1.08
--------- ---------- --------- ---------
     7369 SMITH           800       864
     7499 ALLEN          1600      1728
     7521 WARD           1250      1350
     7566 JONES          2975      3213
     7654 MARTIN         1250      1350
     7698 BLAKE          2850      3078
     7782 CLARK          2450      2646
     7788 SCOTT          3000      3240
     7839 KING           5000      5400
     7844 TURNER         1500      1620
     7876 ADAMS          1100      1188
     7900 JAMES           950      1026
     7902 FORD           3000      3240
     7934 MILLER         1300      1404
```

Operator Precedence

There's usually at least one question on OCP dealing with operator precedence—that high-school math concept regarding which calculation to do first. An easy way to remember operator precedence in mathematics is to use the acronym PEMDAS. You can remember PEMDAS using the mnemonic "Please Excuse My Dear Aunt Sally." PEMDAS stands for parentheses, exponents, multiplication *and* division, addition *and* subtraction. Here are some examples of PEMDAS in action:

- 2 + 6 / 2 equals 5
- (2 + 6) / 2 equals 4
- 2 / 10 + 36 * (84 − 6) is 2808.2
- 2 / 10 + 36 * 84 − 6 is 3018.2.

2 + 2 and the DUAL Table

As mentioned earlier, every `select` statement must have a column clause and a table clause. However, you might not always want to perform arithmetic calculations on data from an actual table. Say, for example, you simply want to add 2 + 2. Conveniently, the column clause in a `select` statement needn't contain actual column names. It can contain fixed numbers or other types of expressions instead. But what about the table clause? Because you're using fixed numbers, you don't want data from a real table. So why not use a fake one? You can use a special table called *DUAL* to fill in the table clause without Oracle actually using its data. Take a look at the following block:

```
SQL> select 2 + 2 from dual;
     2+2
---------
       4
```

The DUAL table consists of one column, called *DUMMY*, containing one value, X. Execute a `select * from DUAL` statement and see for yourself that there is no meaningful data stored here. It simply exists as a SQL construct to support the requirement of a table specification in the `from` clause. The DUAL table is owned by the Oracle built-in user SYS. We can also use the DUAL table in our understanding of schemas. The following example shows you how to obtain the username you used when you logged into Oracle:

```
SQL> select user from dual;
USER
-----
SCOTT
```

Handling NULL Values

Sometimes a query for information produces a nothing result. In database terms, *nothing* is called *NULL*. In set theory, the mathematical foundation for relational databases, NULL represents the value of an empty dataset, or a dataset containing no values. Put another way, NULL is *not* the blank character displayed when you hit the spacebar, nor is it somehow equivalent to zero! NULL is the *absence of information*. Unless specified otherwise, a column in a table is designed to accommodate the placement of nothing into the column. An example of retrieving NULL is listed in the MGR column of the following code block on EMPNO 7839:

```
SQL> select empno, ename, mgr
  2  from emp;
    EMPNO ENAME            MGR
--------- ---------- ---------
     7369 SMITH           7902
     7499 ALLEN           7698
     7521 WARD            7698
     7566 JONES           7839
     7654 MARTIN          7698
     7698 BLAKE           7839
     7782 CLARK           7839
     7788 SCOTT           7566
     7839 KING
     7844 TURNER          7698
     7876 ADAMS           7788
     7900 JAMES           7698
     7902 FORD            7566
     7934 MILLER          7782
```

However, there are times when you may want to substitute a value in place of NULL. Oracle provides this functionality with a special function, called nvl( ). Assume that you do not want to see blank spaces for manager information. Instead, you want the output of the query to contain a zero where a NULL value is listed. The query in the following code block illustrates how you can obtain the desired result:

```
SQL> select empno, ename, nvl(mgr,0)
  2  from emp;
    EMPNO ENAME      NVL(MGR,0)
--------- ---------- ----------
     7369 SMITH            7902
     7499 ALLEN            7698
     7521 WARD             7698
     7566 JONES            7839
```

```
7654 MARTIN          7698
7698 BLAKE           7839
7782 CLARK           7839
7788 SCOTT           7566
7839 KING               0
7844 TURNER          7698
7876 ADAMS           7788
7900 JAMES           7698
7902 FORD            7566
7934 MILLER          7782
```

The basic syntax for nvl( ) is NVL(*column_name*, *value_if_null*). Notice that the column specified in nvl( ) contains an actual value. That value is what Oracle returns; when the column is NULL, the special string is returned. The nvl( ) function can be used on columns of all datatypes, but remember this: *The value specified to be returned if the column value is NULL must be the same datatype as the column specified.*

The distinct Keyword

If you look back at the code block that lists all the employees in the EMP table, you'll notice something interesting in the JOB column. Many of the employees have the same job title. Sometimes, you might have a situation where you want to see only the unique values for a column that you know contains many repeated values. In order to do so, Oracle offers the distinct keyword. To obtain the unique values for a column containing duplicates, you simply precede the column reference with the distinct keyword in your column clause, like this:

```
SQL> select distinct job
  2  from emp;
JOB
---------
ANALYST
CLERK
MANAGER
PRESIDENT
SALESMAN
```

TIP
In order for the distinct keyword to work, it must appear directly after the select keyword in your SQL query.

When more than one column name appears after the distinct keyword in a select statement, then Oracle attempts to identify all the distinct combinations of values in those columns named. Take a look at an example:

```
SQL> select distinct job, empno from emp;
JOB          EMPNO
---------    ---------
ANALYST      7788
ANALYST      7902
CLERK        7369
CLERK        7876
CLERK        7900
CLERK        7934
MANAGER      7566
MANAGER      7698
MANAGER      7782
PRESIDENT    7839
SALESMAN     7499
SALESMAN     7521
SALESMAN     7654
SALESMAN     7844
```

Changing Output Headings with Aliases

In every result set Oracle returns in response to your SQL select commands, Oracle creates headings for each column so that you know what the data is. By default, Oracle reprints the column name exactly as you defined it in the select statement, including functions if there are any. Unfortunately, this method often leaves you with a bad description of the column data. Oracle truncates the expression to fit a certain width corresponding to the datatype of the column returned, making the problem even worse. Fortunately, you can use *aliases* in your column clause to solve this problem. In a column alias, you give the column another name that Oracle uses when the select statement results are displayed. This feature gives you the ability to fit more descriptive names into the space allotted. Here's an example:

```
SQL> select empno, ename, nvl(mgr,0) as mgr
  2  from emp;
    EMPNO ENAME           MGR
--------- ---------- ---------
     7369 SMITH          7902
     7499 ALLEN          7698
     7521 WARD           7698
     7566 JONES          7839
     7654 MARTIN         7698
```

```
7698 BLAKE          7839
7782 CLARK          7839
7788 SCOTT          7566
7839 KING              0
7844 TURNER         7698
7876 ADAMS          7788
7900 JAMES          7698
7902 FORD           7566
7934 MILLER         7782
```

TIP
*You can omit the as keyword in the column alias
and still wind up with substantially the same result.*

Column aliases are useful for adding meaningful headings to output from SQL queries. Aliases can be specified in two ways: either by naming the alias after the column specification separated by a space or by using of the as keyword to mark the alias more clearly. Here's the general rule:

```
SQL> -- SELECT column_name_or_operation alias, ...;
SQL> SELECT nvl(mgr,0) MGR
  2  FROM EMP;
```

or

```
SQL> -- SELECT column_name_or_operation  AS alias, ...;
SQL> SELECT nvl(mgr,0) AS MGR
  2  FROM EMP;
```

You don't need to specify a function in order to use an alias. For example, if you simply wanted to change the column heading for the MGR column to something more descriptive, you could do so using a column alias. The SQL statement might look something like select mgr as "Manager Code" from emp.

Putting Columns Together with Concatenation
You can also glue together column data to produce more interesting or readable output. This is called *concatenation*. The concatenation operator is two pipe characters put together: ||. You can also use the concat ( ) operation, passing it the two column names. In the following example, the ENAME column is concatenated with a text expression and the JOB column using both available methods to produce a meaningful result:

```
SQL> select ename || ', who is the ' ||
  2  concat(job,' for the company')
```

```
  3  as "Name and Role"
  4  from emp;
Name and Role
-------------------------------------------------
SMITH, who is the CLERK for the company
ALLEN, who is the SALESMAN for the company
WARD, who is the SALESMAN for the company
JONES, who is the MANAGER for the company
MARTIN, who is the SALESMAN for the company
BLAKE, who is the MANAGER for the company
CLARK, who is the MANAGER for the company
SCOTT, who is the ANALYST for the company
KING, who is the PRESIDENT for the company
TURNER, who is the SALESMAN for the company
ADAMS, who is the CLERK for the company
JAMES, who is the CLERK for the company
FORD, who is the ANALYST for the company
MILLER, who is the CLERK for the company
```

TIP

*Use column aliases to name your concatenated
column to make the output more readable and
meaningful.*

For Review

1. Understand the two components of `select` statements and what a schema
   is.

2. Know how to perform arithmetic on selected columns and on numeric
   expressions in Oracle and know what the DUAL table is.

3. Know both methods used for concatenating columns and how to define
   column aliases. Also, know what the `distinct` keyword is and how it is
   used.

4. Be able to define what NULL means in the context of Oracle SQL and how
   to use the `nvl ( )` function.

5. Be sure you understand the correct operator precedence using the acronym
   PEMDAS.

Exercises

1. You are identifying a table for use in your `select` clause that was not created by you. Which of the following choices identifies the reference that must be included in your `select` statement so that Oracle knows where to look for the information?

   A. Alias

   B. Schema

   C. Expression

   D. Session

2. Use the following code block to answer this question:

```
SQL> select empno, ename, mgr
  2  from emp;
    EMPNO ENAME          MGR
--------- ---------- ---------
     7369 SMITH         7902
     7499 ALLEN         7698
     7521 WARD          7698
     7566 JONES         7839
     7654 MARTIN        7698
     7698 BLAKE         7839
     7782 CLARK         7839
     7788 SCOTT         7566
     7839 KING
     7844 TURNER        7698
     7876 ADAMS         7788
     7900 JAMES         7698
     7902 FORD          7566
     7934 MILLER        7782
SQL> select empno, ename, nvl(mgr,'none') as mgr
  2  from emp;
```

   Which of the following choices describes what Oracle will return as the output in the MGR column for KING's record from this query?

   A. Oracle returns NULL in the MGR column for KING's record.

   B. Oracle returns MGR in the MGR column for KING's record.

   C. Oracle returns NONE in the MGR column for KING's record.

   D. Oracle returns an error.

3. **You are concatenating information from two columns in an SQL query. Which of the following choices best identifies the special character required for this operation?**

   A. @

   B. #

   C. ||

   D. /

4. **Provide the name of the table containing no meaningful information that can be used to fulfill the table clause requirement for select statements when you perform arithmetic operations on fixed numeric expressions:**

   _____

5. **You may use the contents from the standard EMP table used in this discussion to answer the following question. You are attempting to calculate 20 percent of the salary and commission for all employees of the company. Which of the following SQL statements would be appropriate for the task?**

   A. `select empno, ename, sal/20, comm/20 from emp;`

   B. `select empno, ename, sal*20, comm*20 from emp;`

   C. `select empno, ename, sal/.20, comm/.20 from emp;`

   D. `select empno, ename, sal*.20, comm*.20 from emp;`

6. **You may use the contents of the following code block to answer this question:**

```
SQL> select * from dept;
   DEPTNO DNAME          LOC
--------- -------------- -------------
       10 ACCOUNTING     NEW YORK
       20 RESEARCH       DALLAS
       30 SALES          CHICAGO
       40 OPERATIONS     BOSTON
```

   You issue the following statement in Oracle: select distinct dname, loc from dept. Which of the following choices correctly describes the result Oracle will return?

A. Oracle returns the distinct combinations of values from DNAME and LOC.

B. Oracle returns only three distinct values from DNAME in the DEPT table.

C. Oracle returns only the distinct values from the DEPTNO column.

D. Oracle returns the contents of all four records from the table.

Answer Key
1. B. 2. D. Remember, the datatype in the nvl ( ) function must match the datatype for the column. 3. C. 4. DUAL. 5. D. 6. A.

Differentiating Between SQL and SQL*Plus Commands

Although the SQL*Plus work environment works well when you don't make mistakes, it is unforgiving to the fat-fingered once you have pressed ENTER to move to the next input line. So far, this limitation hasn't presented much difficulty because our queries haven't been long. However, as the queries you write get more and more complicated, you will grow frustrated. SQL*Plus does allow some correction of entered statements with a special command called change, abbreviated as c. Consider the following example, which illustrates this point:

```
SQL> SELECT empno, ename, NVL(mgr,'none') mgr,
  2  hiredate, sal, comm, deptno
  3  FROM EMP;
SELECT empno, ename, NVL(mgr,'none') mgr,
                     *
ERROR at line 1:
ORA-01722: invalid number
SQL> 1
1* SELECT empno, ename, NVL(mgr,'none') mgr,
SQL> c/'none'/0
1* SELECT empno, ename, NVL(mgr,0) mgr,
SQL> /
    EMPNO ENAME      JOB          MGR HIREDATE   SAL COMM DEPTNO
--------- -------- --------- ----- --------- ---- ---- ------
     7369 SMITH      CLERK       7902 17-DEC-80  800        20
     7499 ALLEN      SALESMAN    7698 20-FEB-81 1600  300   30
```

```
7521 WARD      SALESMAN   7698 22-FEB-81 1250  500      30
7566 JONES     MANAGER    7839 02-APR-81 2975           20
7654 MARTIN    SALESMAN   7698 28-SEP-81 1250 1400      30
7698 BLAKE     MANAGER    7839 01-MAY-81 2850           30
7782 CLARK     MANAGER    7839 09-JUN-81 2450           10
7788 SCOTT     ANALYST    7566 19-APR-87 3000           20
7839 KING      PRESIDENT     0 17-NOV-81 5000           10
7844 TURNER    SALESMAN   7698 08-SEP-81 1500    0      30
7876 ADAMS     CLERK      7788 23-MAY-87 1100           20
7900 JAMES     CLERK      7698 03-DEC-81  950           30
7902 FORD      ANALYST    7566 03-DEC-81 3000           20
7934 MILLER    CLERK      7782 23-JAN-82 1300           10
```

In this example, the select statement contains a datatype mismatch error in the nvl( ) function. Oracle notices the error and alerts you to it with the ORA-01722 error message.

Other error messages that may be produced include the following:

ORA-00904: invalid column name

This error indicates that the column you referenced does not exist or was misspelled or misplaced. To resolve this problem, you need to check for typos in your column clause and verify that the column actually exists in the table. Sometimes, a column name may include nonalphanumeric characters, such as underscores, designed to separate two words. Thus, the column name EMPNO is not the same as EMP_NO, even though conceptually they mean about the same thing.

ORA-00923: FROM keyword not found where expected

This error indicates that the from keyword was not included or was misspelled. Sometimes this error occurs when you put a comma after the last column listed in your select clause (that is, select empno, ename, from emp), so watch out for that common mistake.

ORA-00942: table or view does not exist

This error indicates that the table or view typed in does not exist. Usually, the ORA-00942 error message indicates a typo in the name of the table or view, or that the schema owner was not specified in front of the table name. This error is fixed either by correcting the typing problem or by adding the schema owner onto the front of the table name. (An alternative solution for the latter case involves creating synonyms for tables that are accessible to other users. This solution is discussed later in the book.)

In any case, the method used to correct the typing problem is to first type the line number containing the error to activate that line for editing. In the preceding example, we did so by typing the number 1, shown in bold. Then we used the change command, also shown in bold, observing the proper syntax:

```
c/old_value/new_value
```

After the change is made to the *first* appearance of *old_value* in the current line, Oracle redisplays the current line with the change made. Note that the change will be made to the first appearance of *old_value* only. If the change must be made to a specific place in the line, more characters can be added to the *old_value* parameter, as appropriate. Finally, the corrected text can be reexecuted by entering a slash (/) at the prompt, as indicated, or by entering the command run on the SQL*Plus command line.

> **TIP**
> *If you ever get confused about the difference between the use of the slash and semicolon, remember that the slash command reruns the code currently in your SQL*Plus operating buffer, whereas the semicolon is used to end a SQL statement you type into the buffer.*

Using a Text Editor

Oracle makes provisions for you to use your favorite text editor to edit the statement created in afiedt.buf, the file in which SQL*Plus stores the most recently executed SQL statement. You simply type edit (abbreviated ed). This action causes Oracle to bring up the SQL statement from afiedt.buf into the operating system's default text editor. On UNIX systems, that text editor is usually VI or EMACS, whereas Windows environments use Notepad. To change the text editor used, issue the define _editor='youreditor' statement on the SQL*Plus prompt.

> **TIP**
> *You can also define your text editor in the SQL*Plus GUI interface using the Tools | Environment menu option.*

Using a text editor rather than the line editor native to SQL*Plus offers many benefits. By using a text editor you know well, you can create a familiarity with SQL*Plus that is useful for adapting to the application. Also, it is helpful with large queries to have the entire block of code in front of you and immediately accessible.

Writing SQL Commands in Scripts

You can write entire queries in a text editor first and then load the queries into SQL*Plus if you want to. When you do this, try to remember to save the script with a `.sql` extension so that SQL*Plus can identify it easily. Two commands are available to load the file into SQL*Plus. The first is `get`. The `get` command opens the text file specified and places the contents in `afiedt.buf`. Once the script is loaded, you can execute the command using the slash (/) command. Alternatively, you can use the `@` or `start` command, which loads SQL statements from the named file into `afiedt.buf` and executes them in one step. The methods are shown in the following example, with a script called `select_emp.sql`:

```
$/home/oracle> sqlplus scott/tiger
SQL*Plus: Release 8.1.7.0.0 - Production on Fri Jul 06 18:53:11 2001
Copyright (c) Oracle Corporation 1979, 2000.  All rights reserved.
Connected to Oracle9i Release 9.0.1.0.0
With the partitioning option
JServer Release 9.0.1.0.0 - Production
SQL> GET select_emp
SELECT * FROM emp
SQL> /
     EMPNO ENAME      JOB         MGR HIREDATE   SAL COMM DEPTNO
     ----- -------    --------   ----- --------- ---- ---- ------
      7369 SMITH      CLERK      7902 17-DEC-80  800          20
      7499 ALLEN      SALESMAN   7698 20-FEB-81 1600  300     30
      7521 WARD       SALESMAN   7698 22-FEB-81 1250  500     30
      7566 JONES      MANAGER    7839 02-APR-81 2975          20
      7654 MARTIN     SALESMAN   7698 28-SEP-81 1250 1400     30
      7698 BLAKE      MANAGER    7839 01-MAY-81 2850          30
      7782 CLARK      MANAGER    7839 09-JUN-81 2450          10
      7788 SCOTT      ANALYST    7566 19-APR-87 3000          20
      7839 KING       PRESIDENT       17-NOV-81 5000          10
      7844 TURNER     SALESMAN   7698 08-SEP-81 1500          30
      7876 ADAMS      CLERK      7788 23-MAY-87 1100          20
      7900 JAMES      CLERK      7698 03-DEC-81  950          30
      7902 FORD       ANALYST    7566 03-DEC-81 3000          20
      7934 MILLER     CLERK      7782 23-JAN-82 1300          10
SQL> @select_emp
SELECT * FROM emp
     EMPNO ENAME      JOB         MGR HIREDATE   SAL COMM DEPTNO
     ----- -------    --------   ----- --------- ---- ---- ------
      7369 SMITH      CLERK      7902 17-DEC-80  800          20
      7499 ALLEN      SALESMAN   7698 20-FEB-81 1600  300     30
      7521 WARD       SALESMAN   7698 22-FEB-81 1250  500     30
      7566 JONES      MANAGER    7839 02-APR-81 2975          20
      7654 MARTIN     SALESMAN   7698 28-SEP-81 1250 1400     30
```

7698	BLAKE	MANAGER	7839	01-MAY-81	2850		30
7782	CLARK	MANAGER	7839	09-JUN-81	2450		10
7788	SCOTT	ANALYST	7566	19-APR-87	3000		20
7839	KING	PRESIDENT		17-NOV-81	5000		10
7844	TURNER	SALESMAN	7698	08-SEP-81	1500	0	30
7876	ADAMS	CLERK	7788	23-MAY-87	1100		20
7900	JAMES	CLERK	7698	03-DEC-81	950		30
7902	FORD	ANALYST	7566	03-DEC-81	3000		20
7934	MILLER	CLERK	7782	23-JAN-82	1300		10

TIP
The "at" (@) sign in front of your SQL script name in the code block above serves a different purpose than the @ in front of the database name we saw in an earlier example when we started SQL*Plus on the command line. Be sure you don't confuse the two forms of usage.

Notice that the `.sql` extension was left off the end of the filename in the line with the `get` command. SQL*Plus assumes that all scripts containing SQL statements will have the `.sql` extension, so it can be omitted in the `get` and the @ commands. You can store SQL commands in text files with other extensions, such as `.txt` and `.lst`, but if you do, you have to specify the full filename, including the extension, in the `get` command. Notice also that after the file is brought in using `get`, it can then be executed using the slash (/) command. Later in that same code block, we use the @ command to read the same file into `afiedt.buf`. The contents of the buffer are executed in the same step, which eliminates the need for entering the slash (/) command. Again, we omit the `.sql` extension. Finally, if you don't specify the path when typing the filename for the `get` or @ command, Oracle assumes the file is in whatever directory you were in when you started running SQL*Plus.

TIP
When typing SQL statements in a script that you intend to execute in SQL*Plus, do not put a semicolon (;) at the end of these SQL statements. Instead, put a slash (/) character as the first character on the last line in the script. Do this if you encounter problems where Oracle says it encountered an invalid character (the semicolon) in your script.

Other SQL*Plus Commands to Know

The rest of this discussion focuses on identifying other important commands you should know in SQL*Plus, both for your job and for passing the OCP exam. Let's now take a look at explanations for important SQL*Plus commands to know about.

DESCRIBE tablename   This command returns a description of *tablename*, including all columns in that table, the datatype for each column, and an indication of whether the column permits storage of NULL values. If you experience ORA-00904 errors, this command is used for determining the names of columns in the table you referenced. This command is synonymous with its abbreviation, desc. Here's an example:

```
SQL> describe emp
 Name                            Null?    Type
 ------------------------------- -------- ------------
 EMPNO                           NOT NULL NUMBER(4)
 ENAME                                    VARCHAR2(10)
 JOB                                      VARCHAR2(9)
 MGR                                      NUMBER(4)
 HIREDATE                                 DATE
 SAL                                      NUMBER(7,2)
 COMM                                     NUMBER(7,2)
 DEPTNO                                   NUMBER(2)
```

LIST   This command is used to list the contents of the current SQL*Plus working buffer, organized by line number. SQL*Plus buffers the last SQL command you issued. If you haven't entered a SQL command yet, the SP2-0223: No lines in SQL buffer error message is displayed. The current line available for editing and other changes is indicated by an asterisk next to the line number. Here's an example:

```
SQL> select empno, ename
  2  from emp
  3  where empno < 7700;
    EMPNO ENAME
 --------- ----------
     7369 SMITH
     7499 ALLEN
     7521 WARD
     7566 JONES
     7654 MARTIN
     7698 BLAKE
6 rows selected.
SQL> list
```

```
1  select empno, ename
2  from emp
3* where empno < 7700
```

DEL number　　This command deletes line *number* from the SQL*Plus working buffer (not *number* lines!). Each line in the buffer is preceded by a line number, and the last line in the buffer has an asterisk (*) next to the line number. If you want to delete multiple lines, list each line to be removed separated by a space. Here's an example:

```
SQL> del 3
SQL> list
  1  select empno, ename
  2* from emp
```

APPEND string　　This command adds *string* specified to the current line. Blank spaces are permitted in the string, and a leading blank space should be included if the current string already has information in it. The current line is indicated with an asterisk (*) in the output of the append command. See the following append command for displaying current line information along with the contents of the SQL*Plus working buffer:

```
SQL> append  where empno < 7700
  2* from emp where empno < 7700
```

CLEAR BUFFER　　This command clears the contents of the SQL*Plus buffer. Here's an example:

```
SQL> clear buffer
Buffer cleared
```

INPUT　　When entered at the SQL prompt, this command enables you to add contents to your SQL*Plus operating buffer at the current line. If the buffer was cleared, you start at the first line. If the buffer has something in it, you start at the beginning of a new line at the end of the buffer. Here's an example:

```
SQL> input
  1  select ename, sal
  2  from emp    —
  3  where empno < 7600;
ENAME          SAL
---------- ---------
SMITH          800
ALLEN         1600
```

```
WARD          1250
JONES         2975
```

TIP
The append command is different from the input
*command because append allows you to specify
the string you want to append, while* input *is
specified by itself so that you can enter the string
you want added on the next line.*

RUN   This command executes the contents of the SQL*Plus buffer. Here's an
example:

```
SQL> run
  1  select ename, sal
  2  from emp
  3* where empno < 7600
ENAME          SAL
---------- ---------
SMITH          800
ALLEN         1600
WARD          1250
JONES         2975
```

number string   When a number is entered in SQL*Plus followed by a string of
characters, SQL*Plus adds the *string* you specify to the operating buffer as the
line *number* you indicated. If the line number already exists, Oracle replaces it. If
the line number indicated is not contiguous with the existing lines in the buffer,
SQL*Plus adds the string as the last line number in the buffer. Here's an example:

```
SQL> 6 new line being added
SQL> list
  1  select ename, sal
  2  from emp
  3  where empno < 7600
  4* new line being added
SQL> 2 from jason.emp
SQL> list
  1  select ename, sal
  2  from jason.emp
  3  where empno < 7600
  4* new line being added
```

SPOOL {filename|OFF|OUT}   This command writes all output shown in SQL*Plus following issuance of the `spool filename` command to a text file identified by `filename`. If no filename extension is specified, SQL*Plus appends the `.1st` extension. When the `off` or `out` keyword is specified, spooling SQL*Plus output to a file is turned off. Here's an example:

```
SQL> spool jason.out
SQL> select ename, sal
  2  from emp
  3  where empno < 7600;
ENAME           SAL
---------- ---------
SMITH           800
ALLEN          1600
WARD           1250
JONES          2975
SQL> spool off
SQL> exit
C:\WINDOWS> type jason.out
SQL> select ename, sal
  2  from emp
  3  where empno < 7600;
ENAME           SAL
---------- ---------
SMITH           800
ALLEN          1600
WARD           1250
JONES          2975
SQL> spool off
```

SAVE filename   This command places the contents of your SQL*Plus buffer into a text file called `filename`. If no filename extension is specified, SQL*Plus appends `.sql`.

EXIT   This command exits the SQL*Plus interface and returns to the operating system.

TIP
*You can see where having the ability to edit your SQL commands using your favorite text editor is a handy feature of SQL*Plus that makes it possible to avoid learning all the commands of SQL*Plus. Nevertheless, be sure you understand the basics of entering SQL using SQL*Plus before taking the OCP exam.*

For Review

1. Be sure you know the two mechanisms available for entering and modifying SQL statements within SQL*Plus.

2. Know how to use the `edit` command in the SQL*Plus command line and how to load and run the contents of SQL scripts into SQL*Plus.

3. Understand how to use the other SQL*Plus commands identified in this section.

Exercises

1. **You are modifying a text string on line 3 of your SQL*Plus buffer. Which of the following choices best identifies the method you must use if the `edit` command is used?**

   A. Modify the code block using your favorite text editor.

   B. First refer to the line number; then use the `change` command.

   C. First delete the line using the `del` command; then refer to the line number.

   D. Load the SQL you intend to modify using the `input` command.

2. **You would like to list the columns found in an Oracle table. Which of the following SQL*Plus commands are useful for this purpose?**

   A. `get`

   B. `input`

   C. `describe`

   D. `spool`

3. **This command displays the contents of your SQL*Plus buffer:** _____
   _____

4. **This is the name of the file Oracle stores the contents of your SQL*Plus buffer in:** _____

Answer Key
1. A. 2. C. 3. `list` 4. `afiedt.buf`

Chapter Summary

This chapter ambitiously takes you from an introduction to the Oracle database through some basic techniques used in `select` statements. You learned about the theory behind relational database systems such as Oracle's and how they differ from earlier systems for data storage and retrieval. The concept of a table was presented, along with common Oracle datatypes used in those tables. The chapter also described the basic architecture of an Oracle database system and covered such factors as what an object-relational RDBMS is and some of the features for developing code in Oracle's proprietary programming language, PL/SQL. You then focused your attention on the use of `select` statements. We discussed the use of the column and table clauses as well.

Two-Minute Drill

- Data is retrieved from Oracle using `select` statements.

- The syntax for a `select` statement consists of `select ... from ...;`.

- Expressions appearing after the keyword `select` are part of the column clause, and are usually the names of columns from the table storing the data you wish to retrieve.

- Expressions appearing after the `from` keyword are part of the table clause, and are usually the names of tables you want to retrieve data from.

- When you're entering a `select` statement from the prompt using SQL*Plus, a semicolon (;) at the end of the statement or a slash (/) at the beginning of the first empty line appearing after the statement in your operating buffer must be used to terminate the statement.

- Arithmetic operations can be used to perform math operations on data selected from a table or on numbers using the DUAL table.

- The DUAL table is a table with one column and one row used to fulfill the syntactic requirements of SQL `select` statements.

- Values in columns for particular rows may be empty (NULL).

- If a column contains a NULL value, you can use the `nvl( )` function to return meaningful information instead of an empty field.

- Aliases can be used in place of the actual column name or to replace the appearance of the function name in the header.

- Output from two columns can be concatenated together using a double pipe (||). Alternately, the `concat( )` function can be used for this purpose.

- SQL commands can be entered directly into SQL*Plus on the command line.

- You can edit mistakes in SQL*Plus with the `change` command. If a mistake is made, the `change (c/old/new)` command is used.

- Alternatively, the `edit (ed)` command can be used to make changes in your favorite text editor.

- You can specify your favorite text editor by issuing the `define _editor` command at the prompt.

- Use the acronym PEMDAS to remember the correct order for operator precedence.

- There are a host of commands available in SQL*Plus that are not part of Structured Query Language to be aware of. A few to pay close attention to include

    - `get` for retrieving SQL scripts into SQL*Plus

    - `run` for executing retrieved SQL scripts

    - `@` for getting and running a script in one operation

    - `describe` for listing the columns in a particular table, along with their datatypes

    - `spool` for telling SQL*Plus to write the contents of your session to a file

Fill-in-the-Blank Questions

1. This term refers to a logical grouping of tables according to the user who created the tables: _____

2. When you want to perform an operation on two expressions, you can query this table: _____

3. A command-line tool you will use frequently to access Oracle is called: _____

4. The function whose work is performed by placing two pipe characters (||) together is called: _____

5. The Oracle component handling the actual obtainment of data you request is called: _____

6. The command set you request data from Oracle with is called: _____

Chapter Questions

1. **You are formulating queries in SQL*Plus. Which of the following statements correctly describes how to specify a column alias?**

   A. Place the alias at the beginning of the statement to describe the table.

   B. Place the alias after each column, separated by a space, to describe the column.

   C. Place the alias after each column, separated by a comma, to describe the column.

   D. Place the alias at the end of the statement to describe the table.

2. **You wish to use a function in your column clause of a SQL statement. The nvl( ) function accomplishes which of the following tasks?**

   A. Assists in the distribution of output across multiple columns

   B. Enables you to specify alternate output for non-NULL column values

   C. Enables you to specify alternate output for NULL column values

   D. Nullifies the value of the column output

3. **Output from a table called PLAYS with two columns, PLAY_NAME and AUTHOR, is shown next. Which of the following SQL statements produced it?**

```
PLAY_TABLE
---------------------------------------
"Midsummer Nights Dream", SHAKESPEARE
"Waiting For Godot", BECKETT
"The Glass Menagerie", WILLIAMS
```

   A. `select PLAY_NAME|| AUTHOR from PLAYS;`

   B. `select PLAY_NAME, AUTHOR from PLAYS;`

   C. `select PLAY_NAME||', ' || AUTHOR from PLAYS;`

   D. `select PLAY_NAME||', ' || AUTHOR play_table from PLAYS;`

4. **You are configuring your SQL*Plus working environment. Issuing the** `define _editor='emacs'` **will produce which of the following outcomes?**

   A. The EMACS editor will become the SQL*Plus default text editor.

   B. The EMACS editor will start running immediately.

   C. The EMACS editor will no longer be used by SQL*Plus as the default text editor.

   D. The EMACS editor will be deleted from the system.

5. **You are using SQL*Plus to execute some math functions. What is the appropriate table to use when performing arithmetic calculations on values defined within the** `select` **statement (not pulled from a table column)?**

   A. EMP

   B. The table containing the column values

   C. DUAL

   D. An Oracle-defined table

6. **You wish to use SQL*Plus to connect to the Oracle database. Which of the following choices does not indicate a component you must specify when logging into Oracle?**

   A. The `sqlplus` keyword

   B. The username

   C. The password

   D. The database name

7. **Review the following output from a SQL*Plus session:**

   ```
   Name                          Null?     Type
   ----------------------------- --------  ------------
   SYMPTOM                       NOT NULL  VARCHAR2(10)
   CAUSE                                   VARCHAR2(10)
   TREATMENT                               VARCHAR2(9)
   ```

   Which of the following keywords likely produced the output above?

   A. `describe`

   B. `get`

   C. `run`

   D. `spool`

Fill-in-the-Blank Answers

1. Schema

2. DUAL

3. SQL*Plus

4. `concat( )`

5. RDBMS or relational database management system

6. SQL or structured query language

Answers to Chapter Questions

1. B. Place the alias after each column, separated by a space, to describe the column.

Explanation   Aliases do not describe tables; they describe columns, which eliminates choices A and D. Commas are needed between each column appearing in the column clause of the `select` statement. If a column alias appeared after a column, Oracle would either select the wrong column name, based on information provided in the alias, or return an error.

2. C. Enables you to specify alternate output for NULL column values

Explanation   The `nvl( )` function is a simple `if-then` operation that tests column value output to see whether it is NULL. If it is, `nvl( )` substitutes the specified default value for the NULL value. Because this function only operates on one column per call to `nvl( )`, choice A is incorrect. Choice B is incorrect because it is the logical opposite of choice C. Choice D is incorrect because `nvl( )` is designed to substitute actual values for situations where NULL is present, not nullify data.

3. D. `select PLAY_NAME||', ' || AUTHOR play_table from PLAYS;`

Explanation   This question illustrates the need to read carefully. Because the output specified for the question contains a column alias for the output of the statement, choice D is the only one that is correct, even though choice C also performs the correct calculation. Choice A is incorrect because it specifies an inaccurate concatenation method, and choice B is wrong because it doesn't specify concatenation at all.

4. A. The emacs editor will become the SQL*Plus default text editor.

Explanation   The define _editor statement is designed to define the default text editor in SQL*Plus. Changing the definition will not start or stop the editor specified from running, which eliminates choices B and D. Choice C is the logical opposite of choice A and is therefore incorrect.

5. C. DUAL

Explanation   When all data to be processed by the query is present in the statement, and no data will be pulled from the database, users typically specify the DUAL table to fulfill the syntactic requirements of the from clause.

6. D. The database name

Explanation   You needn't specify the name of the database you wish to connect to. If this information is omitted, then Oracle assumes you want to connect to the local database called ORCL on your machine. All other choices identify a component required for connecting to the Oracle database.

7. A. describe

Explanation   The describe command produces a listing of all columns in a table, along with their associated datatypes. Choice B is incorrect because get merely loads the contents of a script into SQL*Plus memory. Choice C is incorrect because run executes a script that has already been loaded into SQL*Plus memory. Finally, choice D is incorrect because the spool command is used for writing the commands from a SQL*Plus session issued after the spool command to flat file.

CHAPTER

2

Limiting, Sorting, and Manipulating Return Data

n this chapter, you will learn about and demonstrate knowledge in the following areas:

- ■ Restricting and sorting row data
- ■ Using single-row functions

This chapter will build on the concepts you learned in Chapter 1 with respect to selecting data from Oracle. In this chapter, we'll discuss how to limit the data selected from the Oracle database and how to tell Oracle to return the data in a specific order. We'll also discuss how to use a category of functions called *single-row* functions to manipulate the results of your queries in a variety of ways. This chapter covers important material comprising 16 percent of the test content of OCP Exam 1.

Restricting and Sorting Row Data

This section will cover the following areas related to restricting and sorting row data:

- ■ Sorting return data with the `order by` clause
- ■ Limiting return data with the `where` clause

Obtaining all output from a table is great, but usually you must be more selective in choosing output. Most database applications contain a lot of data. How much data can a database contain? Some applications contain tables with a million rows or more, and the most recent release of Oracle9*i* will store over 512 petabytes ($512 \times 1{,}024^5$ bytes) of data. Of course, this is only a theoretical limit. The real amount of data you can store with Oracle depends on how much disk space you give Oracle to use, but, needless to say, manipulating vast amounts of data like that requires you to be careful. Always ask for *exactly* what you want, and no more. This section tells you how.

Sorting Return Data with the `order by` Clause

Notice that Oracle does not return data requested in a particular order on any particular column, either numeric or alphabetical. According to the fundamentals of relational database theory, a table is by definition an *unordered* set of row data. That's fine for the ivory tower, but it's not always useful in real-world situations. Oracle enables you to order the output from `select` statements using the `order by` clause. This clause can impose a sort order on one or more columns in ascending *or* descending order in each of the columns specified. If more than one expression is specified for a sort order, then Oracle sorts in the order of data appearing in the first expression. If the first expression has duplicates, Oracle sorts in the order of data appearing in the second expression, and so on. The order by clause usually appears last in the Structured Query Language (SQL) statement, and the general syntax for the order by clause is to include both the clause and the column(s) or column alias(es) by which Oracle will order the results, each optionally followed by a special clause defining the direction of the order (asc for ascending and desc for descending). The default value is asc, and here is an example:

```
SQL> select empno, ename, sal
  2  from emp
  3  order by ename asc;
   EMPNO ENAME           SAL
--------- ---------- ---------
    7876 ADAMS         1100
    7499 ALLEN         1600
    7698 BLAKE         2850
    7782 CLARK         2450
    7902 FORD          3000
    7900 JAMES          950
    7566 JONES         2975
    7839 KING          5000
    7654 MARTIN        1250
    7934 MILLER        1300
    7788 SCOTT         3000
    7369 SMITH          800
    7844 TURNER        1500
    7521 WARD          1250
```

An example of sorting output in descending order using the desc keyword is shown here:

```
SQL> select * from emp
  2  order by ename desc;
```

EMPNO	ENAME	JOB	MGR	HIREDATE	SAL	COMM	DEPTNO
7521	WARD	SALESMAN	7698	22-FEB-81	1250	500	30
7844	TURNER	SALESMAN	7698	08-SEP-81	1500	0	30
7369	SMITH	CLERK	7902	17-DEC-80	800		20
7788	SCOTT	ANALYST	7566	19-APR-87	3000		20
7934	MILLER	CLERK	7782	23-JAN-82	1300		10
7654	MARTIN	SALESMAN	7698	28-SEP-81	1250	1400	30
7839	KING	PRESIDENT		17-NOV-81	5000		10
7566	JONES	MANAGER	7839	02-APR-81	2975		20

```
7900  JAMES      CLERK       7698  03-DEC-81   950              30
7902  FORD       ANALYST     7566  03-DEC-81   3000             20
7782  CLARK      MANAGER     7839  09-JUN-81   2450             10
7698  BLAKE      MANAGER     7839  01-MAY-81   2850             30
7499  ALLEN      SALESMAN    7698  20-FEB-81   1600    300      30
7876  ADAMS      CLERK       7788  23-MAY-87   1100             20
```

TIP
When NULL data appears in a column that Oracle is attempting to sort in ascending order, Oracle lists the NULL records at the end of the list. When sorting in descending order, Oracle places the NULL data at the top of the list.

The `order by` clause can be useful in simple reporting. It can be applied to columns that are NUMBER, text (VARCHAR2 and CHAR), and DATE datatypes. You can even use numbers to positionally indicate the column where Oracle should order the output from a statement. For example, if you issue a statement similar to the one in the following code block, the order for the output will be as shown (the number 2 indicates that the second column specified in the statement should be used to define the order in the output):

```
SQL> select empno, ename from emp
  2 order by 2 desc;
 EMPNO ENAME
------ --------
  7521 WARD
  7844 TURNER
  7369 SMITH
  7788 SCOTT
  7934 MILLER
  7654 MARTIN
  7839 KING
  7566 JONES
  7900 JAMES
  7902 FORD
  7782 CLARK
  7698 BLAKE
  7499 ALLEN
  7876 ADAMS
SQL> select ename, empno from emp
  2  order by 2 desc;
ENAME      EMPNO
--------- ------
```

```
MILLER      7934
FORD        7902
JAMES       7900
ADAMS       7876
TURNER      7844
KING        7839
SCOTT       7788
CLARK       7782
BLAKE       7698
MARTIN      7654
JONES       7566
WARD        7521
ALLEN       7499
SMITH       7369
```

TIP
You can also sort by column alias.

Here's an even more complex example:

```
SQL> select ename, deptno, sal
  2  from emp
  3  order by 2 asc, 3 desc;
ENAME          DEPTNO         SAL
----------  ---------  ---------
KING             10        5000
CLARK            10        2450
MILLER           10        1300
SCOTT            20        3000
FORD             20        3000
JONES            20       -2975
ADAMS            20        1100
SMITH            20         800
BLAKE            30        2850
ALLEN            30        1600
TURNER           30        1500
WARD             30        1250
MARTIN           30        1250
JAMES            30         950
```

For Review

1. Know how to put row data returned from a `select` statement in order and
   know the various sort orders (ascending and descending) that can be used
   with this option. Know also that Oracle can sort based on multiple
   columns.

2. Be sure you understand both the positional and named ways to specify the column on which the sort order should be defined.

Exercises

1. Which of the choices below identifies the `order by` clause that produces the following output?

   ```
   EMPNO ENAME          MGR
   --------- ---------- ---------
       7369 SMITH      7902
       7566 JONES      7839
       7782 CLARK      7839
       7698 BLAKE      7839
       7876 ADAMS      7788
       7934 MILLER     7782
       7499 ALLEN      7698
       7654 MARTIN     7698
       7521 WARD       7698
       7900 JAMES      7698
       7844 TURNER     7698
       7788 SCOTT      7566
       7902 FORD       7566
   ```

   A. `order by empno asc`

   B. `order by ename desc`

   C. `order by hiredate asc`

   D. `order by mgr desc`

2. You are sorting data in a table in your `select` statement in descending order. The column you are sorting on contains NULL records. Where will the NULL records appear?

   A. At the beginning of the list

   B. At the end of the list

   C. In the middle of the list

   D. At the same location they are listed in the unordered table

3. Identify the default sort order used by Oracle when no sort order is specified: _____

4. **The results from an SQL query are shown here:**

```
DEPTNO DNAME            LOC
--------- -------------- --------------
       10 ACCOUNTING     NEW YORK
       40 OPERATIONS     BOSTON
       20 RESEARCH       DALLAS
       30 SALES          CHICAGO
```

Which of the following SQL statements could not have produced this output?

A. `select deptno, dname, loc from dept order by 2 asc, 1 asc, 3 desc;`

B. `select deptno, dname, loc from dept order by 3 asc;`

C. `select deptno, dname, loc from dept order by 2 asc;`

D. `select deptno, dname, loc from dept order by 2 asc, 3 desc, 1 desc;`

Answer Key
1. D. **2.** A. **3.** Ascending. **4.** C.

Limiting Return Data with the where Clause

The where clause in Oracle select statements is where things really become interesting. This important clause in select statements enables you to single out a few rows from hundreds, thousands, or even millions like it. The where clause operates on a basic principle of comparison and must follow the select and from clauses in the SQL statement. Here's an example:

```
SQL> select * from emp
  2  where empno = 7844;
EMPNO ENAME      JOB          MGR HIREDATE    SAL COMM DEPTNO
------ ---------- --------- ----- --------- ----- ----- -------
 7844 TURNER     SALESMAN   7698 08-SEP-81  1500     0      30
```

Assuming the EMPNO column contains all unique values, instead of pulling all rows from EMP, Oracle pulls just one row for display. To determine which row to display, the where clause performs a comparison operation as specified by the query. In this case, the comparison is an equality operation: `where empno = 7844`. However, equality is not the only means by which Oracle can obtain data. Some other examples of comparisons are demonstrated in Table 1-1. Every comparison between two values in Oracle boils down to one or more of the operations from that table.

`x = y`	Comparison to see if *x* is equal to *y*.
`x > y`	Comparison to see if *x* is greater than *y*.
`x >= y`	Comparison to see if *x* is greater than or equal to *y*.
`x < y`	Comparison to see if *x* is less than *y*.
`x <= y`	Comparison to see if *x* is less than or equal to *y*.
`x <> y, x != y, x ^= y`	Comparison to see if *x* is not equal to *y*.
`like`	A special comparison used in conjunction with search wildcards. Two wildcards exist in Oracle. The first, percent (`%`), is for multiple characters, as in `'%ORA%'` for all columns or rows containing string ORA. The second, underscore (`_`), is used for single-character substitution, as in `'OR_CLE'` for all strings where the user may have mistyped I instead of A. An example might be `select ename from emp where ename is like 'S%'`.
`soundex`	A special function used to introduce "fuzzy logic" into text-string comparisons by enabling equality based on similarly spelled words.
`between`	A range comparison operation that enables operations on dates, numbers, and characters that are similar to the following numeric comparison: *y* is between *x* and *z*. An example might be `select * from emp where sal is between 300 and 500`.
`in (set)`	A special comparison that enables you to specify multiple equality statements by defining a set of values, any of which the value can be equal to. An example of its usage would be `select * from emp where deptno in (10,20,30)`.

TABLE 2-1 *Comparison Operations in Oracle*

You can also use the `where` clause and the `order by` clause together in the same statement. The following code block shows an example of all the data from EMP for sales persons in order of the highest salary to the lowest:

```
SQL> select ename, empno, sal
  2  from emp
  3  where job = 'SALESMAN'
  4  order by sal desc;
ENAME           EMPNO        SAL
----------  ---------  ---------
ALLEN            7499       1600
TURNER           7844       1500
WARD             7521       1250
MARTIN           7654       1250
```

Getting Even More Selective

Multiple comparisons can be placed together using the list of operations given in Table 2-2. The operator is listed along with the result that is required to fulfill the criteria based on the presence of this operator. For example, the `and` keyword can be used to join two comparisons together, forcing Oracle to return only the rows that fulfill both criteria. In contrast, the `or` keyword enables a much looser joining of two comparisons, enabling Oracle to return records that fulfill one criteria or the other. In this case, if a record fulfills the criteria of both comparisons, Oracle will return the record as well.

`x and y`	Both comparisons in *x* and *y* must be true.
`x or y`	One comparison in *x* or *y* must be true.
`not x`	The logical opposite of *x*.
`x is NULL`	This returns TRUE if the value is NULL. This operator resolves the problem where comparing variable *x* to NULL produces a NULL result rather than TRUE. An example might be `select ename from emp where mgr is null`.

TABLE 2-2 *Keywords for Joining Comparisons Together*

The OCP exam may or may not contain a question covering the order of precedence between operators in a `where` clause of a `select` statement. The order in which Oracle resolves operators in a `where` clause is as follows:

1. First, Oracle resolves comparison operators.

2. Next, Oracle resolves all `and` operators as a single unit.

3. After that, Oracle resolves all `or` operators as separate units.

4. Finally, Oracle resolves all `not` reversers. You can force a different resolution priority using parentheses.

More Examples

Let's look at a more complex example of a query that uses a where clause so that we can see some other comparison operations and the keywords from Table 2-2 in action. Let's say we want to obtain information on all the employees at our company who make more than $900 per year and also have a last name between QUENTIN and ZYRYRAB. The following code block illustrates how to execute this query:

```
SQL> select empno, ename, sal
  2  from emp
  3  where sal > 900
  4  and ename between 'QUENTIN' and 'ZYRYRAB';
    EMPNO ENAME          SAL
--------- ---------- ---------
     7521 WARD          1250
     7788 SCOTT         3000
     7844 TURNER        1500
```

Perhaps you noticed that the output above doesn't list KING, the president of the company. We know from earlier examples and from Chapter 1 that KING makes more money than SCOTT, WARD, or TURNER, and yet he's not listed among the output. There's a simple reason for this. KING's last name doesn't fall between QUENTIN and ZYRYRAB alphabetically, and because we used the AND operation to concatenate the two comparison criteria, KING was excluded.

So, let's take a look at another example of output where we see the employees that make more than $900 or if their names fall between QUENTIN and ZYRYRAB alphabetically:

```
SQL> select empno, ename, sal
  2  from emp
  3  where sal > 900
  4  OR ename between 'QUENTIN' and 'ZYRYRAB';
    EMPNO ENAME             SAL
```

```
--------- ---------- ---------
    7369  SMITH             800
    7499  ALLEN            1600
    7521  WARD             1250
    7566  JONES            2975
    7654  MARTIN           1250
    7698  BLAKE            2850
    7782  CLARK            2450
    7788  SCOTT            3000
    7839  KING             5000
    7844  TURNER           1500
    7876  ADAMS            1100
    7900  JAMES             950
    7902  FORD             3000
    7934  MILLER           1300
```

As we can see from the output above, we weren't at all selective in our output because apparently everyone in the company falls within the criteria given. In other words, every employee of our company EITHER makes more than $900 or has a last name that falls alphabetically between QUENTIN and ZYRYRAB.

Finally, let's look at an example using the not operator to see how this "reverser" can potentially change the output of a query:

```
SQL> select empno, ename, sal
  2  from emp
  3  where sal > 900
  4  OR ename NOT between 'QUENTIN' and 'ZYRYRAB';
    EMPNO ENAME            SAL
--------- ---------- ---------
    7499  ALLEN            1600
    7521  WARD             1250
    7566  JONES            2975
    7654  MARTIN           1250
    7698  BLAKE            2850
    7782  CLARK            2450
    7788  SCOTT            3000
    7839  KING             5000
    7844  TURNER           1500
    7876  ADAMS            1100
    7900  JAMES             950
    7902  FORD             3000
    7934  MILLER           1300
```

Did you notice who's not listed in the output above? SMITH, whose name is between QUENTIN and ZYRYRAB, is not listed. Thus, you can see how this reverser can eliminate records that would otherwise appear in the set. However, be careful with your use of the `not` keyword. You can include it in contexts where it would appear with other keywords, but not in front of symbols or expressions. For example, using `where empno is not null` is acceptable in Oracle SQL, but using `where sal not > 900` would result in an error.

TIP
A substantial portion of the OCP exam on SQL rides on your ability to formulate queries with `where` *clauses. Thus, it is important that you practice this ability.*

For Review

1. Be able to define what a `where` clause is as well as the principle of comparison that the clause operates on in order to determine the data to return to the user.

2. Know all the operations available that can assist in the purpose of comparison. Also, be sure you know which operations enable you to specify more than one comparison in the `where` clause.

Exercises

1. **You are defining an SQL statement to return a limited number of rows based on specific criteria. Which of the following choices identifies the clause you will use to define the search criteria?**

   A. `select`

   B. `from`

   C. `where`

   D. `order by`

2. **The principle that the search criteria available within SQL `select` statements operate on is _____.**

3. **The operation used when you want to determine whether a NULL value appears in a column (two words) is _____.**

4. **You want to obtain data from the ORDERS table, which contains three columns: CUSTOMER, ORDER_DATE, and ORDER_AMT. Which of the**

following choices identifies how you would formulate the **where** clause in a query against the ORDERS table when you want to see orders for customer LESLIE that exceed 2,700?

A. `where customer = 'LESLIE';`

B. `where customer = 'LESLIE' and order_amt < 2700;`

C. `where customer = 'LESLIE' or order_amt > 2700;`

D. `where customer = 'LESLIE' and order_amt > 2700;`

Answer Key

1. C. 2. Comparison. 3. is NULL 4. D.

Using Single-Row Functions

This section will cover the following areas related to using single-row functions:

- Explanations of various single-row functions
- Using functions in `select` statements
- Date functions
- Conversion functions

Dozens of functions are available in Oracle that can be used for many purposes. Some functions in Oracle are designed to alter the data returned by a query, such as the nvl( ) function already presented. The functions in this category are designed to work on columns of any datatype to return information in different ways. Other single-row functions operate on only one or two datatypes. This section will explain the use of various important single-row functions in the Oracle database. Single-row functions are those designed to operate on individual column records in a row, for every row returned in the result set. You'll also see how these functions are used in SQL commands. Date and conversion functions will be covered in some detail as well.

Various Single-Row Functions Explained

Functions are similar to comparison operators in that they manipulate data items and return a result. The difference is that functions can usually do more complex things than simple comparisons. Several different types of functions exist and they include the following:

- Text functions that perform operations on alphanumeric text strings

- Arithmetic functions that perform operations on numbers

- List functions that perform operations on lists of values

- Other functions, such as decode( ), that perform important or unique operations

Text Functions

Several functions in Oracle manipulate text strings. These functions are similar in concept to nvl( ) and decode( ) in that they can perform a change on a piece of data, but the functions in this family can change only VARCHAR2 and CHAR data. Here are some examples:

- **lpad(x,y[,z]) and rpad(x,y[,z])**   Return data in string or column *x* padded on the left or right side, respectively, to width *y*. The optional value *z* indicates the character(s) that lpad( ) or rpad( ) use to pad the column data. If no character *z* is specified, a space is used.

- **lower(x), upper(x), and initcap(x)**   Return data in string or column *x* in lowercase or uppercase characters, respectively, or change the initial letter in the data from column *x* to a capital letter.

- **length(x)**   Returns the number of characters in string or column *x*.

- **substr(x,y[,z])**   Returns a substring of string or column *x*, starting at the character in position number *y* to the end, which is optionally defined by the character appearing in position *z* of the string. For example, substr('ABCDEFG',3,4) returns CDEF.

- **instr(x,y)**   Determines whether a substring *y* given can be found in string *x*. For example, instr('CORPORATE FLOOR','OR') returns 2.

The trim( ) Function   A single-row function called trim( ) behaves like a combination of ltrim( ) and rtrim( ). The trim( ) function accepts a string describing the data you would like to trim from a column value using the following syntax: trim([[*keyword*]'*x*' from] *column*). Here *keyword* is replaced by leading, trailing, or both, or it's omitted. Also, *x* is replaced with the character to be trimmed, or it's omitted. If *x* is omitted, Oracle assumes it must trim whitespace. Finally, *column* is the name of the column in the table to be trimmed. Note that trim( ) only removes trailing or leading instances of the character specified. If that character appears somewhere in the string, `trim( )` will not remove it. The following code block illustrates the use of `trim( )`:

```
SQL> select col_1,
  2    trim(both '_' from col_1) as trimmed
  3    from example;
LASTNAME TRIMMED
-------- ---------
__thr_   thr
@_593__  @_593
Booga__  Booga
```

Another example appears here:

```
SQL> select trim(0 from 000004439094000)
  2    as example
  3    from dual;
EXAMPLE
-------
4439094
```

TIP
The table used in the previous code block is not created by `utlsampl.sql` *or* `demobld.sql` *and will not exist in your database unless you create and populate it yourself. It's a really trivial example, though, and you're time will be better spent focusing on how to formulate* where *clauses, but if you must recreate the example, instructions for creating tables and adding data to them appear in Chapter 5.*

Arithmetic Functions

Other functions are designed to perform specialized mathematical functions, such as those used in scientific applications such as sine and logarithms. These operations are commonly referred to as *arithmetic* or *number operations*. The functions falling into this category are listed next. These functions are not all that is available in Oracle, but rather they are the most commonly used ones that will likely appear on OCP Exam 1:

- **abs(x)**   Obtains the absolute value for a number. For example, the absolute value of −1 is 1, whereas the absolute value of 6 is 6.

- **round(*x*,*y*)** Rounds *x* to the decimal precision of *y*. If *y* is negative, it rounds to the precision of *y* places to the left of the decimal point. For example, round(134.345,1) = 134.3, round(134.345,0) = 134, round(134.345,-1) = 130. This can also be used on DATE columns.

- **ceil(*x*)** Similar to executing round on an integer (for example, round(*x*,0)), except ceil always rounds up. For example, ceil(1.4) = 2. Note that rounding up on negative numbers produces a value closer to zero (for example, ceil(-1.6) = −1, not −2).

- **floor(*x*)** Similar to ceil, except floor always rounds down. For example, floor(1.6) = 1. Note that rounding down on negative numbers produces a value further away from zero (for example, floor (-1.6) = −2, not −1).

- **mod(*x*,*y*)** The modulus of *x*, defined in long division as the integer remainder when *x* is divided by *y* until no further whole number can be produced. For example, mod(10,3) = 1, and mod(10,2) = 0.

- **sign(*x*)** Displays an integer value corresponding to the sign of *x*: 1 if *x* is positive, −1 if *x* is negative.

- **sqrt(*x*)** The square root of *x*.

- **trunc(*x*,*y*)** Truncates *x* to the decimal precision of *y*. If *y* is negative, it truncates to *y* number of places to the left of the decimal point. This can also be used on DATE columns.

- **vsize(*x*)** The storage size in bytes for value *x*.

TIP
All arithmetic functions containing a NULL value passed in as input will return NULL as the result.

List Functions

The final category of number functions discussed here is the set of list functions. These functions are actually used for many different datatypes, including CHAR, VARCHAR2, NUMBER, and DATE. Let's now take a look at the list functions available in Oracle:

- **greatest(*x*,*y*, . . .)** Returns the highest value from the list of text strings, numbers, or dates (*x*, *y* . . .).

- **least(*x*,*y*, . . .)** Returns the lowest value from the list of text strings, numbers, or dates (*x*, *y* . . .).

TIP
*If you're a little confused after reading about all these functions because you don't know how their output would look in SQL*Plus, don't worry. We're going to look at some examples in the next discussion.*

The decode( ) Function

One commonly used single-row function merits a separate explanation. It is decode( ). The decode( ) function works on the same principle as the if-then-else statement does in many common programming languages, including PL/SQL. You can pass a variable number of values into the call to the decode( ) function, which will appear in the column clause of your select statement. Your first item will always be the name of the column you want to decode. Next, you identify the first specific value Oracle should look for in that column. After that, you pass in the substitute you want Oracle to return if the first specific value is encountered. From there, you can then define as many specific value-substitute pairs as you would like. Once all value-substitute pairs have been defined, you can optionally specify a default value that Oracle will return if the column value doesn't match a specified value. Take a look at the following code block to get a better idea of how this works:

```
SELECT decode(column_name,
          value1, substitute1,
          value2, substitute2,
          ... ,
          return_default)
FROM ... ;
```

The decode( ) function enables a powerful transformation of data from one value to another. Some examples of decode( ) in action will appear shortly. This function is presented first because, like nvl( ), decode( ) can operate on virtually every datatype in Oracle. From this point on, all functions described have limitations on the datatypes that they can perform their operations on. Let's look at an example:

```
SQL>  select ename, decode(deptno, 10, 'Accounting',
  2    20, 'Research',
  3    30, 'Sales',
  4    40, 'Operations', 'Other') Department
  5  from emp
```

```
  6  order by department;
ENAME       DEPARTMENT
----------  ----------
CLARK       Accounting
KING        Accounting
MILLER      Accounting
SMITH       Research
ADAMS       Research
FORD        Research
SCOTT       Research
JONES       Research
ALLEN       Sales
BLAKE       Sales
MARTIN      Sales
JAMES       Sales
TURNER      Sales
WARD        Sales
```

For Review

1. Be sure you can identify the character, math, and date functions available in SQL, as shown in this discussion. Know the two functions that enable you to transform column values regardless of the datatype.

2. Know how to use the `trim( )` function.

3. Understand the list functions presented in this discussion that perform operations on specified sets of information.

Exercises

1. The result of a math function is −97, and the information passed into that function was −97.342. Which of the following choices identifies the single-row function that could have produced this output?

    A. `abs( )`

    B. `ceil( )`

    C. `mod( )`

    D. `sqrt( )`

2. You want to determine the size in bytes of a particular column value. Which of the following single-row functions might be useful for doing so?

    A. `vsize( )`

    B. `trunc( )`

      C. trim( )

      D. greatest( )

  3. **Which of the single-row functions covered in this discussion operates in a way similar to an `if-then-else` expression?**

    _____

Answer Key
1. B. 2. A. 3. decode( )

Using Functions in select Statements

Let's take a look at the functions introduced in the last discussion in action. The first example details the use of the decode( ) function. Assume that you select data from the EMP table. The data in the JOB column identifies the role each employee performs for the company. Instead of displaying the job title, the following code block lets you write out a verb that describes the employee's role so that you know that no slackers exist in the company:

```
SQL> select ename || ' does the ' ||
  2  decode(job, 'ANALYST','analyzing','CLERK','filing',
  3  'MANAGER','managing','PRESIDENT','bossing around',
  4  'SALESMAN','golfing','goofing off') as functions
  5  from emp;
FUNCTIONS
----------------------------------
SMITH does the filing
ALLEN does the golfing
WARD does the golfing
JONES does the managing
MARTIN does the golfing
BLAKE does the managing
CLARK does the managing
SCOTT does the analyzing
KING does the bossing around
TURNER does the golfing
ADAMS does the filing
JAMES does the filing
FORD does the analyzing
MILLER does the filing
```

This decode( ) command has 12 variables. The first is the name of the column to be decoded and must always be present. The next two variables identify, respectively, a value that could be found in the JOB column (ANALYST, in this case) and what decode( ) should substitute if the value is found. This matching of potential values with appropriate substitutes continues until you identify all the cases you would like to decode. The last variable, which is optional, is used for the default substitute value.

Text Function Examples

Now let's look at some text (character) function examples. The first of these examples is for rpad( ) and lpad( ). As shown in the following code, these two functions can be used to place additional filler characters on the right and left sides of data in a column out to a specified column width:

```
SQL> select ename || ' does the ' ||
  2  RPAD(decode(job, 'ANALYST','analyzing','CLERK','filing',
  3  'MANAGER','managing','PRESIDENT','bossing around',
  4  'SALESMAN','golfing','goofing off'), 10, '-') as functions
  5  from emp
  6  where empno < 7600;
FUNCTIONS
-----------------------------
SMITH does the filing----
ALLEN does the golfing---
WARD does the golfing---
JONES does the managing--
```

TIP
This example also illustrates another important principle—the output from one SQL function can be used as input for another!

Some of the simpler character functions are shown next. The following examples show single-row functions that are sometimes referred to as "case translators" because they perform a simple translation of case based on the text string passed:

```
SQL> SELECT lower(ename) as one,
  2  upper(ename) as two,
  3  initcap(ename) as three
  4  FROM emp;
ONE        TWO        THREE
---------- ---------- ----------
```

```
smith      SMITH      Smith
allen      ALLEN      Allen
ward       WARD       Ward
jones      JONES      Jones
martin     MARTIN     Martin
blake      BLAKE      Blake
clark      CLARK      Clark
scott      SCOTT      Scott
king       KING       King
turner     TURNER     Turner
adams      ADAMS      Adams
james      JAMES      James
ford       FORD       Ford
miller     MILLER     Miller
```

Another straightforward and useful character function is the `length( )` function, which returns the length of a text string:

```
SQL> select ename, length(ename) as length
  2  from emp;
ENAME        LENGTH
---------  ---------
SMITH            5
ALLEN            5
WARD             4
JONES            5
MARTIN           6
BLAKE            5
CLARK            5
SCOTT            5
KING             4
TURNER           6
ADAMS            5
JAMES            5
FORD             4
MILLER           6
```

TIP
If the string includes spaces, double quotes, or other special characters, all those special characters are counted as part of the length of the string.

Another extraordinarily useful function related to character strings is the `substr( )` function. This function is commonly used to extract data from a longer text string. The substr( ) function takes as its first variable the full text string to be searched. The second variable contains an integer that designates the character number at which the substring should begin. The third parameter is optional and specifies how many characters to the right of the start of the substring will be included in the substring. By default, it will include all the characters until the end of the string. Observe the following output to understand the effects of omitting the third parameter:

```
SQL> select ename, substr(ename,2,3)
  2  from emp;
ENAME      SUB
---------  ---
SMITH      MIT
ALLEN      LLE
WARD       ARD
JONES      ONE
MARTIN     ART
BLAKE      LAK
CLARK      LAR
SCOTT      COT
KING       ING
TURNER     URN
ADAMS      DAM
JAMES      AME
FORD       ORD
MILLER     ILL
SQL> select ename, substr(ename,2)
  2  from emp;
ENAME      SUBSTR(EN
---------  ---------
SMITH      MITH
ALLEN      LLEN
WARD       ARD
JONES      ONES
MARTIN     ARTIN
BLAKE      LAKE
CLARK      LARK
SCOTT      COTT
KING       ING
TURNER     URNER
ADAMS      DAMS
JAMES      AMES
FORD       ORD
MILLER     ILLER
```

Arithmetic Function Examples

The number (math) functions are frequently used in scientific applications. The first function detailed here is the abs ( ) function, or *absolute value* function, which calculates how far away from zero the parameter passed lies on the number line:

```
SQL> SELECT ABS(25), ABS(-12) FROM DUAL;
ABS(25) ABS(-12)
------- --------
     25       12
```

The next single-value function is the ceil ( ) function, which automatically rounds the number passed as its parameter up to the next highest integer:

```
SQL> SELECT CEIL(123.323), CEIL(45),
  2  CEIL(-392), CEIL(-1.12) FROM DUAL;
CEIL(123.323) CEIL(45) CEIL(-392) CEIL(-1.12)
------------- -------- ---------- -----------
          124       45       -392          -1
```

The next single-value function is the floor ( ) function. The floor ( ) function is the opposite of ceil ( ), because it rounds the value passed down to the next lowest integer:

```
SQL> SELECT FLOOR(123.323), FLOOR(45), FLOOR(-392),
  2  FLOOR(-1.12) FROM DUAL;
FLOOR(123.323) FLOOR(45) FLOOR(-392) FLOOR(-1.12)
-------------- --------- ----------- ------------
           123        45        -392           -2
```

The next function covered in this section is related to long division. The function is called mod ( ), and it returns the remainder (or *modulus*) for a number and its divisor:

```
SQL> SELECT MOD(12,3), MOD(55,4) FROM DUAL;
MOD(12,3)   MOD(55,4)
---------   ---------
        0           3
```

After that, look at round ( ). This important function enables you to round a number off to a specified precision:

```
SQL>
SELECT ROUND(123.323,2), ROUND(45,1),
  2  ROUND(-392,-1), ROUND (-1.12,0) FROM DUAL;
```

```
ROUND(123.323,2) ROUND(45,1) ROUND(-392,-1) ROUND(-1.12,0)
---------------- ----------- -------------- --------------
          123.32          45           -390             -1
```

The next function is called `sign( )`. It assists in identifying whether a number is positive or negative. If the number passed is positive, `sign( )` returns 1, and if the number is negative, `sign( )` returns −1. If the number is zero, `sign( )` returns 0:

```
SQL> SELECT SIGN(-1933), SIGN(55), SIGN(0) FROM DUAL;
SIGN(-1933) SIGN(55) SIGN(0)
----------- -------- -------
         -1        1       0
```

The next example is the `sqrt( )` function. It is used to derive the square root for a number:

```
SQL> SELECT SQRT(34), SQRT(9) FROM DUAL;
SQRT(34) SQRT(9)
-------- -------
5.830951       3
```

The next single-value number function is called `trunc( )`. Similar to `round ( )`, `trunc( )` truncates a value passed into it according to the precision that is also passed in:

```
SQL> SELECT TRUNC(123.232,2), TRUNC(-45,1),
  2  TRUNC(392,-1), TRUNC(5,0) FROM DUAL;
TRUNC(123.232,2) TRUNC(-45,1) TRUNC(392,-1) TRUNC(5,0)
---------------- ------------ ------------- ----------
          123.23          -45           390          5
```

The final single-row operation that is covered in this section is the `vsize( )` function. This function is not strictly for numeric datatypes. The `vsize( )` function gives the size in bytes of any value for VARCHAR2, CHAR, NUMBER, DATE, ROWID, and other column datatypes:

```
SQL> SELECT VSIZE(384838), VSIZE('ORANGE_TABBY'),
  2  VSIZE(sysdate) FROM DUAL;
VSIZE(384838) VSIZE('ORANGE_TABBY') VSIZE(SYSDATE)
------------- --------------------- --------------
            4                    12              8
```

For Review

1. Be sure you understand the purpose of the decode( ) statement and that it accepts all the common Oracle datatypes. Make sure you can set up a call to this function correctly.

2. Know how to use the text functions. Also make sure you understand how to combine two functions using the output of one function as input for the other.

3. Understand the use of the math functions. Be sure you know how to utilize them on real columns and how to use them on fixed expressions using the DUAL table.

Exercises

1. **Use the following output to answer this question (assume that the information shown comes from the EMP table we've been using in the chapter).**

```
ENAME
----------
SMITH-dog-
ALLEN-dog-
WARD-dog-d
JONES-dog-
MARTIN-dog
BLAKE-dog-
CLARK-dog-
SCOTT-dog-
KING-dog-d
TURNER-dog
ADAMS-dog-
JAMES-dog-
FORD-dog-d
MILLER-dog
```

Which of the following choices identifies the SQL statement that produced this output?

A. select trim(trailing '-dog' from ename) as ename from emp;

B. select rpad(ename, 10, '-dog') as ename from emp;

C. select substr(ename, 1, 10) as ename from emp;

D. select lpad(ename, 10, '-dog') as ename from emp;

2. **Use the following code block to answer the question:**

```
SQL> select _____(-45) as output from dual;
OUTPUT
------
   -45
```

   Which of the following choices identifies a single-row function that could not have produced this output?

   A. abs( )

   B. ceil( )

   C. floor( )

   D. round( )

3. **For a certain row in a table, a VARCHAR2 column contains the value SMITHY, padded to the right with seven spaces by the application. When the `length( )` function processes that column value, what will be the value returned?**

   A. 5

   B. 6

   C. 12

   D. 13

4. **You issue the following statement in SQL*Plus:**

```
SQL> select ceil(-97.342),
  2  floor(-97.342),
  3  round(-97.342,0),
  4  trunc(-97.342)
  5  from dual;
```

   Which of the following choices identifies the function that will not return −97 as the result?

   A. ceil( )

   B. floor( )

   C. round( )

   D. trunc( )

5. **You issue the following statement in SQL*Plus:**

```
SQL> select ceil(256.342),
  2  floor(256.342),
  3  round(256.342,0),
  4  trunc(256.342)
  5  from dual;
```

Which of the following choices identifies the function that will not return 256 as the result?

A. `ceil( )`

B. `floor( )`

C. `round( )`

D. `trunc( )`

Answer Key
1. B. **2.** A. **3.** D. **4.** B. `Ceil( )` returns −97 because −97 is closer to 0 and is therefore greater than −98. **5.** A.

Date Functions

You may not see this listed as an official objective on the OCP 9*i* SQL Candidate Guide, but understanding date functions is crucial for your use of the Oracle database. Thus, I like to cover it as a separate topic. To start our discussion of date functions, you should be aware that a special keyword can be specified to give Oracle users the current date. This keyword is `sysdate`. In the same way you calculated simple arithmetic earlier in the chapter using the DUAL table, so too can you execute a `select` statement using `sysdate` to produce the current date. Here's an example:

```
SQL> SELECT sysdate FROM DUAL;
SYSDATE
---------
15-MAR-01
```

TIP
The DATE information you obtain when using the keyword `sysdate` is the date according to the server hosting the Oracle database. Therefore, the date information returned could differ from the date information for your client PC.

Now for a note about the format. Typically, Oracle by default displays date information either in DD-MON-YY format or DD-MON-YYYY format. Thus, DD stands for a two-digit date (01 for the first day of the month, 02 for the second, and so on), while MON is a three-character abbreviation for the month of the year (JAN for January, FEB for February, and so on). YY or YYYY stands for a two- or four-digit year. If you use Oracle in your organization and you retrieve `sysdate` information in a format other than the ones described, don't panic! Chances are, your DBA or someone else in the organization has altered Oracle to display date information in some nondefault format. We'll discuss ways to apply other format masks to Oracle date information shortly.

Some Available Date Functions

The date functions available in Oracle can operate on columns of the DATE datatype. The date functions available in Oracle are very useful for executing well-defined operations on DATE data in a table or on constant values. Make sure you understand these functions for the OCP exam. The functions that can be used on DATE columns are as follows, along with their definitions:

- **add_months(x,y)**   Returns a date corresponding to date x plus y months.
- **last_day(x)**   Returns the date of the last day of the month that contains date x.
- **months_between(x,y)**   Returns a number of months between dates x and y. If date x is earlier than y, the result is positive; otherwise, the result is negative. If dates x and y contain the same day of different months, the result is an integer; otherwise, the result is a decimal.
- **new_time(x,y,z)**   Returns the current date and time for date x in time zone y as it would be in time zone z.
- **next_day(x)**   Identifies the name of the next day from the given date, x.

Let's look at date information and the associated functions in more detail. As mentioned earlier, Oracle stores dates as integers, representing the number of days since the beginning of the Julian calendar. This method enables easy format changes and inherent millennium compliance. The first function is the `add_months( )` function. This function takes as input a date and a number of months to be added. Oracle then returns the new date, which is the old date plus the number of months:

```
SQL> SELECT ADD_MONTHS('15-MAR-00',26)
  2   FROM DUAL;
ADD_MONTHS('15
--------------
      15-MAY-02
```

The next function, `last_day( )`, helps to determine the date for the last day in the month for the date given:

```
SQL> SELECT LAST_DAY('15-MAR-00') FROM DUAL;
LAST_DAY('15-M
--------------
    31-MAR-00
```

The next date function determines the number of months between two different dates. The name of the function is `months_between( )`. The syntax of this command is tricky, so it will be presented here. The syntax of this command is `months_between(x, y)`, and the return value for this function is *x-y*:

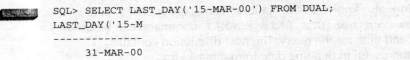

```
SQL> SELECT MONTHS_BETWEEN('15-MAR-00','26-JUN-99') FROM DUAL;
MONTHS_BETWEEN
--------------
    8.6451613
```

TIP

In general, you should try to specify the values passed into `months_between( )`, such that the first value is larger than the second. If you pass a second value that is greater than the first, a negative number will be returned.

The last example of a date function is `new_time( )`. It accepts three parameters—the first being a date and time, the second being the time zone the first parameter belongs in, and the last parameter being the time zone you would like to convert to. Each time zone is abbreviated in the following way: *XST* or *XDT*, where *S* and *D* stands for standard and daylight saving time, respectively, and *X* stands for the first letter of the time zone (for example, *A*tlantic, *B*ering, *C*entral, *E*astern, *H*awaii, *M*ountain, *N*ewfoundland, *P*acific, or *Y*ukon). This function has two exceptions: Greenwich mean time is indicated by GMT, whereas Newfoundland standard time does not use daylight saving. Take a look at the following example:

```
SQL> ALTER SESSION
  2  SET NLS_DATE_FORMAT = 'DD-MON-YYYY HH24:MI:SS';
Session altered.
SQL> SELECT NEW_TIME('15-MAR-1999 14:35:00','AST','GMT')
  2  FROM DUAL;
NEW_TIME('15-MAR-199
--------------------
15-MAR-1999 18:35:00
```

None of the queries used to demonstrate the date functions have required that much precision so far, except for this one. In order to demonstrate the full capability of Oracle in the `new_time( )` function, we altered the format Oracle uses to displays date information, also known as the National Language Set (NLS) date format. The `alter session set NLS_DATE_FORMAT` command can be used to display the full date and time for the query. The next discussion contains information you may find useful in defining date format masks for NLS_DATE_FORMAT.

Date Arithmetic

Oracle stores date information internally as a number, so you can perform arithmetic on dates as though they were numbers too. You can add numbers to or subtract numbers from a date in order to determine a new date value. For example, if you wanted to determine when an employee's 180-day evaluation should take place based on the employee's hire date, you could issue the following query:

```
SQL> select hiredate + 180 as "Review Date"
  2  from emp
  3  where ename = 'TURNER';
Review Da
---------
07-MAR-82
```

Alternately, you could subtract two dates to find the number of weeks between those days if you wanted to determine how many weeks on the job a particular employee had with the company. The following example shows how:

```
SQL> select ename, (hiredate-sysdate)/7 as "Weeks at Work"
  2  from emp
  3  where ename = 'TURNER';
ENAME        Weeks at Work
---------- --------------
TURNER          4176.485
```

For Review

1. Understand that dates are stored as numbers in Oracle to enable the database to display the date information into multiple formats.

2. Know that the date format is defined by the `alter session set nls_date_format` command.

3. Be able to identify and use the date functions described in this section to return information about dates. Also know that only the `months_between( )` function returns information in a datatype other than DATE.

Exercises

1. **You issue the following query in Oracle:**

```
SQL> select sysdate from dual;
SYSDATE
--------------------------------
THURSDAY, MARCH 15 2001 10:35AM
```

Which format mask was used for generating this output?

A. DD, MONTH DAY RRRR HH:MI

B. DAY, MONTH DD YYYY HH:MIAM

C. DAY, MON DD RR HH:MIAM

D. MONTH, DAY DD YYYY HH24:MI

2. **You issue the following query in Oracle:**

```
SQL> select months_between('15-MAR-83', '15-MAR-97') from dual;
```

What will Oracle return?

A. 14

B. −14

C. 168

D. −168

3. **Which command is used for adjusting your date format for the duration of your connection with Oracle (two words)?** _____

Answer Key

1. B. This question was a little tricky—we'll cover date format conventions in the next discussion of the chapter. **2.** D. **3.** `alter session`

Conversion Functions

Conversion functions are designed to convert data from one datatype format to another. These functions do not actually modify the stored data in the table itself; they just return the converted values to the SQL*Plus session. Figure 2-1 displays how information can get converted from one datatype to another using various functions. Several different conversion functions are available in the Oracle database, as listed here:

■ **to_char(x)**   Converts the value x to a character or converts a date to a character string using formatting conventions (see "Date-Formatting Conventions" subtopic below).

■ **to_number(x)**   Converts nonnumeric value x to a number.

■ **to_date(x[,y])**   Converts the nondate value x to a date using the format specified by y.

■ **to_multi_byte(x)**   Converts the single-byte character string x to multibyte characters according to national language standards.

■ **to_single_byte(x)**   Converts the multibyte character string x to single-byte characters according to national language standards.

■ **chartorowid(x)**   Converts the string of characters x into an Oracle ROWID.

■ **rowidtochar(x)**   Converts the ROWID value into the string of characters x of VARCHAR2 datatype.

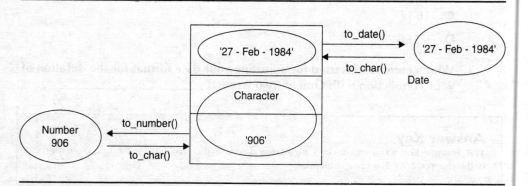

FIGURE 2-1.   *Converting data of different types*

- **hextoraw(x)**   Converts the hexadecimal (base-16) value *x* into a raw (binary) format.

- **rawtohex(x)**   Converts the raw (binary) value *x* into a hexadecimal (base-16) format.

- **convert(x[,y[,z]])**   Executes a conversion of alphanumeric string *x* from the current character set (optionally specified as *z*) to the one specified by *y*.

- **translate(x,y,z)**   Executes a simple value conversion for character or numeric string *x* into something else based on the conversion factors *y* and *z*.

Date-Formatting Conventions

You can use the to_char( ) function to convert DATE column information into a text string. The format is to_char(*column_name*, '*date_format_mask*'). Some of the most popular format masks available in Oracle include the following:

- **DD**   Shows the two-digit date.

- **DAY**   Shows the day spelled out.

- **MON**   Shows a three-letter month abbreviation, such as MAR for March.

- **MONTH**   Shows the month spelled out.

- **YY**   Shows the two-digit year (not millennium-compliant).

- **YYYY**   Shows the four-digit year (not millennium-compliant).

- **RR**   Shows the two-digit year (millennium-compliant).

- **RRRR**   Shows the four-digit year (millennium-compliant).

- **HH**   Shows the two-digit hour in A.M./P.M. format (must be used with the MIAM mask, explained later).

- **HH24**   Shows the two-digit hour in 24-hour format (cannot be used with the MIAM mask).

- **MI**   Shows the two-digit minute (use with HH24 mask).

- **MIAM**   Shows the two-digit minute in A.M./P.M. format (do not use with the HH24 mask).

- **SS**   Shows the two-digit second.

TIP
*Oracle stores hour and minute information as well
as the day, month, and year for a DATE column.
Therefore, if you want to compare dates, you need
to adjust your expectations about what you're
actually comparing or else you will often have
problems because the times won't match on dates
that are otherwise the same. Use the* trunc( )
function to avoid this problem.

Demonstrating Single-Row Functions, Continued

This section illustrates the most commonly used procedures for converting data in
action. These are the to_char( ), to_number( ), and to_date( ) functions.
We'll first examine the to_char( ) function.

In the example of new_time( ), the date function described earlier, the
alter session set nls_date_format statement was used to demonstrate
the full capabilities of Oracle in both storing date information and converting dates
and times from one time zone to another. That exercise could have been
accomplished with the to_char( ) conversion function as well. Using
to_char( ) in this manner saves you from converting nls_date_format,
which, once executed, is in effect for the rest of your session, or until you execute
another alter session set nls_date_format statement. Rather than using
this method, you may want to opt for the less permanent option offered by the
to_char( ) function, as shown here:

```
SQL> SELECT TO_CHAR(NEW_TIME(TO_DATE('15-MAR-2000 14:35:00',
  2  'DD-MON-YYYY HH24:MI:SS'),'AST','GMT'))
  3  FROM DUAL;
NEXT_DAY('15-MAR-200
--------------------
15-MAR-2000 18:35:00
```

Note that this example also uses the to_date( ) function, another conversion
function in the list to be discussed. The to_date( ) function is very useful for
converting numbers, and especially character strings, into properly formatted DATE
fields.

The next function to consider is to_number( ), which converts text or date
information into a number:

```
SQL> SELECT TO_NUMBER('49583') FROM DUAL;
TO_NUMBER('49583')
```

```
------------------
      49583
```

Although not much difference appears to exist between the output of this query and the string that was passed, the main difference is the underlying datatype. Even so, Oracle is intelligent enough to convert a character string consisting of all numbers before performing an arithmetic operation using two values of two different datatypes, as shown in the following code:

```
SQL> SELECT '49583' + 34 FROM DUAL;
'49583'+34
----------
    49617
```

For Review

1. Be sure you can identify the datatype-conversion functions. Also, know which of the functions are most commonly used.

2. Understand the situations where Oracle performs an implicit datatype conversion.

Exercises

1. **You want to use a format mask for date information in Oracle. In which of the following situations is this format mask not appropriate?**

    A. to_date( )

    B. to_char( )

    C. alter session set nls_date_format

    D. to_number( )

2. **State the reason why using to_number( ) to convert a numeric text string into an actual number is unnecessary in the Oracle database (three words):** _____

Answer Key
1. D. 2. Implicit datatype conversion.

Chapter Summary

This chapter adds to your understanding of how to query data in the Oracle database by building on what you learned about `select` statements in Chapter 1. We discussed the use of the comparison clause via the `where` keyword to restrict the data Oracle returns. Then we discussed the use of the `order by` clause to place return data in a specific order based on whatever criteria we want to use. The chapter wrapped up the intermediate coverage of queries by introducing a multitude of single-row functions that you can use to manipulate the data Oracle returns.

Two-Minute Drill

- The `order by` clause in a `select` statement is a useful clause for incorporating a sort order into the output of a file.

- The sort orders that can be used are `ascending` and `descending`, abbreviated as `asc` and `desc`, respectively. The order is determined by the column identified in the `order by` clause. The default is `asc`.

- The `where` clause is used in SQL queries to limit the data returned by a query.

- The `where` clauses contain comparison operations that determine whether a row will be returned by a query.

- The logical comparison operations include =, >, >=, <, <, <=, <>, !=, and ^=.

- In addition to the logical operations, a comparison operation, called `like`, can be used for pattern matching. The `%` and `_` characters are used to designate wildcards.

- The range operation is called `between`.

- The fuzzy logic operation is called `soundex`.

- The `where` clause can contain one or more comparison operations linked together by using `and` or `or` and preceded by `not`.

- SQL functions are broken down into character functions, number functions, and date functions. Be sure you know how to use these functions for the OCP exam.

- Several conversion functions are available for transforming data from text to numeric datatypes and back, numbers to dates and back, text to ROWID and back, and so on.

Fill-in-the-Blank Questions

1. The order by clause lists output in this order by default:
   _____

2. Finish the sentence: The where clause works on the premise of
   _____ one value to another.

3. Two or more where clause criteria can be joined together using this
   keyword to force Oracle to return data only if both criteria are met:
   _____

4. This indicates that two values are compared to each other, yielding a TRUE
   or FALSE result: _____

5. This keyword is considered a reverser because it negates the Boolean result
   of the comparison it precedes: _____

Chapter Questions

1. **You are writing select statements in a SQL*Plus session against the
   Oracle database. Which of the following statements contains an error?**

   A. `select * from EMP where EMPNO = 493945;`

   B. `select EMPNO from EMP where EMPNO = 493945;`

   C. `select EMPNO from EMP;`

   D. `select EMPNO where EMPNO = 56949 and ENAME =
   'SMITH';`

2. **You are using single-row functions in a select statement. Which function
   can best be categorized as similar in function to an if-then-else
   statement?**

   A. `sqrt( )`

   B. `decode( )`

   C. `new_time( )`

   D. `rowidtochar( )`

3. You want to use single-row functions in your SQL statements. Which three of the following are number functions? (Choose three of the four.)

   A. sinh( )

   B. to_number( )

   C. sqrt( )

   D. round( )

4. You are using SQL*Plus to retrieve data from an Oracle database. Which of the following is a valid SQL statement?

   A. `select to_char(nvl(sqrt(59483), '0')) from dual;`

   B. `select to_char(nvl(sqrt(59483), 'INVALID')) from dual;`

   C. `select (to_char(nvl(sqrt(59483), '0')) from dual;`

   D. `select to_char(nvl(sqrt(59483), 'TRUE')) from dual;`

5. You want to utilize an `order by` clause in your `select` statement. Which of the following keywords are used in `order by` clauses? (Choose two.)

   A. abs

   B. asc

   C. desc

   D. disc

6. You are formulating SQL statements in a SQL*Plus session. Which of the following statements are *not* true about `order by` clauses?

   A. The ascending or descending order can be defined with the `asc` or `desc` keyword.

   B. Only one column can be used to define the sort order in an `order by` clause.

   C. Multiple columns can be used to define sort order in an `order by` clause.

   D. Columns can be represented by numbers indicating their listed order in the `select` clause within `order by`.

7. **The following SQL statement was taken from a SQL*Plus session:**

```
select decode(EMPNO, 58385, 'INACTIVE', 'ACTIVE') empno
from EMP
where substr(ENAME,1,1) > to_number('S')
and EMPNO > 02000
order by EMPNO desc, ENAME asc;
```

Which of the following lines in the `select` statement shown in the previous code block contain an error?

A. `select decode(EMPNO, 58385, 'INACTIVE', 'ACTIVE')`
   `empno`

B. `from EMP`

C. `where substr(ENAME,1,1) > to_number('S')`

D. `and EMPNO > 02000`

E. `order by EMPNO desc, ENAME asc;`

F. No errors in this statement

Fill-in-the-Blank Answers

1. ascending

2. Comparing

3. and

4. Boolean

5. not

Answers to Chapter Questions

1. D. `select EMPNO where EMPNO = 56949 and ENAME = 'SMITH';`

Explanation This statement has no `from` clause. Although a `select` statement can be issued without a `where` clause, no `select` statement can be executed without a `from` clause specified. For that reason, the DUAL table exists to satisfy the `from` clause in situations where you define all the data needed within the statement.

2. B. `decode( )`

Explanation The `decode( )` function acts like an `if-then-else` clause in your SQL statements. Choice A is incorrect because `sqrt( )` produces the square root of a number. Choice C is incorrect because the `new_time( )` function returns a new time based on values specified in the call to that function. Finally, choice D is incorrect because `rowidtochar( )` is a function that converts ROWID information to CHAR information.

3. A, C, and D. `sinh( )`, `sqrt( )`, and `round( )`

Explanation The only nonnumber function in this list is the `to_number( )` function, which is a conversion operation. Several questions of this type appear throughout the OCP exams, and for these types of questions you must choose multiple answers.

4. A. `select to_char(nvl(sqrt(59483), '0')) from dual;`

Explanation Functions such as these can be used in conjunction with one another. Although usually the datatype of the value inserted if the column value is NULL and the column specified for `nvl(  )` must match, Oracle performs many datatype conversions implicitly, such as this one.

5. B and C. `asc` and `desc`

Explanation Information returned from Oracle in a query that uses the `order by` clause can be returned either in ascending or descending order, as indicated by the keywords in choices B and C. The `abs(  )` function is the absolute value function, which eliminates choice A. The `disc(  )` function is not an actual option either, thus eliminating choice D.

6. B. Only one column can be used to define the sort order in an `order by` clause.

Explanation Notice, first, that a logical difference exists between choices B and C, meaning you can eliminate one of them on principle. Multiple columns can be used to define order in `order by` statements, thereby eliminating choice C automatically. Choice A is incorrect because you can use `asc` or `desc` to specify ascending or descending order in your `order by` clause. Finally, choice D is incorrect because you can use numbers to represent the column you want to place an order on, based on how the columns are listed in the `select` statement.

7. C. `where substr(ENAME,1,1) > to_number('S')`

Explanation Characters that are alphabetic, such as *S*, cannot be converted into numbers. When this statement is run, it will produce an error on this line. The other lines in this query are correct as composed.

CHAPTER
3

Advanced Data
Selection in Oracle

n this chapter, you will learn about and demonstrate knowledge in the following areas:

- Displaying data from multiple tables
- Group functions and their uses

This chapter will take you to a fairly sophisticated level of understanding how to query data in Oracle. First, we will cover how you can write `select` statements to access data from more than one table. You will also learn how to create joins that display data from different tables even when the information in the two tables does not correspond completely. The chapter discusses how to create and use table self-joins as well. After discussing table joins, the chapter introduces the `group by` clause used in `select` statements and group functions. This clause allows you to treat entire columns of data as a single unit for operation.

The material in this chapter comprises 18 percent of OCP Exam 1.

NOTE
Like Chapters 1 and 2, this chapter also uses the standard demo tables created by `utlsampl.sql` *or* `demobld.sql`*. However, this chapter also uses trivial and not-so-trivial examples from other tables. For nontrivial examples, I've included commands that will create and populate the table used. Because it's so important that you practice your use of Oracle as much as possible for OCP, I don't provide scripts to automatically generate the objects for you.*

Displaying Data from Multiple Tables

This section will cover the following areas related to displaying data from multiple tables:

- Using `select` statements to join data from more than one table
- Creating outer joins
- Joining a table to itself

The typical database contains many tables. Some smaller databases may have only a dozen or so tables, whereas other databases may have hundreds or even thousands. The common factor, however, is that few databases have just one table containing everything you need. Therefore, you usually have to draw data from multiple tables together in a meaningful way. To show data from multiple tables in one query, Oracle allows you to perform *table joins*. Here are the two rules you need to remember for table joins. Data from two (or more) tables can be joined, if the same column (under the same or a different name) appears in *both* tables, and the column is the primary key (or part of that key) in *one* of the tables.

TIP
At least one column must be shared between two tables for you to join the two tables in a select *statement, and that column must be a primary key (or part of the key) in at least one of the tables.*

The Keys to Table Joins

Having a common column in two tables implies a relationship between the two tables. The nature of that relationship is determined by which table uses the column as a primary key. This begs the question, what is a primary key? A *primary key* is a column in a table used for identifying the uniqueness of each row in a table. The table in which the column appears as a primary key is referred to as the *parent table* in this relationship (sometimes also called the *master table*), whereas the column that references the other table in the relationship is often called the *child table* (sometimes also called the *detail table*). The common column appearing in the child table is referred to as a *foreign key*. Figure 3-1 demonstrates how the relationship may work in a database.

select Statements That Join Data from More Than One Table

Recall from Chapters 1 and 2 that a select statement can have three parts: the select clause, the from clause, and the where clause. That final clause, the where clause, contains comparison operators that filter out the unwanted data from what you want to see. To join data from one table to another, you must compare the data in the common column from one table to that same column in the other table in the where clause.

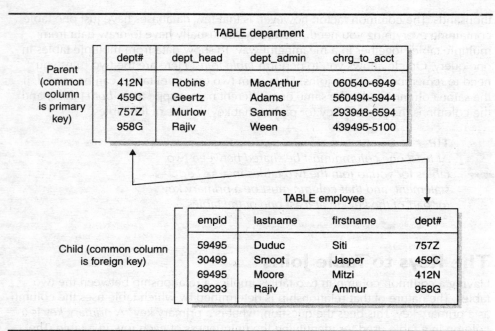

FIGURE 3-1. *Parent and child tables*

Oracle Join Syntax

Let's look at an example of a join statement using the Oracle traditional syntax, where we join the contents of the EMP and DEPT tables together to obtain a listing of all employees, along with the names of the departments they work for:

```
SQL> select e.ename, e.deptno, d.dname
  2  from emp e, dept d
  3  where e.deptno = d.deptno;
ENAME        DEPTNO DNAME
---------- --------- --------------
SMITH          20 RESEARCH
ALLEN          30 SALES
WARD           30 SALES
JONES          20 RESEARCH
MARTIN         30 SALES
BLAKE          30 SALES
CLARK          10 ACCOUNTING
SCOTT          20 RESEARCH
KING           10 ACCOUNTING
```

```
TURNER             30  SALES
ADAMS              20  RESEARCH
JAMES              30  SALES
FORD               20  RESEARCH
MILLER             10  ACCOUNTING
```

Note the many important components in this table join. Listing two tables in the `from` clause clearly indicates that a table join is taking place. Note also that each table name is followed by a letter: E for EMP or D for DEPT. This demonstrates an interesting concept—just as columns can have aliases, so too can tables. The aliases serve an important purpose—they prevent Oracle from getting confused about which table to use when listing the data in the DEPTNO column. Remember, EMP and DEPT both have a column named DEPTNO. Look what happens when we don't use aliases:

```
SQL> select ename, deptno, dname
  2  from emp, dept
  3  where deptno = deptno;
where deptno = deptno
                 *
ERROR at line 3:
ORA-00918: column ambiguously defined
```

You can also avoid ambiguity in table joins by prefixing references to the columns with the table names, but this often requires extra coding. You can also give the column two different names, but then you might forget that the relationship exists between the two tables. It's just better to use aliases! Notice something else, though. Neither the alias nor the full table name needs to be specified for columns appearing in only one table. Take a look at another example:

```
SQL> select ename, emp.deptno, dname
  2  from emp, dept
  3  where emp.deptno = dept.deptno;
ENAME          DEPTNO DNAME
---------- --------- ---------------
SMITH              20  RESEARCH
ALLEN              30  SALES
WARD               30  SALES
JONES              20  RESEARCH
MARTIN             30  SALES
BLAKE              30  SALES
CLARK              10  ACCOUNTING
SCOTT              20  RESEARCH
KING               10  ACCOUNTING
TURNER             30  SALES
```

```
ADAMS          20 RESEARCH
JAMES          30 SALES
FORD           20 RESEARCH
MILLER         10 ACCOUNTING
```

Cartesian Products

Notice also that our where clause includes a comparison on DEPTNO linking data in EMP to that of DEPT. Without this link, the output would have included all data from EMP and DEPT, jumbled together in a mess called a *Cartesian product*. Cartesian products are big, meaningless listings of output that are nearly never what you want. They are formed when you omit a join condition in your SQL statement, which causes Oracle to join all rows in the first table to all rows in the second table. Let's look at a simple example in which we attempt to join two tables, each with three rows, using a select statement with no where clause, resulting in output with nine rows:

```
SQL> select a.col1, b.col_2
  2  from example_1 a, example_2 b;
     COL1 COL_2
--------- -----------------------------
        1 one
        2 one
        3 one
        1 two
        2 two
        3 two
        1 three
        2 three
        3 three
```

TIP
This table isn't created by utlsampl.sql *or* demobld.sql. *It's a trivial example, so unless you want to get some experience creating and populating tables, don't bother trying to execute the query on Oracle. If you want some experience on your own database, run the* select *statement on EMP and DEPT from the previous example, but leave off the* where *clause.*

You must always remember to include join conditions in join queries to avoid Cartesian products. But take note of another important fact. Although you learned in Chapter 2 that where clauses can contain comparison operations other than equality, to avoid Cartesian products, *you must always use equality operations in a comparison joining data from two tables*. If you want to use another comparison operation, you must first join the information using an equality comparison and then perform the other comparison somewhere else in the where clause. This is why table join operations are also sometimes referred to as *equijoins*. Take a look at the following example that shows proper construction of a table join, where the information being joined is compared further using a nonequality operation to eliminate the employees from accounting:

```
SQL> select ename, emp.deptno, dname
  2  from emp, dept
  3  where emp.deptno = dept.deptno
  4  and dept.deptno > 10;
ENAME           DEPTNO DNAME
---------- --------- --------------
SMITH              20 RESEARCH
ALLEN              30 SALES
WARD               30 SALES
JONES              20 RESEARCH
MARTIN             30 SALES
BLAKE              30 SALES
SCOTT              20 RESEARCH
TURNER             30 SALES
ADAMS              20 RESEARCH
JAMES              30 SALES
FORD               20 RESEARCH
```

ANSI/ISO Join Syntax

Oracle**9i** and higher   In Oracle9*i*, Oracle introduces strengthened support for ANSI/ISO join syntax. To join the contents of two tables together in a single result according to that syntax, we must include a join *tablename* on *join_condition* in our SQL statement. If we wanted to perform the same table join as before using this new syntax, our SQL statement would look like the following:

```
SQL> select ename, emp.deptno, dname
  2  from emp join dept
  3  on emp.deptno = dept.deptno;
ENAME           DEPTNO DNAME
---------- --------- --------------
SMITH              20 RESEARCH
ALLEN              30 SALES
WARD               30 SALES
JONES              20 RESEARCH
```

```
MARTIN      30 SALES
BLAKE       30 SALES
CLARK       10 ACCOUNTING
SCOTT       20 RESEARCH
KING        10 ACCOUNTING
TURNER      30 SALES
ADAMS       20 RESEARCH
JAMES       30 SALES
FORD        20 RESEARCH
MILLER      10 ACCOUNTING
```

Note how different this is from Oracle syntax. First, ANSI/ISO syntax separates join comparisons from all other comparisons by using a special keyword, on, to indicate what the join comparison is. You can still include a where clause in your ANSI/ISO-compliant join query, the only difference is that the where clause will contain only those additional conditions you want to use for filtering your data. You also do not list all your tables being queried in one from clause. Instead, you use the join clause directly after the from clause to identify the table being joined.

TIP

Never combine Oracle's join syntax with ANSI/ISO's join syntax! Also, there are no performance differences between Oracle join syntax and ANSI/ISO join syntax.

How Many Comparisons Do You Need?

When using Oracle syntax for table joins, a query on data from more than two tables must contain the right number of equality operations to avoid a Cartesian product. To avoid confusion, use this simple rule: If the number of tables to be joined equals *N*, include at least *N–1* equality conditions in the select statement so that each common column is referenced at least once. Similarly, if you are using the ANSI/ISO syntax for table joins, you need to use *N–1* join *tablename* on *join_condition* clauses for every *N* tables being joined.

TIP

For N joined tables using Oracle or ANSI/ISO syntax for table joins, you need at least N–1 equijoin conditions in the where clause of your select statement or N–1 join tablename on join_condition clauses in order to avoid a Cartesian product, respectively.

Natural Joins

One additional type of join you need to know about for OCP is the natural join. A natural join is a join between two tables where Oracle joins the tables according to the column(s) in the two tables sharing the same name (naturally!). Natural joins are executed whenever the `natural` keyword is present. Let's look at an example. Recall our use of the EMP and DEPT tables from our discussion above. Let's take a quick look at the column listings for both tables:

```
SQL> describe emp
Name                             Null?     Type
------------------------------   --------  ------------
EMPNO                            NOT NULL  NUMBER(4)
ENAME                                      VARCHAR2(10)
JOB                                        VARCHAR2(9)
MGR                                        NUMBER(4)
HIREDATE                                   DATE
SAL                                        NUMBER(7,2)
COMM                                       NUMBER(7,2)
DEPTNO                                     NUMBER(2)
SQL> describe dept
Name                             Null?     Type
------------------------------   --------  ------------
DEPTNO                           NOT NULL  NUMBER(2)
DNAME                                      VARCHAR2(14)
LOC                                        VARCHAR2(13)
```

As you can see, DEPTNO is the only column in common between these two tables, and appropriately enough, it has the same name in both tables. This combination of facts makes our join query of EMP and DEPT tables a perfect candidate for a natural join. Take a look and see:

```
SQL> select ename, deptno, dname
  2  from emp natural join dept;
ENAME          DEPTNO DNAME
----------  ---------  --------------
SMITH           20 RESEARCH
ALLEN           30 SALES
WARD            30 SALES
JONES           20 RESEARCH
MARTIN          30 SALES
BLAKE           30 SALES
CLARK           10 ACCOUNTING
SCOTT           20 RESEARCH
KING            10 ACCOUNTING
TURNER          30 SALES
```

```
ADAMS              20  RESEARCH
JAMES              30  SALES
FORD               20  RESEARCH
MILLER             10  ACCOUNTING
```

We can see that natural joins allow you to greatly simplify your join queries by eliminating table aliases and join comparisons. This is because Oracle assumes the column with the same name in both tables is the one to use for the join comparison. If multiple columns in the tables have the same name, Oracle incorporates join comparisons for all the common columns. We can see where natural joins can aid greatly in consolidating the contents of a where clause in your queries to include only filter criteria. Let's look at an example:

```
SQL> select ename, deptno, dname
  2  from emp natural join dept
  3  where dept.loc = 'NEW YORK';
ENAME           DEPTNO DNAME
----------    --------- --------------
CLARK              10  ACCOUNTING
KING               10  ACCOUNTING
MILLER             10  ACCOUNTING
```

Cartesian Products: An ANSI/ISO Perspective

In some cases, you might actually want to retrieve a Cartesian product, particularly in financial applications where you have a table of numbers that needs to be cross-multiplied with another table of numbers for statistical analysis purposes. ANSI/ISO makes a provision in its syntax for producing Cartesian products through the use of a *cross-join*. A cross-join is produced when you use the cross keyword in your ANSI/ISO-compliant join query. Recall from a previous example that we produced a Cartesian product by omitting the where clause when joining two sample tables, each containing three rows, to produce nine rows of output. We can produce this same result in ANSI/ISO SQL by using the cross keyword, as shown here in bold:

```
SQL> select col1, col_2
  2  from example_1 cross join example_2;
    COL1 COL_2
-------- ------------------------------
       1 one
       2 one
       3 one
       1 two
       2 two
       3 two
       1 three
```

```
2 three
3 three
```

For Review

1. A *table join* is a type of query that obtains data from two or more tables based on common information in both tables.

2. In order to join data from two tables, you must have a common column in both tables, and that column must be a primary key in *one* of the tables.

3. You must use equality comparisons in the where clause joining data between two tables. Nonequality comparisons usually result in Cartesian products.

4. To know how many comparisons to include in a join statement, remember this formula: For *N* tables, use *N*–1 equality comparisons.

5. Be sure you know what natural joins and cross-joins are for OCP.

Exercises

1. **Two tables, PRODUCT and STORAGE_BOX, exist in a database. Individual products are listed in the table by unique ID number, product name, and the box a particular product is stored in. Individual storage boxes (identified by number) listed in the other table can contain many products, but each box can be found in only one location. Which of the following statements will correctly display the product ID, name, and box location of all widgets in this database?**

   A. `select p.prod_id, p.prod_name, b.box_loc from product p, storage_box b where p.prod_id = b.prod_id and prod_name = 'WIDGET';`

   B. `select p.prod_id, p.prod_name, b.box_loc from product p, storage_box b where prod_name = 'WIDGET';`

   C. `select p.prod_id, p.prod_name, b.box_loc from product p, storage_box b where p.stor_box_num = b.stor_box_num and p.prod_name = 'WIDGET';`

   D. `select prod_id, prod_name, box_loc from product, storage_box where stor_box_num = stor_box_num and prod_name = 'WIDGET';`

2. **You want to join information from three tables as part of developing a report. The tables are EMP, DEPT, and SALGRADE. Only records corresponding to employee, department location, and salary range are required for employees in grades 10 and higher for the organization. How many comparison operations are required for this query?**

   A. Two

   B. Three

   C. Four

   D. Five

3. **You wish to join the contents of two tables, PRODUCT and STORAGE, to list the location of all boxes. PRODUCT has three columns, ID, NAME, and BOX#. STORAGE has two columns, BOX# and LOC. Which of the following choices will not give the desired result?**

   A. `select product.id, product.name, storage.loc from product, storage where product.box# = storage.box#;`

   B. `select product.id, product.name, storage.loc from product join storage on product.box# = storage.box#;`

   C. `select product.id, product.name, storage.loc from product natural join storage on product.box# = storage.box#;`

   D. `select product.id, product.name, storage.loc from product natural join storage;`

4. **What is the name of the result when a join statement lacks a where clause (two words)? _____. What ANSI/ISO keywords can be used to obtain this type of result? _____.**

Answer Key

1. C. 2. B. Remember, you must include two equality comparisons to form the join properly, plus an additional filtering comparison to get only records where salary grade is greater than 10. 3. C.
4. Cartesian product, `cross-join`

Creating Outer Joins

Outer joins extend the capacity of Oracle queries to include handling of situations where you want to see information from tables even when no corresponding records exist in the common column. You can see a graphical representation of outer joins in Figure 3-2. For the purposes of this demonstration, let's issue the following statement in our SQL*Plus session:

```
SQL> update emp set deptno = NULL where ename = 'KING';
1 row updated.
```

TIP
We'll talk more about update *statements in Chapter 6.*

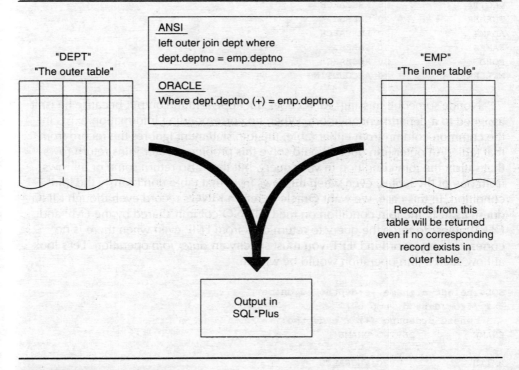

FIGURE 3-2. *Outer joins*

In effect, we're telling Oracle that because KING is the company president, he is no longer reporting to his old department number. Now look at what happens when we try to join the EMP table to the DEPT table using the common DEPTNO column:

```
SQL> select e.ename, e.deptno, d.dname
  2  from dept d, emp e
  3  where d.deptno = e.deptno;
ENAME           DEPTNO DNAME
---------- --------- --------------
SMITH              20 RESEARCH
ALLEN              30 SALES
WARD               30 SALES
JONES              20 RESEARCH
MARTIN             30 SALES
BLAKE              30 SALES
CLARK              10 ACCOUNTING
SCOTT              20 RESEARCH
TURNER             30 SALES
ADAMS              20 RESEARCH
JAMES              30 SALES
FORD               20 RESEARCH
MILLER             10 ACCOUNTING
```

Notice someone missing? KING does not appear in the output because he isn't assigned to a department anymore. When no corresponding information exists in the common column from either table, the join statement ignores the record from that table. An outer join query would solve this problem. Outer joins return rows that satisfy the join condition in your query, but they also return some or all rows from one of the tables, even when the rows from that table don't satisfy the join condition. In this case, we want Oracle to return KING's record even though KING doesn't satisfy the join condition on the DEPTNO column shared by the EMP and DEPT tables. To force the query to return data from EMP even when there is no corresponding record in DEPT, you must specify an *outer join* operation. Let's look at how such a join operation would be written:

```
SQL> select e.ename, e.deptno, d.dname
  2  from dept d, emp e
  3  where d.deptno (+) = e.deptno;
ENAME           DEPTNO DNAME
---------- --------- --------------
SMITH              20 RESEARCH
ALLEN              30 SALES
WARD               30 SALES
JONES              20 RESEARCH
```

```
MARTIN          30 SALES
BLAKE           30 SALES
CLARK           10 ACCOUNTING
SCOTT           20 RESEARCH
KING
TURNER          30 SALES
ADAMS           20 RESEARCH
JAMES           30 SALES
FORD            20 RESEARCH
MILLER          10 ACCOUNTING
```

By using outer join statements, we can get KING listed in the result, even though he is outside the join criteria specified by the query. Notice the use of the (+) marker (in bold) after the reference to the DEPTNO column in the DEPT table; this is called the *outer join operator*. This marker denotes which table can have NULL data corresponding to non-NULL values in the column values from the other table. The outer join marker is on the side of the DEPT table, meaning that data in the EMP table can correspond either to values in DEPT or to NULL if there is no corresponding value in the DEPT table. Had the order been reversed, such that the outer join operator appears next to the column reference in EMP, then values from DEPT with or without corresponding values in EMP would have been listed. Take a look at the following code block to see what I mean:

```
SQL> select e.ename, e.deptno, d.dname
  2  from dept d, emp e
  3  where d.deptno = e.deptno (+);
ENAME          DEPTNO DNAME
---------- --------- --------------
MILLER          10 ACCOUNTING
CLARK           10 ACCOUNTING
SMITH           20 RESEARCH
SCOTT           20 RESEARCH
ADAMS           20 RESEARCH
FORD            20 RESEARCH
JONES           20 RESEARCH
ALLEN           30 SALES
JAMES           30 SALES
TURNER          30 SALES
BLAKE           30 SALES
MARTIN          30 SALES
WARD            30 SALES
                   OPERATIONS
```

TIP
Be careful where you place the (+) symbol for outer joins—if it appears next to the column reference for the wrong table in the join comparison, your result set will contain unexpected data.

ANSI/ISO Syntax for Outer Joins

 Oracle9i extends its compliance with ANSI/ISO by supporting that standard's requirements for outer join syntax and semantics. As with the syntax for standard join operations, the syntax for outer joins in ANSI/ISO seeks to separate the join conditions from the rest of the comparison operations in the where clause of your SQL query. Let's take another look at the query from earlier, where we managed to include KING's record in the output even though he wasn't assigned to a department. For reference, both versions of the query are shown below:

```
SQL> -- earlier version with outer join operator
SQL> -- select e.ename, e.deptno, d.dname
SQL> -- from dept d, emp e
SQL> -- where d.deptno (+) = e.deptno;
SQL>
SQL> -- ANSI/ISO version
SQL> select e.ename, e.deptno, d.dname
  2  from emp e left outer join dept d
  3  on d.deptno = e.deptno;
ENAME         DEPTNO DNAME
---------- --------- --------------
MILLER            10 ACCOUNTING
CLARK             10 ACCOUNTING
FORD              20 RESEARCH
ADAMS             20 RESEARCH
SCOTT             20 RESEARCH
JONES             20 RESEARCH
SMITH             20 RESEARCH
JAMES             30 SALES
TURNER            30 SALES
BLAKE             30 SALES
MARTIN            30 SALES
WARD              30 SALES
ALLEN             30 SALES
KING
```

Let's look at the code shown in bold above in more detail. We can see that the keywords left outer precede the join keyword to signify this is an outer join. Thus, we can see how ANSI/ISO introduces the convention of bidirectionality in outer joins. Earlier, we placed the (+) symbol next to D.DEPTNO on the left side of the join comparison. This signifies to Oracle that records from EMP could be returned even if there were no corresponding record in DEPT. ANSI/ISO replaces the outer join operator with the `left outer join` *tablename* clause. We specify DEPT as the table name in this clause in the same way that we placed the outer join symbol next to D.DEPTNO referenced in the join comparison.

But what if we want to return records from DEPT even if there are no corresponding records in EMP? We can also specify a right join that produces results similar to another earlier query, where we moved the outer join operator to the other side. For reference, both versions of the query are shown below:

```
SQL> -- Earlier version of outer join
SQL> -- select e.ename, e.deptno, d.dname
SQL> -- from dept d, emp e
SQL> -- where d.deptno = e.deptno (+);
SQL>
SQL> -- ANSI/ISO version
SQL> select e.ename, e.deptno, d.dname
SQL> from emp e right outer join dept d
SQL> on d.deptno = e.deptno;
ENAME           DEPTNO DNAME
---------- --------- --------------
SMITH           20 RESEARCH
ALLEN           30 SALES
WARD            30 SALES
JONES           20 RESEARCH
MARTIN          30 SALES
BLAKE           30 SALES
CLARK           10 ACCOUNTING
SCOTT           20 RESEARCH
TURNER          30 SALES
ADAMS           20 RESEARCH
FORD            20 RESEARCH
MILLER          10 ACCOUNTING
JAMES           30 SALES
                   OPERATIONS
```

As you can see above, the right outer join allows us to alter the returned data without making too many drastic changes. We simply substitute the keyword `right` for `left`, and Oracle handles the rest.

TIP
*There is no default outer join option. If you omit the
`left` or `right` keywords from the `outer join`
clause, then Oracle returns an error saying the SQL
command was not properly ended. You must
identify to Oracle whether the outer join is a left
join or a right join.*

Full Outer Joins

Oracle9i also makes it possible for you to easily execute a full outer join,
including all records from the tables that would have been displayed if you
had used both the `left outer join` or `right outer join` clauses. Let's take
a look at an example:

```
SQL> select e.ename, e.deptno, d.dname
2 from emp e full outer join dept d
3 on d.deptno = e.deptno;
ENAME          DEPTNO DNAME
---------- --------- --------------
MILLER             10 ACCOUNTING
CLARK              10 ACCOUNTING
FORD               20 RESEARCH
ADAMS              20 RESEARCH
SCOTT              20 RESEARCH
JONES              20 RESEARCH
SMITH              20 RESEARCH
JAMES              30 SALES
TURNER             30 SALES
BLAKE              30 SALES
MARTIN             30 SALES
WARD               30 SALES
ALLEN              30 SALES
KING
                      OPERATIONS
```

TIP
*Never combine the Oracle outer join syntax with
the ANSI/ISO join syntax!*

Concluding This Lesson

Because we have made a change to KING's record in the EMP table for our sample data, we want to discard those changes using the following command:

```
SQL> rollback;
Rollback complete.
```

TIP
You'll learn more about the `rollback` *command in Chapter 6.*

For Quick Reference

For quick reference, Table 3-1 shows a listing of outer join where clauses using Oracle syntax and the ANSI/ISO equivalents using fictitious tables A and B.

For Review

1. Understand that an outer join accommodates the situation in which you want to display data in a join statement where records from one table don't necessarily all have corresponding records in the other.

2. (+) is the special character used to denote outer joins, however, remember that it's an Oracle convention. Remember the importance of where you

Oracle Outer Join Syntax	ANSI/ISO Equivalent
`from tab_a a, tab_b b` `where a.col_1 (+) = b.col_1`	`from tab_a a left outer join` `tab_b b on a.col_1 = b.col_1`

`from tab_a a, tab_b b`
`where a.col_1 = b.col_1 (+)`
	`from tab_a a right outer`
	`join tab_b b on a.col_1 =`
	`b.col_1`

`from tab_a a, tab_b b`
`where a.col_1 (+) = b.col_1`
`and b.col_2 = 'VALUE'`
	`from tab_a a left outer join`
	`tab_b b on a.col_1 = b.col_1`
	`and b.col_2 = 'VALUE'`

TABLE 3-1. *Oracle Outer Join Syntax and ANSI/ISO Equivalent*

place the outer join operator—it tells Oracle which table in the join can have NULL records corresponding to values from the other table.

3. Oracle's adopting ANSI/ISO conventions for join operations, using the clauses [left|right] outer join *tablename* on *join_condition*, where *tablename* is the name of the table being joined and *join_condition* is the comparison used to join the data.

4. Oracle9i introduces the possibility of executing a full outer join to include records from both tables that would be returned by combining results from left and right outer joins. To do so, use the clause full outer join *tablename* on *join_condition*.

Exercises

1. Identify the Oracle syntax symbol used for outer join operations: _____. Identify the equivalent ANSI/ISO outer join clause: _____.

2. You are defining an outer join statement. Which of the following choices is true concerning outer join statements?

   A. Because outer join operations permit NULL values from one of the tables, you do not have to specify equality comparisons to join those tables.

   B. In outer join statements on tables A and B, you specify the right outer join when you want all of table A's rows, even when no corresponding record exists in table B.

   C. In outer join statements on tables A and B, you specify the left outer join when you want all of table B's rows, even when no corresponding record exists in table A.

   D. Even though outer join operations permit NULL values from one of the tables, you still need to specify equality comparisons to join those tables.

3. Two tables, PRODUCT and STORAGE_BOX, exist in a database. Individual products are listed in the table by unique ID number, product name, and the box a particular product is stored in. Individual storage boxes (identified by number) listed in the other table can contain many products, but the box can be found in only one location. Which of the following statements will correctly display the product ID, name, and box location of all widgets in this database that have or have not been assigned to a storage box?

A. select p.prod_id, p.prod_name, b.box_loc from
   product p left outer join storage_box b on
   p.stor_box_num = b.stor_box_num where p.prod_name =
   'WIDGET'(+);

B. select p.prod_id, p.prod_name, b.box_loc from
   product p left outer join storage_box b on
   p.stor_box_num = b.stor_box_num where p.prod_name =
   'WIDGET';

C. select p.prod_id, p.prod_name, b.box_loc from
   product p right outer join storage_box b where
   b.stor_box_num = p.stor_box_num (+) and p.prod_name
   = 'WIDGET';

D. select p.prod_id, p.prod_name, b.box_loc from
   product p full outer join storage_box b on
   p.stor_box_num = b.stor_box_num where
   b.stor_box_num is NULL;

4. You issue the following command in Oracle:

```
SQL> select e.ename, a.street_address, a.city, a.state, a.post_code
  2  from emp e, addr a
  3  where e.empno = a.empno (+)
  4  and a.state = 'TEXAS';
```

Which of the following choices shows the ANSI/ISO equivalent statement?

A. select e.ename, a.street_address, a.city, a.state,
   a.post_code from emp e outer join addr a on e.empno
   = a.empno where a.state = 'TEXAS';

B. select e.ename, a.street_address, a.city, a.state,
   a.post_code from emp e left outer join addr a on
   e.empno = a.empno where a.state = 'TEXAS';

C. select e.ename, a.street_address, a.city, a.state,
   a.post_code from emp e right outer join addr a on
   e.empno = a.empno where a.state = 'TEXAS';

D. select e.ename, a.street_address, a.city, a.state,
   a.post_code from emp e right outer join addr a
   where e.empno = a.empno (+) and a.state = 'TEXAS';

5. Examine the following output from SQL*Plus:

```
PRODUCT.ID PRODUCT.NAME BOX.LOCATION
---------- ------------ ------------
578-X      WIDGET       IDAHO
                        TENNESSEE
456-Y      WIDGET
```

Which of the following choices identify the type of query that likely produced this result?

A. Full outer join

B. Left outer join

C. Right outer join

D. Equijoin

Answer Key
1. (+), [left|right] outer join tablename on join_condition **2.** D. **3.** B. **4.** C. **5.** A.

Joining a Table to Itself

In special situations, it may be necessary for you to perform a join using only one table. What you are really doing is using two copies of the table to join the data in the table to itself. This SQL programming technique is known as a table *self-join*. This task can be useful in cases where there is a possibility that some slight difference exists between two rows that would otherwise be duplicate records. If you want to perform a self-join on a table, use table aliases to specify the same table so that Oracle understands that a self-join is being performed. This lesson illustrates proper use of a self-join to show how to employ the technique properly. To follow along in your Oracle database, issue the following command:

```
SQL> insert into emp values (7903, 'FORD', 'ANALYST', '7566',
  2  '03-DEC-81', 3000, null, 10);
1 row created.
```

TIP
You'll see more examples of using the insert
command in Chapter 6.

In this case, we've added a new record to table EMP for employee FORD, who is already an employee of the company. Everything about this user is the same, except for her employee number. Once we realize our mistake, we can issue the following simple query to obtain the duplicate records:

```
SQL> select * from emp where ename = 'FORD';
EMPNO ENAME    JOB  MGR HIREDATE    SAL COMM DEPTNO
----- -----  ------- ---- ---------  ---- ---- ------
 7902 FORD   ANALYST 7566 03-DEC-81 3000        20
 7903 FORD   ANALYST 7566 03-DEC-81 3000        20
```

This simple query works fine for this uncomplicated example, but let's make it more complex. Let's pretend that the EMP table stores values for a company with hundreds of employees named FORD, each working in different jobs and under different managers. In this case, we might use the following query to guarantee that the instances of FORD we get are the ones we want:

```
SQL> select e.empno, e.ename, e.job
  2  from emp e, emp e2
  3  where e.empno <> e2.empno
  4  and e.ename = e2.ename
  5  and e.job = e2.job
  6  and e.mgr = e2.mgr;
    EMPNO ENAME      JOB        MGR
--------- ---------- --------- ----
     7903 FORD       ANALYST    7566
     7902 FORD       ANALYST    7566
```

This query says, "OK, Oracle, give me the records for users named FORD who have different employee numbers, but filter out the FORDs working in different jobs for different managers." As you can see, self-joins can be useful for obtaining nearly duplicate records in the event some error occurs. Situations where this might be useful include the following:

- Batch jobs that incorrectly load lots of duplicate records

- Situations where users enter nearly duplicate records by mistake

- Any instance where a record nearly identical to a record already in the table may have been entered

Some Self-Join Caveats

Here's a final note of caution. Although powerful and useful for identifying duplicate records, self-joins should be run with extreme caution because of two important factors. First, self-joins often take a long time to process and can cause performance issues for other users on the database. This is because Oracle must read all table data twice sequentially. Second, because the required number of equality operations is at least *two* in the situation of self-joins (one to join the table to itself and the other to distinguish the duplication), Cartesian products can result when you don't formulate your where clause properly. Without a proper comparison operation set up in the where clause, you may wind up with many copies of every row in the table returned, which will certainly run for a long time and produce a lot of unnecessary output.

TIP
The number of equality operations usually needed in the where clause of a self-join of a table to itself should be two or more—one to join the table to itself and the other to distinguish the duplicates.

In Conclusion

To wrap up this lesson, let's once again make sure that the changes we made to the demo tables are not saved. To do this, issue the following command:

```
SQL> rollback;
Rollback complete.
```

TIP
Once again, you'll learn more about the rollback command in Chapter 6.

For Review

1. Know what a self-join is and how one is formulated and used.

2. When using a self-join, remember that you need enough comparison operations in the where clause to join the table to itself and distinguish the duplicate records.

3. Understand the slow performance and Cartesian product issues that may arise from the use of self-joins.

Exercises

1. **A multinational Fortune 500 company uses internal testing to determine employee promotability and job placement. Tests are offered at multiple locations. Employees are permitted to take tests for any job they want to apply for, with one restriction: An employee may take a specific exam for a corresponding job position only once per year. Recently, Human Resources discovered that some employees were circumventing this restriction by taking the same exam in different test locations. Which of the following queries might be useful in identifying employees who have circumvented this restriction?**

   A. ```
select a.ename, a.test_name, a.test_date,
a.location b.test_date, b.location from tests a,
tests b where a.ename = b.ename and a.test_name =
b.test_name and a.location = b.location and
trunc(a.test_date) > trunc(sysdate-365) and
trunc(b.test_date) > trunc(sysdate-365);
```

   **B.** ```
select a.ename, a.test_name, a.test_date,
a.location b.test_date, b.location from tests a,
tests b where a.ename <> b.ename and a.test_name =
b.test_name and a.location = b.location and
trunc(a.test_date) > trunc(sysdate-365) and
trunc(b.test_date) > trunc(sysdate-365);
```

   C. ```
select a.ename, a.test_name, a.test_date,
a.location b.test_date, b.location from tests a,
tests b where a.ename = b.ename and a.test_name <>
b.test_name and a.location = b.location and
trunc(a.test_date) > trunc(sysdate-365) and
trunc(b.test_date) > trunc(sysdate-365);
```

   **D.** ```
select a.ename, a.test_name, a.test_date,
a.location b.test_date, b.location from tests a,
tests b where a.ename = b.ename and a.test_name =
b.test_name and a.location <> b.location and
a.test_date > trunc(sysdate-365) and b.test_date >
trunc(sysdate-365);
```

2. **Identify a general concern related to the use of self-joins on the Oracle database:** _____

3. **Identify a problem with self-joins resulting from malformed where clauses (two words):** _____

Answer Key
1. D. 2. Performance. 3. Cartesian products.

Group Functions and Their Uses

This section will cover the following topics related to group functions and their uses:

- Identifying and using group functions
- Using the group by clause
- Excluding group data with the having clause

Group functions allow you to perform data operations on several values in a column of data as though the column were one collective group of data. These functions are also called *group-by functions* because they are often used in a special clause of select statements, called the group by clause. A more complete discussion of the group by clause appears later in this section. This discussion also describes how to use the having clause in group by clauses, which can act as a where clause within a where clause.

Identifying and Using Group Functions

Sometimes, you may want to treat the data in a column as if it were a list of items to be manipulated as a group. Think about the contents of the EMP table. Let's say you want to obtain the average salary for employees in the company. The formula for averaging numbers is to add all the numbers in the list together and then divide by the number of elements in that list. Group functions are useful for this sort of activity because, unlike single-row functions, group functions can operate on column data in several rows at a time. Here's a list of the available group functions:

- **avg(x)**   Averages all *x* column values returned by the select statement
- **count(x)**   Counts the number of non-NULL values returned by the select statement for column *x*
- **max(x)**   Determines the maximum value in column *x* for all rows returned by the select statement
- **min(x)**   Determines the minimum value in column *x* for all rows returned by the select statement
- **stddev(x)**   Calculates the standard deviation for all values in column *x* in all rows returned by the select statement

- **sum(x)** Calculates the sum of all values in column *x* in all rows returned by the `select` statement
- **Variance(x)** Calculates the variance for all values in column *x* in all rows returned by the `select` statement

Group Functions in Action

Let's take a closer look at the grouping functions. The `avg( )` function takes the values for a single column on all rows returned by the query and calculates the average value for that column. Based on EMP, the `avg( )` function on the SAL column produces the following result:

```
SQL> select avg(sal) from emp;
 AVG(SAL)
---------
2073.2143
```

The second grouping function listed is `count( )`. This function is bound to become the cornerstone of any Oracle professional's repertoire. The `count( )` function returns a row count for the table, given certain column names, `select` criteria, or both. Note that the fastest way to execute `count( )` is to pass a value that resolves quickly in the SQL processing mechanism. Some values that resolve quickly are integers and the ROWID pseudocolumn. Here's an example:

```
SQL> SELECT COUNT(*), -- Slow
  2  COUNT(1), -- Fast
  3  COUNT(rowid) -- Fast
  4  FROM EMP;

COUNT(*)  COUNT(1) COUNT(rowid)
--------  -------- ------------
      14        14           14
```

TIP
The `count(expr)` function returns the number of rows in the table with a non-NULL value in the column you are counting. In other words, if you specify a column for the `count( )` function, and a row for that column contains a NULL value, then the row won't be counted. Many users of Oracle avoid this problem by using `count(ROWID)`. It's faster than `count(*)`, and every row in a table will have a ROWID value.

The asterisk (*) in the previous query is a wildcard variable that indicates all columns in the table. For better performance, this wildcard should not generally be used because the Oracle SQL processing mechanism must first resolve all column names in the table—a step that is unnecessary if you're simply trying to count rows. Notice that one of these examples uses the special pseudocolumn ROWID, which is a special value that uniquely identifies each row. Each row in a table has one unique ROWID.

TIP

Do not use count (*) *to determine the number of rows in a table. Use* count (1) *or* count (ROWID) *instead. These options are faster because they bypass some unnecessary operations in Oracle's SQL processing mechanism.*

The next pair of grouping functions to be covered is the max( ) and min( ) functions. The max( ) function determines the largest value for the column passed, whereas min( ) determines the smallest value for the column passed, as shown here:

```
SQL> select max(sal), min(sal) from emp;
 MAX(SAL)  MIN(SAL)
--------- ---------
     5000       800
```

You can combine group functions with single-row functions as well. The following example shows how:

```
SQL> select to_char(max(hiredate),'DD-MON-YYYY') "Newest",
  2   to_char(min(hiredate),'DD-MON-YYYY') "Oldest"
  3  from emp;
Newest      Oldest
----------- -----------
23-MAY-1987 17-DEC-1980
```

The final group function, sum( ), is used commonly in simple accounting reports. The sum( ) function gives the total of all values in a column. Here's an example:

```
SQL> select sum(sal) from emp;
 SUM(SAL)
---------
    29025
```

In general, the group functions operate on columns of datatypes NUMBER and DATE because many of the functions they represent in mathematics are numeric operations. It makes little sense to take the standard deviation for a set of 12 words, unless the user wants to take the standard deviation of the length of those words by combining the use of the `length( )` function with the `stddev( )` function. A few notable exceptions to this general rule exist, though. The first exception is the `count( )` function. The `count( )` function operates on a column of any datatype. The other exceptions are `max( )` and `min( )`, which operate on many different Oracle datatypes in addition to NUMBER and DATE.

Group Functions Ignore Null Values!

Group functions ignore NULL values by default. To force Oracle group functions not to ignore NULL values, you can use the `nvl( )` function. For example, let's look at the results of a group function when NULL values are present in the column with and without use of the `nvl( )` function:

```
SQL> select avg(comm) from emp;
AVG(COMM)
---------
      550
SQL> select avg(nvl(comm,0)) from emp;
AVG(NVL(COMM,0))
----------------
      157.142857
```

For Review

1. Know what the group functions are and how they are used in simple `select` statements.

2. Understand specifically how to use the `count( )` function and why using `count(ROWID)` or `count(1)` might be a better idea than using `count(*)`.

3. Understand that group functions ignore NULL values by default, but can be forced not to ignore NULL values through the use of the `nvl( )` function.

Exercises

1. A table containing all 1,232,432 customer orders for the last year has a column, TOTAL, that lists the total amount spent by the customers on their orders. You issue the following command to obtain gross sales for the year:

`select sum(total) from customers`. Which of the following choices identifies the number of rows that will appear in the output?

A. 1

B. 2

C. 500

D. 1,232,432

2. The standard EMP table we have worked with so far in the book contains 14 records corresponding to employees of the corporation. One of those records has a NULL value stored in the MGR column. You issue the following command on that table: `select count(mgr) from emp;`. Which of the following choices identifies the result Oracle will return?

A. 11

B. 12

C. 13

D. 14

3. Identify the type of value that group functions ignore by default: _____. Name the single-row function that can be used in conjunction with group functions to force group functions not to ignore that type of value: _____.

Answer Key

1. A. 2. C. 3. NULL, nvl( )

Using the `group` `by` Clause

So far, you've seen examples of using group functions by themselves in the column clause of your query. This use is well and good, but sometimes it gives more meaning to the output of a `select` statement to collect data into logical groupings in combination with group functions. For example, let's say you want a listing of the different job roles in the corporation, along with the number of employees who fill those roles. For our small company, you could simply list all the information in the EMP table and count by hand. However, that process wouldn't work in a larger organization. Instead, you might want to use a `select` statement with a group function such as count ( ) to produce a meaningful listing of information. Let's try it out:

```
SQL> select job, count(job)
  2  from emp;
SQL> select job, count(job)
            *
ERROR at line 1:
ORA-00937: not a single-group group function
```

What happened? Well, we forgot something. Oracle expects group functions to produce one line of output for all rows in the table whose column you specify. In this case, Oracle became confused when we told it to list the individual values for the JOB column by including a reference to JOB in the column clause, too. The solution is to include a group by clause, which in effect tells Oracle to list each *distinct* value for JOB and then count the number of times that value appears in the EMP table. Let's take another look:

```
SQL> select job, count(job)
  2  from emp
  3  group by job;
JOB          COUNT(JOB)
---------    ----------
ANALYST               2
CLERK                 4
MANAGER               3
PRESIDENT             1
SALESMAN              4
```

TIP

All columns in the column clause of your select *statement that are not in a group function must be listed in the* group *by clause. However, a column listed in the* group *by clause needn't appear in the column clause.*

Perfect! The group by clause in this example saves you from performing a great deal of work by hand. Instead, Oracle shoulders most of the work and shows only the results you need. The group by clause works well in many situations where you want to report calculations on data according to groups or categories.

Now let's consider a more complex example. Suppose you want a list of our company's average salary for a given job within a department. You already saw what happens when the group by clause is left out entirely. But there's something else we need to be careful about. Take a look at a first stab for developing a group by query that satisfies our requirements:

```
SQL> select deptno, avg(sal), job
  2  from emp
  3  group by deptno;
select deptno, avg(sal), job
                         *
ERROR at line 1:
ORA-00979: not a GROUP BY expression
```

When you use a group by clause in your query, all the nongroup expressions in the column clause of the query must appear before the grouped expression in the column clause. Put another way, *no nongroup expression can appear after the group expression in the column clause*. To solve the problem, we can remove the JOB column from the column clause entirely. However, that won't give us the output we need. Instead, we must first rearrange the nongroup expressions in the column clause to appear in front of the group function and then add the JOB column to the group by clause. This way, Oracle knows how to evaluate the aggregate columns in the select statement that are part of the grouping expression. The solution is shown here:

```
SQL> select deptno, job, avg(sal)
  2  from emp
  3  group by deptno, job;
DEPTNO JOB         AVG(SAL)
--------- --------- ---------
       10 CLERK          1300
       10 MANAGER        2450
       10 PRESIDENT      5000
       20 ANALYST        3000
       20 CLERK           950
       20 MANAGER        2975
       30 CLERK           950
       30 MANAGER        2850
       30 SALESMAN       1400
```

Notice something else about this output—the records are listed in order based on the contents of the DEPTNO column. This is because DEPTNO appears first in the group by clause. If we listed JOB first, the output would be alphabetized by job, as shown here:

```
SQL> select deptno, job, avg(sal)
  2  from emp
```

```
3   group by job, deptno;
  DEPTNO JOB         AVG(SAL)
--------- --------- ---------
     20 ANALYST        3000
     10 CLERK          1300
     20 CLERK           950
     30 CLERK           950
     10 MANAGER        2450
     20 MANAGER        2975
     30 MANAGER        2850
     10 PRESIDENT      5000
     30 SALESMAN       1400
```

You can use order by clauses with group by clauses as well—it's actually fairly common to do so. Take a look at the following output, where we've created some additional meaning by ordering the output such that the highest average salaries are listed at the top, so we can figure out which departments and jobs pay the most:

```
SQL> select deptno, job, avg(sal)
  2   from emp
  3   group by deptno, job
  4   order by 3 desc;
  DEPTNO JOB         AVG(SAL)
--------- --------- ---------
     10 PRESIDENT      5000
     20 ANALYST        3000
     20 MANAGER        2975
     30 MANAGER        2850
     10 MANAGER        2450
     30 SALESMAN       1400
     10 CLERK          1300
     20 CLERK           950
     30 CLERK           950
```

TIP

When you're using an order by clause with a group by clause, the order in which you list columns in the group by clause doesn't matter—the order of output is dictated by the order by clause.

OLAP Features in Oracle

Some features for query processing in Oracle include the use of online analytical processing (OLAP) operations in your database. These features are useful for data warehousing and data mart applications used for supporting business decision-making processes. The first of these new operations is a performance enhancement to a specific type of query, called a *top-N* query. We discuss top-N queries more extensively later in the book. The other two new operations make it possible to perform certain OLAP operations in a `group by` clause. These two operations are `cube` and `rollup`. Let's look at each in more detail.

rollup   This `group by` operation is used to produce subtotals at any level of aggregation needed. These subtotals then "roll up" into a grand total, according to items listed in the `group by` expression. The totaling is based on a one-dimensional data hierarchy of grouped information. For example, let's say we wanted to get a payroll breakdown for our company by department and job position. The following code block would give us that information:

```
SQL> select deptno, job, sum(sal) as salary
  2  from emp
  3  group by rollup(deptno, job);
   DEPTNO JOB             SALARY
--------- ---------- ---------
       10 CLERK           1300
       10 MANAGER         2450
       10 PRESIDENT       5000
       10                 8750
       20 ANALYST         6000
       20 CLERK           1900
       20 MANAGER         2975
       20                10875
       30 CLERK            950
       30 MANAGER         2850
       30 SALESMAN        5600
       30                 9400
                         29025
```

TIP
Notice that NULL values in the output of `rollup`
*operations typically mean that the row contains
subtotal or grand total information. If you want, you
can use the* `nvl ( )` *function to substitute a more
meaningful value.*

cube   This is an extension, similar to `rollup`. The difference is that `cube` allows you to take a specified set of grouping columns and create subtotals for all possible combinations of them. The `cube` operation calculates all levels of subtotals on horizontal lines across spreadsheets of output and creates cross-tab summaries on multiple vertical columns in those spreadsheets. The result is a summary that shows subtotals for every combination of columns or expressions in the `group by` clause, which is also known as *n-dimensional cross-tabulation*. In the following example, notice how `cube` not only gives us the payroll breakdown of our company by DEPTNO and JOB, but it also gives us the breakdown of payroll by JOB across all departments:

```
SQL>  select deptno, job, sum(sal) as salary
  2   from emp
  3   group by cube(deptno, job);
DEPTNO JOB          SALARY
------- --------- ---------
    10 CLERK          1300
    10 MANAGER        2450
    10 PRESIDENT      5000
    10                8750
    20 ANALYST        6000
    20 CLERK          1900
    20 MANAGER        2975
    20               10875
    30 CLERK           950
    30 MANAGER        2850
    30 SALESMAN       5600
    30                9400
       ANALYST        6000
       CLERK          4150
       MANAGER        8275
       PRESIDENT      5000
       SALESMAN       5600
                     29025
```

For Review

1. Know that the use of a group function in combination with a nongroup expression in the column clause requires using the group by clause. All nongroup expressions must be listed before the group expression.

2. Understand the relationship between the order in which columns are listed in the group by expression and the order in which Oracle will list records in

the output. Also, know that when an order by clause is used, it overrides the order set by the group by clause.

3. Be sure you can identify the situations in which statements containing the group by clause return errors as well as how to resolve those errors.

4. Know how to use OLAP functionality provided by cube and `rollup` in the group by clause. Also, know that without this functionality, you would have to develop long multiple queries whose output is joined by `union all` operations (don't worry about what a `union all` operation is; just be sure you can identify it as an alternative to the OLAP functions described in this section).

Exercises

1. **You are developing a query on the PROFITS table that stores profit information by company region, product type, and quarterly time period. Which of the following SQL statements will display a cross-tabulation of output showing profits by region, product type, and time period?**

   A. `select region, prod_type, time, sum(profit) from profits group by region, prod_type, time;`

   B. `select region, prod_type, time from profits group by rollup (region, prod_type, time);`

   C. `select region, prod_type, time from profits group by cube (region, prod_type, time);`

   D. `select region, prod_type, time, sum(profit) from profits group by cube (region, prod_type, time);`

2. **Which of the following choices identifies a group by query that will not result in an error from Oracle when run against the database?**

   A. `select deptno, job, sum(sal) from emp group by job, deptno;`

   B. `select sum(sal), deptno, job from emp group by job, deptno;`

   C. `select deptno, job, sum(sal) from emp;`

   D. `select deptno, sum(sal), job from emp group by job, deptno;`

3. **Review the following SQL statement:**

```
SQL> select a.deptno, a.job, b.loc, sum(a.sal)
  2  from emp a, dept b
  3  where a.deptno = b.deptno
  4  group by a.deptno, a.job, b.loc
  5  order by sum(a.sal);
```

Which of the following choices identifies the column upon which the order of output from this query will be returned?

A. A.DEPTNO

B. A.JOB

C. B.LOC

D. sum(A.SAL)

4. **Without the OLAP functionality built into group by statements, you would need to develop multiple SQL queries whose output is joined by these types of statements (two words):**

_____

Answer Key
1. D. 2. A. 3. D. 4. union all

Excluding group Data with having

Once the data is grouped using the group by statement, it is sometimes useful to _weed out_ unwanted data. For example, let's say we want to list the average salary paid to employees in our company, broken down by department and job title. However, for this query, we only care about departments and job titles where the average salary is over $2000. In effect, we want to put a where clause on the group by clause to limit the results we see to departments and job titles where the average salary equals $2001 or higher. This effect can be achieved with the use of a special clause called the having clause, which is associated with group by statements. Take a look at an example of this clause:

```
SQL> select deptno, job, avg(sal)
  2  from emp
  3  group by deptno, job
  4  having avg(sal) > 2000;
  DEPTNO JOB          AVG(SAL)
```

```
10 MANAGER       2450
10 PRESIDENT     5000
20 ANALYST       3000
20 MANAGER       2975
30 MANAGER       2850
```

Consider the output of this query for a moment. First, Oracle computes the average for every department and job title in the entire company. Then, the having clause eliminates departments and titles whose constituent employees' average salary is $2000 or less. This selectivity cannot easily be accomplished with an ordinary where clause, because the where clause selects individual rows, whereas this example requires that groups of rows be selected. In this query, you successfully limit output on the group by rows by using the having clause.

TIP
There is no specific order that the having and group by clauses must appear in. A having clause can appear before the group by clause in the query. However, it is logical that the group by appear first in the SQL statement.

For Review

1. Know what the having clause is and the function that it serves.

2. Know that referencing the group expression in the having clause allows Oracle to filter data based on known or derived criteria.

Exercises

1. You are developing a query on the PROFITS table that stores profit information by company region, product type, and quarterly time period. Which of the following choices identifies a query that will obtain the average profits greater than $100,000 by product type, region, and time period?

   A. select region, prod_type, period, avg(profit) from profits where avg(profit) > 100000 group by region, prod_type, period;

   B. select region, prod_type, period, avg(profit) from profits where avg(profit) > 100000 order by region, prod_type, period;

   C. `select region, prod_type, period, avg(profit) from`
      `profits group by region, prod_type, period having`
      `avg(profit) > 100000;`

   D. `select region, prod_type, period, avg(profit) from`
      `profits group by region, prod_type, period having`
      `avg(profit) < 100000;`

2. A having clause can act like this type of clause inside `group by` expressions: _____

Answer Key
1. C. 2. where

Chapter Summary

This chapter covered a lot of territory. You learned a great deal about advanced selection of data in SQL*Plus. We discussed how to join data in multiple tables into one output result using the premise that two tables with a common column can be used in a join operation. We discussed how to create equijoins, which are joins where the data from one table only appears if a corresponding record can be found in the other table. From there, we covered how to formulate outer joins, where the corresponding record requirement between tables isn't enforced as strictly. We learned how to join data from one table to itself using the self-join process as well. From there, we moved onto discuss group expressions and group by operations. We covered the use of the `having` clause, as well as the use of OLAP expressions like `cube` and `rollup`.

Two-Minute Drill

- `Select` statements that obtain data from more than one table and merge the data together are called *joins*.

- In order to join data from two tables, a common column must exist.

- A common column between two tables can create a foreign key, or *link*, from one table to another. This condition is especially true if the data in one of the tables is part of the primary key—the column that defines uniqueness for rows on a table.

- A foreign key can create a parent/child relationship between two tables.

- One type of join is the inner join, or *equijoin*. An equijoin operation is based on an equality operation linking the data in common columns of two tables.

- When joining tables using Oracle syntax, a join comparison on the common columns in the tables must be included in the `where` clause of the query.

- When joining tables using ANSI/ISO syntax, the `join tablename` on `join_comparison` clause must be used. The join comparison operation is thus kept separate from other filter comparisons that might otherwise appear in the `where` clause.

- ANSI/ISO and Oracle syntax for joins is logically equivalent. There is no performance advantage for using one over the other. However, ANSI/ISO and Oracle syntax for joins cannot be used together in the same SQL query.

- Another type of join is the outer join. An outer join returns data in one table even when there is no data in the other table. The "other" table in the outer join operation is called the *outer table*.

- The common column that appears in the outer table of the join must have a special marker next to it in the comparison operation of the `select` statement that creates the table.

- The Oracle-syntax outer join symbol is "(+)", which is equivalent to the ANSI/ISO `[left|right] outer join` clause. Whether the outer join is a left join or a right join depends on where the outer join symbol is placed.

- If the column name is the same in both tables, the common column in both tables used in Oracle-syntax join operations must be preceded either with a table alias that denotes the table in which the column appears or the entire table name.

- The data from a table can be joined to itself. This technique is useful in determining whether there are rows in the table that have slightly different values but are otherwise duplicate rows. This is called a *self-join* operation.

- Table aliases must be used in self-join `select` statements.

- A Cartesian product is formed when you omit a join comparison from your Oracle-syntax join statement, or when you use the `cross join` keywords in ANSI/ISO syntax.

- A natural join can be used to simplify join operations. Natural joins are possible in ANSI/ISO syntax when all common columns between joined tables have the same name. Use the `natural` keyword to specify to Oracle to execute a natural join. You do not need to specify a join comparison in order to execute a natural join.

- Data output from table `select` statements can be grouped together according to criteria set by the query.

- The `group by` clause assists you in grouping data together.

- Several grouping functions are available that allow you to perform operations on data in a column as though the data were logically one variable.

- The grouping functions are `max( )`, `min( )`, `sum( )`, `avg( )`, `stddev ( )`, `variance( )`, and `count( )`.

- These grouping functions can be applied to the column values for a table as a whole or for subsets of column data for rows returned in `group by` statements.

- Data in a `group by` statement can be excluded or included based on a special set of where criteria defined specifically for the group in a `having` clause.

- The data used to determine the `having` clause can be specified at runtime by the query.

- NULL values are ignored by group functions. To force group functions not to ignore NULL values, use the `nvl( )` function.

Fill-in-the-Blank Questions

1. This SQL command allows you to aggregate data using column functions (two words): _____

2. This phrase describes the result of a join operation on two or more tables when the where clause is poorly defined: _____

3. This SQL keyword extends the functionality of a grouping expression to act as a where clause within a where clause: _____

4. This type of constraint in Oracle is used for defining a relationship between two tables so that join operations can be executed: _____

Chapter Questions

1. **You want to specify a group expression in SQL*Plus. Which of the following is not a group function?**

   A. avg ( )

   B. sqrt ( )

   C. sum ( )

   D. max ( )

2. **You are selecting data from multiple tables in Oracle with the intent of merging the results together. In order to perform an inner join, which criteria must be true?**

   A. The common columns in the join do not need to have shared values.

   B. The tables in the join need to have common columns.

   C. The common columns in the join may or may not have shared values.

   D. The common columns in the join must have shared values.

3. **A user is setting up a join operation between tables EMPLOYEE and DEPT. There are some employees in the EMPLOYEE table that the user wants returned by the query, but the employees are not assigned to department heads yet. Which select statement is most appropriate for this user?**

   A. select e.empid, d.head from EMPLOYEE e, dept d;

B. `select e.empid, d.head from EMPLOYEE e, dept d`
   `where e.dept# = d.dept#;`

C. `select e.empid, d.head from EMPLOYEE e, dept d`
   `where e.dept# = d.dept# (+);`

D. `select e.empid, d.head from EMPLOYEE e, dept d`
   `where e.dept# (+) = d.dept#;`

4. **You are developing group expressions in Oracle. Which of the following uses of the `having` clause are appropriate? (Choose three.)**

   A. To put returned data into sorted order

   B. To exclude certain data groups based on known criteria

   C. To include certain data groups based on unknown criteria

   D. To include certain data groups based on known criteria

5. **You are developing table join statements in Oracle and wish to do so properly. Which of the following statements indicates the proper definition of a Cartesian product?**

   A. A group function

   B. The result of a join `select` statement with no `where` clause

   C. The result of fuzzy logic

   D. A special feature of Oracle server

6. **You develop the following SQL statement containing a group expression. Which line in the following `select` statement, when removed from the statement, will correct the error?**

```
select deptno, avg(sal)
from emp
group by empno;
```

   A. `select deptno, avg(sal)`

   B. `from EMP`

   C. `group by empno;`

   D. There are no errors in this statement, therefore no clauses should be removed.

Fill-in-the-Blank Answers

1. group by
2. Cartesian product.
3. having
4. Foreign key.

Answers to Chapter Questions

1. B. sqrt ( )

Explanation Square root operations are performed on one column value. Choice A is incorrect because avg ( ) is a group function that accepts a set of data and returns the average. Choice C is incorrect because the sum ( ) function is a group function that returns the sum of a set of numbers. Finally, choice D is incorrect because max ( ) is a group function that accepts a set of numbers and returns the highest value.

2. B. The tables in the join need to have common columns.

Explanation It is possible that a join operation will produce no return data, just as it is possible for any select statement not to return any data. Choices A, C, and D represent the spectrum of possibilities for shared values that may or may not be present in common columns. However, joins themselves are not possible without two tables having common columns.

3. C. select e.empid, d.head from EMPLOYEE e, dept d where e.dept# = d.dept# (+);

Explanation Choice C details the outer join operation most appropriate to this user's needs. The outer table in this join is the DEPT table, as identified by the (+) marker next to the DEPT# column in the comparison operation that defines the join. Each of the other choices incorrectly identifies the location of the outer join operator, or else contains some other error.

4. B, C, and D. To exclude certain data groups based on known criteria, to include certain data groups based on unknown criteria, *and* to include certain data groups based on known criteria

Explanation All exclusion or inclusion of grouped rows is handled by the having clause of a select statement. Choice A is not an appropriate answer because sort order is given in a select statement by the order by clause.

5. B. The result of a join `select` statement with no `where` clause

Explanation A Cartesian product is the resultant dataset from a `select` statement in which all data from both tables is returned. Some potential causes of a Cartesian product include not specifying a `where` clause for the join `select` statement.

6. C. `group by empno;`

Explanation Because the EMPNO column does not appear in the original list of columns to be displayed by the query, it cannot be used in a `group by` statement. This question confuses many readers who believe that the ordering of the column references in the column clause is really at fault. To avoid being confused by this thought, remember that if you removed the `group by` expression, the query would execute correctly, while if you removed the column clause the query would still fail.

CHAPTER

4

Subqueries

n this chapter, you will learn about and demonstrate knowledge in the following areas:

- Using subqueries
- Producing readable output from SQL*Plus

This chapter concludes the required coverage of topics related to Oracle data selection. First, we will discuss how to use subqueries in your select statements. You will learn both about straightforward subqueries and about multiple-column subqueries. Finally, this chapter will cover how to specify special formatting in order to use SQL*Plus as a reporting tool. The material in this chapter will complete your knowledge of data selection and comprises 10 percent of OCP Exam 1.

TIP
Of these two subject areas, the topic of subqueries is covered in more detail on the OCP exams. You might want to limit your review of producing readable output to understanding how to use substitution variables and simply use the rest of the information for reference.

Using Subqueries

This section will cover the following topics related to using subqueries:

- Understanding and defining subqueries
- Listing and writing different types of subqueries
- Multiple-column subqueries
- NULL values in subqueries
- Subqueries in a from clause

A *subquery* is a "query within a query." In other words, a subquery is a select statement nested within a select statement, designed to limit the selected output of the parent query by producing an intermediate result set of some sort. There are several different ways to include subqueries in SQL statements' where clauses. We'll talk in this section about the types of problems subqueries can solve, how to develop subqueries, the different subquery types, and how to write single-row and multiple-row subqueries.

TIP
Some of the topics we'll cover here go into slightly further detail than what you might see on the OCP exams. We recommend working through the material so that you understand subqueries thoroughly in order to do well not just on the exam, but in your career as an Oracle professional.

Understanding and Defining Subqueries

Subqueries can be used to obtain values for parent `select` statements when specific search criteria isn't known. To do so, the `where` clause in the parent `select` statement must have a comparison operation where the unknown value being compared is determined by the result of the subquery. The inner subquery executes once, right before the main outer query executes. The subquery returns its results to the main outer query. Consider the following example, where we search for the name, department number, and salary information for employees working in New York. The known criterion is that the employees work in New York. However, without looking at the DEPT table, we won't know which department number corresponds to the New York office. Let's look at how we might obtain the desired result using a join statement:

```
SQL> select ename, emp.deptno, sal
  2  from emp join dept on emp.deptno = dept.deptno
  3. where dept.loc = 'NEW YORK';
ENAME       .  DEPTNO      SAL
---------- --------- ---------
CLARK             10     2450
KING              10     5000
MILLER            10     1300
```

Now, let's take a look at how a subquery can help us out:

```
SQL>  select ename, deptno, sal
  2   from emp
  3   where deptno =
  4   ( select deptno
  5     from dept
  6     where loc = 'NEW YORK' );
ENAME       DEPTNO      SAL
---------- --------- ---------
CLARK             10     2450
KING              10     5000
MILLER            10     1300
```

TIP
Subqueries must appear inside parentheses, or else Oracle will have trouble distinguishing the subquery from the parent query. You should also make sure to place subqueries on the right side of the comparison operator.

The highlighted portion of the SQL statement is the subquery. Notice how the parent query requires the subquery to resolve itself for the DEPTNO value corresponding to the New York office. When this `select` statement is submitted, Oracle will process the subquery *first* in order to resolve all unknown search criteria and then feed that resolved criteria to the outer query. The outer query then can resolve the dataset it is supposed to return.

Consider also that the preceding example uses an equality comparison to connect the parent query to the subquery. This is the most commonly used method for connecting subqueries to their parents, but it isn't the only one. You could use many of the other comparison operations, such as <, >, <=, <>, and >=. You can also use the `in` comparison, which is similar to the `case` statement offered in many programming languages, because resolution can be established based on the parent column's equality with any element in the group. Let's take a look at an example:

```
SQL> select ename, job, sal
  2  from emp
  3  where deptno in
  4    ( select deptno
  5      from dept
  6      where dname in
  7      ('ACCOUNTING', 'SALES'));
ENAME       JOB            SAL
----------  ---------  ---------
ALLEN       SALESMAN      1600
WARD        SALESMAN      1250
MARTIN      SALESMAN      1250
BLAKE       MANAGER       2850
CLARK       MANAGER       2450
KING        PRESIDENT     5000
TURNER      SALESMAN      1500
JAMES       CLERK          950
MILLER      CLERK         1300
```

Another way of including a subquery in the `where` clause of a `select` statement is to use the `exists` clause. This clause enables you to test for the existence of rows in the results of a subquery, and its logical opposite is not exists. When you specify the exists operation in a where clause, you must include a subquery that satisfies the exists operation. If the subquery returns data, the exists operation returns TRUE, and a record from the parent query will be returned. If not, the exists operation returns FALSE, and no record for the parent query will be returned. Let's look at an example in which we obtain the same listing of employees working in the New York office, only this time, we use the exists operation:

```
SQL> select e.ename, e.job, e.sal
  2  from emp e
  3  where exists
  4    ( select d.deptno
  5      from dept d
  6      where d.loc = 'NEW YORK'
  7      and d.deptno = e.deptno);
ENAME      JOB          SAL
---------- --------- ---------
CLARK      MANAGER      2450
KING       PRESIDENT    5000
MILLER     CLERK        1300
```

Notice something very interesting about this subquery example. We used table aliases in both the parent query and the subquery to create a *correlated subquery*. Oracle performs a correlated subquery when the subquery references a column from a table referred to in the parent statement. A correlated subquery is evaluated once for each row processed by the parent statement. Correlated subqueries are used to affect row-by-row processing. Each subquery is executed once for every row produced by the outer query. This technique enables us to "jump" from the subquery to the parent level in order to perform incredibly complex, almost counterintuitive, processing that necessarily must involve some discussion of a programming concept known as *variable scope*.

Variable scope refers to the availability or "viewability" of data in certain variables at certain times. Sometimes a variable has a *local* scope. That is to say that the variable can only be seen when the current block of code is being executed. You can consider the columns in subquery comparison operations to be variables whose scope is *local* to the query. There is also *global* scope. In addition to a variable having local scope within the subquery where it appears, the variable also has *global* scope, meaning that it is available in all subqueries to that query. In the previous example, all variables or columns named in comparison operations in the outermost select operation are local to that operation and global to all the nested subqueries.

TIP
You've only seen some simple examples, but you should know that subqueries can be nested inside other subqueries to a surprisingly deep level – up to 255 subqueries in a single select *statement! Subqueries are also the topic of many OCP questions, so you should make sure you have plenty of experience writing them before taking the exam —and make sure you know the subquery discussions in this book cold!*

We can use many different types of functions in subqueries. In general, whatever functions are permitted in a parent query are also permitted in a subquery. For example, to obtain a listing of employees earning the minimum salary for a company might ordinarily present a small problem, especially if that minimum salary is an unknown value. You can solve this problem by using a group function in your subquery to obtain the unknown value, then use the parent query to search the EMP table for all employees whose salary is that value. The following code block shows the SQL:

```
SQL> select empno, ename, sal
  2  from emp
  3  where sal = (select min(sal) from emp);
     EMPNO ENAME           SAL
---------- ---------- ----------
      7369 SMITH           800
```

For Review

1. Know what a subquery is as well as when you might want to incorporate a subquery into a database select statement.

2. Be sure you can identify and give examples of how to write subqueries that are linked to their parent query by means of equality comparison, the in comparison, and the exists comparison.

Exercises

1. **The company has an employee expense application with two tables. One table, called EMP, contains all employee data. The other, called EXPENSE, contains expense vouchers submitted by every employee in the company. Which of the following queries will obtain the employee ID and name for**

those employees who have submitted expenses whose total value exceeds their salary?

A.
```
select e.empno, e.ename from emp e where e.sal <
(select sum(x.vouch_amt) from expense x) and
x.empno = e.empno;
```

B.
```
select e.empno, e.ename from emp e where e.sal <
(select x.vouch_amt from expense x where x.empno =
e.empno);
```

C.
```
select e.empno, e.ename from emp e where sal <
(select sum(x.vouch_amt) from expense x where
x.empno = e.empno);
```

D.
```
select e.empno, e.ename from emp e where exists
(select sum(x.vouch_amt) from expense x where
x.empno = e.empno);
```

2. **Take a look at the following statement:**

```
SQL> select ename
  2    from emp
  3    where empno in
  4      ( select empno
  5        from expense
  6        where vouch_amt > 10000 );
```

Which of the following choices identifies a SQL statement that will produce the same output as the preceding, rewritten to use the `exists` operator?

A.
```
select e.ename from emp e where exists (select
x.empno from expense x where x.vouch_amt > 10000)
and x.empno = e.empno;
```

B.
```
select e.ename from emp e where exists (select
x.empno from expense x where x.vouch_amt > 10000
and x.empno = e.empno);
```

C.
```
select e.ename from emp e where x.empno = e.empno
and exists (select x.empno from expense x where
x.vouch_amt > 10000);
```

D.
```
select e.ename from emp e, expense x where x.empno
= e.empno and x.vouch_amt > 10000 and exists
(select x.empno from expense x where x.vouch_amt >
10000);
```

3. In order to jump levels in nested subqueries, the availability of data from the parent query is often useful. Therefore, the variables from the parent query are said to be _____ in scope.

Answer Key

1. C. 2. B. 3. Global.

Listing and Writing Different Types of Subqueries

The following list identifies several different types of subqueries you may need to understand and use on the OCP exam:

- **Single-row subqueries** The main query expects the subquery to return only one value.

- **Multirow subqueries** The main query can handle situations where the subquery returns more than one value.

- **Inline views** A subquery in a `from` clause used for defining an intermediate result set to query from. These types of subqueries will be discussed later in the chapter.

- **Multiple-column subqueries** A subquery that contains more than one column of return data in addition to however many rows are given in the output. These types of subqueries will be discussed later in the chapter.

Writing Single-Row Subqueries

Check out the following example, which should look familiar:

```
SQL>  select ename, deptno, sal
  2   from emp
  3   where deptno =
  4   ( select deptno
  5     from dept
  6     where loc = 'NEW YORK' );
ENAME          DEPTNO      SAL
----------   ---------   ---------
CLARK            10         2450
KING             10         5000
MILLER           10         1300
```

Believe it or not, this is a single-row subquery. Why, you ask? Because, although the resulting set of data contains multiple rows of output from the EMP table, the subquery on the DEPT table to derive the output from EMP returns only one row of data. If you don't believe me, check out the following code block and see for yourself:

```
SQL> select deptno
  2  from dept
  3  where loc = 'NEW YORK';
   DEPTNO
---------
       10
```

Sure enough, there's only one column returned from one row of data by this query. Sometimes, single-row subqueries are also referred to as *scalar subqueries*. What makes the difference between whether a subquery can handle a single value or multiple values has to do with the comparison operation used for linking the parent query to the subquery. Notice in this situation that we used an equal sign. Therefore, we can generalize a simple rule: *When subqueries are linked to the parent by equality comparisons, the parent query expects only one row of data from the subquery.* Therefore, parent queries with subqueries linked by equality comparison operations are single-row subqueries.

TIP
Other comparison operations that indicate single-row subqueries include <, >, <=, >, and <>.

Writing Multirow Subqueries
Check out what happens when a parent query gets more than it bargained for:

```
SQL> select ename, job, sal
  2  from emp
  3  where deptno =
  4  (select deptno
  5  from dept
  6  where dname in ('ACCOUNTING','SALES'));
  (select deptno
   *
ERROR at line 4:
ORA-01427: single-row subquery returns more than one row
```

To solve the problem that arises in this example, you must transform the single-row subquery into a multirow subquery. How, you ask? You should transform the equality comparison that links the subquery to its parent into a comparison operation that handles multiple rows of output from the subquery—an operation such as in (shown in bold in the following example):

```
SQL> select ename, job, sal
  2  from emp
  3  where deptno in
  4  (select deptno
  5  from dept
  6  where dname in ('ACCOUNTING','SALES'));
ENAME        JOB           SAL
---------    ---------  ---------
ALLEN        SALESMAN      1600
WARD         SALESMAN      1250
MARTIN       SALESMAN      1250
BLAKE        MANAGER       2850
CLARK        MANAGER       2450
KING         PRESIDENT     5000
TURNER       SALESMAN      1500
JAMES        CLERK          950
MILLER       CLERK         1300
```

having Clauses and Subqueries

The having clause can use subqueries, too. Let's say you want to look at the average salaries of people in the company, broken out by department and job title again. This time, however, you only want to see departments and job titles where the average salary is higher than what the company is paying MARTIN, a salesman. There's just one small problem—you don't remember what MARTIN's salary is. We know that subqueries are useful when you need valid data that you don't know the value of, but you do know how to obtain it. You'll see how to use subqueries with the having clause in the following example:

```
SQL> select deptno, job, avg(sal)
  2  from emp
  3  group by deptno, job
  4  having avg(sal) >
  5    ( select sal
  6      from emp
  7      where ename = 'MARTIN');
   DEPTNO JOB        AVG(SAL)
--------- --------- ---------
       10 CLERK         1300
```

```
10  MANAGER         2450
10  PRESIDENT       5000
20  ANALYST         3000
20  MANAGER         2975
30  MANAGER         2850
30  SALESMAN        1400
```

TIP

The order *by clause can be used in a query that uses subqueries, but this clause must appear in the outermost query only. The subquery cannot have the* order *by clause defined for it.*

The with Clause and Subqueries

Sometimes complex queries may need to process the same subquery several times, once for each row obtained by the main query. This situation causes a great deal of processing overhead for Oracle, which could slow down the database's ability to provide you with the result requested quickly. Rather than force repeated processing of the subquery, Oracle9*i* provides you with the with clause that lets you factor out the subquery, give it a name, then reference that name multiple times within the original complex query. This technique lets the optimizer choose how to deal with the subquery results. The optimizer may perform either of the following. It might create a temporary table and query that table, and you'll learn more about temporary tables in Chapter 5. Alternately, the Oracle optimizer might rewrite the subquery using an inline view, and you'll learn about inline views later in this chapter. For example, the following query joins two tables and computes the aggregate sum of salaries redundantly, creating additional performance overhead, in order to list the sum of salaries for departments comprising more than $1/3$ of the firm's annual salary budget. The bold text represents the parts of the query that are repeated:

```
SQL> select dname, sum(sal) as dept_total
  2   from emp, dept
  3   where emp.deptno = dept.deptno
  4   group by dname having sum(sal) >
  5   (select sum(sal)*1/3
  6    from emp, dept
  7    where emp.deptno = dept.deptno)
  8   order by sum(sal) desc;
DNAME                DEPT_TOTAL
-------------------- ----------
RESEARCH                  10875
```

You can improve the performance of this query by having Oracle9i execute the subquery only once, then simply letting Oracle9i reference it at the appropriate points in the main query. The following code block gives a better logical idea of the work Oracle must perform to give you the result. In it, the bold text represents the common parts of the subquery that are performed only once, and the places where the subquery is referenced:

```
SQL> with summary as
  2  (select dname, sum(sal) as dept_total
  3   from emp, dept
  4   where emp.deptno = dept.deptno
  5   group by dname)
  6  select dname, dept_total
  7  from summary
  8  where dept_total >
  9  (select sum(dept_total) * 1/3
 10   from summary)
 11  order by dept_total desc;
DNAME                  DEPT_TOTAL
---------------------- ----------
RESEARCH                    10875
```

For Review

1. Know what the four different types of subqueries are. Also, be sure you can write and understand examples of single-row and multirow subqueries.

2. Know what happens when a parent query expecting a subquery to return only one row receives more than one row from the subquery.

3. Know that you can substitute the in operator for equality or other single-row comparison operations in order to let the parent query support multiple rows returned.

4. Understand the use of the with clause to minimize redundancy in defining steps to be performed in subqueries.

Exercises

1. Use the following code block to answer the question:

```
SQL> select deptno, job, avg(sal)
  2  from emp
  3  group by deptno, job
  4  having avg(sal) >
  5     ( select sal
```

```
6        from emp
7        where ename = 'MARTIN');
```

Which of the following choices identifies the type of subquery used in the preceding statement?

A. A single-row subquery

B. A multirow subquery

C. A from clause subquery

D. A multicolumn subquery

2. **The company's sales database has two tables. The first, PROFITS, stores the amount of profit made on products sold by the different corporate regions in different quarters. The second, REGIONS, stores the name of each departmental region, the headquarter location for that region, and the name of the region's vice president. Which of the following queries will obtain total profits on toys for regions headed by SMITHERS, FUJIMORI, and LAKKARAJU?**

A. `select sum(profit) from profits where region in (select region from regions where reg_head in ('SMITHERS', 'FUJIMORI', 'LAKKARAJU')) and product = 'TOYS';`

B. `select sum(profit) from profits where region in (select region from regions where reg_head in ('SMITHERS', 'FUJIMORI', 'LAKKARAJU') and product = 'TOYS');`

C. `select sum(profit) from profits where region = (select region from regions where reg_head in ('SMITHERS', 'FUJIMORI', 'LAKKARAJU')) and product = 'TOYS';`

D. `select sum(profit) from profits where region in (select region from regions where reg_head in ('SMITHERS', 'FUJIMORI', 'LAKKARAJU')) and product = 'TOYS';`

3. **Provide the name of the operator used for transforming single-row subqueries returning more than one row into a subquery capable of handling multiple rows returned to the main query:**

_____

4. **The following code block shows a query containing a subquery:**

```
SQL> select dname, avg(sal) as dept_avg
  2  from emp, dept
  3  where emp.deptno = dept.deptno
  4  group by dname having avg(sal) >
  5  (select avg(sal) * 1/4
  6   from emp, dept
  7   where emp.deptno = dept.deptno)
  8  order by avg(sal);
```

Which of the following choices identifies a clause you might use to redefine this query to remove redundancy of group function execution in the subquery and in the main query?

A. group by

B. order by

C. with

D. having

Answer Key

1. A. 2. A. 3. In 4. C.

Writing Multiple-Column Subqueries

Notice that in all the prior examples, regardless of whether one row or multiple rows were returned from the subquery, each of those rows contained only one column's worth of data to compare at the main query level. The main query can be set up to handle multiple columns in each row returned, too. To evaluate how to use multiple-column subqueries, let's consider an example. Let's say we want to find out the highest-paid employee in each department. Check out the following code block to see how we might perform this task:

```
SQL> select deptno, ename, job, sal
  2  from emp
  3  where (deptno, sal) in
  4    (select deptno, max(sal)
  5     from emp
  6     group by deptno);
```

```
DEPTNO ENAME      JOB          SAL
--------- ---------- ---------- ----------
    10 KING       PRESIDENT    5000
    20 SCOTT      ANALYST      3000
    20 FORD       ANALYST      3000
    30 BLAKE      MANAGER      2850
```

A couple of noteworthy points need to be made concerning multiple-column subqueries and syntax. For multiple-column subqueries only, you must enclose the multiple columns requested in the main query in parentheses; otherwise, the query will result in an "invalid relational operator" error. Also, your column references in both the main query's where clause and the subquery must match positionally—in other words, because DEPTNO is referenced first in the main query, it must be selected first in the subquery.

For Review
Be sure you understand the syntax and semantics of multiple-column subqueries.

Exercises

1. **The database for an international athletic competition consists of one table, ATHLETES, containing contestant name, age, and represented country. To determine the youngest athlete representing each country, which of the following queries could be used?**

    A. `select name, country, age from athletes where (country, age) in (select min(age), country from athletes group by country);`

    B. `select name, country, age from athletes where (country, age) in (select country, min(age) from athletes) group by country;`

    C. `select name, country, age from athletes where age in (select country, min(age) from athletes group by country);`

    D. `select name, country, age from athletes where (country, age) in (select country, min(age) from athletes group by country);`

2. **You are developing a multiple-column subquery on an Oracle database. Which of the following statements is true about SQL statements containing multiple-column subqueries?**

   A. The parent query must use a single-column subquery.

   B. The order of multiple columns being referenced in the where clause must match the column order in the subquery.

   C. The parent query must use an inline view, or else the query must be rewritten.

   D. The parent query must contain a group by expression in order to obtain the correct result.

Answer Key
1. D. 2. B.

NULL Values and Subqueries

If you're planning to follow along on your own EMP table built by demobld.sql, you need to execute the following statement for this lesson to flow properly:

```
SQL> update emp set deptno = null where ename = 'KING';
1 row updated.
```

TIP
You'll learn more about update statements in Chapter 6.

Now, review the following code block, where we rerun the multiple-column subquery from the previous example:

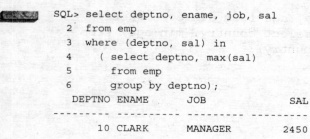

```
SQL> select deptno, ename, job, sal
  2  from emp
  3  where (deptno, sal) in
  4    ( select deptno, max(sal)
  5      from emp
  6      group by deptno);
  DEPTNO ENAME      JOB           SAL
--------- ---------- --------- ---------
      10 CLARK      MANAGER      2450
```

```
20  SCOTT     ANALYST      3000
20  FORD      ANALYST      3000
30  BLAKE     MANAGER      2850
```

Notice someone missing from the output? Even though KING is still listed in the EMP table, he is no longer the highest-paid employee in his department. That's strange, especially when we review the output from the subquery in our example:

```
DEPTNO  MAX(SAL)
-------- ----------
    10      2450
    20      3000
    30      2850
            5000
```

You can see that KING was listed among the highest paid in his respective department. However, notice that his department is set to NULL. If you're thinking that the problem must have something to do with how subqueries handle NULL values, you're right. Unfortunately, the subquery only returns non-NULL values to the parent query. Therefore, we don't see KING listed in the output from that main query. In order to ensure that your queries don't miss any NULL values, you should rewrite them in such a way that they don't use the group by expression. This step can be done using a correlated subquery, as demonstrated in the following code block:

```
SQL> select e.deptno, e.ename, e.job, e.sal
  2  from emp e
  3  where e.sal =
  4  (select max(e2.sal)
  5  from emp e2
  6* where nvl(e.deptno,99) = nvl(e2.deptno,99));
DEPTNO ENAME       JOB         SAL
-------- ---------- ---------- ----------
    30  BLAKE      MANAGER      2850
    10  CLARK      MANAGER      2450
    20  SCOTT      ANALYST      3000
        KING       PRESIDENT    5000
    20  FORD       ANALYST      3000
```

Notice something interesting about this query? The use of the nvl( ) function in the subquery substitutes the value 99 for NULL on KING's record. This is an arbitrary value picked simply because it wasn't already in use as a department number. However, you're probably wondering why the output doesn't display 99 in the DEPTNO column for KING. The reason is because the subquery is not actually returning a value for DEPTNO to the parent query—it only returns the maximum salary for that department! We use nvl( ) in the subquery only so we have a non-NULL value to compare E.DEPTNO and E2.DEPTNO in the subquery. Because the department number for KING's record is still NULL, that is what the parent query displays.

TIP
When writing queries that use subqueries, remember that certain operations, such as group by, may return NULL values and that NULL values are ignored by subqueries when the subquery returns its dataset to the main query. If you need to include NULL values in your output, experiment with rewriting the query in other ways.

In Conclusion

Remember to discard the change to KING's record in the EMP table when you're done:

```
SQL> rollback;
Rollback complete.
```

For Review

Be sure you understand that certain operations, such as group by, may generate NULL values, which are ignored by subqueries when the dataset is returned to the main query. Know how to rewrite a subquery if you need to handle NULL values.

Exercises

1. Subqueries ignore this value by default: _____

2. Use the output in the code block to answer the following question:

```
SQL> select e.deptno, e.ename, e.job, e.sal
  2  from emp e
  3  where e.sal =
  4  (select max(e2.sal)
  5    from emp e2
  6* where nvl(e.deptno,99) = nvl(e2.deptno,99));
DEPTNO ENAME        JOB          SAL
--------- ---------- --------- ---------
    30 BLAKE        MANAGER      2850
```

```
10 CLARK      MANAGER      2450
20 SCOTT      ANALYST      3000
   KING       PRESIDENT    5000
20 FORD       ANALYST      3000
```

In order to display a value of 99 in the DEPTNO column in the preceding return set, which of the following SQL statements might be appropriate?

A. `select nvl(e.deptno,99), e.ename, e.job, e.sal from emp e where (e.deptno, e.sal) =(select max(e2.sal) from emp e2 where nvl(e.deptno,99) = nvl(e2.deptno,99));`

B. `select nvl(e.deptno,99), e.ename, e.job, e.sal from emp e where e.sal =(select max(e2.sal) from emp e2 where nvl(e.deptno,99) = nvl(e2.deptno,99));`

C. `select nvl(e.deptno,99), e.ename, e.job, e.sal from emp e where (e.deptno, e.sal) =(select e2.deptno, max(e2.sal) from emp e2 where nvl(e.deptno,99) = nvl(e2.deptno,99));`

D. `select nvl(e.deptno,99), e.ename, e.job, e.sal from emp e where (e.deptno, e.sal) =(select e2.deptno, max(e2.sal) from emp e2 where nvl(e.deptno,99) = nvl(e2.deptno,99) group by e2.deptno);`

Answer Key
1. NULL. 2. B.

Subqueries in a `from` Clause

If you're planning to follow along on your own EMP table built by `demobld.sql`, you need to execute the following statement for this lesson to flow properly:

```
SQL> update emp set deptno = null where ename = 'KING';
1 row updated.
```

TIP
You'll learn more about `update` statements in Chapter 6.

You can also write subqueries that appear in your `from` clause. Writing subqueries in the `from` clause of the main query can be a handy way to collect an intermediate set of data that the main query treats as a table for its own query-access purposes. This subquery in the `from` clause of your main query is called an *inline view*. You must enclose the query text for the inline view in parentheses and also give a label for the inline view so that columns in it can be referenced later. The subquery can be a `select` statement that utilizes joins, the `group by` clause, or the `order by` clause. The following code block shows you a very simple example of using an inline view that accomplishes the same result as a regular table join. In the following code block, the query in parenthesis is given an alias, SUBQ. SUBQ contains an inline view listing the DEPTNO information for the New York and Dallas locations. The main query uses this information to determine which employees work in those locations:

```
SQL> select e.ename, subq.loc
  2  from emp e,
  3     ( select deptno, loc
  4       from dept
  5       where loc in ('NEW YORK', 'DALLAS')) subq
  6  where e.deptno = subq.deptno;
ENAME        LOC
----------   -------------
SMITH        DALLAS
JONES        DALLAS
CLARK        NEW YORK
SCOTT        DALLAS
ADAMS        DALLAS
FORD         DALLAS
MILLER       NEW YORK
```

TIP
In some cases, the columns referenced in your inline view might call single-row or group functions. This is permitted; however, if you want to refer to those columns in the main query's where clause, you will need to supply column aliases for that column in the inline view, in addition to supplying a table alias for the entire inline view.

Inline Views and Top-N Queries

Top-N queries use inline views and are handy for displaying a short list of table data, based on "greatest" or "least" criteria. For example, let's say that profits for our company were exceptionally strong this year, and we want a list of the three lowest-paid employees in our company so that we could give them a raise. A top-N query would be useful for this purpose. Take a look at a top-N query that satisfies this business scenario:

```
SQL> select ename, job, sal, rownum
  2  from (select ename, job, sal from emp
  3        order by sal)
  4  where rownum <=3;
ENAME      JOB            SAL    ROWNUM
---------- --------- --------- ---------
SMITH      CLERK          800        1
JAMES      CLERK          950        2
ADAMS      CLERK         1100        3
```

You need to know two important things about top-N queries for OCP. The first is their use of the inline view to list all data in the table in sorted order. The second is their use of ROWNUM—a virtual column identifying the row number in the table—to determine the top number of rows to return as output. Conversely, if we have to cut salaries based on poor company performance and want to obtain a listing of the highest-paid employees, whose salaries will be cut, we would reverse the sort order inside the inline view, as shown here:

```
SQL> select ename, job, sal, rownum
  2  from (select ename, job, sal from emp
  3        order by sal desc)
  4  where rownum <=3;
ENAME      JOB            SAL    ROWNUM
---------- --------- --------- ---------
KING       PRESIDENT     5000        1
SCOTT      ANALYST       3000        2
FORD       ANALYST       3000        3
```

TIP
Inline views support the use of the order by
*clause. However, they are the only view in Oracle
that does so. Other types of views that you will
learn about in Chapter 7 do not support the use of
the* order by *clause.*

In Conclusion

Remember to discard the change to KING's record in the EMP table when you're done:

```
SQL> rollback;
Rollback complete.
```

For Review

1. Understand the syntax and semantics of creating basic inline views. Be able to remember that inline views are the only views in Oracle that support the use of the order by clause.

2. Know what a top-N query is and how to use an inline view to create one. Also, be sure you understand the use of ROWNUM in these types of queries.

Exercises

1. This is the name of the pseudo-column often utilized for obtaining information for top-N queries: _____

2. Your company's sales database contains one table, PROFITS, which stores profits listed by product name, sales region, and quarterly time period. If you wanted to obtain a listing of the five best-selling products in company history, which of the following SQL statements would you use?

   A. select p.prod_name, p.profit from (select prod_name, profit from profits order by profit desc) where rownum <= 5;

   B. select p.prod_name, p.profit from (select prod_name, sum(profit) from profits group by prod_name order by sum(profit) desc) subq where p.prod_name = subq.prod_name;

   C. select prod_name, profit from (select prod_name, sum(profit) from profits group by prod_name order by sum(profit) desc) where rownum <=5;

   D. select prod_name, profit from (select prod_name, sum(profit) from profits order by sum(profit) desc) where rownum <=5;

Answer Key

1. ROWNUM. **2.** C. Remember, you must account for the fact that the profits for the same products will appear once for each quarter.

Producing Readable Output with SQL*Plus

This section will cover the following topics related to using runtime variables:

- Entering variables
- Customizing SQL*Plus environments
- Producing readable output
- Creating and executing scripts
- Saving customizations

SQL*Plus is a powerful tool that can be used interactively to enter commands, as demonstrated so far throughout the book, or silently through batch processing and reporting. It is on this second topic thatwe will focus considerable attention in the next section. In this section, you will learn more about how entering variables into statements in SQL*Plus, customizing your work environment, producing readable output for reporting, creating and executing scripts, and saving your environment customizations.

TIP
*At any point in SQL*Plus operation, you can enter the `help SQLPLUS_command` command, and SQL*Plus will give you more information about use of that command.*

Entering Variables

In order to prepare for OCP, you should spend a little extra time on this topic, and treat the rest of the other topics in this section as background or reference material. Thus, if you've already been working with SQL for a while, you'll have less work to do in preparation for OCP. Let's say you have to pull up data for several different employees manually for the purpose of reviewing some aspect of their data. The following example shows how you've learned to do it so far:

```
SQL> select ename, job, deptno, sal
  2  from emp
  3  where empno = 7844;
ENAME       JOB         DEPTNO       SAL
----------  --------  ---------  ---------
TURNER      SALESMAN         30      1500
```

Now, let's say you wanted to pull up the same data for KING, whose employee number is 7839. You've seen how to edit SQL commands in SQL*Plus and how to reexecute them using the slash (/) command. In light of these facts, you could edit the SQL statement with either the `change` or `edit` command to change the EMPNO information and then reissue the command. However, let's face it, you'll have to do a lot of typing and mouse clicking, and all that work is tedious. First, you have to open the text editor; then you have to find the text to change, modify it, and then save it to the SQL*Plus buffer—all before you reexecute the command. An easier way exists. Take a look at the following code block:

```
SQL> select ename, job, deptno, sal
  2  from emp
  3  where empno = &empno;
Enter value for empno: 7844
old   3: where empno = &empno
new   3: where empno = 7844
ENAME       JOB         DEPTNO       SAL
----------  --------  ---------  ---------
TURNER      SALESMAN         30      1500
```

Now, all you have to do is issue the slash command and then enter a new employee number every time you want to see this information from the EMP table, as shown here:

```
SQL> /
Enter value for empno: 7839
old   3: where empno = &empno
new   3: where empno = 7839
ENAME       JOB         DEPTNO       SAL
----------  --------  ---------  ---------
KING        PRESIDENT        10      5000
```

You can repeat this activity as often as you want until you enter a new SQL statement, which is great when you have repetitive SQL operations that you need to execute. Notice two important things about this output. First, notice the ampersand (&) preceding the reference to EMPNO in the where clause. This ampersand indicates to Oracle that you want to specify a value for that column before Oracle processes the query. This combination of ampersand and column identifier creates a *lexical substitution variable*. Second, Oracle shows you the line as it appeared in the buffer and then shows you the value you substituted. This presentation lets you know what data was changed by your input.

TIP
You can also use the double-ampersand (&&) keyword in Oracle to define variable values in SQL*Plus. The && keyword has an advantage over & in that && will preserve the value you define for the variable after you define it the first time you execute the statement, whereas & will prompt you to specify a value every time you execute the statement.

If you don't want to use the ampersand to create the substitution variable, the input can be changed with the set define command at the SQL prompt in SQL*Plus. You can reexecute the statement containing a runtime variable declaration by using the slash (/) command at the prompt in SQL*Plus. The following code block illustrates this:

```
SQL> set define ?
SQL> select ename, job, deptno, sal
  2  from emp
  3  where empno = ?empno;
Enter value for empno: 7839
old   3: where empno = ?empno
new   3: where empno = 7839
ENAME      JOB         DEPTNO      SAL
---------- ---------- ---------- ---------
KING       PRESIDENT       10       5000
SQL> /
Enter value for empno: 7844
old   3: where empno = ?empno
new   3: where empno = 7844
ENAME      JOB         DEPTNO      SAL
---------- ---------- ---------- ---------
TURNER     SALESMAN        30       1500
```

Now, for your own sanity, go ahead and switch back to the default:

```
SQL> set define &
```

> **TIP**
> *You can find more information about the* set
> define *command in the "Customizing SQL*Plus
> Environments" discussion appearing later in this
> chapter.*

Defining lexical substitution variables that handle text information is done slightly differently. Because text information must appear within single quotes in SQL queries in Oracle, you must therefore define the lexical substitution variable inside single-quotes as well. Also, remember that Oracle stores the text information literally as you typed it when the data was first added to Oracle, so pay attention to issues like spaces between words, case sensitivity, and so on. The following code block illustrates how to set up lexical substitution variables for text data:

```
SQL> select empno, deptno, sal
  2  from emp
  3  where ename = '&empname';
Enter value for empname: SMITH
old   3: where ename = '&empname'
new   3: where ename = 'SMITH'
    EMPNO     DEPTNO        SAL
---------- ---------- ----------
     7369         20        800
```

Finally, setting up lexical substitution variables that accommodate date information should be enclosed in single-quotes. The data entered should conform to whatever date format mask is used by Oracle to display data. The following code block illustrates both how to discover the format mask being used and how to enter it properly in a lexical substitution variable:

```
SQL> select ename, job, sal
  2  from emp where hiredate = '&startdate';
Enter value for startdate: 23-JAN-82
old   2: from emp where hiredate = '&startdate'
new   2: from emp where hiredate = '23-JAN-82'
ENAME      JOB           SAL
---------- --------- ----------
MILLER     CLERK        1300
SQL> /
```

```
Enter value for startdate: 23-jan-82
old   2: from emp where hiredate = '&startdate'
new   2: from emp where hiredate = '23-jan-82'
ENAME      JOB           SAL
---------- --------- ----------
MILLER     CLERK        1300
```

Automatic Definition of Runtime Variables

In some cases, it may not be useful to enter new values for a runtime variable every time the statement executes. For example, assume you must perform some onerous reporting process weekly for every person in a company. A great deal of value is added to the process by having a variable that can be specified at runtime because you can then simply execute the same statement over and over again with new EMPNO values each time. However, even this improvement does not streamline the process as much as one might like. Instead of running the statement over and over again with new values specified each time, you could create a script similar to the following:

```
------------------------
-- empinfo.sql -
-- This script selects information
-- from EMP and returns it to
-- the user
------------------------
define var_empno = 7844
select ename, job, deptno, sal
from emp
where empno = &var_empno;
undefine var_empno
define var_empno = 7839
select ename, job, deptno, sal
from emp
where empno = &var_empno;
```

TIP
You'll get the most out of your preparation time for OCP if you teach yourself by example. Therefore, spend the extra time coding in these scripts by hand to test them on your system. The more experience you have with Oracle, the better you will do on your OCP exam. Also, if you don't want to use the set define *command to use the question mark to identify substitution variables, just replace every instance of ? previously with &.*

When you use the @ command to run this script in SQL*Plus, the following output is produced:

```
SQL> @c:\windows\empinfo
old   3: where empno = &var_empno
new   3: where empno = 7844
ENAME      JOB        DEPTNO       SAL
---------- ---------  ---------  ---------
TURNER     SALESMAN        30       1500
old   3: where empno = &var_empno
new   3: where empno = 7839
ENAME      JOB        DEPTNO       SAL
---------- ---------  ---------  ---------
KING       PRESIDENT       10       5000
```

TIP

*The @@ command can also be used to execute scripts in SQL*Plus when the contents of one script call for execution of another script. When used, @@ tells SQL*Plus to look for the script in the same path where it found the currently executing script.*

The time spent actually keying in values for the variables named in the SQL `select` statement is eliminated with the `define` statement. Notice, however, that in between each execution of the SQL statement is a special statement using a command called `undefine`. In Oracle, the data that is defined with the `define` statement will remain defined for the variable for the entire session, unless the variable is undefined. By *undefining* a variable, you allow another `define` statement to reuse the variable in another execution of the same or a different statement.

TIP

You can also use the `define` command if you want to reuse substitution variables over different SQL statements, allowing you to pass a value from one statement to another.

accept: Another Way to Define Variables

You may have noticed that Oracle's method for identifying input, though not exactly cryptic, is fairly nonexpressive. You need not stick with Oracle's default messaging to identify the need for input. Instead, you can define a more expressive message that Oracle will use to prompt for input data. The name of the command that provides this functionality is the `accept` command. Check out the following code block, where it shows a slight modification to `empinfo.sql` that uses the `accept` command:

```
------------------------
--  empinfo2.sql -
--  This script selects information
--  from EMP and returns it to
--  the user
------------------------
accept var_empno prompt 'Enter EMPNO now => '
select ename, job, deptno, sal
from emp
where empno = &var_empno;
```

TIP
You'll get the most out of your preparation time for OCP if you teach yourself by example. Therefore, spend the extra time coding in these scripts by hand to test them on your system. The more experience you have with Oracle, the better you will do on your OCP exam. Also, notice the use of two dashes next to each other in the first few lines of this code block. That usage indicates a comment.

We can then run the script, as follows:

```
SQL> @c:\windows\empinfo2
Enter EMPNO now => 7844
old    3: where empno = &var_empno
new    3: where empno = 7844
ENAME        JOB          DEPTNO       SAL
----------   ----------   ----------   ----------
TURNER       SALESMAN           30      1500
```

Using the `accept` command can be preferable to Oracle's default output message in situations where you want to define a more accurate or specific prompt or when you want more output to display as the values are defined.

TIP
By default, the datatype for a variable defined with the `accept` *command is CHAR. Fortunately, Oracle can execute implicit type conversions from CHAR to the datatype required for the input variable, so usually, you won't have a problem. You can also explicitly specify the datatype in the* `accept` *command.*

For Review

1. Know the special character used to specify a lexical substitution variable (it's the ampersand).

2. Understand how to use the `accept` command and the benefits offered by the `accept` command.

3. Be sure you can tell how variables are defined within the SQL*Plus session using the `define` and `undefine` commands.

4. Know that two dashes next to each other (--) in a script indicates to SQL*Plus that everything else on that line is a comment.

Exercises

1. **Your sales database consists of one table, PROFITS, which lists profits for every product type the company sells, listed by quarter and by sales region. You need to develop a report that users can run interactively to show them the profits on toys for a given quarter. You have concerns about the users of this report because they have frequently complained about the readability and usability of your reports. Which of the following choices shows the contents of the script you should use for your report?**

   A. ```
select profit from profits
where prod_type = 'TOYS'
and time_period = '&v_period';
```

   B. ```
define v_period
select profit from profits
where prod_type = 'TOYS'
and time_period = '&v_period';
```

    C. `accept v_period prompt 'Enter the time period =>`
       `select profit from profits`
       `where prod_type = 'TOYS'`
       `and time_period = '&v_period';`

    D. `accept v_period`
       `select profit from profits`
       `where prod_type = 'TOYS'`
       `and time_period = '&v_period';`

2. **Review the following code block containing the contents of a script called `dates.sql`:**

```
accept v_hiredate prompt 'enter hire date => '
select empno, ename, job
from emp
where trunc(hiredate) = trunc('&v_hiredate');
```

    Which of the following aspects of the script must be changed in order for the script to function properly?

    A. Variable `v_hiredate` must be changed to accept DATE information.

    B. The `trunc( )` function in the query should be eliminated.

    C. The `prompt` clause in the `accept` command is unnecessary.

    D. Nothing, the script will work fine as is.

3. **This is the string that must prefix lexical substitution variables if you want the value saved between statement executions:** _____

Answer Key

1. C. Remember, part of your goal is pleasing the users. **2.** A. **3.** &&

Customizing SQL*Plus Environments

You can customize your SQL*Plus operating environment with the `set system_variable value` command, where *system_variable* is the name of a system variable you can set in SQL*Plus, and *value* is the value you would like to set that system variable to. We'll cover some common system variables and their acceptable values in this discussion. Each of the headers for the following subtopics contains the full name of the system variable, followed by its abbreviation in brackets ([ ]), followed by its valid values in curly braces ({ }).

NOTE
This section is provided primarily for reference purposes and for your OCP study. No examples are provided, but it is assumed that you will practice using each of these commands on your own. Recognizing that this list of SQL*Plus commands is extensive, you may want to focus mainly on ARRAYSIZE, COLSEP, FEEDBACK, HEADING, LINESIZE, LONG, PAGESIZE, PAUSE, and TERMOUT for OCP and use the rest of this information as a reference.

ARRAYSIZE [ARRAY] {15|n}   This command sets the number of rows that SQL*Plus fetches from the database at one time. Valid values are 1 to 5,000. A large value increases the efficiency of queries and subqueries that fetch many rows, but it requires more memory.

AUTOCOMMIT [AUTO] {OFF|ON|IMMEDIATE|n}   This controls when Oracle commits pending changes to the database. ON commits pending changes to the database after Oracle executes each successful data change command or PL/SQL block. OFF suppresses automatic committing so that you must commit changes manually. IMMEDIATE functions in the same manner as the ON option. The value *n* commits pending changes to the database after Oracle executes *n* successful data change commands or PL/SQL blocks, where *n* cannot be less than zero or greater than 2,000,000,000.

AUTOTRACE [AUTOT] {OFF|ON|TRACEONLY|EXPLAIN|STATISTICS}
This command displays a report on the execution of successful SQL statements. The report can include execution statistics and the query execution path. OFF does not display a trace report. ON displays a trace report. TRACEONLY displays a trace report but does not print query data, if any. Before using autotrace, you must run the plustrce.sql script found in the sqlplus/admin directory under your Oracle software home directory. The EXPLAIN and STATISTICS options can be used for performance tuning as well by displaying SQL statement execution plans and statistics from the cost-based optimizer, respectively.

CMDSEP [CMDS] {;|c|OFF|ON}   This sets the nonalphanumeric character used to separate multiple SQL*Plus commands entered on one line to *c*. ON or OFF controls whether you can enter multiple commands on a line; ON automatically sets the command separator character to a semicolon (;).

COLSEP [COLSEP] { |text}   This command sets the text to be printed between selected columns. If the colsep variable contains blanks or punctuation characters, you must enclose it with single quotes. The default value for text is a single space. In multiline rows, the column separator does not print between columns that begin on different lines.

COMPATIBILITY [COM] {V7|V8|NATIVE}   This specifies the version of Oracle to which you are currently connected. Set compatibility to V7 for Oracle7 or V8 for Oracle8 and Oracle8*i*. Set compatibility to NATIVE if you want the database to determine the setting (for example, if you're connected to Oracle8 or Oracle8*i*, compatibility would default to V8). The compatibility variable must be correctly set for the version of Oracle to which you are connected; otherwise, you will be unable to run any SQL commands. However, you can set compatibility to V7 when connected to Oracle8*i*. This enables you to run Oracle7 SQL against Oracle8*i*.

CONCAT [CON] {.|c|OFF|ON}   This sets the character you can use to terminate a substitution variable reference if you want to immediately follow the variable with a character that SQL*Plus would otherwise interpret as a part of the substitution variable name. SQL*Plus resets the value of concat to a period when you switch concat on.

COPYCOMMIT [COPYC] {0|n}   This command controls the number of batches after which the copy command commits changes to the database. copy commits rows to the destination database each time it copies n row batches. Valid values are 0 to 5,000. You can set the size of a batch with the arraysize variable. If you set copycommit to 0, copy performs a commit operation only at the end of a copy operation.

COPYTYPECHECK [COPYTYPECHECK] {OFF|ON}   This sets the suppression of the comparison of datatypes while inserting or appending to tables with the copy command. This is to facilitate copying to DB2, which requires that a CHAR be copied to a DB2 DATE.

DESCRIBE [DESCRIBE] DEPTH {1|n|ALL} LINENUM {ON|OFF} INDENT {ON|OFF}   This command sets the depth of the level to which you can recursively describe an object. The valid range of the depth clause is from 1 to 50. If you issue the set describe depth ALL command, the depth will be set to 50, which is the maximum level allowed. You can also display the line number and indentation of the attribute or column name when an object contains multiple object types. Use the `set linesize` command to control the width of the data displayed.

ECHO [ECHO] {OFF|ON}   This controls whether the `start` command lists each command in a command file as the command is executed. `ON` lists the commands; `OFF` suppresses the listing.

EDITFILE [EDITF] {file_name[.ext]}   This command sets the default filename for the `edit` command. You can include a path and/or file extension. For information on changing the default extension, see the `suffix` variable of this command. The default filename and maximum filename length are operating system specific.

EMBEDDED [EMB] {OFF|ON}   This controls where on a page each report begins. `OFF` forces each report to start at the top of a new page. `ON` enables a report to begin anywhere on a page. Set `embedded` to `ON` when you want a report to begin printing immediately following the end of the previously run report.

ESCAPE [ESC] {\|c|OFF|ON}   This command defines the character you enter as the escape character. `OFF` undefines the escape character. `ON` enables the escape character. `ON` also changes the value of *c* back to the default (\). You can use the escape character before the substitution character (set through `set define`) to indicate that SQL*Plus should treat the substitution character as an ordinary character rather than as a request for variable substitution.

FEEDBACK [FEED] {6|n|OFF|ON}   This displays the number of records returned by a query when a query selects at least *n* records. `ON` or `OFF` turns this display on or off. Turning feedback `ON` sets *n* to 1. Setting feedback to 0 is equivalent to turning it `OFF`.

FLAGGER [FLAGGER] {OFF|ENTRY |INTERMEDIATE|FULL}   This command checks to make sure that SQL statements conform to the ANSI/ISO SQL92 standard. If any nonstandard constructs are found, the Oracle server flags them as errors and displays the violating syntax. This is the equivalent of the SQL language `alter session set flagger` command. You may execute `set flagger` even if you are not connected to a database. Flagging will remain in effect across SQL*Plus sessions until a `set flagger OFF` (or `alter session set flagger = OFF`) command is successful or you exit SQL*Plus.

FLUSH [FLU] {OFF|ON}   This controls when output is sent to the user's display device. `OFF` enables the host operating system to buffer output. `ON` disables buffering. Use OFF only when you run a command file noninteractively. The use of flush OFF may improve performance by reducing the amount of program I/O.

HEADING [HEA] {OFF|ON}   This command controls the printing of column headings in reports. ON prints column headings in reports; OFF suppresses column headings. The set heading OFF command will not affect the column width displayed; it only suppresses the printing of the column header itself.

HEADSEP [HEADS] {||c|OFF|ON}   This defines the character you enter as the heading separator character. The heading separator character cannot be alphanumeric or whitespace. ON or OFF turns heading separation on or off. When heading separation is OFF, SQL*Plus prints a heading separator character like any other character. ON changes the value of c back to the default (|).

INSTANCE [instance_path|LOCAL]   This command changes the default instance for your session to the specified instance path. Using this command does not connect you to the database. The default instance is used for commands when no instance is specified. Any commands preceding the first use of this command cause SQL*Plus to communicate with the default instance.

LINESIZE [LIN] {80|n}   This sets the total number of characters that SQL*Plus displays on one line before beginning a new line. You can define linesize as a value from 1 to a system-dependent maximum.

LOBOFFSET [LOBOF] {n|1}   This command sets the starting position from which large object (LOB) data is retrieved and displayed.

LONG [LONG] {80|n}   This sets the maximum width (in bytes) for displaying LONG, CLOB, and NCLOB values as well as for copying LONG values. The maximum value of n is 2GB.

LONGCHUNKSIZE [LONGC] {80|n}   This command sets the size (in bytes) of the increments in which SQL*Plus retrieves a LONG, CLOB, or NCLOB value.

NEWPAGE [NEWP] {1|n|NONE}   This sets the number of blank lines to be printed from the top of each page to the top title. A value of 0 places a form feed at the beginning of each page (including the first page) and clears the screen on most terminals. If you set newpage to NONE, SQL*Plus does not print a blank line or formfeed between the report pages.

NULL [NULL] {text}   This command sets the text that represents a NULL value in the result of a select command.

NUMFORMAT [NUMF] {format} This sets the default format for displaying numbers. Enter a number format for `format`.

NUMWIDTH [NUM] {10|n} This command sets the default width for displaying numbers.

TIP
More information about formatting numbers as output in SQL*Plus is offered in the next discussion.

PAGESIZE [PAGES] {24|n} This sets the number of lines in each page. You can set `pagesize` to 0 to suppress all headings, page breaks, titles, the initial blank line, and other formatting information.

PAUSE [PAU] {OFF|ON|text} This command enables you to control scrolling of your terminal when running reports. ON causes SQL*Plus to pause at the beginning of each page of report output. You must press ENTER after each pause. The text you enter specifies the text to be displayed each time SQL*Plus pauses. If you enter multiple words, you must enclose the text in single quotes. You can embed terminal-dependent escape sequences in the `pause` command. These sequences enable you to create inverse video messages or other effects on terminals that support such characteristics.

RECSEP [RECSEP] {WRAPPED|EACH|OFF} This tells SQL*Plus where to make the record separation. For example, if you set `recsep` to WRAPPED, SQL*Plus prints a record separator only after wrapped lines. If you set `recsep` to EACH, SQL*Plus prints a record separator following every row. If you set `recsep` to OFF, SQL*Plus does not print a record separator.

RECSEPCHAR [RECSEPCHAR] { |c} This command displays or prints record separators. A record separator consists of a single line of the record-separating character (`recsepchar`) repeated `linesize` times. The `recsepchar` command defines the record-separating character. A single space is the default.

SERVEROUTPUT [SERVEROUT] {OFF|ON} SIZE {N} This controls whether to display the output from `DBMS_OUTPUT.put_line( )` calls in PL/SQL blocks in SQL*Plus. OFF suppresses the output of `DBMS_OUTPUT.put_line( )`; ON displays the output. The `size` clause sets the number of bytes of the output that can be buffered within Oracle8i. The default for n is 2,000, and it cannot be less than 2,000 or greater than 1,000,000. This command can handle other values like WRAPPED, TRUNCATED, and FORMAT, but this functionality probably won't appear in the OCP exam.

SHIFTINOUT [SHIFT] {VISIBLE]|INVISIBLE]}   This command enables correct alignment for terminals that display shift characters. The `set shiftinout` command is useful for terminals that display shift characters together with data (for example, IBM 3270 terminals). You can only use this command with shift-sensitive character sets (for example, JA16DBCS). Use `VISIBLE` for terminals that display shift characters as a visible character (for example, a space or a colon). `INVISIBLE` is the opposite and does not display any shift characters.

SHOWMODE [SHOW] {OFF|ON}   This controls whether SQL*Plus lists the old and new settings of a SQL*Plus system variable when you change the setting with `set`. `ON` lists the settings; `OFF` suppresses the listing.

SQLBLANKLINES [SQLBL] {ON|OFF}   This command controls whether SQL*Plus enables blank lines within a SQL command. `ON` interprets blank lines and new lines as part of a SQL command. `OFF`, the default value, does not enable blank lines or new lines in a SQL command. SQL*Plus returns to the default behavior when a SQL statement terminator or PL/SQL block terminator is encountered.

SQLCASE [SQLC] {MIXED|LOWER|UPPER}   This converts the case of SQL commands and PL/SQL blocks just prior to execution. SQL*Plus converts all text within the command, including quoted literals and identifiers, as follows:

- Uppercase if `sqlcase` equals `UPPER`
- Lowercase if `sqlcase` equals `LOWER`
- Unchanged if `sqlcase` equals `MIXED`

TIP
The `sqlcase` keyword does not change the SQL buffer itself.

SQLCONTINUE [SQLCO] {>|text}   This command sets the character sequence SQL*Plus displays as a prompt after you continue a SQL*Plus command on an additional line using a hyphen (-).

SQLNUMBER [SQLN] {OFF|ON}   This sets the prompt for the second and subsequent lines of a SQL command or PL/SQL block. `ON` sets the prompt to be the line number. `OFF` sets the prompt to the value of `sqlprompt`.

SQLPREFIX [SQLPRE] {#|c}   This command sets the SQL*Plus prefix character. While you are entering a SQL command or PL/SQL block, you can enter a SQL*Plus command on a separate line, prefixed by the SQL*Plus prefix character. SQL*Plus will execute this command immediately without affecting the SQL command or PL/SQL block that you are entering. The prefix character must be a nonalphanumeric character.

SQLPROMPT [SQLP] {SQL>|text}   This sets the SQL*Plus command prompt.

SQLTERMINATOR [SQLT] {;|c|OFF|ON}   This command sets the character used to end and execute SQL commands to c. OFF means that SQL*Plus recognizes no command terminator; you terminate a SQL command by entering an empty line. ON resets the terminator to the default—a semicolon (;).

SUFFIX [SUF] {SQL|text}   This sets the default file extension that SQL*Plus uses in commands that refer to command files. The value for suffix does not control extensions for spool files.

TAB [TAB] {OFF|ON}   This command determines how SQL*Plus formats whitespace in terminal output. OFF uses spaces to format whitespace in the output. ON uses the tab character. The tab character creates a space setting of eight blank characters. The default value for tab is system dependent.

TERMOUT [TERM] {OFF|ON}   This controls the display of output generated by commands executed from a command file. OFF suppresses the display so that you can spool output from a command file without seeing the output on the screen. ON displays the output. Setting termout OFF does not affect output from commands you enter interactively.

TIME [TI] {OFF|ON}   This command controls the display of the current time. ON displays the current time before each command prompt. OFF suppresses the time display.

TIMING [TIMI] {OFF|ON}   This controls the display of timing statistics. ON displays timing statistics on each SQL command or PL/SQL block run. OFF suppresses timing of each command.

TRIMOUT [TRIM] {OFF|ON}   This command determines whether SQL*Plus enables trailing blanks at the end of each displayed line. ON removes blanks at the end of each line, thus improving performance, especially when you access SQL*Plus from a slow communications device. OFF enables SQL*Plus to display trailing blanks. Setting trimout ON does not affect spooled output.

TRIMSPOOL [TRIMS] {ON|OFF}   This determines whether SQL*Plus enables trailing blanks at the end of each spooled line. ON removes blanks at the end of each line. OFF enables SQL*Plus to include trailing blanks. Using trimspool ON does not affect terminal output.

VERIFY [VER] {OFF|ON}   This command controls whether SQL*Plus lists the text of a SQL statement or PL/SQL command before and after SQL*Plus replaces substitution variables with values. ON lists the text; OFF suppresses the listing.

> **TIP**
> *In most cases, if you want to see the value set for a particular SQL*Plus attribute, you can precede that attribute with the show command. For example, to see the value set for linesize, use the show linesize command.*

For Review

Be sure you know how to customize the SQL*Plus running environment using the set command, including the use of common system variables such as pagesize, linesize, termout, feedback, sqlprompt, and echo.

Exercises

1. **This SQL*Plus command is useful for determining whether the "N rows selected" message will appear:** _____

2. **This SQL*Plus command is useful for determining what extension SQL*Plus expects for files containing SQL commands:**
   _____

3. **Use of this command requires that you first run the plustrce.sql script:** _____

Answer Key
1. feedback 2. suffix 3. autotrace

Producing Readable Output

Certain commands are also available to improve the look of your SQL*Plus output. These commands are explained in the following subtopics. If an abbreviation is available for the command, the abbreviation will be given inside brackets ([ ]). The valid values for this command will be given inside curly braces ({ }).

COLUMN {col} FORMAT {fmt} HEADING {string}   The most commonly used command for injecting readability into your SQL*Plus output by controlling column output format is the column *col* command, where *col* is the name of your column in the SQL query. You can turn formatting on and off by specifying column *col* on or column *col* off, respectively. You can also clear any setting by issuing column *col* clear. You can change the heading used for a column by using the heading '*string*' clause. You can also refine the format of output appearing in that column using the format *fmt* clause. For alphanumeric information appearing in a column, *fmt* is specified in the form a*num*, where *num* is a number representing how many characters wide the column should be. For numbers, *fmt* can be specified as a series of 9s representing the number of digits you want to see, optionally with currency symbols (L for local currency), commas, and/or periods. For example, column sal format $9,999.99 would display all numbers in the salary column of a query as follows:

```
SQL> column sal format $9,999.99
SQL> select sal from emp;
      SAL
----------
   $800.00
 $1,600.00
 $1,250.00
 $2,975.00
 $1,250.00
 $2,850.00
 $2,450.00
 $3,000.00
 $5,000.00
 $1,500.00
 $1,100.00
   $950.00
 $3,000.00
 $1,300.00
```

UNDERLINE [UND] {-|c|ON|OFF}   This command sets the character used to underline column headings in SQL*Plus reports to *c*. Note, *c* cannot be an alphanumeric character or a whitespace character. ON or OFF turns underlining on or off. ON changes the value of *c* back to the default (-). For example, you can use asterisks to underline column headings in the following way:

```
SQL> column empno format 99999
SQL> column ename format a12
SQL> set underline *
SQL> select empno, ename, sal
```

```
  2  from emp;
 EMPNO ENAME               SAL
 ****** ************* **********
   7369 SMITH           $800.00
   7499 ALLEN         $1,600.00
   7521 WARD          $1,250.00
   7566 JONES         $2,975.00
   7654 MARTIN        $1,250.00
   7698 BLAKE         $2,850.00
   7782 CLARK         $2,450.00
   7788 SCOTT         $3,000.00
   7839 KING          $5,000.00
   7844 TURNER        $1,500.00
   7876 ADAMS         $1,100.00
   7900 JAMES           $950.00
   7902 FORD          $3,000.00
   7934 MILLER        $1,300.00
```

WRAP [WRA] {OFF|ON}   The heading string specified for column can also contain a pipe character (|). For example, column dname heading 'd|name' denotes that you would like to split the heading into two separate lines. In some cases when you format column output in this way, the value for the column may not fit in the space allotted. The wrap variable controls whether SQL*Plus truncates the display of a selected row if it is too long for the current line width. OFF truncates the selected row; ON enables the selected row to wrap to the next line. If you want, you can also specify recsep and recsepchar to print separators between word-wrapped lines to make output clearer. Here's an example:

```
SQL> column dname heading d|name format a4
SQL> set recsep wrapped
SQL> set recsepchar '-'
SQL> select * from dept;
           d
   DEPTNO name LOC
--------- ---- -------------
       10 ACCO NEW YORK
          UNTI
          NG
-------------------------------------------------
       20 RESE DALLAS
          ARCH
-------------------------------------------------
       30 SALE CHICAGO
          S
-------------------------------------------------
```

```
    40 OPER BOSTON
       ATIO
       NS
------------------------------------------------
```

BREAK   Sometimes when the information returned by your SQL query is ordered on a column, you may have multiple rows of data, each with the same value in the ordered column. The output can be changed so that only the first in a series of rows, where the ordered column value is the same, will show the column value. Observe how this is accomplished in the following code block using the break command:

```
SQL> break on deptno
SQL> select deptno, ename from emp
  2  order by deptno;
   DEPTNO ENAME
--------- ----------
       10 CLARK
          KING
          MILLER
       20 SMITH
          ADAMS
          FORD
          SCOTT
          JONES
       30 ALLEN
          BLAKE
          MARTIN
          JAMES
          TURNER
          WARD
```

TIP
You can also use the skip n or skip page clauses in the break command to insert n blank lines or page breaks, respectively.

COMPUTE   You can also generate simple reports in SQL*Plus using the compute command in conjunction with the break command. The compute command performs one of several grouping functions on the column you are breaking on, including sum, minimum, maximum, avg (average), std (standard deviation), variance, count, and number (number of rows in the column). The following block illustrates a couple of uses for this command, in conjunction with break:

```
SQL> -- example 1
SQL> break on deptno skip 1
SQL> compute sum of sal on deptno
SQL> select deptno, ename, sal
  2  from emp order by deptno;
    DEPTNO ENAME           SAL
---------- ---------- ---------
        10 CLARK           2450
           KING            5000
           MILLER          1300
********                ---------
sum                        8750

        20 SMITH            800
           ADAMS           1100
           FORD            3000
           SCOTT           3000
           JONES           2975
********                ---------
sum                       10875

        30 ALLEN           1600
           BLAKE           2850
           MARTIN          1250
           JAMES            950
           TURNER          1500
           WARD            1250
********                ---------
sum                        9400
SQL> -- example 2
SQL> clear breaks
breaks cleared
SQL> clear computes
computes cleared
SQL> break on report
SQL> compute sum of sal on report
SQL> /
    DEPTNO ENAME           SAL
---------- ---------- ---------
        10 CLARK           2450
        10 KING            5000
        10 MILLER          1300
        20 SMITH            800
        20 ADAMS           1100
        20 FORD            3000
        20 SCOTT           3000
```

```
20  JONES           2975
30  ALLEN           1600
30  BLAKE           2850
30  MARTIN          1250
30  JAMES            950
30  TURNER          1500
                ---------
sum                29025
```

TTITLE and BTITLE   The use of break and compute segues into a larger discussion of using SQL*Plus to write reports. If you want a top or bottom title to appear on each page of a report, you can place one through the use of the ttitle and btitle commands, respectively. The syntax is [btitle|ttitle] *position 'title_text'*, where *position* can be LEFT, CENTER, RIGHT, or COL *n* to indicate a fixed number of characters from the left to start the title line.

TIP
*Using linesize and pagesize to determine
page width and how many lines of text appear on a
page will also determine where btitle and
ttitle place your top and bottom title lines,
respectively.*

For Review
Practice writing SQL*Plus reports using the commands covered in this and the previous discussion.

Exercises

1. **This SQL*Plus command can be used for calculating sums of data on columns in the same way as a group function:** _____

2. **This SQL*Plus command can be used to enhance report readability by reducing the number of times a duplicate value appears in a sorted column:** _____

3. **This SQL*Plus command can be used for placing a footer title on the bottom of a report page:** _____

Answer Key
1. compute 2. break 3. btitle

Creating and Executing Scripts

Each time you execute a SQL statement in SQL*Plus, that statement gets saved to a buffer used by SQL*Plus for repeat execution. One thing you might want to do when you have SQL statements you execute routinely in SQL*Plus is to save those statements as scripts. You can do this in a few different ways, one of which is to simply open up a text editor available on your operating system, enter the statements you want to execute routinely, and save the script to your host machine as a plain-text file. Another method available to you within SQL*Plus is to use the save command with a .sql extension, as follows:

```
SQL> select empno, ename, sal, deptno, hiredate
  2  from emp;
    EMPNO ENAME            SAL    DEPTNO HIREDATE
--------- ---------- --------- --------- ---------
     7369 SMITH            800        20 17-DEC-80
     7499 ALLEN           1600        30 20-FEB-81
     7521 WARD            1250        30 22-FEB-81
     7566 JONES           2975        20 02-APR-81
     7654 MARTIN          1250        30 28-SEP-81
     7698 BLAKE           2850        30 01-MAY-81
     7782 CLARK           2450        10 09-JUN-81
     7788 SCOTT           3000        20 19-APR-87
     7839 KING            5000        10 17-NOV-81
     7844 TURNER          1500        30 08-SEP-81
     7876 ADAMS           1100        20 23-MAY-87
     7900 JAMES            950        30 03-DEC-81
     7902 FORD            3000        20 ?3-DEC-81
     7934 MILLER          1300        10 ?-JAN-82
SQL> save employee.sql
Created file employee.sql
```

You have already seen that, when you want to execute the script again, you can use the @ command within SQL*Plus. Let's take one more look for review:

```
SQL> @employee.sql
SQL> @employee.sql
    EMPNO ENAME            SAL    DEPTNO HIREDATE
--------- ---------- --------- --------- ---------
     7369 SMITH            800        20 17-DEC-80
     7499 ALLEN           1600        30 20-FEB-81
     7521 WARD            1250        30 22-FEB-81
     7566 JONES           2975        20 02-APR-81
     7654 MARTIN          1250        30 28-SEP-81
     7698 BLAKE           2850        30 01-MAY-81
```

```
7782  CLARK          2450      10 09-JUN-81
7788  SCOTT          3000      20 19-APR-87
7839  KING           5000      10 17-NOV-81
7844  TURNER         1500      30 08-SEP-81
7876  ADAMS          1100      20 23-MAY-87
7900  JAMES           950      30 03-DEC-81
7902  FORD           3000      20 03-DEC-81
7934  MILLER         1300      10 23-JAN-82
```

For Review

Be sure you understand which commands to use for saving and executing your scripts in SQL*Plus.

Exercises

1. This is the command for storing the contents of your SQL*Plus buffer as a command file: _____

2. This is a command for loading a SQL command file into the operating buffer and executing it: _____

Answer Key

1. save 2. @

Saving Customizations

To save customizations to a file, you should use the `store` command, which accepts the `set` keyword along with a filename to save the environment settings to. The following code block illustrates this principle:

```
SQL> set termout on
SQL> set pagesize 132
SQL> store set myfile.out
Created file myfile.out
SQL>
```

Once your settings are saved, you can look at them in the file SQL*Plus created. To restore your settings, you must execute the contents the file in SQL*Plus. Both of these points are demonstrated in the following code block:

```
SQL> get myfile.out
  1  set appinfo ON
```

```
 2  set appinfo "SQL*Plus"
 3  set arraysize 15
 4  set autocommit OFF
 5  set autoprint OFF
 6  set autotrace OFF
 7  set shiftinout invisible
 8  set blockterminator "."
 9  set cmdsep OFF
10  set colsep " "
11  set compatibility NATIVE
12  set concat "."
13  set copycommit 0
14  set copytypecheck ON
15  set define "&"
16  set echo OFF
17  set editfile "afiedt.buf"
18  set embedded OFF
19  set escape OFF
20  set feedback 6
21  set flagger OFF
22  set flush ON
23  set heading ON
24  set headsep "|"
25  set linesize 100
26  set long 80
27  set longchunksize 80
28  set newpage 1
29  set null ""
30  set numformat ""
31  set numwidth 9
32  set pagesize 132
33  set pause OFF
34  set recsep WRAP
35  set recsepchar " "
36  set serveroutput OFF
37  set showmode OFF
38  set sqlcase MIXED
39  set sqlcontinue "> "
40  set sqlnumber ON
41  set sqlprefix "#"
42  set sqlprompt "SQL> "
43  set sqlterminator ";"
44  set suffix "sql"
45  set tab ON
46  set termout ON
47  set time OFF
```

```
48  set timing OFF
49  set trimout ON
50  set trimspool OFF
51  set underline "-"
52  set verify ON
53* set wrap ON
SQL> @myfile.out
SQL>
```

NOTE
Your settings for column, break, compute,
btitle, *and* ttitle *will not be included in the*
output file.

Alternately, if your environment file is stored in a file called login.sql, SQL*Plus can automatically execute the contents of the file so that the next time you log into SQL*Plus, your environment will be exactly the way you want it. This file must be stored either in the local directory from where you start SQL*Plus or on an operating system–specific path.

For Review

Be sure you understand how to store your environment settings and what the use of the login.sql file is.

Exercises

1. This is the command for writing all SQL*Plus environment data to a script for executing later: _____

2. This is the name of the script that will run whenever you start SQL*Plus to configure your environment settings: _____

Answer Key
1. store 2. login.sql

Chapter Summary

This chapter covered a lot of territory. You learned a great deal about advanced selection of data in SQL*Plus, including how to structure single-row, multiple-row, and correlated subqueries, as well as how to identify all those different types of queries. You also learned that subqueries ignore NULL results—a crucial fact to remember for OCP. After that, we discussed the many commands in SQL*Plus for formatting output for reports, how to write scripts, and how to enter variables into SQL queries for ease of use.

Two-Minute Drill

- The data used to determine the `having` clause can either be specified at runtime by the query or by a special embedded query, called a *subquery*, which obtains unknown search criteria based on known search methods.

- Subqueries can be used in other parts of the `select` statement to determine unknown search criteria, as well. Subqueries are generally included in this fashion in the `where` clause.

- Subqueries can use columns in comparison operations that are local to the table specified in the subquery, or they can use columns that are specified in tables named in any parent query to the subquery. This use is based on the principles of variable scope, as presented in this chapter.

- Various types of subqueries you might encounter when using Oracle include the following:

  - **Single-row subqueries** The main query expects the subquery to return only one value.

  - **Multiple-row subqueries** The main query can handle situations where the subquery returns more than one value.

  - **Inline views** A subquery in a `from` clause used for defining an intermediate result set to query from.

  - **Multiple-column subqueries** A subquery that contains more than one column of return data in addition to however many rows are given in the output.

- Be sure you understand how to set up and use a correlated subquery in Oracle to retrieve data.

- Recall that most subqueries (even those returning multiple rows) generally only return one column of output per row. However, you can construct subqueries that return multiple columns. Review the chapter to refresh your understanding of the syntax and semantics involved.

■ Subqueries that contain group by expressions will ignore rows if the group by column contains NULL values for those rows. Be sure you understand how to rewrite such queries, if necessary, to obtain those NULL values.

■ A subquery found in a from clause of the parent SQL query is called an *inline view*. Be sure you recall the syntax and semantics involved in using inline views, especially if you want to refer directly to columns in an inline view. Recall the use of inline views for top-N queries as well.

■ Review the SQL*Plus environment characteristics that can be configured using the set command.

■ In addition, be sure you understand completely how to use the following SQL*Plus commands for enhancing output readability:

   ■ format

   ■ btitle

   ■ ttitle

   ■ break

   ■ compute

■ Variables can be set in a select statement at runtime with use of runtime variables. A runtime variable is designated with the ampersand character (&) preceding the variable name.

■ The special character that designates a runtime variable can be changed using the set define command.

■ The define command can identify a runtime variable value to be picked up by the select statement automatically.

■ Once defined, the variable remains defined for the rest of the session or until it is undefined by the user or process with the undefine command.

■ You can modify the message that prompts the user to input a variable value. This activity is performed with the accept command.

Fill-in-the-Blank Questions

1. In order to generate reports that display sums of information by report, you might use this SQL*Plus command: _____

2. After assigning a value to a variable in a SQL*Plus command, you can reassign that variable a value using this SQL*Plus command:

_____

3. This SQL*Plus keyword is used for defining formats for how SQL*Plus displays column information: _____

4. This phrase describes a query that feeds one row of results to a parent query for the purpose of selection when the exact where clause criteria is not known: _____

Chapter Questions

1. **Once a variable is defined, how long will it remain defined in SQL*Plus?**

    A. Until the database is shut down

    B. Until the instance is shut down

    C. Until the statement completes

    D. Until the session completes

2. **You want to change the prompt Oracle uses to obtain input from a user. Which of the following choices are used for this purpose? (Choose two.)**

    A. Change the prompt in the `config.ora` file.

    B. Alter the `prompt` clause of the `accept` command.

    C. Enter a new prompt in the `login.sql` file.

    D. There is no way to change a prompt in Oracle.

3. **What is the default character for specifying substitution variables in `select` statements?**

    A. Ampersand

    B. Ellipses

    C. Quotation marks

    D. Asterisk

4. **The default character that identifies runtime variables is changed by which of the following?**

   A. Modifying the init*sid*.ora file

   B. Modifying the login.sql file

   C. Issuing the define *variablename* command

   D. Issuing the set define command

5. **You are developing a multiple-row query to handle a complex and dynamic comparison operation for the Olympics. Two tables are involved. CONTESTANT lists all contestants from every country, and MEDALS lists every country and the number of gold, silver, and bronze medals they have. If a country has not received one of the three types of medals, a zero appears in the column. Therefore, a query will always return data, even for countries that haven't won a medal. Which of the following queries shows only the contestants from countries with more than ten medallists of any type?**

   A. SELECT NAME FROM CONTESTANT C, MEDALS M WHERE
   C.COUNTRY = M.COUNTRY;

   B. SELECT NAME FROM CONTESTANT WHERE COUNTRY C IN
   (SELECT COUNTRY FROM MEDALS M WHERE C.COUNTRY =
   M.COUNTY)

   C. SELECT NAME FROM CONTESTANT WHERE COUNTRY C =
   (SELECT COUNTRY FROM MEDALS M WHERE C.COUNTRY =
   M.COUNTY)

   D. SELECT NAME FROM CONTESTANT WHERE COUNTRY IN
   (SELECT COUNTRY FROM MEDALS WHERE NUM_GOLD +
   NUM_SILVER + NUM_BRONZE > 10)

6. **You issue the following query in a SQL*Plus session:**

```
SELECT NAME, AGE, COUNTRY FROM CONTESTANT
WHERE (COUNTRY, AGE) IN ( SELECT COUNTRY, MIN(AGE)
FROM CONTESTANT GROUP BY COUNTRY);
```

   Which of the following choices identifies both the type of query and the expected result from the Oracle database?

   A. Single-row subquery, the youngest contestant from one country.

   B. Multiple-row subquery, the youngest contestant from all countries.

C. Multiple-column subquery, the youngest contestant from all countries.

D. Multiple-column subquery; Oracle will return an error because = should replace IN.

7. **The contents of the CONTESTANT table are listed as follows:**

```
NAME                      AGE COUNTRY
-------------      -------------- ---------------
BERTRAND                  24 FRANCE
GONZALEZ                  29 SPAIN
HEINRICH                  22 GERMANY
TAN                       39 CHINA
SVENSKY                   30 RUSSIA
SOO                       21
```

You issue the following query against this table:

```
SELECT NAME FROM CONTESTANT
WHERE (COUNTRY, AGE) IN ( SELECT COUNTRY, MIN(AGE)
FROM CONTESTANT GROUP BY COUNTRY);
```

Which of the following contestants will not appear in the output from this query?

A. SOO

B. HEINRICH

C. BERTRAND

D. GONZALEZ

8. **User JANKO would like to insert a row into the EMPLOYEE table. The table has three columns: EMPID, LASTNAME, and SALARY. This user would like to enter data for EMPID 59694, LASTNAME Harris, but no salary. Which statement would work best?**

A. `insert into EMPLOYEE values (59694,'HARRIS', NULL);`

B. `insert into EMPLOYEE values (59694,'HARRIS');`

C. `insert into EMPLOYEE (EMPID, LASTNAME, SALARY)`
    `values (59694,'HARRIS');`

D. `insert into EMPLOYEE (select 59694 from 'HARRIS');`

9. **Omitting the `where` clause from a `delete` statement has which of the following effects?**

   A. The `delete` statement will fail because there are no records to delete.

   B. The `delete` statement will prompt the user to enter criteria for the deletion.

   C. The `delete` statement will fail because of a syntax error.

   D. The `delete` statement will remove all records from the table.

Fill-in-the-Blank Answers

1. compute

2. undefine

3. Set

4. Single-row subquery

Answers to Chapter Questions

1. D. Until the session completes

Explanation   A variable defined by the user during a session with SQL*Plus will remain defined until the session ends or until the user explicitly undefines the variable. Refer to the discussion of defining variables earlier in the chapter.

2. B and C. Alter the prompt clause of the accept command *and* enter a new prompt in the login.sql file.

Explanation   Choice D should be eliminated immediately, leaving choices A, B, and C. Choice A is incorrect because config.ora is a feature associated with Oracle's client/server network communications product. Choice C is correct because you can use the set sqlprompt command within your login.sql file. This is a special file Oracle users can incorporate into their use of Oracle that will automatically configure aspects of the SQL*Plus session, such as the default text editor, column and NLS data formats, and other items.

3. A. Ampersand

Explanation   The ampersand (&) character is used by default to define runtime variables in SQL*Plus. Review the discussion of the definition of runtime variables and the set define command.

4. D. Issuing the set define command

Explanation   Choice A is incorrect because a change to the initsid.ora file will alter the parameters Oracle uses to start the database instance. Use of this feature will be covered in the next unit. Choice B is incorrect because, although the login.sql file can define many properties in a SQL*Plus session, the character that denotes runtime variables is not one of them. Choice C is incorrect because the define command is used to define variables used in a session, not an individual statement. Review the discussion of defining runtime variables in select statements.

5. D. SELECT NAME FROM CONTESTANT WHERE COUNTRY IN (SELECT COUNTRY FROM MEDALS WHERE NUM_GOLD + NUM_SILVER + NUM_BRONZE > 10)

Explanation The SELECT NAME FROM CONTESTANT WHERE COUNTRY IN (SELECT COUNTRY FROM MEDALS WHERE NUM_GOLD + NUM_SILVER + NUM_BRONZE > 10) query is correct because it contains the subquery that correctly returns a subset of countries that have contestants who won ten or more medals of any type. Choice A is incorrect because it contains a join operation, not a subquery. Choice B is simply a rewrite of choice A to use a multiple-row subquery; however, it does not go far enough to restrict return data and is therefore incorrect. Choice C is a single-row subquery that does essentially the same thing as choice B and is therefore incorrect.

6. C. Multiple-column subquery, the youngest contestant from all countries.

Explanation Because the main query compares against the results of two columns returned in the subquery, this is a multiple-column subquery that will return the youngest contestant from all countries in the table. This multiple-column subquery is also a multiple-row subquery, but because the defining factor is the fact that two columns are present, you should focus more on that fact than on the rows being returned. This fact eliminates choices A and B. The subquery does return multiple rows, however. You should also be sensitive to the fact that the main query must use an IN clause, not the equals sign (=), thus making choice D incorrect as well.

7. A. SOO

Explanation If you guessed SOO, great job! The correct answer is SOO because the subquery operation specified by the IN clause ignores NULL values implicitly. Therefore, because SOO has no country defined, that row is not selected as part of the subquery. As a result, the output lists each of the youngest contestants from the named countries, so choices B, C, and D will all appear in the result set.

8. A. insert into EMPLOYEE values (59694,'HARRIS', NULL);

Explanation This choice is acceptable because the positional criteria for not specifying column order is met by the data in the values clause. When you would like to specify that no data be inserted into a particular column, one method of doing so is to insert a NULL. Choice B is incorrect because not all columns in the table have values identified. When you're using positional references to populate column data, values must be present for every column in the table. Otherwise, the columns that will be populated should be named explicitly. Choice C is incorrect because when a column is named for data insert in the insert into clause, a value must definitely be specified in the `values` clause. Choice D is incorrect because using the multiple-row `insert` option with a `select` statement is not appropriate in this situation. Refer to the discussion of `insert` statements for more information.

9. D. The `delete` statement will remove all records from the table.

Explanation   There is only one effect produced by leaving off the `where` clause from any statement that enables one—the requested operation is performed on all records in the table.

CHAPTER
5

Creating Oracle
Database Objects

n this chapter, you will learn about and demonstrate knowledge in the following topics:

- Creating the tables of an Oracle database
- Including constraints

The topics covered in this chapter include creating tables and including constraints. With mastery of these topics, your experience with Oracle moves from the level of casual user to the world of application development. Application developers usually create database objects and determine how casual users will access those objects in production environments. The database administrator (DBA) is the person who is responsible for migrating developed objects into production and then managing the needs of production systems. This chapter will lay the foundation for discussion of Oracle database object and constraint creation, which is important for both developers and DBAs, so pay close attention to this material. The OCP Exam 1 test questions in this subject area are worth 15 percent of the final score.

Creating the Tables of an Oracle Database

This section covers the following topics related to creating tables:

- Describing tables
- Creating tables
- Datatypes and column definitions
- Altering table definitions
- Dropping, renaming, and truncating tables

This section will explain the basic syntax required of developers and DBAs in order to produce the logical database objects in Oracle known as *tables*. You will learn the syntax and semantics of creating tables and related database objects. You will also learn how to identify characteristics of tables already created. The section will cover how to change the definition of existing tables and other advanced types of table manipulation in the database as well. Finally, you will see a fast, neat way for deleting records from tables while leaving the definition of the table intact.

Describing Tables

The best way to think of a table for most Oracle beginners is to envision a spreadsheet containing several records of data. Across the top, try to see a horizontal list of column names that label the values in these columns. Each record listed across the table is called a *row*. In SQL*Plus, the command `describe` enables you to obtain a basic listing of characteristics about the table. We've already seen this command earlier in the book, but let's take another look at it using our trusty standby demo table, EMP, owned by SCOTT:

```
SQL> describe scott.emp
 Name                        Null?     Type
 -------------------- -------- --------------
 EMPNO                NOT NULL NUMBER(4)
 ENAME                         VARCHAR2(10)
 JOB                           VARCHAR2(9)
 MGR                           NUMBER(4)
 HIREDATE                      DATE
 SAL                           NUMBER(7,2)
 COMM                          NUMBER(7,2)
 DEPTNO                        NUMBER(2)
```

TIP
The `describe` command can be abbreviated as `desc` to obtain the same result with fewer keystrokes. This is not to be confused with the `desc` keyword used in conjunction with `order by` clauses to list output in descending order!

Note some interesting characteristics about the output in the preceding code block. First, the `describe` command lists the columns in the EMP table by name. Sometimes, columns in a table are also referred to as *fields*. We prefixed table EMP with its schema owner, SCOTT. If we didn't, Oracle would assume we wanted to see a description of the EMP table in our own schema, if one existed. Second, notice the column with the heading *Null?* This information indicates whether the column listed allows NULL information. A listing of not NULL for the table column usually (although not always) indicates that the table column is the primary key for identifying unique rows in the table. Finally, notice that the output shows detailed information about the datatype for that table column.

TIP
You've progressed quite a bit in your knowledge of Oracle. Therefore, the demo tables we used in prior chapters are of less and less use to you. From here on out in the book, we're going to work with our own database objects, creating them first, then populating them, and then selecting information from them if necessary. You'll probably want to continue using the SCOTT user ID, however, because it has the privileges you need to execute these examples!

For Review

Know how to use the `describe` command and what its abbreviation is. Understand what three pieces of information are listed in the output for this command as well as what that information means.

Exercises

1. You issue the following command in SQL*Plus: `describe PROFITS`. Which of the following choices identifies information that will not be shown in the results listed by this command?

   A. Columns in the table

   B. Foreign keys from this table to other tables

   C. Datatypes of columns in the table

   D. The primary key of the table

2. You issue the following command in SQL*Plus: `describe PROFITS`. Potential primary key information given in the output of the `describe` command will be listed under which of the following headings in the output?

   A. NAME

   B. NULL?

   C. TYPE

   D. None of the above

3. This is the keyword you can enter as an abbreviation for the `describe` command: _____

Answer Key
1. B. 2. B. 3. desc

Creating Tables

To create a table in Oracle, you use the `create table` command. This statement is one of many database object creation statements known in Oracle as the data definition language (DDL). For our purposes in the next several examples, we're going to create our own table of employees in a company of our own making. The following code block provides the basic `create table` statement that will create our new EMPLOYEE table:

```
SQL>  create table employee
  2   (empid varchar2(5),
  3    firstname varchar2(10),
  4    lastname varchar2(10),
  5    salary number(7));
Table created.
```

TIP
In order to create tables in the Oracle database, you need the `create table` privilege. User SCOTT has this privilege. You can find information for granting the needed privileges to other users in Chapter 8. Alternatively, you can ask your DBA at work to grant the `create table` privilege to the user ID you intend to use for working through the examples in this chapter.

Notice the important aspects of this basic `create table` statement. We define the table's name and then define all the columns we want in our table inside parentheses and separated by commas. The absolute maximum number of columns that a table may have is 1,000. Each column has an associated datatype that the information stored in that column must conform to. We make sure to close off the parentheses properly, and then Oracle creates our table for us. If a table called

EMPLOYEE already existed in our user schema, Oracle would give the following error and no table would be created:

```
SQL> create table employee
  2  (empid varchar2(5));
create table employee
            *
ERROR at line 1:
ORA-00955: name is already used by an existing object
```

> **TIP**
> *In the case where a table name you select is in use by an existing object in your schema, you can create the object in a different user schema, rename the object you want to create, rename the object that already exists, or remove the object that already exists.*

Creating Temporary Tables

Most of the time, when you create a table in Oracle, the records that eventually populate that table will live inside your database forever (or at least until someone removes them). However, there might be situations where you want records in a table to live inside the database only for a short while. In this case, you can create temporary tables in Oracle, where the data placed into the tables persists for only the duration of the user session, or for the length of your current transaction. A *transaction* is a span of time during which all data changes made are treated as one logical unit of work. You'll learn more about transactions later in Chapter 6.

A temporary table is created using the `create global temporary table` command. Why does a temporary table have to be global? So that the temporary table's definition can be made available to every user on the system. However, the contents of a temporary table are visible only to the user session that added information to the temporary table, even though everyone can see the definition. Temporary tables are a relatively new feature in Oracle, and Oracle hasn't had enough time yet to implement "local" temporary tables (that is, temporary tables that are only available to the user who owns them). Look for this functionality in later database releases. The appropriate `create global temporary table` command is shown in the following code block:

```
SQL> create global temporary table temp_emp
  2  (empno number,
```

```
 3   ename varchar2(10));
Table created.
```

So, to summarize quickly, let's review the following bullets with respect to temporary tables:

■ The `create global temporary table` statement creates a temporary table that can be transaction-specific or session-specific.

■ For transaction-specific temporary tables, data inserted into the temporary table persists for the life of the transaction.

■ For session-specific temporary tables, data inserted into the temporary table persists for the life of the session.

■ Data in a temporary table is private to the session, meaning that each session can see and modify only its own data in the temporary table.

Creating One Table with Data from Another

In most cases, when a developer creates a table in Oracle, the table is empty—it has no data in it. Once the table is created, the users or developers are then free to populate it as long as proper access has been granted. However, in some cases, the developer can create a table that already has data in it. The general statement used to create tables with data built in is the `create table as select` statement, as shown here:

```
SQL> create table emp_copy
  2  as select * from emp
  3  where deptno = 10;
Table created.
```

Two things are worthy of note about the `create table as select` statement. First, notice we didn't have to define any column names in table EMP_COPY. This is because we used a wildcard in the column clause to obtain data from the EMP table, telling Oracle to create the columns in EMP_COPY just as they appear in EMP—same names, same datatype definitions. The second thing is that any `select` statement you can issue from SQL*Plus can also be included in the `create table as select` statement. Oracle then automatically obtains whatever data you selected from EMP and populates EMP_COPY with that data. However, if the `select` statement includes a specific list of columns named in the column clause, your `create table` clause must list the columns you want the table to include, enclosed in parentheses. Here's an example of what I mean:

```
SQL> create table emp_copy_2
  2  (empno, sal) as
```

```
   3   select empno, sal from emp
   4   where deptno = 10;
Table created.
SQL> describe emp_copy_2
 Name                                Null?    Type
 -------------------------------     -------- ----------------
 EMPNO                               NOT NULL NUMBER(4)
 SAL                                          NUMBER(7,2)
SQL> select * from emp_copy_2;
    EMPNO        SAL
 --------- ---------
     7782       2450
     7839       5000
     7934       1300
```

Table-Naming Conventions

Many philosophies about the naming of variables, tables, columns, and other items in software come from the early days of computing. Available memory and disk space was limited on those early machines, so the names of tables and columns in those environments were often small and cryptic. In systems today, however, developers are not faced with that restriction. The names of columns and tables need not be bound by the naming rules of yesteryear. However, standards for naming tables and columns still have value, if only for the sake of readability. There are also some hard-and-fast rules about table and column names in Oracle. For our purposes, we'll divide our rules into two categories: hard-n-fast and soft-n-stylish.

Keep Names Short and Descriptive   Your table- and column-naming conventions in your Oracle database may be compact, but someone viewing the tables and columns in your database for the first time should also have some idea of what the tables and columns represent.

- **Hard-n-fast**   Oracle database object names must begin with a letter and can usually be between 1 and 30 characters long, except for databases (which have a maximum of eight characters) and database links (with a maximum of 128 characters). Names are not case-sensitive.

- **Soft-n-stylish**   Calling a table EMP_LN_FN_SAL might not be as easily understood as simply calling the table EMPLOYEE, or even EMP.

Relate Names for Child Tables to Their Parent   In certain situations, the developers of an application may find themselves creating multiple tables to define a logical entity representing a parent-child relationship. Consider an example where an employee expense application contains two tables—one called EXPENSE, listing information such as total invoiced amount and employee name, and the other called EXPENSE_DETAIL, containing individual entries for airfare, car rental, hotel, and so on. Both are descriptive names, and it is obvious from those names that there is some relationship between the tables.

- **Hard-n-fast**   A user cannot own or refer to two objects with the same name, so if both you and SCOTT own a table called EMPLOYEE, you must prefix references to EMPLOYEE with the schema owner.

- **Soft-n-stylish**   Tables related by foreign key (that is, parent/child relationships) should share part of the same table name.

Foreign-Key Columns Should Have the Same Name in Both Tables   If you are creating foreign-key relationships between columns in two different tables, it also helps if the column appearing in both tables has the same name in both places, implying the potential existence of a foreign key a bit more obviously. Remember, you can use table aliases in your join statements when you reference columns that have the same name in both tables in order to avoid ambiguity.

- **Hard-n-fast**   Don't name a table DUAL, because, as you know, Oracle already has a table called DUAL that is accessible by everyone.

- **Soft-n-stylish**   Give columns shared in multiple tables for parent-child relationships the same name.

Names of Associated Objects Should Relate to the Table   Sometimes other objects exist in conjunction with tables in Oracle. These objects include integrity constraints, triggers, and indexes. You'll learn what all these objects are later. For now, just know that they exist, and that it is useful to give these objects meaningful names that relate back to the table.

- **Soft-n-stylish**   Give objects that are associated with tables meaningful names that relate back to the table: for example, PK_EMP_01 (primary key for EMP table), IDX_EMP_01 (index on EMP table), and TRIG_EMP_01 (trigger on EMP table).

Avoid Quotes, Keywords, and Nonalphanumeric Characters   You can't use quotes in the name of a table or column, nor can you use most nonalphanumeric characters, with three exceptions: the dollar sign ($), the underscore (_), and the hash mark (#), sometimes also called the *pound sign*. The dollar sign is most notable in naming dynamic performance views, whereas the hash mark is used in some data dictionary tables owned by a privileged user called SYS in Oracle. In general, you should steer clear of using $ or #. The underscore is useful for separating two words or abbreviations.

- ■ **Hard-n-fast** Don't use table names beginning with SYS.

- ■ **Hard-n-fast** You can only use the following three special characters in table and column names: #, $, and _.

- ■ **Hard-n-fast** Don't use special characters from European or Asian character sets in a database name, global database name, or database link names.

- ■ **Hard-n-fast** An object name cannot be an Oracle reserved word, such as select or from; a datatype, such as NUMBER; or a built-in function, such as decode( ). Oracle may not complain when you create the object, but it may give you an unpleasant surprise when you refer to the object in your SQL statement.

- ■ **Hard-n-fast** Depending on the product you plan to use to access a database object (for example, WebDB, JDeveloper, or Developer), names might be further restricted by other reserved words. For a list of a product's reserved words, see the manual for that specific product.

For Review

1. Know how to use the statements for creating tables, temporary tables, and tables with data already populated in them. Know that the maximum number of columns a table may have is 1,000.

2. Be sure you can identify some table-naming conventions for descriptiveness, syntactic and semantic correctness, and relatedness to other objects.

Exercises

1. **You are defining database tables in Oracle. Which of the following choices identifies a table name that is not valid for use?**

   A. TEST_NUMBER

   B. P$$#_LOC

   C. 1_COPY_OF_EMP

   D. FLOP_TEST_#3

2. **You are creating tables in the Oracle database. Which of the following statements identifies a table-creation statement that is not valid?**

   A. create table cats (c_name varchar2(10), c_weight number, c_owner varchar2(10));

    B. `create table my_cats as select * from cats where owner = 'ME';`

    C. `create global temporary table temp_cats (c_name varchar2(10), c_weight number, c_owner varchar2(10));`

    D. `create table cats_over_5_lbs as select c_name, c_weight from cats where c_weight > 5;`

3. Your attempt to create a table in Oracle results in the following error: `ORA-00955-name is already used by existing object.` Which of the following choices does not identify an appropriate correction for this situation?

    A. Create the object as a different user.

    B. Drop the existing object with the same name.

    C. Change the column names in the object being created.

    D. Rename the existing object.

4. In Oracle, all temporary tables are available to all users, implying the need for this keyword: _____

Answer Key
1. C. 2. D. 3. C. 4. `global`

Datatypes and Column Definitions

The need for and use of datatypes when identifying the type of data columns in a table can hold has already been mentioned in Chapter 1. When we initially discussed it, we limited our discussion to only the datatypes used in the EMP table (VARCHAR2, DATE, and NUMBER) so that we could get busy learning how to develop queries. However, it is now necessary for us to discuss all the available datatypes in the Oracle database so that you know about all the datatypes available in order to pass the OCP exam. Here is a list of all the datatypes in Oracle, along with their descriptions:

Datatype	Description
VARCHAR2(n)	Contains variable-length text strings of length n bytes, where n can be of up to 4,000 bytes.
NVARCHAR2(n)	Contains single-byte or multibyte variable-length text strings of n bytes, where n can be up to 4,000 bytes in Oracle.
CHAR(n)	Contains fixed text strings of n bytes, where n can be up to 2,000 bytes in Oracle.
NCHAR(n)	Contains single-byte or multibyte fixed-length text strings of n bytes, where n can be up to 2,000 bytes in Oracle. Considered a unicode datatype because it stores unicode character data.
NUMBER($n[,m]$)	Contains numeric data up to n digits in length, where n can be up to 38 digits in Oracle. A NUMBER can also have an optional m number of digits to the right of the decimal point. This collection of digits is called a *mantissa*. The mantissa can have up to 38 digits as well. If no value is specified for n, Oracle defaults to 38.
DATE	Contains date information. DATE columns are seven bytes in length.
RAW	Contains binary data of up to 2,000 bytes in Oracle. This is a variable length datatype like VARCHAR2 in Oracle.
LONG	Contains text data of up to 2GB.
LONG RAW	Contains binary data of up to 2GB.
ROWID	Contains the address for rows in your table. These could be physical ROWIDs or logical ROWIDs.
BLOB	Stores large unstructured binary object data (available in Oracle8 and later versions only) of up to 4GB.
CLOB	Stores large database character set data (available in Oracle8 and later versions only) of up to 4GB.
NCLOB	Stores large single-byte or multibyte character-based unicode character set data (available in Oracle8 and later versions only) of up to 4GB.
BFILE	Stores pointers to large unstructured operating system files outside the Oracle database (available in Oracle8 and later versions only).

Text Datatypes Explained

There are two text datatypes that can contain alphanumeric information—CHAR and VARCHAR2. Although both CHAR and VARCHAR2 hold character strings, some subtle differences exist. First, the CHAR datatype only supports character strings up to a length of 2,000 bytes for Oracle, whereas the VARCHAR2 datatype supports character strings up to a length of 4,000 bytes for Oracle. The more important difference is demonstrated in the following code block:

```
SQL> create table tester
  2  (col1 char(10),
  3   col2 varchar2(10));
Table created.
SQL> insert into tester values ('BRADY','BRADY');
1 row created.
SQL> select vsize(col1), vsize(col2) from tester;
VSIZE(COL1) VSIZE(COL2)
----------- -----------
         10           5
```

TIP

We'll discuss data manipulation statements such as insert *in Chapter 6. For now, simply understand that* insert *is used for adding rows to a table in Oracle. Otherwise, nothing issued in this code block should be unfamiliar to you. If you don't remember what the* vsize( ) *function tells us, review its explanation in Chapter 2.*

Notice that in our TESTER table, the value BRADY that we stored in COL1 takes up ten bytes. This is because Oracle pads the value stored in CHAR columns with blanks up to the declared length of the column. In contrast, Oracle does not store padded blank spaces if the same value is stored in a column defined as datatype VARCHAR2.

TIP

VARCHAR2 has the 2 on the end of its name because there was once a VARCHAR datatype defined in early releases of Oracle. Although VARCHAR and VARCHAR2 are currently synonymous, they may not be in the future, so Oracle recommends using VARCHAR2. VARCHAR is a valid datatype complying with the ANSI standard and Oracle includes that datatype so they can say they are ANSI-compliant.

The NUMBER Datatype

The NUMBER datatype stores number data and can be specified to store integers or real numbers. In order to understand how to define NUMBER columns, let's say you were defining a column as shown in the following code block:

```
SQL> create table tester2
  2  (col1 number(15,2));
Table created.
```

The overall number of digits that this NUMBER column will store is 15 in this case. Thirteen digits can appear in front of the decimal point, whereas two digits are reserved for the mantissa. Therefore, 1234567891011 can be stored in this column as shown below:

```
SQL> insert into tester2 values (1234567891011);
1 row created.
```

However, 12345678910111 cannot fit into this column, as you see here:

```
SQL> insert into tester2 values (12345678910111);
insert into tester2 values (12345678910111)
                          *
ERROR at line 1:
ORA-01438: value larger than specified precision allows
 for this column
```

Interesting things happen when we try to insert values in this column that exceed the mantissa's specified length of two digits, as you see here:

```
SQL> insert into tester2 values (1234567891011.121)
1 row created.
```

Wait a minute, you say. When we tried to add a number to this column that was more than 13 digits to the left of the decimal point, Oracle gave us an error. Yet, when we add a value with more than 15 digits, where the overflow digits appear after the decimal point, Oracle accepts the value. Well, that's only partially true. To better understand what happened, let's take a look at the contents of TESTER2:

```
\SQL> column col1 format 9999999999999.99
SQL> select * from tester2;
          COL1
-----------------
 1234567891011.00
 1234567891011.12
```

The first command in the code block formats the output from COL1 so that we can read it more easily. Had we omitted that formatting command, Oracle would have returned the data in scientific notation. Second, notice in the second row of values from COL1 that Oracle changed our inserted value 1234567891011.121 to 1234567891011.12! Therefore, we can extrapolate two simple rules:

■ Oracle always rounds off when you try to insert values that exceed the number of digits allowed, so long as those extra digits appear after the decimal point.

■ If the extra digits appear in front of the decimal point, Oracle returns an error.

Other Datatypes in Oracle

Let's briefly cover the remaining datatypes in Oracle. We've seen the DATE datatype in action, which stores date values in a special Oracle format represented as the number of days since December 31, 4713 B.C.E. This datatype offers a great deal of flexibility when you want to perform date-manipulation operations, such as adding 30 days to a given date. Recall also that there are many functions that handle complex date operations. Another nice feature of Oracle's method for date storage is that it is inherently millennium-compliant.

Beyond the DATE datatype, there is an entire set of important type declaration options dedicated to the storage of small and large amounts of text and unformatted binary data. These datatypes include LONG, RAW, and LONG RAW. RAW datatypes in Oracle store data in binary format up to 2,000 bytes. It is useful to store graphics and sound files, used in conjunction with LONG, to form the LONG RAW datatype, which can accommodate up to 2GB of data. You can also declare columns as type LONG, which stores up to 2GB of alphanumeric text data. However, because data in a LONG or LONG RAW column is stored contiguously or *inline* with the rest of the table data, there can be only one column declared to be of type LONG in a table.

Storing large blocks of data has been enhanced significantly in Oracle8 and Oracle with the introduction of the BLOB, CLOB, and NCLOB datatypes. These four types can each contain up to 4GB of binary, single-byte, and multibyte character-based data, respectively. Data in a BLOB, CLOB, or NCLOB column is stored in the following way. If the value is less than 4KB, the information can also be stored contiguously (inline) with the rest of table data. Otherwise, a pointer to where Oracle has stored this data outside of the table is stored inline with the rest of the table. This is in contrast to earlier versions of Oracle, where the actual LONG or LONG RAW data must *always* be stored inline with the rest of the table information. As a result of this new way for storing large blocks of data, Oracle allows more than one BLOB, CLOB, or NCLOB column per table.

TIP
Storing data "inline" means that the data in a LONG datatype column is stored literally "in line" with the rest of the data in the row, as opposed to Oracle storing a pointer inline with row data, pointing to LONG column data stored somewhere else.

Finally, the ROWID datatype stores information related to the disk location of table rows. Generally, no column should be created to store data using type ROWID, but this datatype supports the ROWID pseudocolumn associated with every table. A *pseudocolumn* can be thought of as a virtual column in a table. Every table has several pseudocolumns, including one called ROWID. ROWIDs are critical to your ability to store information in tables because they identify how Oracle can locate the rows. They also uniquely identify the rows in your table. Every table contains a ROWID pseudocolumn that contains the ROWID for the rows of the table. The following code block illustrates that we can query data in the ROWID column of a table, just as if it were any other column:

```
SQL> select rowid from emp;
ROWID
------------------

AAACwdAABAAAJGdAAA
AAACwdAABAAAJGdAAB
AAACwdAABAAAJGdAAC
AAACwdAABAAAJGdAAD
AAACwdAABAAAJGdAAE
AAACwdAABAAAJGdAAF
AAACwdAABAAAJGdAAG
AAACwdAABAAAJGdAAH
AAACwdAABAAAJGdAAI
AAACwdAABAAAJGdAAJ
AAACwdAABAAAJGdAAK
AAACwdAABAAAJGdAAL
AAACwdAABAAAJGdAAM
AAACwdAABAAAJGdAAN
```

TIP
Although ROWIDs are essential for Oracle database processing, you don't need to know too much about how they work. ROWIDs are tested more extensively on the OCP DBA Fundamentals I exam.

Column Default Values

You can define tables to populate columns with default values as well using the `default` clause in a `create table` command. This clause is included as part of the column definition to tell Oracle what the default value for that column should be. When a row is added to the table and no value is defined for the column in the row being added, Oracle populates the column value for that row using the default value for the column. The following code block illustrates this point:

```
SQL> create table display
  2   (col1 varchar2(10),
  3    col2 number default 0);
Table created.
SQL> insert into display (col1) values ('MYCOL');
1 row created.
SQL> select * from display;
COL1            COL2
---------- ---------
MYCOL              0
```

For Review

1. Be sure you can name all the datatypes available in Oracle. Know the format of data stored in the DATE datatype and what the ROWID datatype is.

2. Know how to define NUMBER columns and know the significance of the value specified both for overall length and for the mantissa. Know what may happen when the value added to a NUMBER column exceeds the specified length both before and after the mantissa.

3. Understand the difference between the LONG and CLOB datatypes with respect to where data is stored in relation to the overall table.

4. Be able to describe the differences between the CHAR and the VARCHAR2 datatypes—particularly with respect to CHAR's use of additional padding when storing text strings.

5. Know how to use the `default` clause within the `create table` command.

Exercises

1. **The PROFITS column inside the SALES table is declared as NUMBER(10,2). Which of the following values cannot be stored in that column?**

    A. 5392845.324

    B. 871039453.1

    C. 75439289.34

    D. 60079829.25

2. Employee KING was hired on November 17, 1981. You issue the following query on your Oracle database: `select vsize(hiredate) from emp where ename = 'KING;`. Which of the following choices identifies the value returned?

    A. 4

    B. 7

    C. 9

    D. 17

3. You define the PRODUCT_NAME column in your SALES table to be CHAR(40). Later, you add one row to this table with the value "CAT_TOYS" for PRODUCT_NAME. You then issue the following command: `select vsize(product_name) from sales`. Which of the following choices best identifies the value returned?

    A. 8

    B. 12

    C. 40

    D. 4,000

4. Data in LONG RAW columns over 4KB in size is stored _____ with respect to the rest of the data in the table.

5. The JOB table contains three columns: JOB_NAME, JOB_DESC, and JOB_WAGE. You insert a new row into the JOB_DESC table using the following command:

```
SQL> insert into job (job_name, job_desc)
  2  values ('LACKEY','MAKES COFFEE');
```

Later, you query the table, and receive the following result:

```
SQL> select * from job where job_name = 'LACKEY';
JOB_NAME   JOB_DESC        JOB_WAGE
---------- --------------- --------
LACKEY     MAKES COFFEE         35
```

Which of the following choices identify how JOB_WAGE was populated with data?

A. The row for LACKEY in the JOB table already existed with JOB_WAGE set to 35.

B. A `default` clause on the JOB_WAGE column defined when the table was created specified the value when the row was inserted.

C. The `values` clause in the `insert` statement contained a hidden value that was added when the row was added.

D. The only possible explanation is that a later `update` statement issued against the JOB table added the JOB_WAGE value.

Answer Key

1. B. **2.** B. **3.** C. **4.** inline. **5.** B. Choice D is not correct because either an `update` statement or the `default` clause explain the output given in the question.

Altering Table Definitions

Suppose that, after you create a table in Oracle, you discover there is some fact that the table needs to store that you forgot to include. Is this a problem? Absolutely not! You can modify existing Oracle tables with ease using the `alter table` statement. There are several basic changes you might want to make using this statement, as listed below:

- You can add more columns to a table.

- You can modify the size of existing columns in a table.

- You can remove columns from a table (but only in Oracle8*i*, Oracle9*i*, and later versions).

- You can add or modify constraints on columns in the table. Constraints in Oracle prevent users from entering invalid data into tables. We'll defer most of the discussion of this topic until later in the chapter.

TIP
A third type of change you can make with the `alter table` statement has to do with the way tables are stored inside the Oracle database. This is a big topic on OCP Exam 2 in the DBA track. You don't need to worry about this type of modification for OCP Exam 1.

Adding New Columns to a Table

You can use the `alter table` statement to add new columns to a table in Oracle. However, there are some restrictions on doing so. First, no two columns can have the same name in an Oracle table. Second, only one column of the LONG or LONG RAW datatype can appear in a table in Oracle. Third, the maximum number of columns a table may have is 1,000. The following code block shows an example of the `alter table` statement:

```
SQL> alter table employee add (hire_date date);
Table altered.
```

As mentioned, only one column in the table may be of type LONG within a table. That restriction includes the LONG RAW datatype. However, many columns of datatype BLOB, CLOB, NCLOB, and BFILE can appear in one table, in Oracle8 and later versions. It is sometimes useful to emulate Oracle in Oracle7 databases as well, by having a special table that contains the LONG column and a foreign key to the table that would have contained the column; this reduces the amount of data migration and row chaining on the database.

TIP

Row chaining *and* row migration *occurs when the Oracle RDBMS has to move row data around or break it up and save it in pieces inside the files on disk that comprise an Oracle database. This activity is a concern to DBAs because it hurts database performance.*

Modifying Column Datatypes

Another important aspect of table columns that can be modified using the `alter table` statement is the configuration of the column's datatype. Suppose that our newly formed company using our new EMPLOYEE table has just hired a woman named Martha Paravasini-Clark. Recall at the beginning of the chapter that we created our EMPLOYEE table with a LASTNAME column of type VARCHAR2(10). Unfortunately, Ms. Paravasini-Clark's last name has 16 characters, so we need to change the LASTNAME column to accept larger text strings. To resolve the issue, you can issue the following statement, making the LASTNAME column length longer:

```
SQL> alter table products modify (lastname varchar2(25));
Table altered.
```

When you're modifying existing columns' datatypes, the general rule of thumb is that increases are generally okay, but decreases are usually a little trickier. Here are some examples of operations that are generally acceptable:

- Increasing the size of a VARCHAR2 or CHAR column

- Increasing the size of a NUMBER column

However, decreasing the size of column datatypes usually requires special steps. Take a look at the following code block, where we reduce the size of COL2 from our TESTER table:

```
SQL> desc tester
 Name                      Null?    Type
 ----------------------- -------- ------------
 COL1                               CHAR(10)
 COL2                               VARCHAR2(10)
SQL> alter table tester modify (col2 varchar2(5));
alter table tester modify (col2 varchar2(5))
                            *
ERROR at line 1:
ORA-01441: column to be modified must be empty to decrease length
SQL> create table tester_col2
  2  (col2) as select col2 from tester;
Table created.
SQL> update tester set col2 = null;
1 row updated.
SQL> alter table tester modify (col2 varchar2(5));
Table altered.
SQL> update tester set col2 = (select col2 from tester_col2);
1 row updated.
```

TIP

You've already seen examples of every statement used in the code block, and you know what a subquery is, so there shouldn't be anything confusing going on here. You'll learn more about the update *statement later in Chapter 6.*

Let's walk through the statements in the preceding code block. First, we described the TESTER table to see how large COL2 was. Then, we attempted to reduce it from ten to five bytes. Oracle didn't like that, because COL2 contained data. Therefore, we had to copy all the data in COL2 to a temporary location using the create table as select command. We then changed the column values to NULL on the column we want to reduce the size of, and we made the actual change to the datatype size. Finally, we added the data back into the TESTER table using an `update` statement containing a subquery. Here are some other allowable operations that follow this principle:

- Reducing the size of a NUMBER column (empty column for all rows only)

- Reducing the length of a VARCHAR2 or CHAR column (empty column for all rows only)

- Changing the datatype of a column (empty column for all rows only)

Dropping Columns in Oracle

You can also drop columns in Oracle using the `alter table` statement. There are two ways to do so. The first is to instruct Oracle to ignore the column by using the `set unused column` clause. In this situation, no information is removed from the table column. Oracle simply pretends the column isn't there. Later, we can remove the column using the `drop unused columns` clause. Both steps are shown in the following block:

```
SQL> alter table employee set unused column salary;
Table altered.
SQL> alter table employee drop unused columns;
Table altered.
```

The second option is to remove the column and all contents entirely from the table immediately. This statement is shown in the following block:

```
SQL> alter table employee drop column salary;
Table altered.
```

TIP
If you're following along in your Oracle database, make sure you add the SALARY column back to the EMPLOYEE table when you're done practicing both methods for dropping columns. We refer back to the EMPLOYEE table quite often later.

For Review

1. Be sure you know how to add columns using the `alter table` statement with the `add` clause.

2. Know how to modify column datatype definitions using the `alter table` statement with the `modify` clause.

3. Understand both uses of the `alter table` command for dropping columns—one using the `set unused column` and `drop unused columns` syntax, and the other with the `drop column` syntax.

Exercises

1. You want to reduce the size of a non-NULL NUMBER(10) column to NUMBER(6). Which of the following steps must be completed after the appropriate **alter table** command is issued?

   A. Copy column records to a temporary storage location.

   B. Set the NUMBER column to NULL for all rows.

   C. Create a temporary location for NUMBER data.

   D. Copy column records from the temporary location back to the main table.

2. You just issued the following statement: **alter table sales drop column profit;**. Which of the following choices identifies when the column will actually be removed from Oracle?

   A. Immediately following statement execution

   B. After the `alter table drop unused columns` command is issued

   C. After the `alter table set unused column` command is issued

   D. After the `alter table modify` command is issued

3. You want to increase the size of a non-NULL VARCHAR2(5) column to VARCHAR2(10). Which of the following steps must be accomplished after executing the appropriate **alter table** command?

   A. Set the VARCHAR2 column to NULL for all rows.

   B. Create a temporary location for VARCHAR2 data.

   C. Copy the column records from the temporary location back to the main table.

   D. Nothing. The statement is executed automatically.

4. You want to increase the size of the PRODUCT_TYPE column, declared as a VARCHAR(5) column, to VARCHAR2(10) in the SALES table. Which of the following commands is useful for this purpose?

   A. `alter table sales add (product_type varchar2(10));`

   B. `alter table sales modify product_type varchar2(10));`

   C. `alter table sales set unused column product_type varchar2(10));`

   D. `alter table sales drop column product_type;`

Answer Key
1. D. 2. A. 3. D. 4. B.

Dropping, Renaming, and Truncating Tables

Some additional operations are available for the modification of tables; they are designed for handling various situations, such as removing a table, changing the name of a table, and removing all the data from a table while still leaving the definition of the table intact. Let's talk about each of these operations in detail.

Dropping Tables

First, let's talk about how to eliminate a table. In order for a table to be deleted from the database, the `drop table` command must be executed:

```
SQL> drop table emp_copy_2;
Table dropped.
```

As mentioned earlier, sometimes objects are associated with a table that exists in a database along with the table. These objects may include indexes, constraints, and triggers. If the table is dropped, Oracle automatically drops any index, trigger, or constraint associated with the table as well. Here are two other factors to be aware of with respect to dropping tables:

■ You cannot roll back a `drop table` command.

■ To drop a table, the table must be part of your own schema, or you must have the `drop any table` privilege granted to you.

Truncating Tables

Let's move on to discuss how you can remove all data from a table quickly using a special option available in Oracle. In this situation, the DBA or developer may use the `truncate table` statement. This statement is a part of the data definition language (DDL) of Oracle, much like the `create table` statement and completely unlike the `delete` statement. Truncating a table removes all row data from a table quickly, while leaving the definition of the table intact, including the definition of constraints and any associated database objects such as indexes, constraints, and triggers on the table. The `truncate` statement is a high-speed data-deletion statement that bypasses the transaction controls available in Oracle for recoverability in data changes. Truncating a table is almost always faster than executing the `delete` statement without a `where` clause, but once this operation has been completed, the data cannot be recovered unless you have a backed-up copy of the data. Here's an example:

```
SQL> truncate table tester;
Table truncated.
```

> **TIP**
> *Truncating tables affects a characteristic about them that Oracle calls the high-water mark. This characteristic is a value Oracle uses to keep track of the largest size the table has ever grown to. When you truncate the table, Oracle resets the high-water mark to zero.*

Renaming Tables

You can rename a table in Oracle by using either the `rename` command or the `alter table rename` command. These commands allow you to change the name of a table without actually moving any data physically within the database. The following code block demonstrates the use of these commands:

```
SQL> rename tester to tester2;
Table renamed.
SQL> alter table tester3 rename to tester;
Table altered.
```

Commenting Objects

You can also add comments to a table or column using the `comment` command. This is useful especially for large databases where you want others to understand some specific bits of information about a table, such as the type of information stored in the table. An example of using this command to add comments to a table appears in the following block:

```
SQL> comment on table employee is
  2   'This is a table containing employees';
Comment created.
```

You can see how to use the `comment` command for adding comments on table columns in the following code block:

```
SQL> comment on column employee.empid is
  2   'unique text identifier for employees';
Comment created.
```

> **TIP**
> *Comment information on tables is stored in an object called USER_TAB_COMMENTS, whereas comment information for columns is stored in a different database object, called USER_COL_COMMENTS. These objects are part of the Oracle data dictionary. You'll find out more about the Oracle data dictionary later in the book.*

For Review

1. Understand how to remove a table from your database. Be sure you can describe what happens to any objects associated with the dropped table, such as indexes, constraints, and triggers.

2. Be sure you know how to rename and truncate tables. Understand what is meant by a table's *high-water mark* and how it is affected by the `truncate` command. Know how to add comments to a table as well.

3. Make sure you understand the difference between dropping and truncating a table. Dropping the table removes the table and all its data completely from the Oracle database. Truncating the table removes the table data but preserves the table definition for data added later.

Exercises

1. **You want to change the name of an existing database table. Which of the following choices does not identify a practical method for doing so?**

    A. Use the `create table as select` statement; then drop the original table.

    B. Use the `rename` command.

    C. Drop the table; then re-create it with its new name.

    D. Use the `alter table rename` command.

2. This is the name of the database object containing all comment information on tables: _____

3. BONUS QUESTION: You drop a table in an Oracle database that is the parent table in a parent-child data relationship. Which of the following objects will not be dropped when you drop the parent table?

    A. Associated constraints

    B. The child column

    C. Associated triggers

    D. Associated indexes

Answer Key

1. C. **2.** USER_TAB_COMMENTS **3.** B. In fact, you will have trouble dropping the parent table if there is a child table due to Oracle's enforcement of existing foreign key constraints. You'll learn more about constraints in the next section.

Including Constraints

This section covers the following topics related to including constraints in your database:

- Describing constraints
- Creating and maintaining constraints

Constraints have already been mentioned in some earlier discussions. This section will expand your understanding of constraints—those rules you can define in your Oracle tables that restrict the type of data you can place in the tables. In this section, you will learn more about the different types of constraints available in an Oracle system. You will also learn how to create and maintain the constraints you define in your Oracle database. This section also covers the different things you can do to modify, redefine, and manipulate your constraints. A note of caution: Constraints are one of the hardest areas to understand if you haven't used Oracle before. Proceed at your own pace.

Describing Constraints

Constraints accomplish three goals in an Oracle database. First, they create real and tangible relationships between the many tables that comprise the typical database application. We've already seen this to be the case in parent-child table relationships. Second, constraints prevent "unwanted" data from making its way into the database against your wishes. I put "unwanted" in quotes because ultimately, the definition of what constitutes unwanted data is entirely arbitrary and up to you as the developer of your system. But the point should be clear: *Constraints hold your database together and keep the bad data out.* Constraints perform an important third function as well—they also prevent the deletion of data if dependencies exist between tables.

Types of Constraints

Five basic types of constraints are available in Oracle, and they are listed in Table 5-1. The types of constraints are described in the following subsections.

Constraint	Description
Primary Key	Stipulates that values in the constrained column(s) must be unique and not NULL. If the primary key applies to multiple columns, then the combination of values in the columns must be unique and not NULL.
Foreign Key	Enforces that only values in the primary key of a parent table may be included as values in the constrained column of the child table.
Unique	Enforces uniqueness on values in the constrained column.
Check	Enforces that values added to the constrained column must be present in a static list of values permitted for the column.
Not Null	Enforces that a value must be defined for this column such that the column may not be NULL for any row.

TABLE 5-1. *Constraints in Oracle*

Primary Key   A constraint of this type identifies the column or columns whose singular or combined values identify uniqueness in the rows of your Oracle table. Every row in the table must have a value specified for the primary key column(s). Recall the EMP table used in earlier chapters. In it, EMPNO is a unique identifier for every row in the table. EMPNO, then, is the primary key because no two employees have the same number assigned to them in the EMPNO column. In relational database parlance, other columns in the EMP table are said to be *functionally dependent* on the primary key, EMPNO. This simply means that every other column describes a potentially non-unique attribute of this unique row. In other words, many employees could be named SMITH, but only one can be the employee named SMITH who has an EMPNO of 7369. Figure 5-1 diagrams this relationship in more detail.

Foreign Key   A constraint of this type signifies a parent-child relationship between two tables based on a shared column. The foreign key constraint is enforced on the shared column in the child table, whereas the shared column in the parent table must be enforced by a primary key constraint. When a foreign key

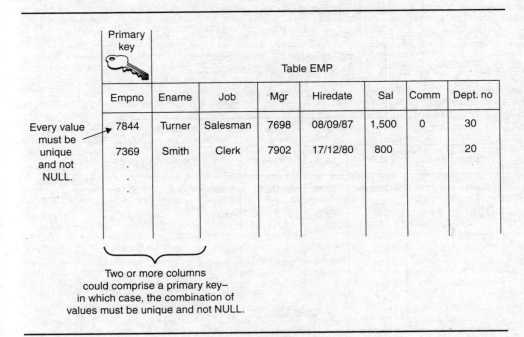

FIGURE 5-1.   *Primary key constraints in Oracle*

constraint exists on a shared column in the child table, Oracle checks to make sure that there is a corresponding value in the shared column of the parent table for every value placed in the shared column of the child table. Note that potentially many values in the parent table may not appear in the child table, but every value in the child table must have an associated value in the parent. Figure 5-2 diagrams this relationship in more detail.

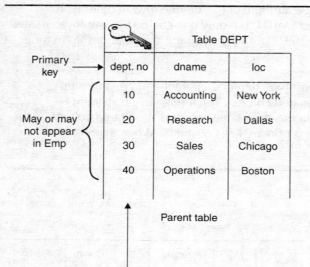

FIGURE 5-2. *Foreign key relationships in Oracle*

Unique Constraint   A constraint of this type enforces uniqueness on the values placed in this column. A good example of data requiring a unique constraint would be social security or government ID number. Every employee needs a unique one for tax purposes, so we want to store it in a table of employee information. However, it isn't an appropriate number to use as the primary key for that table of employee information, because many people want to keep their government ID number private. Therefore, you might store social security or government ID numbers, but apply a unique constraint to prevent duplicated entries rather than use them as a primary key.

Check Constraint   A constraint of this type enforces that values placed in this column meet specified static criteria. For example, a company may use check constraints to make sure that the salary entry for employees does not list an employee's salary as being over $250,000 per year. This is a static value that can easily be measured against an entered column value. Notice the repeated emphasis on *static* criteria. In the next discussion, you'll see what I mean by this.

TIP
Unique constraints, foreign keys, and check constraints usually allow NULL values to be placed in the column.

Not NULL Constraint   A constraint of this type enforces that values placed in the column will not be NULL. This is actually a specific type of check constraint that only checks to see whether the value being entered into the column is NULL.

For Review
Be sure you can identify the five types of constraints in Oracle. With respect to primary key constraints, be sure you can identify what is meant by functional dependency between columns in a table and the primary key as well.

Exercises
1. This type of constraint enforces uniqueness on column values and prevents NULL data from being entered for the column:

   _____

2. This type of constraint indicates a parent-child relationship between this child table and another table: _____

3. This type of constraint enforces that values entered for the column meet some predefined static criteria: _____

Answer Key

1. Primary key. Remember, the constraint enforces uniqueness *and* does not allow NULL values to be entered. **2.** Foreign key. **3.** Check.

Creating and Maintaining Constraints

So much for the easy part, now let's get down to the tough stuff. Two methods exist for defining constraints: the *table constraint method* and the *column constraint method*. How can you tell the difference between the two? Well, here's how. The constraint is defined as a table constraint if the `constraint` clause syntax appears after the column and datatype definitions. The constraint is defined as a column constraint if the constraint definition syntax appears as part of an individual column's definition. All constraints can be defined either as table constraints or as column constraints, with two exceptions:

- Not NULL constraints can only be defined as column constraints.

- Primary keys consisting of two or more columns (known also as *composite primary keys*) can only be defined as table constraints. However, single-column primary keys can be defined either as column or table constraints.

Creating Primary Key Constraints

Enough with the definitions, already. Let's start by taking a look at some examples for defining primary key constraints. Take a look at the following code listing, which displays a `create table` statement for creating our own EMPLOYEE table using constraints defined as table constraints (note that the `constraint` clause appears in bold):

```
SQL>   create table employee
  2    (empid varchar2(5),
  3    lastname varchar2(25),
  4    firstname varchar2(25),
  5    salary number(10,4),
  6    constraint pk_employee_01
  7    primary key (empid));
Table created.
```

TIP

If we wanted to create a composite primary key consisting of two or more columns, we would include the names of two (or more) columns

> inside the parentheses appearing after keywords
> `primary key`.

Only one primary key is permitted per table. Now, take a look at a `create table` statement for generating the same EMPLOYEE table. This time, the code listing shows the definition of the primary key as a column constraint. The `constraint` clause appears in bold in the following example:

```
SQL> create table employee
  2  (empid varchar2(5)
  3   constraint pk_employee_01 primary key,
  4   lastname varchar2(25),
  5   firstname varchar2(25),
  6   salary number(10,4));
Table created.
```

TIP
Both constraint declaration methods allow you to define your own names for your constraints. Remember that this feature is useful because constraints are database objects associated with tables, and from our earlier discussion, you know it's helpful to give associated database objects similar names.

Notice in the previous examples that each primary key constraint was given a meaningful name when defined. Oracle strongly recommends that you give your constraints meaningful names in this way so that you can easily identify the constraint later. With so many similarities between table and column constraint declarations, you may ask, are there any differences between constraints declared as table constraints and those declared as column constraints? Absolutely! Remember, *you can declare composite primary keys only by using the table constraint syntax, and you can declare not NULL constraints only using the column constraint syntax.* Another difference is that you can simplify the constraint declaration by merely indicating to Oracle that you want a constraint on the column (shown in bold), as you can see in the following block:

```
SQL> create table department
  2  (department_num number(5) primary key,
  3   department_name varchar2(25),
  4   location varchar2(25));
Table created.
```

TIP
*When you simplify your column constraint
definition in this way, Oracle names the constraint
for you. When Oracle names the constraint for you,
the naming convention is SYS_Cnnnnn.*

Composite Primary Keys

So that you understand the nature of composite primary keys in Oracle for OCP, the following code block shows how to define a composite primary key:

```
SQL> create table names
  2  (firstname varchar2(10),
  3   lastname  varchar2(10),
  4   constraint pk_names_01
  5   primary key (firstname, lastname));
Table created.
```

Uniqueness in a composite primary key is determined by combining the values in all columns of the composite primary key. If the combination is unique, then the key is unique. Check out the following code block to see some examples:

```
SQL> insert into names values ('JASON','COUCHMAN');
1 row created.
SQL> insert into names values ('JASON','LEE');
1 row created.
SQL> insert into names values ('COUCHMAN','JASON');
1 row created.
SQL> insert into names values ('JASON','COUCHMAN');
insert into names values ('JASON','COUCHMAN')
            *
ERROR at line 1:
ORA-00001: unique constraint (SCOTT.PK_NAMES_01) violated
```

In the second statement above, we add JASON LEE to the NAMES table. This is OK, even though we already have a record where FIRSTNAME is JASON because Oracle enforces uniqueness on the combination of values in FIRSTNAME and LASTNAME. Thus, we can even reverse the values as we did in the third statement above. However, the fourth statement causes an error because it is an exact duplicate of the first.

Defining Foreign Key Constraints

To help you understand how to define foreign key constraints, let's think in terms of an example. Let's say we have our own table called DEPARTMENT, which we just created in the last code block. It lists the department number, name, and location for all departments in our own little company. Let's also say that we want to create our EMPLOYEE table with another column, called DEPARTMENT_NUM. Because there is an implied parent-child relationship between these two tables with the shared column, let's make that relationship official by using a foreign key constraint, shown in bold in the following block:

```
SQL>  create table employee
  2   (empid varchar2(5) primary key,
  3   lastname varchar2(25),
  4   firstname varchar2(25),
  5   salary number(10,4),
  6   department_num number(5)
  7   references department (department_num)
  8   on delete set null);
Table created.
```

For a foreign-key constraint to be valid, the same column appearing in both tables must have exactly the same datatype. You needn't give the columns the same names, but it's a good idea to do so. The foreign key constraint prevents the DEPARTMENT_NUM column in the EMP table from ever storing a value that can't also be found in the DEPT table. The final clause, on `delete set null`, is an option relating to the deletion of data from the parent table. If someone attempts to remove a row from the parent table that contains a referenced value from the child table, Oracle sets all corresponding values in the child to NULL. The other option is on `delete cascade`, where Oracle allows remove all corresponding records from the child table when a referenced record from the parent table is removed.

Let's also test your eyes for distinguishing table and column constraints. Is the foreign key in the previous example a table or column constraint? At first, it might seem like a table constraint because the constraint definition appears after all the columns. However, close examination yields two important features. For one, there is no `constraint` clause. Table constraints must have a `constraint` clause; otherwise, Oracle returns an error. For another, there is no comma separating the constraint definition from the rest of the columns defined. If you flip back to our other constraint definition examples and look again carefully, you'll realize that this example shows the foreign key defined as a column constraint, not a table constraint.

TIP
A foreign key constraint cannot be created on the child table until the parent table is created and the primary key is defined on that parent table.

Defining Unique Key Constraints

Let's say we also want our employee table to store social security or government ID information. The definition of a UNIQUE constraint on the GOVT_ID column prevents anyone from defining a duplicate government ID for any two employees in the table. Take a look at the following example, where the unique constraint definition is shown in bold:

```
SQL>  create table employee
  2   (empid varchar2(5) primary key,
  3   lastname varchar2(25),
  4   firstname varchar2(25),
  5   salary number(10,4),
  6   department_num number(5)
  7     references department (department_num),
  8   govt_id number(10) unique);
Table created.
```

TIP
Unlike primary keys, which require that the column value not be NULL in addition to enforcing uniqueness, a unique constraint permits NULL values to be added to the column. Only non-NULL column values must be unique when unique constraints are present on the column.

Defining Other Types of Constraints

The last two types of constraints are not NULL and CHECK constraints. By default, Oracle allows columns to contain NULL values. The not NULL constraint prevents the data value defined by any row for the column from being NULL. By default, primary keys are defined to be not NULL. All other columns can contain NULL data, unless you explicitly define the column to be not NULL. CHECK constraints allow Oracle to verify the validity of data being entered on a table against static criteria. For example, you could specify that the SALARY column cannot contain values over $250,000. If someone tries to create an employee row with a salary of

$1,000,000 per year, Oracle would return an error message saying that the record data defined for the SALARY column has violated the CHECK constraint for that column. Let's look at a code example where both not NULL and check constraints are defined in bold:

```
SQL> create table employee
  2  (empid varchar2(5) primary key,
  3   lastname varchar2(25) not null,
  4   firstname varchar2(25),
  5   salary number(10,4) check (salary <=250000),
  6   department_num number(5)
  7     references department (department_num),
  8   govt_id number(10) unique);
Table created.
```

TIP
Here's what is meant by static criteria for CHECK constraints: CHECK constraints can only compare data in that column to a specific set of constant values or operations on those values. A CHECK constraint cannot refer to any other column or row in this or any other table. It also cannot refer to special keywords, such as user, sysdate, currval, nextval, level, uid, userenv, rownum, and rowid.

Indexes Created by Constraints

Indexes are created automatically by Oracle to support integrity constraints that enforce uniqueness. The two types of integrity constraints that enforce uniqueness are PRIMARY KEY and UNIQUE constraints. When the primary key or UNIQUE constraint is declared, a unique index to support the column's uniqueness is also created, and all values in all columns that were defined as part of the primary key or UNIQUE constraint are placed into the index.

The name of the unique index created automatically to support unique and primary key constraints is the same name as the one given to the constraint. Therefore, if you were to explicitly name the primary key on your EMP table PK_EMPLOYEE_01, Oracle calls the unique index PK_EMPLOYEE_01 as well. If, however, you choose not to name your unique or primary key constraint, Oracle generates the name of your constraint for you. In this case, Oracle also gives the unique index the same name it gives the constraint.

TIP
When a primary key or unique constraint is created,
a unique index corresponding to that constraint of
the table is created to enforce uniqueness.

Adding Integrity Constraints to Existing Tables

Another constraint-related activity that you may need to do involves adding new constraints to an existing table. This can be easy if there is no data in the table already, but it can be a nightmare if data already exists in the table that doesn't conform to the constraint criteria. The simplest scenario for adding the constraint is to add it to the database before data is inserted. Take a look at the following code block:

```
SQL> create table employee
  2  (empid varchar2(5),
  3   lastname varchar2(25),
  4   firstname varchar2(25),
  5   salary number(10,4),
  6   department_num number(5),
  7   govt_id number(10));
Table created.
SQL> alter table employee add constraint
  2  pk_employee_01 primary key (empid);
Table altered.
SQL> alter table employee add constraint
  2  fk_employee_01 foreign key (department_num)
  3  references department (department_num);
Table altered.
SQL> alter table employee add constraint
  2  ck_employee_01 check (salary <=250000);
Table altered.
SQL> alter table employee add constraint
  2  uk_employee_01 unique (govt_id);
Table altered.
SQL> alter table employee modify
  2  (lastname not null);
Table altered.
```

Notice that all the examples follow a general pattern of `alter table` *table_name* `add constraint` *constraint_name type* (*definition*), except for `not NULL` constraints, which use the `alter table modify` statement we saw in earlier discussions. The column on which the constraint is added must already exist in the database table; no constraint can be created for a column that does not exist in the table. Some of the other restrictions on creating constraints when data already exists in the table are listed here:

- **Primary keys** Columns cannot contain NULL values, and all values must be unique.

- **Foreign keys** Referenced columns in the other table must contain all values found in this one; otherwise, this column's value must be NULL.

- **UNIQUE constraints** Columns must contain all unique values or NULL values, or a combination of the two.

- **CHECK constraints** The new constraint will only be applied to data added or modified after the constraint is created.

- **Not NULL** Columns cannot contain NULL values. If you want to add a column with a not NULL constraint to a table, you should use a `default` clause to identify a value Oracle can populate in this column for existing rows. If you want to define a not NULL constraint on an existing column, the table must be empty or else the column must already have no NULL values defined for any rows.

Disabling Constraints

A constraint can be turned on and off. When the constraint is disabled, it will no longer do its job of enforcing rules on the data entered into the table. The following code block demonstrates some sample statements for disabling constraints:

```
SQL> alter table employee disable primary key;
Table altered.
SQL> alter table employee disable constraint uk_employee_01;
Table altered.
```

You may experience a problem if you attempt to disable a primary key when existing foreign keys depend on that primary key. This problem is shown in the following situation:

```
SQL> alter table department disable primary key;
alter table department disable primary key
*
ERROR at line 1:
ORA-02297: cannot disable constraint (SCOTT.SYS_C001913) -
dependencies exist
```

If you try to drop a primary key when there are foreign keys depending on it, the cascade option is required as part of `alter table disable` *constraint*, as shown in the following code block:

```
SQL> alter table department disable primary key cascade;
Table altered.
```

TIP
Disabling a constraint leaves the table vulnerable to inappropriate data being entered! Care should be taken to ensure that the data loaded during the period the constraint is disabled will not interfere with your ability to enable the constraint later. The cascade clause disables dependent integrity constraints. Disabling a primary or unique key removes the associated index from Oracle.

Enabling a Disabled Constraint

When the constraint is later enabled, the rules defined for the constraint are once again enforced, rendering the constraint as effective as it was when it was first added to the table. You can enable a disabled constraint as follows:

```
SQL> alter table department enable primary key;
Table altered.
SQL> alter table employee enable uk_employee_01;
Table altered.
```

TIP
Only constraints that have been successfully defined and are currently disabled can be enabled by this code. A constraint that fails on creation will not exist in the disabled state, waiting for you to correct the problem and reenable it. Enabling a unique or primary key constraint automatically rebuilds the index for that constraint.

When Existing Data in a Column Violates a Disabled Constraint

This topic is a bit advanced, so be forewarned. There are situations where you may want to disable a constraint for some general purpose, such as disabling a primary key in order to speed up a large number of `insert` statements. *Be careful when using this approach*! If you disable a constraint and then load data into the table column that violates the integrity constraint while the constraint is disabled, your attempt to enable the constraint later with the `alter table enable constraint` statement will fail. You will need to use a special table called EXCEPTIONS (created by running the `utlexcpt.sql` script in `rdbms/admin` under the Oracle software home directory) to identify and correct the offending records. The following example involving a primary-key constraint should give you an idea of how this works:

```
SQL> @@C:\ORACLE\ORA81\RDBMS\ADMIN\UTLEXCPT
Table created.
SQL> create table example_1 (col1 number);
Table created.
SQL> insert into example_1 values (10);
1 row created.
SQL> insert into example_1 values (1);
1 row created.
SQL> alter table example_1 add (constraint pk_01 primary key (col1));
Table altered.
SQL> select * from example_1;
COL1
---------
        10
         1
SQL> alter table example_1 disable constraint pk_01;
Table altered.
SQL> insert into example_1 values (1);
1 row created.
SQL> alter table example_1 enable constraint pk_01
  2   exceptions into exceptions;
alter table example_1 enable constraint pk_01
*
ERROR at line 1:
ORA-02437: cannot enable (SCOTT.PK_01) - primary key violated
SQL> desc exceptions
 Name                            Null?    Type
 ------------------------------- -------- ----
 ROW_ID                                   ROWID
 OWNER                                    VARCHAR2(30)
 TABLE_NAME                               VARCHAR2(30)
 CONSTRAINT                               VARCHAR2(30)
SQL> select e.row_id, a.col1
  2   from exceptions e, example_1 a
  3   where e.row_id = a.rowid;
ROW_ID                  COL1
```

```
------------------- --------
AAAAvGAAGAAAAPWAAB        1
AAAAvGAAGAAAAPWAAD        1
```

At this point, you have identified the ROWIDs of the offending rows in EXAMPLE_1 that break the rules of the primary key, which you can use either to modify the value of one of these rows or to remove one of the rows so the primary key can be unique. In the future, to ensure that enabling the constraint will be a smooth process, try not to load any data into columns with disabled constraints that would violate the constraint rules.

Removing Constraints

Usually, there is little about a constraint that will interfere with your ability to remove it, so long as you either own the table or have been granted appropriate privileges to do so. When a constraint is dropped, any index associated with that constraint (if there is one) is also dropped. Here is an example:

```
SQL> alter table employee drop unique (govt_id);
Table altered.
SQL> alter table employee drop primary key cascade;
Table altered.
SQL> alter table employee drop constraint ck_employee_01;
Table altered.
```

An anomaly can be found when disabling or dropping not NULL constraints. You cannot disable a not NULL constraint, per se—a column either accepts NULL values or it doesn't. Therefore, you must use the alter table modify clause in all situations where the not NULL constraints on a table must be added or removed. Here's an example:

```
SQL> alter table employee modify (lastname null);
Table altered.
SQL> alter table employee modify (lastname not null);
Table altered.
```

Dropping Parent Tables with Foreign Key Constraint References

In the same way that disabling a primary key constraint can be a problem when the primary key is referenced by a foreign key in a child table, dropping parent tables can also pose a problem when a child table is involved. If we wanted to drop the parent table DEPARTMENT in our parent-child relationship, the foreign key in the child table EMPLOYEE may interfere with our doing so. Let's take a look at what happens:

```
SQL> drop table department;
drop table department
              *
ERROR at line 1:
ORA-02449: unique/primary keys in table referenced by foreign keys
```

When there are constraints on other tables that reference the table to be dropped, you can use the `cascade constraints` clause in your `drop table` statement. The constraints in other tables that refer to the table being dropped are also dropped with `cascade constraints`:

```
SQL> drop table department cascade constraints;
Table dropped.
```

TIP
Alternately, you can disable or drop the foreign key in the child table before dropping the parent table by using the `alter table drop constraint` statement from earlier in the chapter.

Constraint Deferability in Oracle

When records are added to a database table, Oracle immediately validates the incoming records against any constraints that may exist on the columns in the table. If the data doesn't conform to the constraint criteria, Oracle returns an error immediately. However, you can modify this default behavior so that Oracle does not return an error immediately. Instead, you can force Oracle not to return an error until you are ready to end your transaction. Remember from an earlier discussion that a *transaction* is a series of data-change statements issued in a user session that comprise a logical unit of work. You will learn more about transaction processing later in Chapter 6. The concept of forcing Oracle not to return constraint violation errors until the end of your transaction is called *constraint deferability*.

In order for constraint deferability to work, you must define your constraint to be deferrable using the `deferrable initially deferred` syntax. For primary keys and unique constraints, this means that Oracle uses a nonunique index to store primary key values rather than a unique index. The nonunique index allows temporary storage of data in the primary key column until the transaction is completed and constraint violation errors can be reported. If you use the other deferability option, `deferrable initially immediate`, Oracle still creates a nonunique index to support the primary key, but it enforces the primary key when data is entered, not when the transaction ends. If you omit either of these clauses entirely, Oracle also enforces the constraint when data is entered, not when the transaction ends. Finally, remember that the keyword `deferrable` contains two Rs, not one.

The options you have for enabling or disabling deferrable constraints include `enable validate` and `enable novalidate`. If you try to enable your constraint without specifying one of these options, Oracle uses `enable validate` by default. Using the `enable validate` option when you're enabling constraints forces Oracle to validate all the data in the constrained column to ensure that it meets the constraint criteria. This is the default behavior unless otherwise specified. The `enable validate` command is the same as simply using the `enable` keyword—validate is the default behavior of Oracle. However, Oracle also allows you to use the `enable novalidate` option when you want to enforce the constraint for new data entering the table but don't care about data that already exists in the table.

Let's look at an example. Assume that a table called PRODUCTS is used for storing products our company sells. The following code block illustrates how to create, disable, and enable a deferrable primary key constraint using appropriate syntax, which is shown in bold:

```
SQL> create table products
  2  (product# number,
  3   product_name varchar2(15),
  4   quantity number,
  5   color varchar2(10),
  6   prod_size varchar2(10));
Table created.
SQL> insert into products values
  2  (1, 'FLIBBER', 34, 'GREEN', 'XXL');
1 row created.
SQL> insert into products values
  2  (2, 'blobber', 4, 'GREEN', 'P');
1 row created.
SQL> select * from products;
PRODUCT# PRODUCT_NAME    QUANTITY COLOR      PROD_SIZE
-------- --------------- -------- ---------- ----------
       1 FLIBBER             34 GREEN      XXL
       2 blobber              4 GREEN      P
SQL> alter table products add
  2  (constraint pk_products_01 primary key (product#)
  3  deferrable initially deferred);
Table altered.
SQL> alter table products disable primary key;
Table altered.
SQL> update products set product# = 1
  2  where product_name = 'blobber';
1 row updated.
SQL> commit;
```

```
Commit complete.
SQL> alter table products enable validate primary key;
alter table products enable validate primary key
*
ERROR at line 1:
ORA-02437: cannot enable (SCOTT.PK_PRODUCTS_01) - primary
key violated
SQL> alter table products enable novalidate primary key;
Table altered.
SQL> select * from products;
PRODUCT# PRODUCT_NAME    QUANTITY COLOR      PROD_SIZE
-------- ------------- --------- ---------- ----------
       1 FLIBBER              34 GREEN      XXL
       1 blobber               4 GREEN      P
SQL> insert into products
  2 (product#, product_name, quantity, color, prod_size)
  3 values (1,'FLOBBER',23,'GREEN','L')
insert into products
*
ERROR at line 1:
ORA-00001: unique constraint (SCOTT.PK_PRODUCTS_01) violated
```

TIP

*disable novalidate is the same as disable;
however, new in Oracle is disable validate,
which disables the constraints, drops the index, and
disallows any modification on the constrained
columns. The enable keyword implies validate
option unless novalidate is specified. The
disable keyword implies novalidate unless the
validate option is specified.*

For Review

1. Be sure you can identify some differences between defining constraints as table constraints and as column constraints. Know how to define all five constraints on existing tables and as part of new table definitions. Know why defining a not NULL constraint is not like defining other types of constraints.

2. Know how to enable a disabled constraint. Be sure you know the restrictions on enabling constraints and how to create and use the EXCEPTIONS table for enabling constraints when data that violates these constraints exists in the table.

3. Be sure you can explain the concept of constraint deferability and the use of appropriate syntax for defining, enabling, and disabling deferrable constraints.

4. Understand that Oracle creates unique indexes in support of unique and primary key constraints. Know what determines the name given to an index created automatically.

Exercises

I. **The PROFITS table in your database has a primary key on the PRODUCT_NAME and SALE_PERIOD columns. Which of the following statements could *not* have been used to define this primary key?**

A. `create table profits ( product_name varchar2(10), sale_period varchar2(10), profit number, constraint pk_profits_01 primary key (product_name, sale_period));`

B. `alter table profits add constraint pk_profits_01 primary key (product_name, sale_period) deferrable initially immediate;`

C. `alter table profits add (constraint pk_profits_01 primary key (product_name, sale_period));`

D. `create table profits ( product_name varchar2(10) primary key, sale_period varchar2(10) primary key, profit number);`

2. **You are defining check constraints on your SALES table, which contains two columns, PRODUCT_TYPE and UNIT_SALES. Which of the following choices identify a properly defined check constraint? (Choose two.)**

A. `alter table sales add constraint ck_sales_01 check (product_type in ('TOYS', 'HOT DOGS', 'PALM PILOTS'));`

B. `alter table sales add constraint ck_sales_01 check (product_type in (select product_type from valid_products));`

C. `alter table sales modify (product_type varchar2(30) check (product_type in ('TOYS', 'HOT DOGS', 'PALM PILOTS')));`

D. `alter table sales add (product_name varchar2(30) check (product_name <> 'AK-47'));`

3. **Use the following code block to answer the question:**

```
SQL> create table prices
  2  ( product_name varchar2(30),
  3    price number(10,4));
Table created.
SQL> alter table prices add constraint pk_prices_01
  2  primary key (product_name);
Table altered.
SQL> insert into prices values ('DOGGY', 499.99);
1 row created.
SQL> alter table prices disable constraint pk_prices_01;
Table altered.
SQL> insert into prices values ('DOGGY', 449.99);
1 row created.
SQL> alter table prices enable novalidate pk_prices_01;
Table altered.
```

What happens next?

A. Existing entries are checked for violations, PK_PRICES_01 is enabled, and Oracle checks subsequent entries for violations immediately.

B. Existing entries are checked for violations, PK_PRICES_01 is not enabled, and Oracle does not check subsequent entries for violations immediately.

C. Existing entries are not checked for violations, PK_PRICES_01 is enabled, and Oracle checks subsequent entries for violations immediately.

D. Existing entries are checked for violations, PK_PRICES_01 is not enabled, Oracle checks subsequent entries for violations immediately.

4. **Your attempt to disable a constraint yields the following error: ORA-02297: cannot disable constraint - dependencies exist. Which of the following types of constraints is likely causing interference with your disablement of this one?**

A. Check constraint

B. Not NULL constraint

C. Foreign key constraint

D. Unique constraint

5. **You are disabling a not NULL constraint on the UNIT_PRICE column in the SALES table. Which of the following choices identifies the correct statement for performing this action?**

   A. `alter table sales modify (unit_prices null);`

   B. `alter table sales modify (unit_prices not null);`

   C. `alter table sales add (unit_prices null);`

   D. `alter table sales add (unit_prices not null);`

Answer Key

1. D. **2.** A and D. Nothing in the question said you can't add a new column. **3.** B. Remember, when a constraint cannot be enabled, it does not perform its job. **4.** C. **5.** A.

Chapter Summary

We covered a great deal of ground in this chapter. At the beginning, we discussed how to create tables in the Oracle database. We talked about how to alter our table definitions as well. After covering how to define and change the definition of tables with respect to columns, we spent a great deal of time discussing database constraints. You learned about the five different types of database constraints as well as how to create them when initially defining the table. You also learned how to create constraints after the fact using the `alter table` command. We then moved on to discuss indexes that can be created with constraints. We covered constraint deferability and how to correct problems where the data in a table column might violate the constraint on that column—two complex topics to know for OCP.

Two-Minute Drill

- The basic types of data relationships in Oracle include primary keys and functional dependency within a table as well as foreign key constraints from one table to another.

- A relational database is composed of objects that store data, objects that manage access to data, and objects that improve performance when accessing data.

- A table can be created with five different types of integrity constraints: `PRIMARY KEY`, `FOREIGN KEY`, `UNIQUE`, `not NULL`, and `CHECK`.

■ Referential integrity often creates a parent/child relationship between two tables—the parent being the referenced table and the child being the referring table. Often, a naming convention that requires child objects to adopt and extend the name of the parent table is useful in identifying these relationships.

■ The datatypes available for creating columns in tables are CHAR, VARCHAR2, NUMBER, DATE, RAW, LONG, LONG RAW, ROWID, BLOB, CLOB, NCLOB, and BFILE.

■ A table column can be added or modified with the `alter table` statement.

■ Columns can be added with little difficulty if they are nullable, using the `alter table add (column_name datatype)` statement. If a not NULL constraint is desired, add the column, populate the column with data, and then add the `not NULL` constraint separately.

■ Column datatype size can be increased with no difficulty by using the `alter table modify (column_name datatype)` statement. Column size can be decreased, or the datatype can be changed, only if the column contains NULL for all rows.

■ Constraints can be added to a column only if the column already contains values that will not violate the added constraint.

■ `PRIMARY KEY` constraints can be added with a table constraint definition by using the `alter table add (constraint constraint_name primary key (column_name))` statement or with a column constraint definition by using the `alter table modify (column_name constraint constraint_name primary key)` statement.

■ `UNIQUE` constraints can be added with a table constraint definition by using the `alter table add (constraint constraint_name unique (column_name))` statement or with a column constraint definition by using the `alter table modify (column_name constraint constraint_name unique)` statement.

■ `FOREIGN KEY` constraints can be added with a table constraint definition by using the `alter table add (constraint constraint_name foreign key (column_name) references OWNER.TABLE (column_name) [on delete cascade])` statement or with a column constraint definition by using the `alter table modify (column_name constraint constraint_name references OWNER.TABLE (column_name) [on delete cascade])` statement.

■ CHECK constraints can be added with a table constraint definition by using the alter table add (constraint *constraint_name* check (*check_condition*)) statement or with a column constraint definition by using the alter table modify (*column_name* constraint *constraint_name* check (*check_condition*)) statement.

■ The check condition cannot contain subqueries, references to certain keywords (such as user, sysdate, and rowid), or any pseudocolumns.

■ Not NULL constraints can be added with a column constraint definition by using the alter table modify (*column_name* NOT NULL) statement.

■ A named PRIMARY KEY, UNIQUE, CHECK, or FOREIGN KEY constraint can be dropped with the alter table drop constraint *constraint_name* statement. A not NULL constraint is dropped using the alter table modify (*column_name* NULL) statement.

■ If a constraint that created an index automatically (such as a primary key or UNIQUE constraint) is dropped, the corresponding index is also dropped.

■ If the table is dropped, all constraints, triggers, and indexes created for the table are also dropped.

■ Removing all data from a table is best accomplished with the truncate command rather than the delete from table_name statement because truncate resets the table's high-water mark and deallocates all the table's storage quickly, thus improving performance on select count( ) statements issued after the truncation.

■ An object name can be changed with the rename statement or with the use of synonyms.

■ Indexes are created automatically in conjunction with primary key and UNIQUE constraints. These indexes are named after the constraint name given to the constraint in the definition of the table.

■ Tables are created without any data in them, except for tables created with the create table as select statement. These tables are created and prepopulated with data from another table.

Fill-in-the-Blank Questions

1. This constraint is useful for verifying data entered for a column against a static list of values identified as part of the table definition: _____

2. This datatype is used for identifying each row uniquely in the table: _____

3. The definition of the object can be made available to every user on the system. However, its contents are visible only to the user session that added the information to this object: _____

4. This keyword for constraint enablement specifies that Oracle not check to see whether the data conforms to the constraint until the user commits the transaction: _____

5. This database object in Oracle, created when the primary key is defined, is dropped when the table is dropped: _____

Chapter Questions

1. **Which of the following integrity constraints automatically create an index when defined? (Choose two.)**

   A. Foreign keys

   B. Unique constraints

   C. Not NULL constraints

   D. Primary keys

2. **Developer ANJU executes the following statement: `create table ANIMALS as select * from MASTER.ANIMALS;`. What is the effect of this statement?**

   A. A table named ANIMALS will be created in the MASTER schema with the same data as the ANIMALS table owned by ANJU.

   B. A table named ANJU will be created in the ANIMALS schema with the same data as the ANIMALS table owned by MASTER.

C. A table named ANIMALS will be created in the ANJU schema with the same data as the ANIMALS table owned by MASTER.

D. A table named MASTER will be created in the ANIMALS schema with the same data as the ANJU table owned by ANIMALS.

3. **No relationship officially exists between two tables. Which of the following choices is the strongest indicator that a parent/child relationship exists between these tables?**

A. The two tables in the database are named VOUCHER and VOUCHER_ITEM, respectively.

B. The two tables in the database are named EMPLOYEE and PRODUCTS, respectively.

C. The two tables in the database were created on the same day.

D. The two tables in the database contain none of the same columns.

4. **Which of the following are valid database datatypes in Oracle? (Choose three.)**

A. CHAR

B. VARCHAR2

C. BOOLEAN

D. NUMBER

E. NUMERIC

F. ROWNUM

5. **Which line of the following statements produces an error?**

A. `create table GOODS`

B. `(GOODNO number,`

C. `GOOD_NAME varchar2(20) check(GOOD_NAME in (select NAME from AVAIL_GOODS)),`

D. `constraint PK_GOODS_01`

E. `primary key (GOODNO));`

F. There are no errors in this statement.

6. **You are adding columns to a table in Oracle. Which of the following choices indicates what you would do to increase the number of columns accepting NULL values in a table?**

   A. Use the `alter table` statement.

   B. Ensure that all column values are NULL for all rows.

   C. First, increase the size of adjacent column datatypes and then add the column.

   D. Add the column, populate the column, and then add the not NULL constraint.

7. **A user issues the statement `select count(*) from employee`. The query takes an inordinately long time and returns a count of zero. What is the most cost-effective solution to this problem?**

   A. Upgrade the hardware.

   B. Truncate the table.

   C. Upgrade the version of Oracle.

   D. Delete the high-water mark.

8. **You are creating some tables in your database as part of the logical data model. Which of the following constraints has an index associated with it that is generated automatically by Oracle?**

   A. Unique

   B. Foreign key

   C. CHECK

   D. Not NULL

9. **Each of the following statements is true about referential integrity, except one. Which is it?**

   A. The referencing column in the child table must correspond with a primary key in the parent.

   B. All values in the referenced column in the parent table must be present in the referencing column in the child.

C. The datatype of the referenced column in the parent table must be identical to the referencing column in the child.

D. All values in the referencing column in the child table must be in present in the referenced column in the parent.

10. **You are managing constraints on a table in Oracle. Which of the following choices correctly identifies the limitations on check constraints?**

A. Values must be obtained from a lookup table.

B. Values must be part of a fixed set defined by `create` or `alter table`.

C. Values must include reserved words, such as SYSDATE and USER.

D. The column cannot contain a NULL value.

Fill-in-the-Blank Answers

1. Check

2. ROWID

3. Global temporary table

4. `novalidate`

5. Index

Answers to Chapter Questions

1. B and D. Unique constraints and primary keys

Explanation   Every constraint that enforces uniqueness creates an index to assist in the process. The two integrity constraints that enforce uniqueness are unique constraints and primary keys. Other types of integrity constraints like check, not NULL, and foreign keys, do not use indexes in any capacity for enforcing data integrity.

2. C. A table named ANIMALS will be created in the ANJU schema with the same data as the ANIMALS table owned by MASTER.

Explanation   This question requires you to look carefully at the `create table` statement in the question and to know some things about table creation. First, a table is always created in the schema of the user who created it. Second, because the `create table as select` clause was used, choices B and D are both incorrect because they identify the table being created as something other than ANIMALS, among other things. Choice A identifies the schema into which the ANIMALS table will be created as MASTER, which is incorrect for the reasons just stated. Refer to the discussion of creating tables for more information.

3. A. The two tables in the database are named VOUCHER and VOUCHER_ITEM, respectively.

Explanation   This choice implies the use of a naming convention similar to the one we discussed in this chapter, where tables with foreign key relationships have similar names. Although there is no guarantee that these two tables are related, the possibility is strongest in this case. Choice B implies the same naming convention, but because the two tables' names are dissimilar, there is little likelihood that the two tables are related in any way. Choice C is incorrect because the date a table is created has absolutely no bearing on what function the table serves in the database.

Choice D is incorrect because two tables *cannot* be related if there are no common columns between them. Refer to the discussion of creating tables using integrity constraints, naming conventions, and data modeling.

4.   A, B, and D. CHAR, VARCHAR2, and NUMBER

Explanation   BOOLEAN is the only invalid datatype in this listing. Although BOOLEAN is a valid datatype in PL/SQL, it is not a datatype available on the Oracle database, meaning that you cannot create a column in a table that uses the BOOLEAN datatype. Review the discussion of allowed datatypes in column definitions.

5.   C. `GOOD_NAME varchar2(20) check(GOOD_NAME in (select NAME from AVAIL_GOODS)),`

Explanation   A check constraint cannot contain a reference to another table, nor can it reference a virtual column, such as ROWID or SYSDATE. The other lines of the `create table` statement contain the correct syntax.

6.   A. Use the `alter table` statement.

Explanation   The `alter table` statement is the only choice offered that allows you to increase the number of columns per table. Choice B is incorrect because setting a column to all NULL values for all rows does simply that. Choice C is incorrect because increasing the adjacent column sizes simply increases the sizes of the columns, and choice D is incorrect because the listed steps outline how to add a column with a not NULL constraint—something not specified by the question.

7.   B. Truncate the table.

Explanation   Choices A and C may work, but an upgrade of hardware and software will cost far more than truncating the table. Choice D is partly correct, because there will be some change required to the high-water mark. However, the change will reset the high-water mark, not eliminate it entirely, and the method used is to issue the `truncate table` command.

8.   A. Unique

Explanation   Only unique and primary-key constraints require Oracle to generate an index that supports or enforces the uniqueness of the column values. Foreign keys, CHECK constraints, and not NULL constraints do not require indexes. Therefore, choices B, C, and D are incorrect.

9. B. All values in the referenced column in the parent table must be present in the referencing column in the child.

Explanation   Referential integrity is from child to parent, not vice versa. The parent table can have many values that are not present in child records, but the child record must correspond to something in the parent. Therefore, the correct answer is in this case is choice B.

10. B. Values must be part of a fixed set defined by `create table` or `alter table`.

Explanation   A check constraint may only use fixed expressions defined when you create or alter the table with the constraint definition. Reserved words such as SYSDATE and USER and values from a lookup table are not permitted, thus making choices A and C incorrect. Finally, NULL values in a column are constrained by not NULL constraints, a relatively unsophisticated form of check constraints. Therefore, choice D is incorrect.

CHAPTER

6

Manipulating
Oracle Data

his chapter covers the following topics related to manipulating Oracle data:

- Adding new rows to a table
- Making changes to existing row data
- Deleting data from the Oracle database
- Merging data in an Oracle table
- The importance of transaction control

I've shown some data-manipulation operations from time to time in the previous several chapters. Every time I've done so, I've promised to explain what these statements meant later. Well, now is my chance. This section will introduce you to all forms of data-change manipulation. The three types of data-change manipulation in the Oracle database are updating, deleting, and inserting data. These statements are collectively known as the *data-manipulation language* of Oracle, or DML for short. A collection of DML statements that form a logical unit of work is called a transaction. We'll also look at *transaction processing*, which is a mechanism that the Oracle database provides in order to facilitate the act of changing data. Without transaction-processing mechanisms, Oracle cannot guarantee that users won't overwrite one another's changes in midprocess or select data that is in the process of being changed by another user.

Adding New Rows to a Table

The first data-change manipulation operation that will be discussed is the act of inserting new rows into a table. Once a table is created, no data is in the table, unless the table is created and populated by rows selected from another table. Even in this case, the data must come from somewhere. This "somewhere" is from users who enter data into the table via `insert` statements. An `insert` statement has a different syntax from a `select` statement. The general syntax for an `insert` statement is `insert into tablename (column_list) values (values_list)`, where *tablename* is the name of the table you want to insert data into, *column_list* is the list of columns for which you will define values on the record being added, and *values_list* is the list of those values you will define. The datatype of the data you add as values in the values list must correspond to the datatype for the column identified in that same position in the column list. We can see the columns in the EMPLOYEE table we defined in Chapter 5 listed in the following code block:

```
SQL> desc employee
 Name                                  Null?    Type
```

```
-----------------------------   -------- -------------
EMPID                           NOT NULL VARCHAR2(5)
LASTNAME                        NOT NULL VARCHAR2(25)
FIRSTNAME                                VARCHAR2(25)
SALARY                                   NUMBER(10,4)
HIRE_DATE                                DATE
DEPT                                     VARCHAR2(10)
```

TIP

We're dealing with our own EMPLOYEE table that we created in Chapter 5 in this example, so as not to disturb the contents of the EMP table shipped with every Oracle database.

The following code block shows three examples of how to use the `insert` command to add new values to this table:

```
SQL> insert into employee (empid, lastname, firstname,
  2    salary, dept, hire_date)
  3   values ('39334','SMITH','GINA',75000, null, '15-MAR-97');
1 row created.
SQL> insert into employee (empid, lastname, firstname, salary,
  2   dept, hire_date)
  3   values ('49539','LEE','QIAN',90000, '504A', '25-MAY-99');
1 row created.
SQL> insert into employee (empid, lastname, firstname, salary,
  2   dept, hire_date)
  3   values ('60403','HARPER','ROD',45000, '504A', '30-APR-79');
1 row created.
```

TIP

If you want to follow along on your Oracle database, remember that we've created several different versions of EMPLOYEE in the earlier discussion about constraints. Therefore, you need to ensure that your version of the EMPLOYEE table contains all the columns listed in the preceding `describe` statement, using the appropriate `alter table` statements, before inserting data into your table.

The preceding `insert` statements each have two parts. In the first part, the table to receive the inserted row is defined, along with the columns of the table that will have the column values inserted into them. The second portion of the statement defines the actual data values for the row to be added. This latter portion of the statement is denoted by the `values` keyword. Notice how each value in the values list matches up positionally to a column defined in the column list. If you look back at the description information for the table, you'll also notice that the datatype for each value matches the datatype Oracle expects for that column. Also, make sure you enclose character and date values in single quotation marks.

A Variation on a Theme

Oracle is capable of handling several variations on the `insert` statement. For example, you may not necessarily need to define explicit columns of the table. You only need to do that when you don't plan to populate every column in the record you are inserting with a value. Let's look at an example where we don't identify explicit columns because we intend to define values for every column listed in the EMPLOYEE table:

```
SQL> insert into employee values
  2  ('02039','WALLA','RAJENDRA',60000,'01-JAN-96','604B');
1 row created.
SQL> insert into employee values
  2  ('49392','SPANKY','STACY',100000,null,'604B');
1 row created.
SQL> insert into employee values
  2  ('49394','SMITH','BOB',50000,sysdate,'604B');
1 row created.
```

TIP
Notice how we used the NULL to insert a NULL value for HIRE_DATE in the row entry for user SPANKY. We had to do this because Oracle expects us to define explicitly a value for every column in the table.

Position, Position, Position

How does Oracle know which column to populate with what data? The answer is position. Position can matter in tables on the Oracle database; the position of the data in the `insert` statement must correspond to the position of the columns in the table. The user can determine the position of each column in a table by using the `describe` command or the output from the USER_TAB_COLUMNS dictionary view using COLUMN_ID to indicate position as part of the `order by` clause. The order in which the columns are listed in the output from the describe command is the same order in which values should be placed to insert data into the table without explicitly naming the columns of the table. Take a look for yourself:

```
SQL> select column_name, column_id
  2  from user_tab_columns
  3  where table_name = 'EMPLOYEE'
  4  order by column_id;
COLUMN_NAME              COLUMN_ID
-----------------        -----------
EMPID                        1
LASTNAME                     2
FIRSTNAME                    3
SALARY                       4
HIRE_DATE                    5
DEPT                         6
SQL> describe employee
Name                            Null?      Type
-----------------------------   --------   ------------
EMPID                           NOT NULL   VARCHAR2(5)
LASTNAME                        NOT NULL   VARCHAR2(25)
FIRSTNAME                                  VARCHAR2(25)
SALARY                                     NUMBER(10,4)
HIRE_DATE                                  DATE
DEPT                                       VARCHAR2(10)
```

I cannot stress enough the fact that inserting data of the correct datatype into the correct column by matching the position of the value in the value listing to the position of the column in the column listing is not as easy as it sounds. If the datatype of data you add to a column does not match the datatype defined for the table, Oracle returns an error. Let's look at an example where we try to add text information to a NUMBER column:

```
SQL> insert into emp (empno, ename, sal)
  2  values ('SMITHERS',7444,900);
values ('SMITHERS',7444,900)
        *
ERROR at line 2:
ORA-01722: invalid number
```

Luckily, Oracle notified us of the mismatched datatypes so that we could then make the correction. You won't always be so luckily, especially if the datatype of the value added matches the datatype Oracle expects for the column, but the data is otherwise incorrect for the column. Let's look at another example where we accidentally add a new record to EMP with the job information incorrectly placed in the ENAME column:

```
SQL> insert into emp (empno, ename, job, sal)
  2  values (7444,'LACKEY','SMITHERS',900);
1 row created.
```

We know that LACKEY isn't this employee's name, nor is his or her job accurately described as SMITHERS. However, Oracle didn't produce an error, so if you're not careful, you could wind up adding a lot of junk data to your tables. So, the moral of the story is this: be careful to insert new records to a table so as to avoid errors, but be even more careful to avoid problems where you add data that doesn't cause an error but is contextually incorrect.

Another Variation

Another variation on the `insert` theme is the option to populate a table using data obtained from other tables using a `select` statement. This method of populating table data is similar to the method used by the `create table as select` statement. In this case, the `values` clause can be omitted entirely. However, the rules regarding column position of the inserted data still apply in this situation, meaning that if you can select data for all columns of the table having data inserted into it, you need not name the columns in the `insert into` clause. The following is an example:

```
SQL> insert into scott.employee (select * from master.employee);
```

TIP
In order to put data into a table, a special privilege must be granted from the table owner to the user who needs to perform the `insert` operation. A more complete discussion of object privileges appears in Chapter 8.

Can I Insert Into More Than One Table at a Time?

Sometimes, newcomers to Oracle think that because you can insert more than one row of data at a time into a single table with the `insert` command, you should also be able to insert data into more than one table at a time with a single issuance of the `insert` command. However, this would be too confusing both for Oracle and for us. You would need to tell Oracle explicitly what data to put in which table.

If you have to specify which data goes into what table, you'd be better off issuing two separate `insert` statements anyway. Thus, you can use the `insert` command to add data to only one table at a time. You can insert into one table using data from another table, however, and we've already seen how to accomplish this task.

Inserting Data and Integrity Constraints

No data can be inserted into a table when a column value for that new record being added violates an integrity constraint on the table. For example, if you used the `utlsampl.sql` script to build the EMP table we used in previous discussions, Oracle built a primary key constraint on the EMPNO column, designed to enfoce uniqueness on that column. The following code block shows how Oracle would react if you tried to insert a new row into EMP for an employee named SMITHERS using the EMPNO value defined for SMITH:

```
SQL> insert into emp (empno, ename, job)
  2  values (7369,'SMITHERS','LACKEY');
insert into emp (empno, ename, job)
*
ERROR at line 1:
ORA-00001: unique constraint (SCOTT.PK_EMP) violated
```

When you attempt to add new data to a table that violates an integrity constraint on that table, Oracle returns an error as we see in the previous example. However, you should also know that Oracle does not add the record to the table. See for yourself in the following code block that SMITHERS was not added to the table or overwrite SMITH's record in any way:

```
SQL> select empno, ename, job
  2  from emp
  3  where empno = 7369;
    EMPNO ENAME      JOB
---------- ---------- ---------
     7369 SMITH      CLERK
```

TIP
For inserting records into tables with foreign key constraints, you must first insert the new row into the parent table, and then insert new rows into the child(ren) table(s).

Specifying Explicit Default Values

Oracle **9i** and higher — Recall from Chapter 5 that we can define our table columns to carry default values. If no value is specified for a particular column by an `insert` statement adding new rows to the table, Oracle can populate that column anyway using the default value. To refresh your memory, consider the following code block where we define a table with a default column value, populate that table without specifying a value for the column, and then look at the result:

```
SQL> create table sample
  2   (col1 number,
  3    col2 varchar2(30) default 'YOU FORGOT ME');
Table created.
SQL> insert into sample (col1) values (1);
1 row created.
SQL> select * from sample;
      COL1 COL2
--------- ------------------------------
         1 YOU FORGOT ME
```

We can see in the previous code block that Oracle populated the column we forgot to specify data for anyway. We can invoke this feature explicitly as well by using the `default` keyword in our `insert` statement. Check out the following code block to understand how:

```
SQL> insert into sample (col1, col2) values (2, default);
1 row created.
SQL> select * from sample;
      COL1 COL2
--------- ------------------------------
         1 YOU FORGOT ME
         2 YOU FORGOT ME
```

For Review

Know the statement used to place new data into an Oracle table. Know how to code several derivatives of this statement as well.

Exercises

1. You are adding data to the PRODUCTS table in an Oracle database. This table contains three columns: PRODUCT_NAME, PRODUCT_TYPE, and PRICE. Which of the following choices does not identify a well-formed `insert` statement on this table?

    A. `insert into products (product_name, product_type, price) ('BARNEY DOLL','TOYS',49.99);`

B. insert into products (product_name, product_type, price) values ('BARNEY DOLL','TOYS',49.99);

C. insert into products values ('BARNEY DOLL','TOYS',49.99);

D. insert into products (select product_name, product_type, price from master_products);

2. **Examine the following statement:**

   insert into SALES values ('BARNEY DOLL','31-MAR-93',29483854.39);

   Which of the following choices identifies a statement you cannot use to verify whether the correct information is placed into the correct columns?

   A. select * from sales;

   B. select column_name, column_id from all_tab_columns where table_name = 'SALES';

   C. describe sales

   D. select column_name, column_position from all_ind_columns where table_name = 'SALES';

3. **The absence of a values clause in an insert statement indicates that the insert statement contains a** _____.

4. **This keyword enables us to tell Oracle explicitly to populate a column with its default value:** _____.

Answer Key
1. A. **2.** D. **3.** subquery. **4.** default

Making Changes to Existing Row Data

Data manipulation on Oracle tables does not end after you add new records to your tables. Often, the rows in a table will need to be changed. In order to make those changes, the update statement can be used. Updates can be made to any row in a database except in two cases. One case is where you don't have enough access privileges to update the data. You will learn more about access privileges in Chapter 8. The other case is where some other user on the database is making changes to the row you want to change. You will learn more about transaction control at the end of this section in the discussion titled "The Importance of Transaction Control."

Otherwise, you can change data by issuing an `update` statement, as shown in the following example:

```
SQL> update employee set salary = 99000
  2  where lastname = 'SPANKY';
1 row updated.
```

The typical `update` statement has three clauses:

■ An `update` clause, where the table that will be updated is named.

■ A `set` clause, where all columns whose values will be changed are named and the new values assigned.

■ The `where` clause (optional), which lists one or more comparison operations to determine which rows Oracle will update. Omitting the `where` clause in an `update` statement has the effect of applying the data change to every row that presently exists in the table. Specific rows are modified whenever you specify the `where` clause.

Advanced Data Changes in Oracle

You can modify the values in more than one column using a single `update` statement, and you can also use subqueries in `update` statements. The following code block illustrates examples of both these statements:

```
SQL> update employee
  2  set firstname = 'ATHENA', lastname = 'BAMBINA'
  3  where empid = '49392';
1 row updated.
SQL> update employee
  2   set lastname = (select ename from emp where empno = 7844)
  3  where empid = '49392';
1 row updated.
```

Can I Update Data in More Than One Table at a Time?

Like the `insert` command, the `update` command permits you to make changes to records in only one table at a time, for largely the same reasons. You would have to indicate which columns to change in what tables, and this additional layer of granularity would make the `update` statement too burdensome and complex.

Data Changes and Integrity Constraints

Your data changes cannot violate the integrity constraints defined for the table. For example, you can't change the value set for EMPNO in the EMP table if it would cause a duplicate value to exist in that column. If you try to issue this kind of change, Oracle will return an error and will not make the change. However, be sensitive to issues related to context that we saw in the previous discussion on the `insert` statement. Also, if you try to update a record in a parent table where a corresponding record exists in the child table, Oracle will return an error if your change would create orphan records in the child table and disallow your change. You should first modify the records in the child table, and then modify the records in the parent.

Using the `default` Keyword

You can use the `default` keyword to set a column value to its specified default value in `update` statements as well. To do so, you simply set the column whose default value you want to use using the `default` keyword. For the next example, we'll use the SAMPLE table I defined in the earlier discussion about the use of the `default` keyword in `insert` commands. Observe the following code block:

```
SQL> insert into sample (col1, col2) values (3,'NO I DID NOT');
1 row created.
SQL> select * from sample;
     COL1 COL2
--------- ------------------------------
        1 YOU FORGOT ME
        2 YOU FORGOT ME
        3 NO I DID NOT
SQL> update sample set col2 = default where col1 = 3;
1 row updated.
SQL> select * from sample;
     COL1 COL2
--------- ------------------------------
        1 YOU FORGOT ME
        2 YOU FORGOT ME
        3 YOU FORGOT ME
```

For Review

Know how to use `update` statements to change data in an Oracle table. Understand the two mandatory clauses, `update` and `set`, and the optional clause, `where`. Also, understand the use of the `default` keyword in `update` statements to populate columns with their default values explicitly.

Exercises

1. You are updating data in an Oracle table. Which of the following
    statements best describes how you may use the `where` clause in an
    `update` statement?

    A. You may use whatever expressions are appropriate, except for single-
    row functions.

    B. You may use whatever expressions are appropriate, except for
    subqueries.

    C. You may use whatever expressions are appropriate, except for `in`
    expressions.

    D. You may use whatever expressions are appropriate with no limitations.

2. You are updating data in an Oracle table. Which of the following choices
    identifies the keyword that indicates the columns you would like to update
    the values of?

    A. `update`

    B. `set`

    C. `where`

    D. `order by`

Answer Key
1. D. 2. B.

Deleting Data from the Oracle Database

The removal of data from a database is as much a fact of life as putting the data
there in the first place. The `delete` statement in SQL*Plus is used to remove
database rows from tables. The syntax for the `delete` statement is detailed in the
following code block. Note that in this example, you cannot delete data from
selected columns in a row in the table; this act is accomplished with the `update`
statement, with the columns that are to be deleted being set to NULL by the
`update` statement:

```
SQL> delete from employee where lastname = 'TURNER';
1 row deleted.
```

As in the case with database updates, `delete` statements use the `where` clause to help determine which rows are meant to be removed. Like an `update` or `select` statement, the `where` clause in a `delete` statement can contain any type of comparison operation, range operation, subquery, or any other operation acceptable for a `where` clause. Like an `update` statement, if the `where` clause is left off the `delete` statement, the deletion will be applied to all rows in the table.

TIP
Data deletion should be undertaken with care. It can be costly to replace data that has been inappropriately deleted from the database, which is why the privilege of deleting information should only be given out to those users who really should be able to delete records from a table.

Don't Forget the `where` Clause!

I cannot overemphasize the importance of using a `where` clause in your `delete` commands. If you don't use a `where` clause, you'll delete every row from your table. Only specific rows from the table that conform to the criteria noted in your `where` clause are removed when you include a `where` clause in your `delete` command. Let's take a look at an example of a `delete` command where we use the `where` clause to limit removal of data to a few particular records:

```
SQL> delete from emp where deptno = 20;
5 rows deleted.
SQL> select empno, ename, job from emp;
    EMPNO ENAME      JOB
--------- ---------- ---------
     7499 ALLEN      SALESMAN
     7521 WARD       SALESMAN
     7654 MARTIN     SALESMAN
     7698 BLAKE      MANAGER
     7782 CLARK      MANAGER
     7839 KING       PRESIDENT
     7844 TURNER     SALESMAN
     7900 JAMES      CLERK
     7934 MILLER     CLERK
9 rows selected.
```

Now, take a look at what would have happened if we omitted the where clause from the delete command in the previous example:

```
SQL> delete from emp;
14 rows deleted.
SQL> select * from emp;
no rows selected
```

Can I Delete Data from More Than One Table at a Time?

In general, removing data from a database with the delete command can be dangerous because once eliminated, it is tough to get the data back again without requiring some database downtime. Oracle does not let you remove data from more than one table at a time with the delete command for both this reason and for the rationale already presented for limiting the application of an insert or update command to only one table at a time.

Deleting Data and Integrity Constraints

You can remove data from a table without regard for integrity constraints on that table, except for one small detail. You must be careful when deleting records from a parent table with foreign key constraints on it. If your removal of a record from the parent table would produce orphan records in the child table, then Oracle returns an error and prevents you from making the deletion. You should first remove the records in the child table, and then remove the records from the parent table.

For Review

Be sure you understand how to use delete statements to remove data from an Oracle table. Also, understand how to use the mandatory clause, delete from, and the optional clause where.

Exercises

1. This is the clause in a delete statement that identifies which rows to remove: _____

2. You would like to delete data in the PROFITS column of the SALES table for all rows where PRODUCT_TYPE is set to 'TOYS'. Which of the following choices identifies how to accomplish this task?

   A. delete from sales where product_type = 'TOYS';

   B. delete profits from sales where product_type = 'TOYS';

C. `update sales set profits = NULL where product_type = 'TOYS';`

D. `delete from sales;`

Answer Key
1. where **2.** C.

Merging Data in Oracle Tables

 Oracle 9i and higher   Consider the following scenario. Say you manage a movie theater that is part of a national chain. Everyday, the corporate headquarters sends out a data feed that you put into your digital billboard over the ticket sales office, listing out all the movies being played at that theater, along with showtimes. The showtime information changes daily for existing movies in the feed. Let's create the example using the following code block:

```
SQL> create table movies
  2  (movie_name varchar2(30),
  3   showtime varchar2(30),
  4   constraint pk_movies primary key (movie_name));
Table created.
SQL> insert into movies ('GONE WITH THE WIND','6:00 PM');
1 row created.
SQL> select * from movies;
MOVIE_NAME          SHOWTIME
------------------  ------------------------
GONE WITH THE WIND  6:00 PM
```

Every week, new movies are added to the lineup and existing movies have their showtimes changed. Past versions of Oracle SQL were not able to handle this situation. For example, if we tried first to `insert` a new record for movies being added and then tried to `update` existing records with new movie times in our MOVIES table, Oracle would give us an error on either the `insert` (for existing movies) or the `update` (for new movies). Take a look at the following example, where we try to add a new record for the movie *Gone With The Wind*, even though that record already exists in our table:

```
SQL> insert into movies ('GONE WITH THE WIND','7:30 PM');
insert into movies ('GONE WITH THE WIND','7:30 PM');
*
```

```
ERROR at line 1:
ORA-00001: unique constraint (SCOTT.PK_EMP) violated
```

If we wanted to avoid errors, we would have to program a PL/SQL routine. This routine would need to use an `if-then` statement to test for the presence of a row when the showtime for an existing movie needed to be changed, or else add a new row if that movie isn't currently being shown.

The `merge` Command: Concept

In Oracle9i, however, we can use the `merge` command to handle the work for us. The merge command syntax is `merge into table1 using table2 on (join_condition) when matched update set col1 = value when not matched insert (column_list) values (column_values)`. The statement components work in the following way:

1. In the `merge into table1` clause, you identify a table into which you would like to update data in an existing row or add new data if the row doesn't already exist as `table1`.

2. In the `using table2` clause, you identify a second table from which rows will be drawn in order to determine if the data already exists as `table2`. This can be a different table or the same table as `table1`. However, if `table2` is the same table as `table1`, or if the two tables have similar columns, then you must use table aliases to preface all column references with the correct copy of the table. Otherwise, Oracle will return an error stating that your column references are ambiguously defined.

3. In the `on (join_condition)` clause, you define the join condition to link the two tables together. This join condition follows the same requirements as table joins in Chapter 3, meaning that you should include both an equality comparison to avoid any Cartesian products and any filter conditions required to eliminate unneeded data. If `table2` in the `using` clause is the same table as `table1` in the `merge into` clause, or if the two tables have similar columns, then you must use table aliases or the `table.column` syntax when referencing columns in the join or filter conditions. Otherwise, Oracle will return an error stating that your column references are ambiguously defined.

4. In the `when matched then update set col1 = value` clause, you define the column(s) Oracle should `update` in the first table if a match in the second table is found. If `table2` in the `using` clause is the same table as `table1` in the `merge into` clause, or if the two tables have similar columns, then you must use table aliases or the `table.column` syntax

when referencing columns in the update operation. Otherwise, Oracle will return an error stating that your column references are ambiguously defined.

5. In the when not matched then insert(*column_list*) values (*value_list*) clause, you define what Oracle should insert into the first table if a match in the second table is not found. If *table2* in the using clause is the same table as *table1* in the merge into clause, or if the two tables have similar columns, then you must use table aliases or the table.column syntax to preface all column references in *column_list*. Otherwise, Oracle will return an error stating that your column references are ambiguously defined.

TIP

Implicit in the use of the merge command is the concept that you are merging the contents of one table into another based on whether values exist in the second table, extending the table join principles you learned about in Chapter 3. For this discussion, we'll work with only one table using the self-join concept you learned in that chapter as well.

The merge Command: Implementation

At first glance, this command can seem to be a tricky solution to a seemingly easy problem. Let's take a look at an example of how we would implement the addition of data to an existing row in our MOVIES table using the merge statement shown in the following code block:

```
SQL> merge into movies M1
  2    using movies M2 on (M2.movie_name = M1.movie_name
  3                        and M1.movie_name = 'GONE WITH THE WIND')
  4    when matched then update set M1.showtime = '7:30 PM'
  5    when not matched then insert (M1.movie_name, M1.showtime)
  6    values ('GONE WITH THE WIND','7:30 PM');
1 row merged.
SQL> select * from movies;
MOVIE_NAME          SHOWTIME
------------------  -------------------------
GONE WITH THE WIND  7:30 PM
```

Let's examine the code block in more detail. The first line instructs Oracle to merge rows in the MOVIES table. The second line tells Oracle how to match the data using a copy of the MOVIES table. Essentially, we're telling Oracle to use the contents of a second copy of the MOVIES table in order to determine whether a record for *Gone With The Wind* already exists in the table. If so, I want Oracle to change the showtime to 7:30 P.M. If not, I want Oracle to add a new record for that movie with the correct showtime. Notice also that I've used table aliases everywhere to eliminate ambiguity. Now, let's look at what happens when we want to merge data into our MOVIES table for a movie not currently present in that table:

```
SQL> merge into movies M1
  2    using movies M2 on (M2.movie_name = M1.movie_name
  3                        and M2.movie_name = 'LAWRENCE OF ARABIA')
  4    when matched then update set M1.showtime = '9:00 PM'
  5    when not matched then insert (M1.movie_name, M1.showtime)
  6    values ('LAWRENCE OF ARABIA','9:00 PM');
1 row merged.
SQL> select * from movies;
MOVIE_NAME          SHOWTIME
------------------- -------------------------
GONE WITH THE WIND  7:30 PM
LAWRENCE OF ARABIA  9:00 PM
```

Everything is the same in this code block as it was in the previous, except that I want Oracle to check for a record for the movie *Lawrence of Arabia* instead. Because no record exists for that movie, Oracle used the `insert` operation I specified in my `when not matched` clause to add a new record to the MOVIES table.

TIP
It would be nice if the `merge` *command enabled the* `using` *clause to be optional so that we could simplify our command for situations where we want to operate only on one table. Perhaps Oracle will include this feature in a future edition of the database. Until then, be sure you are familiar with the multitabular nature of this command.*

Watch Out for Errors in Your Join and Filter Conditions!

As with table joins, the merge command is fraught with peril especially if you don't formulate your join and filter conditions properly in the on clause. Let's consider what happens if I do not specify my join condition to include a filter condition to identify which movie Oracle should look for. Take a look at the following code block:

```
SQL> merge into movies M1
  2   using movies M2 on (M2.movie_name = M1.movie_name )
  3   when matched then update set M1.showtime = '9:30 PM'
  4   when not matched then insert (M1.movie_name, M1.showtime)
  5   values ('THE MUMMY','9:30 PM');
2 row merged.
SQL> select * from movies;
MOVIE_NAME            SHOWTIME
------------------    ------------------------

GONE WITH THE WIND    9:30 PM
LAWRENCE OF ARABIA    9:30 PM
```

In this situation, I correctly defined my join condition to avoid a Cartesian product in my self-join. However, I forgot to include a filter condition telling Oracle to verify whether a record for the movie *The Mummy* exists in my MOVIES table. Thus, Oracle simply went ahead and changed every row in the table according to the value set in my when matched clause. Now, watch what happens if I forget about the join condition and include only a filter condition instead:

```
SQL> merge into movies m1
  2   using movies m2 on (m2.movie_name = 'THE MUMMY')
  3   when matched then update set m1.showtime = '12:00 AM'
  4   when not matched then insert (m1.movie_name, m1.showtime)
  5   values ('THE MUMMY','12:00 AM');
merge into movies m1
*
ERROR at line 1:
ORA-00001: unique constraint (SCOTT.PK_MOVIES) violated
```

At first glance, it might seem strange that Oracle returns a constraint violation. After all, the row we're trying to add for the movie *The Mummy* does not violate the primary key constraint on the MOVIE_NAME column. Actually, the reason you receive this error relates back to the fact that we forgot our join condition between the two copies of the MOVIES table. Behind the scenes, Oracle formed a Cartesian product, which generated duplicate rows for the movie *The Mummy*. The error was produced when Oracle tried to insert a duplicate row for *The Mummy* into the MOVIES table. Take another look at what happens when we disable the primary key on the MOVIES table:

```
SQL> alter table movies disable constraint pk_movies;
Table altered.
SQL> merge into movies m1
  2   using movies m2 on (m2.movie_name = 'THE MUMMY')
  3   when matched then update set m1.showtime = '12:00 AM'
  4   when not matched then insert (m1.movie_name, m1.showtime)
```

```
   5  values ('THE MUMMY','12:00 AM');
2 rows merged.
SQL> select * from movies;
MOVIE_NAME          SHOWTIME
------------------  -------------------------
GONE WITH THE WIND  9:30 PM
LAWRENCE OF ARABIA  9:30 PM
THE MUMMY           12:00 AM
THE MUMMY           12:00 AM
```

For Review

1. Know the business problem the merge command is intended to solve.

2. Understand the complex syntax for the merge command, including the clauses for joining the tables and determining what to do if a match does or does not occur between the records.

3. Be sure you can employ a merge command properly. Know how to correct the errors caused by incorrect join and/or filter conditions on the joining tables.

Exercises

1. **Review the following code block:**

```
SQL> merge into emp e1
  2  using emp e2 on (e2.ename = 'SMITHERS')
  3  when matched then update set e1.sal = e1.sal *1.1
  4  when not matched then insert (e1.empno, e1.ename, e1.sal)
  5  values (7999,'SMITHERS',800);
```

Which of the following choices identify a line in the preceding merge command that will cause Oracle to return an error?

A. merge into emp e1

B. using emp e2 on (e2.ename = 'SMITHERS')

C. when matched then update set e1.sal = e1.sal * 1.1

D. when not matched then insert (e1.empno, e1.ename, e1.sal)

E. values (7999,'SMITHERS',800);

2. **You want to use the merge command in Oracle. Which of the following statements are *not* true concerning merge commands?**

A. A `merge` command can operate effectively on as few as one table.

B. A `merge` command must include reference to at least two distinct tables.

C. A `merge` command must contain properly defined join conditions or else a Cartesian product is formed.

D. A `merge` command must contain filter conditions in order to determine if the row is or is not present in the table.

Answer Key

1. B. 2. B. Remember, you can use two copies of the same table and then conduct a self-join.

The Importance of Transaction Control

We've made a great deal of changes to our Oracle database over the last several chapters. Some might say we've even made quite a mess of our data. *However, not a single one of those changes was actually saved to the database, and none are visible to any other user on your database besides you*. How can that be, you ask? It's because of the magic of Oracle transaction control! One of the great benefits Oracle provides you is the ability to make changes and then decide later whether we want to save or discard them. Oracle enables you to execute a series of data-change statements together as one logical unit of work, called a *transaction*, that's terminated when you decide to save or discard the work. A transaction begins with your first executable SQL statement. Some advantages for offering transaction processing in Oracle include the following:

- Transactions enable you to ensure read-consistency to the point in time a transaction began for all users in the Oracle database.

- Transactions enable you to preview changes before making them permanent in Oracle.

- Transactions enable you to group logically related SQL statements into one logical unit of work.

Underlying Transaction Controls

Transaction processing consists of a set of controls that enable a user issuing an `insert`, `update`, or `delete` statement to declare a beginning to the series of data-change statements he or she will issue. When the user has finished making the changes to the database, the user can save the data to the database by explicitly ending the transaction. Alternatively, if a mistake is made at any point during the transaction, the user can have the database discard the changes made to the database in favor of the way the data existed before the transaction.

Transactions are created with the use of two different elements in the Oracle database. The first element is the set of commands that define the beginning, breakpoint, and end of a transaction. The second element is the special locking mechanisms designed to prevent more than one user at a time from making a change to row information in a database. Locks will be discussed after the transaction control commands are defined. The commands that define transactions are as follows:

- **set transaction** Initiates the beginning of a transaction and sets key features. This command is optional. A transaction will be started automatically when you start SQL*Plus, commit the previous transaction, or roll back the previous transaction.

- **commit** Ends the current transaction by saving database changes and starts a new transaction.

- **rollback** Ends the current transaction by discarding database changes and starts a new transaction.

- **savepoint** Defines breakpoints for the transaction to enable partial rollbacks.

set transaction

This command can be used to define the beginning of a transaction. If any change is made to the database after the set transaction command is issued but before the transaction is ended, all changes made will be considered part of that transaction. The set transaction statement is not required, because a transaction begins under the following circumstances:

- As soon as you log onto Oracle via SQL*Plus and execute the first command

- Immediately after issuing a rollback or commit statement to end a transaction

- When the user exits SQL*Plus

- When the system crashes

- When a data control language command such as alter database is issued

By default, a transaction will provide both read and write access unless you override this default by issuing `set transaction read only`. You can set the transaction isolation level with `set transaction` as well. The `set transaction isolation level serializable` command specifies serializable transaction isolation mode as defined in SQL92. If a serializable transaction contains data manipulation language (DML) that attempts to update any resource that may have been updated in a transaction uncommitted at the start of the serializable transaction, the DML statement fails. The `set transaction isolation level read committed` command is the default Oracle transaction behavior. If the transaction contains DML that requires row locks held by another transaction, the DML statement waits until the row locks are released. The following is an example:

```
SQL> SET TRANSACTION READ ONLY;
Transaction set.
SQL> rollback;
Rollback complete.
SQL> SET TRANSACTION READ WRITE;
Transaction set.
SQL> rollback;
Rollback complete.
SQL> SET TRANSACTION ISOLATION LEVEL SERIALIZABLE;
Transaction set.
SQL> rollback;
Rollback complete.
SQL> SET TRANSACTION ISOLATION LEVEL READ COMMITTED;
Transaction set.
SQL> rollback;
Rollback complete.
```

TIP

A `set transaction` command can appear only as the first statement in the beginning of a transaction. Therefore, we must explicitly end each transaction with the `rollback` command before starting another with the `set transaction` command.

commit

The `commit` statement in transaction processing represents the point in time where the user has made all the changes he or she wants to have logically grouped together, and because no mistakes have been made, the user is ready to save the work. The work keyword is an extraneous word in the commit syntax that is designed for readability. Issuing a commit statement also implicitly begins a new transaction on the database because it closes the current transaction and starts a new one. By issuing a commit, data changes are made permanent in the database. The previous state of the data is lost. All users can view the data, and all savepoints are erased. It is important also to understand that an implicit commit occurs on the database when a user exits SQL*Plus or issues a data-definition language (DDL) command such as a create table statement, used to create a database object, or an alter table statement, used to alter a database object. The following is an example:

```
SQL> COMMIT;
Commit complete.
SQL> COMMIT WORK;
Commit complete.
```

rollback

If you have at any point issued a data-change statement you don't want, you can discard the changes made to the database with the use of the rollback statement. The previous state of the data is restored. Locks on the affected rows are released. After the rollback command is issued, a new transaction is started implicitly by the database session. In addition to rollbacks executed when the rollback statement is issued, implicit rollback statements are conducted when a statement fails for any reason or if the user cancels a statement with the CTRL-C cancel command. The following is an example:

```
SQL> ROLLBACK;
Rollback complete.
SQL> ROLLBACK WORK;
Rollback complete.
```

Once you issue a commit in Oracle, you cannot rollback the change. You can see this in the following example:

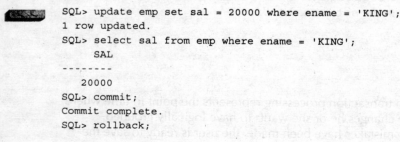

```
SQL> update emp set sal = 20000 where ename = 'KING';
1 row updated.
SQL> select sal from emp where ename = 'KING';
    SAL
---------
   20000
SQL> commit;
Commit complete.
SQL> rollback;
```

```
Rollback complete.
SQL> select sal from emp where ename = 'KING';
     SAL
--------
   20000
```

savepoint

In some cases involving long transactions or transactions that involve many data changes, you may not want to scrap all your changes simply because the last statement issued contains unwanted changes. Savepoints are special operations that enable you to divide the work of a transaction into different segments. You can execute rollbacks to the savepoint only, leaving prior changes intact. Savepoints are great for situations where part of the transaction needs to be recovered in an uncommitted transaction. At the point the `rollback to savepoint so_far_so_good` statement completes in the following code block, only changes made before the savepoint was defined are kept when the `commit` statement is issued:

```
SQL> UPDATE products
  2    SET quantity = 55
  3    WHERE product# = 59495;
1 row updated.
SQL> SAVEPOINT so_far_so_good;
Savepoint created.
SQL> UPDATE spanky.products
  2    SET quantity = 504;
1 row updated.
SQL> ROLLBACK TO SAVEPOINT so_far_so_good;
Rollback complete.
SQL> COMMIT;
Commit complete.
SQL> select quantity from spanky.products
  2    where product# = 59495;
QUANTITY
--------
      55
```

A Word about Read-Consistency

Read-consistency is a feature of crucial importance in Oracle, especially because the database permits multiple users to access the database at the same time. Consider the importance of read-consistency by point of example. Let's say two users are on the Oracle database. User A is reading the contents of the EMP table to making changes elsewhere in the database, while User B is changing the records A is reading within the EMP table. If User A had access to User B's changes before

User B was ready to make them permanent in the database by issuing the `commit` command, User A could wind up making changes elsewhere in the database based on faulty information. Thus, all users must have a read-consistent view of data for the duration of their Oracle transaction. Oracle provides this functionality, and it is crucial for preventing conflicting data changes in the Oracle database.

Locks

The final aspect of the Oracle database that enables the user to employ transaction processing is the lock, the mechanism by which Oracle prevents data from being changed by more than one user at a time. Several different types of locks are available, each with its own level of scope. Locks available on a database are categorized into table-level locks and row-level locks.

A table-level lock enables only the user holding the lock to change any piece of row data in the table, during which time no other users can make changes anywhere on the table. A table lock can be held in any of several modes: row share (RS), row exclusive (RX), share (S), share row exclusive (SRX), and exclusive (X). The restrictiveness of a table lock's mode determines the modes in which other table locks on the same table can be obtained and held.

A row-level lock gives the user the exclusive ability to change data in one or more rows of the table. However, any row in the table that is not held by the row-level lock can be changed by another user.

TIP
An update *statement acquires a special row-level lock called a row-exclusive lock, which means that for the period of time the* update *statement is executing, no other user in the database can view or change the data in the row. The same goes for* delete *or* insert *operations. Another* update *statement—the* select for update *statement— acquires a more lenient lock called the share row lock. This lock means that for the period of time the* update *statement is changing the data in the rows of the table, no other user may change that row, but users may look at the data in the row as it changes.*

For Review

1. Be sure you can identify what a transaction is. Know when a transaction begins and when it ends. Be able to use the `set transaction`, `savepoint`, `commit`, and `rollback` keywords with respect to transaction processing.

2. Know how locks support transactions by preventing other users from seeing the data in your table.

Exercises

1. You are done with your transaction and would like to issue another. Which of the following statements can only appear at the very beginning of the transaction and sets up many characteristics about the transaction?

A. `set transaction`

B. `rollback`

C. `savepoint`

D. `commit`

2. You are engaged in transaction processing on your Oracle database. Which command can you use to define logical breakpoints within the transaction?

A. `set transaction`

B. `rollback`

C. `savepoint`

D. `commit`

3. This is the database component that prevents other users from changing data that you are in the process of changing: _____

Answer Key

1. A. 2. C. 3. Lock.

Chapter Summary

In this chapter, we covered how to manipulate data with `insert`, `update`, and `delete` statements as well as how to engage in Oracle transaction processing. This information comprises just one topic objective for the OCP exam on SQL. However, just because we covered only one topic in this chapter does not mean we didn't review important material. A full 10 percent of the OCP exam deals exclusively with the topic of adding, changing, and removing user data via the `update`, `insert`, and `delete` commands, as well as the use of transaction control.

Two-Minute Drill

- New rows are put into a table with the insert statement. The user issuing the insert statement can insert one row at a time with one statement or can perform a mass insert operation with insert into table_name (select . . . .).

- Existing rows in a database table can be modified using the update statement. The update statement contains a where clause similar in function to the where clause of select statements.

- Existing rows in a table can be deleted using the delete statement. The delete statement also contains a where clause similar in function to the where clause in update and select statements.

- Transaction processing controls the change of data in an Oracle database.

- Transaction controls include commands that identify the beginning, breakpoint, and end of a transaction as well as the locking mechanisms that prevent more than one user at a time from making changes in the database.

Fill-in-the-Blank Questions

1. This transaction-processing command identifies a logical break within the transaction, not an end to the current transaction:

   _____

2. This five-word command specifies that the transaction should execute every DML statement serially and in isolation, as defined in SQL92:

   _____

Chapter Questions

1. **User JANKO would like to insert a row into the EMPLOYEE table. The table has three columns: EMPID, LASTNAME, and SALARY. This user would like to enter data for EMPID 59694, LASTNAME Harris, but no salary. Which statement would work best?**

   A. `insert into EMPLOYEE values (59694,'HARRIS', NULL);`

   B. `insert into EMPLOYEE values (59694,'HARRIS');`

   C. `insert into EMPLOYEE (EMPID, LASTNAME, SALARY) values (59694,'HARRIS');`

   D. `insert into EMPLOYEE (select 59694 from 'HARRIS');`

2. **Omitting the `where` clause from a `delete` statement has which of the following effects?**

   A. The `delete` statement will fail because there are no records to delete.

   B. The `delete` statement will prompt the user to enter criteria for the deletion.

   C. The `delete` statement will fail because of a syntax error.

   D. The `delete` statement will remove all records from the table.

3. **The transaction control that prevents more than one user from updating data in a table is which of the following?**

   A. `lock`

   B. `commit`

   C. `rollback`

   D. `savepoint`

4. Two tables exist, EXPENSES and EXPENSE_ITEMS, for handling employee expense disbursements. Rows for expense #2701 for employee SMITHERS, which had 5 expense items, were added to the EXPENSES and EXPENSE_ITEMS tables a week ago. SMITHERS received reimbursement for #2701 yesterday. The expense disbursements manager now wants to get rid of the data. An excerpt from his SQL*Plus session appears in the following block:

```
SQL> delete from expenses where expense_id = 2701;
```

What happens next?

A. Oracle returns an error and does not remove the record.

B. Oracle returns an error but removes the record from the EXPENSES table anyway.

C. Oracle returns a warning but removes the record anyway.

D. Oracle removes the record from EXPENSES without warning or error.

5. You are adding new records to the PROFITS table. The excerpt from your SQL*Plus session can be found in the following code block:

```
SQL> describe profits
 Name                    Null?     Type
 --------------------- -------- --------------
 PRODUCT_NAME          NOT NULL VARCHAR2(10)
 PRODUCT_ID                     NUMBER(10)
 QTR_END_DATE                   DATE
 SALESPERSON                    VARCHAR2(10)
 PROFIT                         NUMBER
SQL> insert into profits
  2  values ('TURNER',12345,'1-MAR-01','BARNEY TOY',54938);
```

What happens next?

A. Oracle returns a datatype mismatch error and does not add the record.

B. Oracle returns an invalid number error and does not add the record.

C. Oracle returns a warning but adds the record anyway.

D. Oracle adds the record to the table without warnings or errors.

Fill-in-the-Blank Answers

1. savepoint

2. set transaction isolation level serializable

Answers to Chapter Questions

1. A. insert into EMPLOYEE values (59694,'HARRIS', NULL);

Explanation   This choice is acceptable because the positional criteria for not specifying column order is met by the data in the values clause. When you would like to specify that no data be inserted into a particular column, one method of doing so is to insert a NULL. Choice B is incorrect because not all columns in the table have values identified. When you're using positional references to populate column data, values must be present for every column in the table. Otherwise, the columns that will be populated should be named explicitly. Choice C is incorrect because when a column is named for data insert in the insert into clause, a value must definitely be specified in the values clause. Choice D is incorrect because using the multiple-row insert option with a select statement is not appropriate in this situation. Refer to the discussion of insert statements for more information.

2. D. The delete statement will remove all records from the table.

Explanation   One effect is produced by leaving off the where clause from any statement that enables one—the requested operation is performed on all records in the table.

3. A. Lock

Explanation   A *lock* is the mechanism that prevents more than one user at a time from making changes to a database. All other options refer to the commands that are issued to mark the beginning, middle, and end of a transaction. Review the discussion of transaction controls.

4. A. Oracle returns an error and does not remove the record.

Explanation   When you try to remove a record from a table that has a foreign key constraint with child records, Oracle will not let you do so if removal would produce orphan records. Thus, choices B and C are incorrect. Choice D is incorrect because Oracle will return an error indicating that a child record exists.

5. D.

Explanation Even though the data being added will cause the record to have some problems with context, Oracle will not return an error or prevent the record from being added to the table. Thus, choices A, B, and C are incorrect, because the dataypes technically have no errors or the like in this record being added.

CHAPTER
7

Creating Other
Database Objects
in Oracle

In this chapter, you will learn about and demonstrate knowledge in the following areas:

- Creating views
- Other database objects

At this point, you should already know how to select data from tables, design database tables, create relationships between those tables, restrict data from entering the tables, and populate tables with data. These functions represent important cornerstones of functionality that Oracle can provide. However, the design of a database does not stop there. The Oracle architecture has features that can make certain data available to some users but not to others, speed access to data, and generate sequential numbers for primary keys or other purposes. These are advanced database features of Oracle tested in the OCP Exam 1. The material in this chapter comprises 11 percent of the material covered on the exam.

Creating Views

This section covers the following topics concerning views:

- Creating simple views
- Creating views that enforce constraints
- Creating complex views
- Modifying and removing views

It has been said that the eyes are the windows to the soul. Although this may or may not be true, it is true that your eyes can be used to look at data in a table. In order to make sure the right eyes see the right data, however, some special "windows" on the data in a table can be created. These special windows are called *views*. Views are queries stored in Oracle that dynamically assemble data into a virtual table. You can treat this virtual table as though it were a real one, which is exactly what we did on the Oracle data dictionary views of the last chapter. To the person using the view, manipulating the data from the view is just like manipulating the data from a table. In some cases, it is even possible for the user to change data in a view as though the view *were* a table. Let's now explore the topic of creating, using, and managing views in more detail.

TIP
We are deviating somewhat from the Oracle DBA
OCP Candidate Guide with respect to titles for the

topic areas. Although the titles and organization of this content are different from the Candidate Guide, the content covers all the information you need to know for OCP. You covered the information you need to know for inline views and Top-N analysis techniques back in Chapter 4 in the discussion of subqueries in `from` clauses.

Creating Simple Views

Views act like tables by enabling you to query them like tables. However, views are logical representations of data, whereas tables physically store data. Views do not actually store any data. The data in a view comes from a table that the view queries to obtain its own contents. Views can be used to restrict access to data in tables. This is because views use queries to obtain and display selective information. That said, let's start by looking at the simplest example of a `create view` statement—the statement used for creating views in the Oracle database—and perform some simple table-like actions on the view we create. The `create view` statement is shown in bold in the following example:

```
SQL> create view emp_view as
  2  (select * from emp
  3   where job = 'ANALYST');
View created.
SQL> describe emp_view
 Name                          Null?    Type
 ----------------------------- -------- ------------
 EMPNO                         NOT NULL NUMBER(4)
 ENAME                                  VARCHAR2(10)
 JOB                                    VARCHAR2(9)
 MGR                                    NUMBER(4)
 HIREDATE                               DATE
 SAL                                    NUMBER(7,2)
 COMM                                   NUMBER(7,2)
 DEPTNO                                 NUMBER(2)
SQL> select empno, ename from emp_view;
    EMPNO ENAME
--------- ----------
     7788 SCOTT
     7902 FORD
```

TIP
A view will not be created if the base table you specify does not exist. However, you can overcome this restriction by using the `force` *keyword in the* `create view` *command. This keyword forces Oracle to create the view anyway. However, the view will be invalid because no underlying table data is available to draw from.*

Notice the two components of our basic `create view` statement. In the first part, we identify the name of the view we want Oracle to create. In the second part, we define in parentheses the query Oracle should use for obtaining data to populate our virtual table. The underlying table whose information is used as the basis for data in the view is sometimes called the *base table*. You can create views based on the contents of other views as well. Once the view is created, we can do anything with it that we might have done with the underlying table. Everything in our view, EMP_VIEW, looks just like the underlying EMP table, except for one small detail: EMP_VIEW only contains employee data for the analysts! Therefore, *a view can add extra security to data by enabling you to restrict data shown to users looking at the view instead of at the real table.* For example, let's say you have a table containing data across an entire corporation and you want to allow employees in particular departments to access data in the table pertaining only to their department. A view would be useful in this context because you could define the view to contain data only for a specific department, and then have the employees of that department query the view instead of the underlying table.

TIP
Once a view is created, you can list the columns of the view using the `describe` *command, just as you would for a table.*

Appropriately enough, the type of view we just created is known as a *simple view*. Oracle considers this a simple view because it uses data from only one table. Because views contain `select` statements, you should know some things about what sorts of `select` statements are accepted in simple views:

■ Most any `select` statement on a single table you can issue from SQL*Plus can be used for creating a simple view. Basic queries on single tables in Oracle containing single-row operations such as `decode( )`, `nvl( )`, and so on are permitted.

■ Query operations containing `order` by clauses are also permitted, so long as the `order` by clause appears outside the parentheses. The following is an example of what I mean: `create view my_view as (select * from emp) order by empno`.

■ Oracle also permits view queries to contain `group` by clauses, `connect` by clauses, and group functions such as `count ( )`, so long as each function has an alias.

■ Oracle permits views containing the `distinct` keyword, using syntax similar to `create view my_view as (select distinct(job) as my_jobs from emp`.

■ Although references to more than one table are permitted in the queries used in `create view` commands, the view created is not a simple view. It is a complex view (sometimes called a *join view*). We'll talk more about those views in the next discussion.

TIP
Information about views in your database are stored in the data dictionary in a view titled USER_VIEWS. Also, you cannot create a view containing a `for update` clause.

Hierarchical Queries: A Brief Digression

A word of warning: Read this section only if my point about views not accepting queries containing `connect` by clauses has piqued your interest about the type of query known in Oracle as a *hierarchical query*. This topic usually isn't tested on OCP. The hierarchical query can link together the table's rows into a hierarchy. Like most companies, the one whose employees are listed in EMP is a hierarchical one, where every employee reports to another employee all the way up to KING, the president of the company. It is possible to obtain a listing of all employees in that hierarchy using a hierarchical query such as this one:

```
SQL>  select empno, ename, job
  2   from emp
  3   connect by prior empno = mgr;
```

TIP
Like Shakespeare's Polonius, I believe "brevity is the soul of wit." Therefore, I won't show the output of this query because we are digressing from the heart

of our topic—views and the OCP exam. However, if
you find that you like hierarchical queries and want
to play with them on your own time, the Oracle
documentation has some interesting things to say
about them. Good luck!

And Now, Back to Simple Views

Related to the idea that views can help you secure your data against prying eyes, let's explore the use of certain keywords to ensure data security as well. For example, consider our trusty EMP table. It contains data about employee salaries—something that most organizations typically don't like to publish widely. To batten down the hatches on SAL and COMM data in the EMP table from SCOTT's prying eyes (which are disgruntled by being underpaid), consider the following code block:

```
SQL> create or replace view emp_view as
  2  ( select empno, ename, job, mgr, hiredate,
  3           decode(ename, user, sal, 'KING', sal, 0) as sal,
  4           decode(ename, user, comm, 'KING', sal, 0) as comm,
  5           deptno from emp);
View created.
SQL> select ename, sal from emp_view
  2  where job = 'ANALYST';
ENAME          SAL
---------- ---------
SCOTT         3000
FORD             0
```

Notice a few things about the bold code in the preceding example. We used the decode ( ) function to determine what to return for SAL and COMM information, which we know is allowed. Also notice that we used the keyword user, which is a function that identifies the name of the user logged into the system, in order to figure out whose salary and commission information we'll show and to whom. Next, notice that we also built in some functionality so that KING can see everyone's salary (he is the president of the company, after all). After that, notice that we had to create an alias for that column so Oracle would know what to call the column in our virtual table. Besides being required to create the view, column aliases, as you'll recall, simplify the otherwise confusing column name Oracle would generate based on our use of the single-row function.

Finally, observe our use of the create or replace view EMP_VIEW syntax in this example. Before, we simply said create view EMP_VIEW, but in this case our view creation would have failed because EMP_VIEW already exists, if we hadn't included the or replace keywords. These keywords are useful when you want to redefine an existing view based on new needs or criteria. Why not simply use the alter view command, you ask? Because the only job alter view can perform is recompiling an invalid view. We'll discuss alter view in more detail later in the section.

Changing Underlying Table Data Through Simple Views

Now, let's try doing something completely different. Say securing the salary data about other employees from the prying eyes of SCOTT wasn't enough to persuade him not to begrudge the company for his lousy pay. Now SCOTT is irritated enough to take matters into his own hands by changing his pay against company rules. Assuming SCOTT doesn't know about the underlying EMP table, let's see if he can change information in that table, anyway, via EMP_VIEW:

```
SQL> update emp_view set sal = 6000
  2  where ename = 'SCOTT';
update emp_view set sal = 6000
                    *
ERROR at line 1:
ORA-01733: virtual column not allowed here
```

Apparently, he can't. Remember, we didn't use simple column references for SAL and COMM in our view. Instead, we referred to them by way of the decode( ) function, which effectively created virtual columns in EMP_VIEW containing salary and commission information that can't be updated. You might think that this security measure is more of a technicality than a way to enhance security, and in truth, you're probably right. Nevertheless, we thwarted SCOTT's attempt to defraud the company. However, let's say that now SCOTT is fighting mad and is willing to do anything to get even with the company, even if it means calling the president a fool in front of everyone, as shown in the following code block:

```
SQL> update emp_view set ename = 'FOOL! '
  2  where job = 'PRESIDENT';
1 row updated.
SQL> select ename from emp
  2  where job = 'PRESIDENT';
ENAME
----------
FOOL!
```

Sure enough, SCOTT can call the president of the company a fool by modifying the EMP table via an update on EMP_VIEW, although no doubt SCOTT will pay the consequences when KING discovers SCOTT's destructive act.

Changing Data in Underlying Tables
Through Simple Views: Restrictions

Now let's extrapolate a general rule. *You can insert, update, or delete information on an underlying table via simple views*, subject to the following restrictions:

- In general, all constraint restrictions defined on the underlying table also apply to modifying data via the view. For example, you can't add data to an underlying table via a view that violates the table's primary key constraint.

- If the underlying table has not NULL constraints on columns not appearing in your view, you will likely have trouble when you try to insert data into a view. This problem can be solved by using default values for the not NULL column(s) in the table definition.

- Generally speaking, you can delete records from underlying tables using the view, even when the view doesn't contain all the columns or all the rows the underlying table contains.

- You cannot update data in a column of an underlying table via a simple view if the column was defined using a single-row function or function-based keywords such as `user` or `sysdate`. You *can* update a column of an underlying table if the simple view did *not* use a single-row function to define the column.

- You may not insert, update, or delete data on the table underlying the simple view if the `select` statement creating the view contains a `group by` clause, group function, or `distinct` clause.

- You cannot modify data in a view if the pseudocolumn ROWNUM keyword is used or if the columns are defined by expressions.

TIP

If you yearn for some adventure as you follow along in your own database, try creating simple views that don't violate these restrictions but otherwise do odd things. Then see if you can add, change, or remove rows from the underlying table. The following is an example. Try to insert a row into the EMP table via a view created as follows: `create view my_view as (select rowid as row_id, empno from emp)`. *If you find any restrictions in your adventures that I may have missed in the bulleted list, send an e-mail to jcouchman@mindspring.com and I'll acknowledge you by name in my next book.*

For Review

1. Understand what a view is and what it is not. A view is a select statement that generates the contents of a virtual table dynamically. Although views behave like tables, they do not actually contain table data.

2. Know the basic syntax for creating a view in Oracle. Understand the kinds of queries you can use to create a view. Basically, just about anything goes.

3. Be able to identify situations where it is possible to add data to a table via a view and when it is not possible to add data to a table via a view.

Exercises

1. SCOTT creates a view on the EMP table using the following code block:

```
SQL> create or replace view emp_view as
  2  ( select empno, ename, job, mgr, hiredate,
  3           decode(ename, user, sal, 'KING', sal, 0) as sal,
  4           decode(ename, user, comm, 'KING', sal, 0) as comm,
  5           deptno from emp);
View created.
```

Which of the following DML statements will successfully make a change to data in the EMP table?

A. insert into emp_view values (2345, 'SMITHERS','MANAGER', 7839, 4500, 0, 10);

B. update emp_view set job = 'CLERK', comm = 0 where ename = 'TURNER';

C. delete from emp_view where ename = 'SMITH';

D. update emp_view set comm = comm*1.3 where ename = 'TURNER';

2. Use the view shown in the preceding code block to answer this question. User SCOTT logs into Oracle and issues the following query:

```
SQL> select ename, sal from emp_view
  2  where job = 'ANALYST';
ENAME            SAL
---------- ---------
SCOTT           3000
FORD               0
```

Later, TURNER logs into Oracle and issues the same query. What will be the result listed for SCOTT in TURNER's output?

    A. 0

    B. 1500

    C. 3000

    D. 6000

3. **User SCOTT creates a view using the statement in the following code block:**

```
SQL> create or replace view my_view as
  2  (select user as orcl_user, rowid as row_id, empno
  3   from emp
  4   where ename = user)
  5   order by empno;
View created.
```

    Then SCOTT issues the following DML statement: `insert into my_view values ('JASON','weraqwetrqwer',3421);`. Which of the following choices correctly identifies how Oracle will respond and why?

    A. Oracle will return an error because you cannot perform DML on views created with an `order` by clause.

    B. Oracle will return an error because no data can be added on a column defined using `user`.

    C. Oracle will return an error because no data can be added on a column defined using the ROWID pseudocolumn.

    D. Oracle will insert the new row into the underlying table because the statement contains no errors.

4. **Use the code defined for creating MY_VIEW in the previous question to answer this question. You issue the following statement in Oracle: `delete from my_view where orcl_user = 'SCOTT';`. How many rows are removed from the EMP table?**

    A. 0

    B. 1

    C. 2

    D. 14

Answer Key
1. C. 2. A. 3. B. 4. B.

Creating Views That Enforce Constraints

Tables that underlie views often have constraints that limit the data that can be added to those tables. As I said earlier, views cannot add data to the underlying table that would violate the table's constraints. However, you can also define a view to restrict the user's ability to change underlying table data even further, effectively placing a special constraint for data manipulation through the view. This additional constraint says that `insert` or `update` statements issued against the view are cannot create rows that the view cannot subsequently select. In other words, if after the change is made, the view will not be able to select the row you changed, the view will not let you make the change. This viewability constraint is configured when the view is defined by adding the `with check option` to the `create view` statement. Let's look at an example to clarify my point:

```
SQL> create or replace view emp_view as
  2  (select empno, ename, job, deptno
  3   from emp
  4   where deptno = 10)
  5  with check option constraint emp_view_constraint;
View created.
SQL> update emp_view set deptno = 20
  2  where ename = 'KING';
update emp_view set deptno = 20
       *
ERROR at line 1:
ORA-01402: view WITH CHECK OPTION where-clause violation
```

TIP
On some systems, you may not get the ORA-01402 error in this context. Instead, Oracle may simply state that zero rows were updated by your change.

Notice, first, the code in bold in the preceding block where the viewability constraint is defined. We've effectively said that no user can make a change to the EMP table via this view that would prevent the view from selecting a row. After that, we test this constraint by attempting to update the DEPTNO column for KING from

10 to 20, thus causing the view not to be able to pick up that row later. Oracle prevents this data change with an ORA-01402 error, as you can see. Finally, take a look again at the `constraint` clause in the line in bold. This optional clause lets us define a name for our view constraint. If we omitted the clause, Oracle would generate its own name for the constraint. By naming it ourselves, we can easily identify the constraint later in dictionary views containing data about constraints, such as USER_CONSTRAINTS. Output for USER_CONSTRAINTS listing our viewability constraint is shown in the following example:

```
SQL> select constraint_name, constraint_type
  2  from user_constraints;
CONSTRAINT_NAME                 C
------------------------------  -
SYS_C00905                      P
SYS_C00903                      C
PK_EMPLOYEE_01                  P
SYS_C00921                      C
CK_EMPLOYEE_01                  C
EMP_VIEW_CONSTRAINT             V
PK_01                           P
PK_PRICES_01                    P
```

TIP
*The CONSTRAINT_TYPE column in
USER_CONSTRAINTS and ALL_CONSTRAINTS
will list the first character of the first word that best
describes each type of constraint in Oracle: primary
key, foreign key, check, not NULL, unique key, or
viewability.*

Creating Simple Views That Can't Change Underlying Table Data

In some cases, you may find that you want to create views that don't let your users change data in the underlying table. In this case, you can use the `with read only` clause. This clause will prevent any user of the view from making changes to the base table. Let's say that after reprimanding SCOTT severely for calling him a fool, KING wants to prevent all employees from ever changing data in EMP via the EMP_VIEW again. The following shows how he would do it:

```
SQL> create or replace view emp_view
  2  as (select * from emp)
  3  with read only;
```

The next time SCOTT tries to call KING a fool, the following happens:

```
SQL> update emp_view set ename = 'FOOL!'
  2  where ename = 'KING';
where ename = 'KING'
       *
ERROR at line 2:
ORA-01733: virtual column not allowed here
```

For Review

1. Be sure you can explain how viewability constraints placed on views work and how to use the `with check option` and `constraint` clause in `create view` statements in order to create this type of constraint.

2. Understand how to use the `with read only` clause in order to prevent users from making changes to underlying base tables via a view on those tables.

Exercises

1. Use the code in the following block to answer this question:

```
SQL> create or replace view emp_view as
  2  (select empno, ename, job, deptno
  3   from emp
  4   where job = 'MANAGER')
  5   with check option;
View created.
SQL> select * from emp_view;
    EMPNO ENAME      JOB        DEPTNO
--------- ---------- --------- ---------
     7566 JONES      MANAGER       20
     7698 BLAKE      MANAGER       30
     7782 CLARK      MANAGER       10
```

Which of the following data changes will *not* be accepted by Oracle on this view?

A. update emp set job = 'ANALYST' where job = 'MANAGER' and empno = 7566;

B. update emp set ename = 'BARNEY' where job = 'MANAGER' and ename = 'JONES';

C. update emp set empno = 7999 where job = 'MANAGER' and deptno = 10;

D. update emp set deptno = 30 where job = 'MANAGER' and empno = 7782;

2. **Use the contents of the following code block to answer this question:**

```
SQL> create or replace view emp_view as
  2  (select empno, ename, job, deptno
  3   from emp
  4   where job = 'MANAGER')
  5   with check option;
View created.
SQL> select constraint_name, constraint_type
  2  from user_constraints;
CONSTRAINT_NAME                    C
------------------------------     -
SYS_C00905                         P
SYS_C00903                         C
SYS_C00921                         C
SYS_C00929                         V
```

Which of the following constraints is the viewability constraint created in support of EMP_VIEW?

A. SYS_C00905

B. SYS_C00903

C. SYS_C00929

D. SYS_C00921

3. **Use the following code block to answer this question:**

```
SQL> create or replace view emp_view as
  2  (select empno, ename, job, deptno
  3   from emp
  4   where job = 'MANAGER')
  5   with read only;
View created.
```

Which of the following data-change statements will Oracle accept to make changes to the underlying table?

A. insert into emp_view values (2134, 'SMITHERS','MANAGER',10);

B. update emp_view set ename = 'JOHNSON' where empno = 7844;

C. delete from emp_view where ename = 'KING';

D. None of the above

Creating Complex Views

I mentioned earlier that you can create views that join data from more than one table. These are called *complex views*. Complex views provide complicated data models where many base tables are drawn together into one virtual table. Let's take a look at your basic complex view where we join the contents of the EMP and DEPT tables together to form one virtual table:

```
SQL> create view emp_dept_view as
  2   (select empno, ename, job, dname, loc
  3    from emp e, dept d
  4    where e.deptno = d.deptno
  5    and job in ('ANALYST','CLERK','MANAGER'));
View created.
```

The contents of this view are listed as follows:

```
SQL> select * from emp_dept_view;
    EMPNO ENAME      JOB       DNAME          LOC
--------- ---------- --------- -------------- -------------
     7782 CLARK      MANAGER   ACCOUNTING     NEW YORK
     7934 MILLER     CLERK     ACCOUNTING     NEW YORK
     7369 SMITH      CLERK     RESEARCH       DALLAS
     7566 JONES      MANAGER   RESEARCH       DALLAS
     7876 ADAMS      CLERK     RESEARCH       DALLAS
     7902 FORD       ANALYST   RESEARCH       DALLAS
     7788 SCOTT      ANALYST   RESEARCH       DALLAS
     7698 BLAKE      MANAGER   SALES          CHICAGO
     7900 JAMES      CLERK     SALES          CHICAGO
```

TIP

The same sort of select *statements permitted for defining simple views are generally accepted on complex views as well. You may want to refer back to the list of* select *statements that are accepted in simple views for a refresher on complex views. You can even define complex views using the outer join (+) operator as well!*

Updating Base Tables of a Complex View

For the most part, complex views will not enable you to change data in any of the base tables if you haven't properly defined foreign key and primary key relationships between the joined tables using appropriate Oracle integrity constraints. Let's take a look at what I mean by this statement. The dictionary view USER_UPDATABLE_COLUMNS can tell you whether the columns in a complex view can be modified. Let's take a look:

```
SQL> create or replace view emp_dept_view as
  2  (select empno, ename, job, loc
  3  from emp e, dept d
  4  where e.deptno = d.deptno);
View created.
SQL> select column_name, updatable
  2  from user_updatable_columns
  3  where table_name = 'EMP_DEPT_VIEW';
COLUMN_NAME                     UPD
------------------------------- ---
EMPNO                           NO
ENAME                           NO
JOB                             NO
LOC                             NO
```

However, after I properly define my foreign key and primary key relationships between the EMP and DEPT tables, I can create a complex view that will enable partial modification of data in the base tables via the view. Let's look at an example of such a view, which is called an *updatable join view* or *modifiable join view*. A *join view* is simply another name for a complex view, which makes sense, considering that complex views contain join operations. Let's look at the code:

```
SQL> alter table emp add constraint pk_emp_01
  2  primary key (empno);
Table altered.
SQL> alter table dept add constraint pk_dept_01
  2  primary key (deptno);
Table altered.
SQL> alter table emp add constraint fk_emp_01
  2  foreign key (deptno) references dept (deptno);
Table altered.
SQL> create or replace view emp_dept_view as
  2  (select empno, ename, job, loc
  3  from emp e, dept d
  4  where e.deptno = d.deptno);
View created.
SQL> select column_name, updatable
```

```
  2  from user_updatable_columns
  3  where table_name = 'EMP_DEPT_VIEW';
COLUMN_NAME                       UPD
------------------------------    ---
EMPNO                             YES
ENAME                             YES
JOB                               YES
LOC                               NO
```

TIP
Views containing outer joins generally won't contain key-preserved tables unless the outer join generates no NULL values. Even in such a case, the updatability is dependent on your data, so for all intents and purposes, you should just assume that outer join views are not updatable.

That's more like it. Now, when we issue an `update` statement on EMP_DEPT_VIEW that modifies the EMPNO, ENAME, or JOB column, Oracle will let us make the change. Yet, notice that we still cannot update one column. To understand why, we have to talk about the concept of a key-preserved table. A key-preserved table is a table in a complex view whose primary key column is present in the view *and whose values are all unique and not NULL in the view*. In a sense, the key-preserved table's primary key can also be thought of as the primary key for the data in the view. In some cases, many tables in the complex view may be key-preserved if the primary key for the view is the primary key in several of the joined tables. Only columns from the key-preserved table can be modified via the complex view. Columns from the non-key-preserved table (the LOC column in DEPT, in this case) cannot be modified via the complex view. In conclusion, you can execute data-change statements on a complex view only when all the following conditions are met:

- The statement must affect only one of the tables in the join.

- For `update` statements, all columns changed must be extracted from a key-preserved table. In addition, if the view is created using the `with check option` clause, join columns and columns taken from tables that are referenced more than once in the view cannot be part of the `update`.

- For `delete` statements, the join may only have one key-preserved table. This table may be present more than once in the join, unless the view has been created using the `with check option` clause.

- For `insert` statements, all columns in which values are inserted must come from a key-preserved table, and the view must not have been created using the `with check option` clause.

- The complex view does not contain group functions, `group by` expressions, set operations, the `distinct` keyword, `start with` or `connect by` clauses, or the ROWNUM pseudocolumn. Pseudocolumns are virtual columns in a table that you cannot add data to or change data on.

TIP
Set operations include the UNION, UNION ALL, INTERSECT, and MINUS keywords, which are used for joining the output of one select statement with the output of another. For example, select empno from emp UNION select sal from emp is a set operation. Set operations are typically not tested on the OCP exam and therefore will not be covered in this book in any great detail.

For Review

1. Be able to define the meaning of a complex or join view. Know how a complex view differs from a simple view. Be sure you can identify the types of `select` statements permitted in defining a complex view.

2. Know the factors that limit your ability to make changes to underlying base tables in a complex view. In particular, understand the importance of constraints in the underlying tables to solidify the relationship between the two tables, and the concept of key-preserved tables.

3. Be sure you can list the items a complex view cannot contain if you want the ability to modify the underlying tables.

Exercises

1. **Your database of sales information consists of four tables: PROFITS lists the profit amount for every product sold by the company, listed by product name, type, sales region, and quarter; PRODUCT_TYPES lists all valid product types that are sold by your company; PRICES lists the name of every product, along with the associated price; and UNIT_SALES lists**

every product sold by the company and units sold of the product by quarter. You create a view on this database using the following block:

```
SQL> create or replace view profits_view as
  2  (select a.product_name, a.product_type, b.product_desc,
  3  c.product_price,
  4  d.unit_sale, a.quarter
  5  from profits a, product_types b, prices c, unit_sales d
  6  where a.product_type = b.product_type
  7  and a.product_name = c.product_name
  8  and a.product_name = d.product_name
  9  and a.quarter = d.quarter);
View created.
```

Assuming all the proper integrity constraints are in place, which of the following tables in this view is not a key-preserved table?

A. PROFITS

B. PRODUCT_TYPES

C. PRICES

D. UNIT_SALES

2. You are developing complex views in Oracle. Which of the following choices identifies an item that may not be included in the query defining the view if you intend to allow users to update key-preserved tables joined in the view?

A. avg( )

B. decode( )

C. nvl( )

D. to_char( )

3. Key-preserved tables share this in common with the output of complex views they underlie: _____

Answer Key
1. B. **2.** A. **3.** Primary key.

Modifying and Removing Views

Notice that on several occasions, we have altered the definition of views that already existed in the database. However, we didn't follow the same precedent with views that we used for other objects, such as tables, when we wanted to modify them. That's because views don't follow the syntax conventions of other database objects. Although an `alter view` statement appears in the Oracle SQL language, it is used for recompiling or revalidating the view *as it exists already*. The following is an example:

```
SQL> alter view emp_dept_view compile;
View altered.
```

When we wanted to alter the underlying data used in the definition of a view, we used the `create or replace view` statement. When a `create or replace view` statement is issued, Oracle will disregard the error that arises when it encounters the view that already exists with that name, and it will overwrite the definition for the old view with the definition for the new one. The following code block illustrates the use of the `create or replace view` statement from the first exercise in the previous discussion:

```
SQL> create or replace view profits_view as
  2  (select a.product_name, a.product_type, b.product_desc,
  3  c.product_price,
  4  d.unit_sale, a.quarter
  5  from profits a, product_types b, prices c, unit_sales d
  6  where a.product_type = b.product_type
  7  and a.product_name = c.product_name
  8  and a.product_name = d.product_name
  9  and a.quarter = d.quarter);
View created.
```

TIP
You'll have to create your own versions of each of these four tables in order to follow along in your Oracle database, using what you know about. When doing so, make sure the datatypes for the shared PRODUCT_NAME, PRODUCT_TYPE, and QUARTER columns match in each of the tables those columns appear in. Also, make sure you define the appropriate primary and foreign key integrity constraints between the tables. No script is available for creating these tables automatically—I

believe it's very important that you get hands-on
practice developing complex views for OCP!

We see from the last line in the block that Oracle created the view with no
errors. If we wanted to verify the status of the view, we could look in the
USER_OBJECTS view, as shown in the following example:

```
SQL> column object_name format a20
SQL> select object_name, status
  2  from user_objects
  3  where object_name = 'PROFITS_VIEW';
OBJECT_NAME          STATUS
-------------------- -------
PROFITS_VIEW         VALID
```

TIP
The USER_VIEWS view does not contain the validity
status of your view. Be sure you memorize that the
status of all your database objects is found in
USER_OBJECTS or ALL_OBJECTS for OCP.

Let's now drop the PRICES table, which is a base table for PROFITS_VIEW, as
you'll recall from the question. Notice what happens to PROFITS_VIEW:

```
SQL> drop table prices;
Table dropped.
SQL> select object_name, status
  2  from user_objects
  3  where object_name = 'PROFITS_VIEW';
OBJECT_NAME          STATUS
-------------------- -------
PROFITS_VIEW         INVALID
```

So you see, Oracle doesn't remove views from the database if a base table is
destroyed. Instead, Oracle simply marks PROFITS_VIEW as invalid to indicate that
the object dependency that PROFITS_VIEW had on PRICES is now fractured. This is
what happens when you try to obtain data from PROFITS_VIEW:

```
SQL> select * from profits_view;
select * from profits_view
              *
ERROR at line 1:
ORA-04063: view "SCOTT.PROFITS_VIEW" has errors
```

The way to solve this problem is to re-create the PRICES table and recompile PROFITS_VIEW, as shown in the following block. When the view recompiles successfully, you will be able to select data from the view again:

```
SQL> create table prices
  2  (product_name varchar2(10) primary key,
  3   product_price number(10,4));
Table created.
SQL> alter view profits_view compile;
View altered.
```

TIP
Alternately, to fix a view that has become invalid due to the redefinition or deletion of a table that underlies it, you can modify the view with the `create or replace view` *statement.*

Removing Views

A time may come when you need to remove a view. The command for executing this function is the `drop view` statement. No cascading scenarios exist that the person dropping a view must be aware of, except in situations where the view being dropped acts as a base table for another view. In this case, the view that's left will be marked invalid. The `drop view` statement removes the view definition from the database. Dropping views has no effect on the tables on which the view was based. The following statement illustrates the use of `drop view` for deleting views from the database:

```
SQL> drop view profits_view;
View dropped.
```

For Review

1. Know how to use the `alter view` statement for recompiling views and the `create or replace view` statement for redefining the view query.

2. Know that object dependency is when a database object depends on another database object for information. Views have object dependencies on their base tables. Know what happens to the status of a view when its base table gets dropped as well as how to repair the problem.

Exercises

1. You have just replaced a base table for a view that was dropped inadvertently. Which two of the following statements cannot be used to update the status of the view in one step? (Choose two.)

   A. `create view`

   B. `create or replace view`

   C. `alter view`

   D. `drop view`

2. What is the term that describes the relationship between a view and its base table (two words)? _____

3. You would like to identify the status of views in your database. Which of the following dictionary views would you use?

   A. USER_VIEWS

   B. USER_TAB_COLUMNS

   C. USER_OBJECTS

   D. USER_TABLES

Answer Key

1. B and C. 2. Object dependency. 3. C.

Other Database Objects

This section covers the following topics related to other database objects in Oracle:

- Overview of other database objects
- Using sequences
- Using indexes
- Using public and private synonyms

So far, you've gotten some exposure to a few of the types of objects available for use in an Oracle database. This section will change that. In this section, you get an overview of many other important objects available in Oracle. You will also get some hands-on exposure to the creation and use of sequences in the Oracle database. After that, you will gain exposure to indexes, Oracle's performance-giving objects in the database. Finally, you will learn about the use of both public and private synonyms on an Oracle database.

Overview of Other Database Objects

Some of the objects that are part of the relational database produced by Oracle and that are used in the functions just mentioned are as follows:

- **Tables, views, and synonyms**   Used to store and access data. Tables are the basic unit of storage in Oracle. Views logically represent subsets of data from one or more tables. Synonyms provide alternate names for database objects.

- **Indexes and the Oracle RDBMS**   Used to speed access to data.

- **Sequences**   Used for generating numbers for various purposes.

- **Triggers and integrity constraints**   Used to maintain the validity of data entered.

- **Privileges, roles, and profiles**   Used to manage database access and usage.

- **Packages, procedures, and functions**   Application PL/SQL code used in the database.

TIP
This is only a partial listing of all the different types of objects available in Oracle. In reality, dozens of different types of objects are available that aren't covered in this book. But, you do not need to know how to create or use the database object types not listed here in order to pass OCP Exam 1. You should know what the objects listed previously are, however, because we either have discussed or will discuss these objects at some point during this book.

For Review
Be sure you can identify the different basic types of objects found in Oracle databases that are listed in this brief discussion. They are discussed in this book.

Other database objects exist in Oracle; however, they are not covered on the OCP exam.

Exercises

1. This is the database object comprised of PL/SQL code stored in the database that performs some programmatic task:

   _____

2. This is the database object designed to enforce validity rules on data added to the database that does not use PL/SQL code:

   _____

3. This is a database object that generates numbers in order:

   _____

Answer Key

1. Package. (*Procedure* or *function* is also acceptable.) 2. Constraint. 3. Sequence.

Using Sequences

A *sequence* is a database object that generates integers according to rules specified at the time the sequence is created. A sequence automatically generates unique numbers and is sharable between different users in Oracle. Sequences have many purposes in database systems—the most common of which is to generate primary keys automatically. However, nothing binds a sequence to a table's primary key, so in a sense it's also a sharable object. This task is common in situations where the primary key is not generally used for accessing data in a table. The common use of sequences to create primary keys has one main drawback. Because it is simply a sequential number, the primary key itself and the index it creates are somewhat meaningless. However, if you only need the key to guarantee uniqueness and don't care that you're creating a nonsense key, it is perfectly all right to do so. Sequences are created with the `create sequence` statement. The following explains each clause in the statement:

- **start with** *n* Enables the creator of the sequence to specify the first value generated by the sequence. Once created, the sequence will generate the value specified by `start with` the first time the sequence's NEXTVAL virtual column is referenced. If no `start with` value is specified, Oracle defaults to a start value of 1.

- **increment by** *n*   Defines the number by which to increment the sequence every time the NEXTVAL virtual column is referenced. The default for this clause is 1 if it is not explicitly specified. You can set *n* to be positive for incrementing sequences or negative for decrementing or countdown sequences.

- **minvalue** *n*   Defines the minimum value that can be produced by the sequence. If no minimum value is specified, Oracle will assume the default, `nominvalue`.

- **maxvalue** *n*   Defines the maximum value that can be produced by the sequence. If no maximum value is desired or specified, Oracle will assume the default, `nomaxvalue`.

- **cycle**   Enables the sequence to recycle values produced when `maxvalue` or `minvalue` is reached. If cycling is not desired or not explicitly specified, Oracle will assume the default, `nocycle`. You cannot specify `cycle` in conjunction with `nomaxvalue` or `nominvalue`. If you want your sequence to cycle, you must specify `maxvalue` for incrementing sequences or `minvalue` for decrementing or countdown sequences.

- **cache** *n*   Enables the sequence to cache a specified number of values to improve performance. If caching is not desired or not explicitly specified, Oracle will assume the default, which is to cache 20 values.

- **order**   Enables the sequence to assign values in the order in which requests are received by the sequence. If order is not desired or not explicitly specified, Oracle will assume the default, `noorder`.

Consider now an example for defining sequences. The integers that can be specified for sequences can be negative as well as positive. The following example uses a decrementing sequence. The `start with` integer in this example is positive, but the `increment by` integer is negative, which effectively tells the sequence to decrement instead of increment. When zero is reached, the sequence will start again from the top. This sequence can be useful in programs that require a countdown before an event will occur. The following shows an example:

```
SQL> CREATE SEQUENCE countdown_20
  2   START WITH 20
  3   INCREMENT BY -1
  4   MAXVALUE 20
  5   MINVALUE 0
  6   CYCLE
  7   ORDER
  8   CACHE 2;
Sequence created.
```

TIP
Some real-world uses for sequences include automatic generation of tracking numbers, invoice numbers, or other numerical information.

Once the sequence is created, it is referenced using the CURRVAL and NEXTVAL pseudocolumns. The users of the database can view the current value of the sequence by using a `select` statement. Similarly, the next value in the sequence can be generated with a `select` statement. Because sequences are not tables—they are only objects that generate integers via the use of virtual columns—the DUAL table acts as the "virtual" table from which the virtual column data is pulled. As stated earlier, values cannot be placed into the sequence; instead, they can only be selected from the sequence.

The following example demonstrates how COUNTDOWN_20 cycles when `minvalue` is reached:

```
SQL> select countdown_20.nextval from dual;
   NEXTVAL
---------
        20
SQL> /
   NEXTVAL
---------
        19

...

SQL> /
NEXTVAL
---------
         1
SQL> /
NEXTVAL
---------
         0
SQL> /
NEXTVAL
---------
        20
```

TIP
References to sequences cannot be used in subqueries of `select` statements (including those with `having`), views, `select` statements using set

> *operations (such as* union *and* minus)*, or any*
> select *statement that requires a sort to be*
> *performed.*

Once the NEXTVAL column is referenced, the value in CURRVAL is updated to match the value in NEXTVAL, and the prior value in CURRVAL is lost. The next code block illustrates this point:

```
SQL> select countdown_20.currval from dual;
  CURRVAL
---------
       20
SQL> select countdown_20.nextval from dual;
  NEXTVAL
---------
       19
SQL> select countdown_20.currval from dual;
  CURRVAL
---------
       19
```

TIP
CURRVAL is set to the start with *value until NEXTVAL is referenced for the first time after sequence creation. After that, CURRVAL is set to the value for NEXTVAL. Every time NEXTVAL is referenced, CURRVAL changes. Interestingly, the first time you reference NEXTVAL, it gets set to the* start with *value also, so effectively that the value for CURRVAL doesn't change!*

Referencing Sequences in Data Changes

Sequence-value generation can be incorporated directly into data changes made by insert and update statements. This direct use of sequences in insert and update statements is the most common use for sequences in a database. In the situation where the sequence generates a primary key for all new rows entering the database table, the sequence would likely be referenced directly from the insert statement. Note, however, that this approach sometimes fails when the sequence is referenced by triggers. Therefore, it is best to reference sequences within the user interface or within stored procedures. The following statements illustrate the use of sequences directly in changes made to tables:

```
SQL> INSERT INTO expense(expense_no, empid, amt, submit_date)
  2   VALUES(countdown_20.nextval, 59495, 456.34, '21-NOV-99');
1 row inserted.
SQL> UPDATE product
  2   SET product_num = countdown_20.currval
  3   WHERE serial_num = 34938583945;
1 row updated.
```

TIP
These trivial code block examples are for tables that we may or may not have referred to in earlier discussions. You can formulate your own sequences for similar use on tables we have already worked on or tables of your own design.

Modifying Sequence Definitions

The time may come when the sequence of a database will need its rules altered in some way. For example, you may want COUNTDOWN_20 to decrement by a different number. Any parameter of a sequence can be modified by issuing the `alter sequence` statement. The following is an example:

```
SQL> select countdown_20.nextval from dual;
NEXTVAL
-------
     16
SQL> alter sequence countdown_20
  2   increment by -4;
Sequence altered.
SQL> select countdown_20.nextval from dual
  2   ;
  NEXTVAL
---------
      12
SQL> /
  NEXTVAL
---------
       8
```

The effect is immediate. In this example, the statement will change COUNTDOWN_20 to decrement each NEXTVAL by 4 instead of 1.

Any parameter of a sequence that is not specified by the `alter sequence` statement will remain unchanged. Therefore, by altering the sequence to use `nocycle` instead of `cycle`, we cause the COUNTDOWN_20 sequence in the following listing to run through one countdown from 20 to 0 only. After the sequence hits 0, no further references to COUNTDOWN_20.NEXTVAL will be allowed:

```
SQL> alter sequence countdown_20
  2  nocycle;
Sequence altered.
SQL> select countdown_20.nextval from dual;
  NEXTVAL
---------
        4
SQL> /
  NEXTVAL
---------
        0
SQL> /
select countdown_20.nextval from dual
*
ERROR at line 1:
ORA-08004: sequence COUNTDOWN_20.NEXTVAL goes below MINVALUE
and cannot be instantiated
```

Beware of Effects of Modifying Sequences

Modifying sequences is a simple process. However, the impact of the changes can be complex, depending on how an application uses these sequences. The main concern with changing sequences is monitoring the effect on tables or other processes that use the values generated by the sequences.

For example, resetting the value returned by a sequence from 1,150 to 0 is not difficult to execute. However, if the sequence was being used to generate primary keys for a table, for which several values between 0 and 1,150 had already been generated, you will encounter problems when the sequence begins generating values for `insert` statements that depend on the sequence to create primary keys. This problem won't show up when the sequence is altered, but later `insert` operations will have primary key constraint violations on the table. The only way to solve the problem (other than deleting the records already existing in the table) is to alter the sequence again. Gaps can arise in the values of the primary key from this same premise as well.

Dropping Sequences

When a sequence is no longer needed, it can be removed. To do so, the DBA or owner of the sequence can issue the `drop sequence` statement. Dropping the sequence renders its virtual columns, CURRVAL and NEXTVAL, unusable. However, if the sequence was being used to generate primary key values, the values generated by the sequence will continue to exist in the database. No cascading effect occurs on the values generated by a sequence when the sequence is removed. The following shows an example:

```
SQL> DROP SEQUENCE countdown_20;
Sequence dropped.
SQL> select countdown_20.currval from dual;
select countdown_20.currval from dual
            *
ERROR at line 1:
ORA-02289: sequence does not exist
```

> **TIP**
> *You can find information about your sequences and the sequences available to you in the USER_SEQUENCES and ALL_SEQUENCES dictionary views, respectively. Also, sequences are not tied to a table. Generally, you should name the sequence after its intended use; however, the sequence can be used anywhere, regardless of its name.*

Gaps in Sequence
Although sequence generators issue sequential numbers without gaps, this action occurs independent of a `commit` or `rollback`. Therefore, if you roll back a statement containing a sequence, the number is lost. Also, another event that can cause gaps in the sequence is a system crash. If the sequence caches values in the memory, then those values are lost if the system crashes. Finally, because sequences are not tied directly to tables, the same sequence can be used for multiple tables. If you do so, each table can contain gaps in the sequential numbers.

For Review
1. Be sure you know that a sequence is an object that generates numbers in a sequence you define. Sequences can be used for many purposes, but they are most commonly used for generating unique numbers for primary key columns.

2. Know how to use the `create sequence`, `alter sequence`, and `drop sequence` statements. Also, be sure you can identify the information

contained in the CURRVAL and NEXTVAL pseudocolumns of a sequence as well as what happens to CURRVAL when NEXTVAL is selected.

3. Understand the different ways to refer to a sequence with `select`, `update`, and `insert` statements. Know how to use sequences in conjunction with the DUAL table as well.

Exercises

1. **This sequence pseudocolumn contains the most recently generated value the sequence has derived:** _____

2. **This sequence pseudocolumn contains the last value the sequence has derived:** _____

Answer Key
1. NEXTVAL. 2. CURRVAL.

Using Indexes

Indexes are objects in the database that provide a mapping of all the values in a table column, along with the ROWID(s) for all rows in the table that contain that value for the column. A ROWID is a unique identifier for a row in an Oracle database table. Indexes have multiple uses on the Oracle database. Indexes can be used to ensure uniqueness on a database, and they can also boost performance when you're searching for records in a table. Indexes are used by the Oracle Server to speed up the retrieval of rows by using a pointer. The improvement in performance is gained when the search criteria for data in a table include a reference to the indexed column or columns. In Oracle, indexes can be created on any column in a table except for columns of the LONG datatype. Especially on large tables, indexes make the difference between an application that drags its heels and an application that runs with efficiency. However, many performance considerations must be weighed before you make the decision to create an index. Performance is not improved simply by throwing a few indexes on the table haphazardly. Indexes can reduce disk I/O by using a rapid path access method to locate data quickly. Indexes are used and maintained automatically by the Oracle server. Indexes can be created either manually or automatically.

B-tree Index Structure

The traditional index in the Oracle database is based on a highly advanced algorithm for sorting data called a *B-tree*. A B-tree contains data placed in layered, branching order, from top to bottom, resembling an upside-down tree. The midpoint of the entire list is placed at the top of the "tree" and is called the *root node*. The midpoints of each half of the remaining two lists are placed at the next level, and so on, as illustrated in Figure 7-1.

By using a divide-and-conquer method for structuring and searching for data, the values of a column are only a few hops away on the tree, rather than several thousand sequential reads through the list away. However, traditional indexes work best when many distinct values are in the column or when the column is unique.

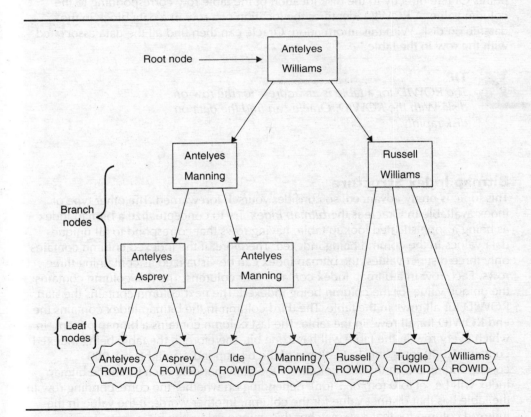

FIGURE 7-I. *A B-tree index, displayed pictorially*

The algorithm works as follows:

1. Compare the given value to the value in the halfway point of the list. If the value at hand is greater, discard the lower half of the list. If the value at hand is less, discard the upper half of the list.

2. Repeat step 1 for the remaining part of the list until a value is found or the list exhausted.

Along with the data values of a column, each individual node of an index also stores a piece of information about the column value's row location on disk. This crucial piece of lookup data is called a ROWID. The ROWID for the column value points Oracle directly to the disk location of the table row corresponding to the column value. A ROWID identifies the location of a row in a data block in the datafile on disk. With this information, Oracle can then find all the data associated with the row in the table.

TIP
The ROWID for a table is an address for the row on disk. With the ROWID, Oracle can find the data on disk rapidly.

Bitmap Index Structure

This topic is pretty advanced, so consider yourself forewarned. The other type of index available in Oracle is the *bitmap index*. Try to conceptualize a bitmap index as being a sophisticated lookup table, having rows that correspond to all unique data values in the column being indexed. Therefore, if the indexed column contains only three distinct values, the bitmap index can be visualized as containing three rows. Each row in a bitmap index contains four columns. The first column contains the unique value for the column being indexed. The next column contains the start ROWID for all rows in the table. The third column in the bitmap index contains the end ROWID for all rows in the table. The last column contains a bitmap pattern, in which every row in the table will have one bit. Therefore, if the table being indexed contains 1,000 rows, this last column of the bitmap index will have 1,000 corresponding bits in this last column of the bitmap index. Each bit in the bitmap index will be set to 0 (off) or 1 (on), depending on whether the corresponding row in the table has that distinct value for the column. In other words, if the value in the indexed column for that row matches this unique value, the bit is set to 1; otherwise, the bit is set to 0. Figure 7-2 displays a pictorial representation of a bitmap index containing three distinct values.

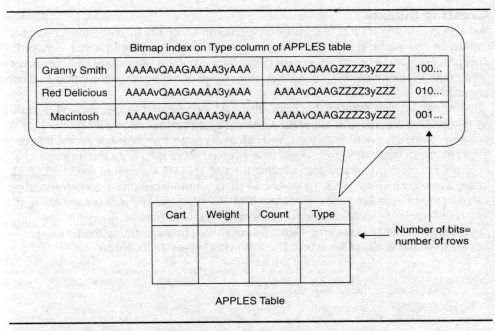

Bitmap index on Type column of APPLES table			
Granny Smith	AAAAvQAAGAAAA3yAAA	AAAAvQAAGZZZZ3yZZZ	100...
Red Delicious	AAAAvQAAGAAAA3yAAA	AAAAvQAAGZZZZ3yZZZ	010...
Macintosh	AAAAvQAAGAAAA3yAAA	AAAAvQAAGZZZZ3yZZZ	001...

Cart	Weight	Count	Type

Number of bits= number of rows

APPLES Table

FIGURE 7-2.   *A bitmap index, displayed pictorially*

Each row in the table being indexed adds only a bit to the size of the bitmap pattern column for the bitmap index, so growth of the table won't affect the size of the bitmap index too much. However, each distinct value adds another row to the bitmap index, which adds another entire bitmap pattern with one bit for each row in the table. Be careful about adding distinct values to a column with a bitmap index, because these indexes work better when few distinct values are allowed for a column. The classic example of using a bitmap index is where you want to query a table containing employees based on a GENDER column, indicating whether the employee is male or female. This information rarely changes about a person, and only two distinct possibilities, so a traditional B-tree index is not useful in this case. However, this is exactly the condition where a bitmap index would aid performance. Therefore, the bitmap index improves performance in situations where traditional indexes are not useful, and vice versa.

TIP
Up to 32 columns from one table can be included in a single B-tree index on that table, whereas a bitmap index can include a maximum of 30 columns from the table.

Creating Indexes

You can create a unique B-tree index on a column manually by using the `create index` *name* on *table* (*column*) statement containing the `unique` keyword. This process is the manual equivalent of creating a unique or primary key constraint on a table. (Remember, unique indexes are created automatically in support of those constraints.)

You can index a column that contains NULL or repeated values, as well, simply by eliminating the `unique` keyword. Creating a composite index with more columns named is possible as well. You can also create a *reverse-key index*, where the contents of the index correspond to a reversed set of data from the indexed column. For example, if you are indexing the LASTNAME column of the EMPLOYEE table, a row containing "COUCHMAN" in that column would have a corresponding value in the reverse-key index of "NAMHCOUC." Reverse-key indexes are often found in Oracle Parallel Server environments to improve parallel query performance. Finally, you can create a bitmap index by substituting the `bitmap` keyword for the `unique` keyword. The following shows an example:

```
SQL> -- unique indexes
  2  CREATE UNIQUE INDEX emp_empno_01
  3  ON emp (empno);
Index created.
SQL> -- nonunique indexes
  2  CREATE INDEX emp_sal_01
  3  ON emp (sal);
Index created.
SQL> -- composite indexes
  2  CREATE UNIQUE INDEX employee_empno_ename_indx_01
  3  ON emp (empno, ename);
Index created.
SQL> -- reverse key indexes
  2  CREATE INDEX emp_ename_reverse_indx
  3  ON emp (ename) REVERSE;
Index created.
SQL> -- bitmap indexes
  2  CREATE BITMAP INDEX emp_deptno_indx_01
  3  ON emp (deptno);
Index created.
```

TIP
You can create all these indexes on the EMP table we've been using throughout the book. Alternatively, you can use these code blocks as templates for creating these types of indexes on tables of your own design.

To create an index in your schema, you must have the CREATE TABLE privilege. To create an index in any schema, you need the CREATE ANY INDEX privilege or the CREATE TABLE privilege on the table on which you are creating the index.

In order to replace the definition of the index, the entire index must be dropped and re-created. However, information about the index can be found in several different ways. The ALL_INDEXES dictionary view displays storage information about the index, along with the name of the table with which the index is associated. The ALL_OBJECTS dictionary view displays object information about the index, including the index status. The ALL_IND_COLUMNS view displays information about the columns that are indexed on the database. This last view is especially useful for determining the order of columns in a composite index.

Creating Function-Based Indexes

To create a function-based index in your own schema on your own table, you must have the CREATE INDEX and QUERY REWRITE system privileges. To create the index in another schema or on another schema's table, you must have the CREATE ANY INDEX and GLOBAL QUERY REWRITE privileges. The table owner must also have the EXECUTE object privilege on the functions used in the function-based index.

The function-based index is a new type of index in Oracle that is designed to improve query performance by making it possible to define an index that works when your where clause contains operations on columns. Traditional B-tree indexes won't be used when your where clause contains columns that participate in functions or operations. For example, suppose you have table EMP with four columns: EMPID, LASTNAME, FIRSTNAME, and SALARY. The SALARY column has a B-tree index on it. However, if you issue the select * from EMP where (SALARY*1.08) > 63000 statement, the RDBMS will ignore the index, performing a full table scan instead. Function-based indexes are designed to be used in situations like this one, where your SQL statements contain such operations in their where clauses. The following code block shows a function-based index defined:

```
SQL> CREATE INDEX ixd_emp_01
  2  ON emp(SAL*1.08);
Index created.
```

By using function-based indexes like this one, you can optimize the performance of queries containing function operations on columns in the where clause, like the query shown previously. As long as the function you specify is repeatable, you can create a function-based index around it. A *repeatable function* is one whose result will never change for the same set of input data. For example,

2 + 2 will always equal 4. In other words, it will never change one day so that it equals 5. Therefore, the addition operation is repeatable. To enable the use of function-based indexes, you must issue two `alter session` statements, as follows:

```
SQL> alter session set query_rewrite_enabled = true;
Session altered.
SQL> alter session set query_rewrite_integrity=trusted;
Session altered.
```

TIP
Bitmap indexes can also be function-based indexes, and function-based indexes can also be partitioned.

Removing Indexes

When an index is no longer needed in the database, the developer can remove it with the `drop index` command. Once an index is dropped, it will no longer improve performance on searches using the column or columns contained in the index. No mention of that index will appear in the data dictionary any more either. You cannot drop the index that is used for a primary key.

The syntax for the `drop index` statement is the same, regardless of the type of index being dropped (unique, bitmap, or B-tree). If you want to rework the index in any way, you must first drop the old index and then create the new one. The following is an example:

```
SQL> DROP INDEX employee_last_first_indx_01;
Index dropped.
```

Guidelines for Creating Indexes

Although the best performance improvement can be seen when a column containing all unique values has an index created on it, similar performance improvements can be made on columns containing some duplicate values or NULL values. Therefore, data in a column need not be unique in order for you to create an index on the column. Some guidelines are available for ensuring that the traditional index produces the performance improvements desired. The guidelines for evaluating performance improvements given by traditional indexes and some consideration of the performance and storage trade-offs involved in creating these indexes will be presented later in this section of the chapter.

Using indexes for searching tables for information can provide incredible performance gains over searching tables using columns that are not indexed.

However, care must be taken to choose the right index. Although a completely unique column is preferable for indexing with a B-tree index, a non-unique column will work almost as well if only about 10 percent of its rows, or even less, have the same values. Switch or flag columns, such as ones for storing the sex of a person, are not appropriate for B-tree indexes. Neither are columns used to store a few valid values, or columns that store a token value representing valid or invalid, active or inactive, yes or no, or any such types of values. Bitmap indexes are more appropriate for these types of columns. Finally, you will typically use reverse-key indexes in situations where Oracle Parallel Server is installed and running and you want to maximize parallelism in the database. Table 4-1 summarizes some handy rules of thumb on the topic of when to create and when not to create indexes.

TIP
The uniqueness of the values in a column is referred to as cardinality. *Unique columns or columns that contain many distinct values have* high cardinality, *whereas columns with few distinct values have* low cardinality. *Use B-tree indexes for columns with high cardinality and bitmap indexes for columns with low cardinality. Also, the USER_INDEXES data dictionary view contains the name of the index and its uniqueness. The USER_IND_COLUMNS view contains the index name, the table name, and the column name.*

When to Create an Index	When Not to Create an Index
When you have a large table	When you have a small table
When the table is used mainly for queries	When users make DML changes to the table frequently
When you generally query the table for one or a few distinct values	When your query results contain substantial portions of the data the table actually stores
When a large number of NULLs are in the column	When the table is updated frequently

TABLE 7-1.   *When to Create and When Not to Create an Index*

For Review

1. Know what an index is and how to create one. Understand the difference between a unique index and a nonunique index. Also, be sure you can create B-tree, bitmap, function-based, reverse-key, and composite indexes.

2. Be sure you understand that, on unique indexes containing more than one column, uniqueness for the row is determined by unique combinations of all columns in the index.

3. Understand what is meant by cardinality. Know when you might use a B-tree index to improve performance and when you might you might use a bitmap index to improve performance instead. Know also that you can look in USER_INDEXES and USER_IND_COLUMNS for information about indexes.

Exercises

1. You want to create an index that will improve performance on salary reviews. The query needs to determine what an employee's salary would be if the employee were given a 12 percent raise. Which of the following `create index` commands would handle this situation?

   A. create index my_idx_1 on employee (salary * 1.12);

   B. create unique index my_idx_1 on employee (salary);

   C. create bitmap index my_idx_1 on employee (salary);

   D. create index my_idx_1 on employee (salary) reverse;

2. Your table, which contains name and telephone number information for the states of California, New York, and Texas, needs an index on the LASTNAME column. In order to improve performance, which of the following indexes would be most appropriate?

   A. create unique index my_idx_1 on people_phone (lastname);

   B. create index my_idx_1 on people_phone (lastname);

   C. create bitmap index my_idx_1 on people_phone (lastname);

   D. create index my_idx_1 on people_phone (lastname) reverse;

3. **You are creating an index for the US_GOVT_SS table in the U.S. Government Social Security application on the SS_NUM column. Which of the following choices best identifies the statement you will use on this column?**

    A. `create index my_idx_1 on US_govt_SS (ss_num);`

    B. `create bitmap index my_idx_1 on US_govt_SS (ss_num);`

    C. `create unique index my_idx_1 on US_govt_SS (ss_num);`

    D. `create index my_idx_1 on US_govt_SS (ss_num) reverse;`

4. **This word describes the uniqueness of values in an indexed column:**
   _____

Answer Key

1. A. **2.** B. **3.** C. **4.** Cardinality.

Using Public and Private Synonyms

The objects in Oracle you create are available only in your schema unless you grant access to the objects explicitly to other users. We'll discuss privileges and user access in the next section. However, even when you grant permission to other users for using an object, the boundary created by schema ownership will force other users to prefix the object name with your schema name in order to access your object. For example, SCOTT owns the EMP table. If TURNER wants to access SCOTT's EMP table, he must refer to EMP as SCOTT.EMP. If TURNER doesn't, the following happens:

```
SQL> connect turner/ike
Connected.
SQL> SELECT * FROM emp
  2  WHERE empno = 7844;
SELECT * FROM emp
              *
ORA-00942: table or view does not exist.
```

TIP
*We'll cover the issue of creating TURNER's user ID
and the privileges associated with accessing a table
in the next section. For now, focus on the issue of
schema ownership.*

So, TURNER can't even see his own employee data—in fact, Oracle tells him
that the EMP table doesn't even exist (pretty sneaky, eh?). Yet, as soon as TURNER
prefixes the EMP table with its schema owner, SCOTT, a whole world of data opens
up for TURNER, as you can see in the following code block:

```
SQL> connect turner/ike
SQL> SELECT empno, ename, sal FROM SCOTT.emp
  2  WHERE empno = 7844;
    EMPNO ENAME            SAL
--------- ---------- ---------
     7844 TURNER          1500
```

How Synonyms Can Help
If remembering which user owns which table seems unnecessarily complicated,
synonyms can be used on the database for schema transparency. *Synonyms* are
alternative names that can be created as database objects in Oracle to refer to a
table or view. You can refer to a table owned by another user using synonyms.
Creating a synonym eliminates the need to qualify the object name with the schema
and provides you with an alternative name for a table, view, sequence, procedure,
or other objects. Synonyms are also used to shorten lengthy object names. Two types
of synonyms exist in Oracle: private synonyms and public synonyms. You can use a
private synonym within your own schema to refer to a table or view by an
alternative name. Private synonyms are exactly that—they are private to your
schema and therefore usable only by you. A private synonym name must be distinct
from all other objects owned by the same user.

Think of private synonyms as giving you the ability to develop "pet names" for
database objects in Oracle. You can use public synonyms to enable all users in
Oracle to access database objects you own without having to prefix the object
names with your schema name. This concept of referencing database objects .
without worrying about the schema the objects are part of is known as *schema
transparency*. Public synonyms are publicly available to all users of Oracle;
however, you need special privileges to create public synonyms. We'll talk more
about the privilege required for creating public synonyms in the next section. For
now, the following code block demonstrates how to create private and public
synonyms, respectively:

```
SQL> create synonym all_my_emps for emp;
Synonym created.
SQL> create public synonym emp for scott.emp;
Synonym created.
```

TIP
*Neither public nor private synonyms alter the details
of the table's or view's definition. They just simply
act as alternative names for the table or view.*

Now that SCOTT has his own private synonym for the EMP table, he can start referring to EMP by his pet name right away:

```
SQL> connect scott/tiger
Connected.
SQL> select empno, ename, sal
  2  from all_my_emps
  3  where empno = 7369;
   EMPNO ENAME            SAL
--------- ---------- ---------
    7369 SMITH            800
```

Meanwhile, TURNER no longer needs to refer to EMP using SCOTT's schema prefixed to the table name. He can simply call it EMP, as he does in the following example:

```
SQL> connect turner/ike
Connected.
SQL> select empno, ename, sal
  2  from emp
  3  where empno = 7844;
   EMPNO ENAME            SAL
--------- ---------- ---------
    7844 TURNER          1500
```

Note another interesting thing about private synonyms. If no public synonym existed for TURNER to use for referencing the EMP table without prefixing SCOTT's schema, TURNER could create his own private synonym for the object, as shown in the following:

```
SQL> connect turner/ike
Connected.
SQL> create synonym emp for scott.emp;
Synonym created.
```

```
SQL> select empno, ename, sal
  2  from emp
  3  where empno = 7844;
   EMPNO ENAME             SAL
--------- ---------- ---------
    7844 TURNER           1500
```

TIP
Synonyms do not give you access to data in a table that you do not already have access to. Only privileges can do that. Synonyms simply enable you to refer to a table without prefixing the schema name to the table reference. When resolving a database table name, Oracle looks first to see whether the table exists in your schema. If Oracle doesn't find the table, Oracle searches for a private synonym. If none is found, Oracle looks for a public synonym.

Dropping Synonyms

Synonyms are dropped using the `drop synonym` command, as shown in the following code block:

```
SQL> connect turner/ike
Connected.
SQL> drop synonym emp;
Synonym dropped.
SQL> connect scott/tiger
Connected.
SQL> drop public synonym emp;
Synonym dropped.
SQL> drop synonym all_my_emps;
Synonym dropped.
```

For Review

1. Understand how synonyms are used to facilitate schema transparency.

2. Know the difference between public synonyms and private synonyms. Know that private synonyms can be referenced only by the user who created them, whereas public synonyms can be referenced by every user in Oracle.

Exercises

1. User DAVIS would like to access table PROFITS, which is owned by user WATTERSON, without prefixing the schema owner. Assuming the privilege issue is worked out, which of the following choices do *not* resolve the schema transparency issue? (Choose two.)

   A. `create synonym profits for watterson.profits;`
   `(issued by WATTERSON)`

   B. `create public synonym for watterson.profits;`
   `(issued by WATTERSON);`

   C. `create synonym profits for watterson.profits;`
   `(issued by DAVIS)`

   D. `create synonym profits for profits; (issued by`
   `DAVIS)`

2. This type of synonym is accessible by every user in the Oracle database (two words): _____

3. This type of synonym is accessible only by the user in the Oracle database who created the synonym (two words): _____

Answer Key
1. A and D. 2. Public synonym. 3. Private synonym.

Chapter Summary

This chapter **has** covered a great deal of information you need to know about objects other than tables in the Oracle database. We started the chapter with a lengthy discussion on how to define both simple and complex views. You learned about how to modify data in base tables using a view as well as when this is not possible in certain circumstances using complex views. We then moved on to cover how to use indexes in the Oracle database. You learned about the different types of indexes available to Oracle as well as the different uses for those types of indexes. The chapter then covered the use of sequences for generating numbers for various purposes in Oracle. Finally, the chapter covered the use of synonyms for creating schema transparency in your database.

Two-Minute Drill

- A view is a virtual table defined by a `select` statement.

- Views can distill data from tables that may be inappropriate for some users, and they can hide the complexity of data joined from several tables. You can also mask the complexity that arises when you perform many single-row or group operations on the data returned by the view's query.

- The two types of views are simple and complex.

- Simple views are those that have only one underlying table.

- Complex views are those with two or more underlying tables that have been joined together.

- Data may be inserted into simple views, except in the following cases:

  - If the `with check option` clause is used, the user may not insert, delete, or update data on the table underlying the simple view if the view itself is not able to select that data for the user.

  - The user may not insert, delete, or update data on the table underlying the simple view if the `select` statement creating the view contains `group by`, `order by`, or a single-row operation.

  - No data may be inserted in simple views that contain references to any virtual columns, such as ROWID, CURRVAL, NEXTVAL, and ROWNUM.

  - No data may be inserted into simple views that are created with the `read only` option.

- Data may be inserted into complex views when all the following conditions are true:

  - The statement affects only one of the tables in the join.

  - For `update` statements, all columns changed are extracted from a key-preserved table. In addition, if the view is created with the `with check option` clause, join columns and columns taken from tables that are referenced more than once in the view are not part of the update.

  - For `delete` statements, the join has only one key-preserved table. This table may be present more than once in the join, unless the view has been created with the `with check option` clause.

- For `insert` statements, all columns where values are inserted must come from a key-preserved table, and the view must not have been created with the `with check option` clause.

- The `with check option` clause, upon creating a view, enables this simple view to limit the data that can be inserted or otherwise changed on the underlying table by requiring that the data change be selectable by the view.

- Modifying the data selected by a view requires re-creating the view with the `create or replace view` statement or dropping the view first and issuing the `create view` statement.

- An existing view can be recompiled by executing the `alter view` statement if for some reason it becomes invalid due to object dependency.

- A view is dropped with the `drop view` statement.

- A sequence generates integers based on rules that are defined by sequence creation.

- Options that can be defined for sequences include the first number generated, how the sequence increments, the maximum value, the minimum value, whether the sequence can recycle numbers, and whether numbers will be cached for improved performance.

- Sequences are used by selecting from the CURRVAL and NEXTVAL virtual columns.

- The CURRVAL column contains the current value of the sequence.

- Selecting from NEXTVAL increments the sequence and changes the value of CURRVAL to whatever is produced by NEXTVAL.

- The rules that a sequence uses to generate values can be modified using the `alter sequence` statement.

- A sequence can be deleted with the `drop sequence` statement.

- Some indexes in a database are created automatically, such as those supporting the primary key and the unique constraints on a table.

- Other indexes are created manually to support database performance improvements.

- Indexes created manually are often on non-unique columns.

- B-tree indexes work best on columns that have high cardinality—that is, columns that contain a large number of distinct values and few duplicates.

- B-tree indexes improve performance by storing data in a binary search tree and then searching for values in the tree using a divide-and-conquer methodology, as outlined in this chapter.

- Bitmap indexes improve performance on columns with low cardinality—that is, columns that contain few distinct values and many duplicates.

- Columns stored in an index can be changed only by dropping and recreating the index.

- Indexes can be deleted by issuing the `drop index` statement.

- The Oracle database security model consists of two parts: limiting user access with password authentication and controlling object use with privileges.

- Available privileges in Oracle include system privileges, for maintaining database objects, and object privileges, for accessing and manipulating data in database objects.

- Changing a password can be performed by a user with the `alter user identified by` statement.

- Granting system and object privileges is accomplished with the `grant` command.

- Taking away system and object privileges is accomplished with the `revoke` command.

- Creating a synonym is accomplished with the `create public synonym` command.

Fill-in-the-Blank Questions

1. Schema transparency can be created in an Oracle database through the use of this type of database object: _____

2. Obtaining a sequence's value without actually changing that value is done by referencing this Oracle pseudocolumn: _____

3. A view containing data from two or more tables where the user can actually modify values in the underlying tables is called what?
_____

4. This type of database index is used for applying a repeatable programmatic operation to all values in a column: _____

5. This type of constraint automatically creates an underlying index in your database: _____

6. This clause enables a view to enforce the rule that if the view itself cannot see the data change, the data change is not allowed:
_____

7. Obtaining a new value from a sequence is accomplished by querying this Oracle pseudocolumn: _____

Chapter Questions

1. **Dropping a table has which of the following effects on a non-unique index created for the table?**

   A. No effect.

   B. The index will be dropped.

   C. The index will be rendered invalid.

   D. The index will contain NULL values.

2. **Which of the following statements about indexes is true?**

   A. Columns with low cardinality are handled well by B-tree indexes.

   B. Columns with low cardinality are handled poorly by bitmap indexes.

   C. Columns with high cardinality are handled well by B-tree indexes.

3. **Which of the following choices represents the step you would take to add the number of columns selected by a view?**

   A. Add more columns to the underlying table.

   B. Issue the `alter view` statement.

   C. Use a correlated subquery in conjunction with the view.

   D. Drop and re-create the view with references to select more columns.

4. **You are creating a sequence on the Oracle database. Which of the following choices is a valid parameter for sequence creation?**

   A. `identified by`

   B. `using temporary tablespace`

   C. `maxvalue`

   D. `on delete cascade`

4. **The following statement is issued against the Oracle database:**

   ```
   create view EMP_VIEW_01
   as select E.EMPID, E.LASTNAME, E.FIRSTNAME, A.ADDRESS
   from EMPLOYEE E, EMPL_ADDRESS A
   where E.EMPID = A.EMPID
   with check option;
   ```

   Which line will produce an error?

   A. `create view EMP_VIEW_01`

   B. `as select E.EMPID, E.LASTNAME, E.FIRSTNAME, A.ADDRESS`

   C. `from EMPLOYEE E, EMPL_ADDRESS A`

   D. `where E.EMPID = A.EMPID`

   E. `with check option;`

   F. This statement contains no errors.

5. **You are working with sequences in Oracle. After referencing NEXTVAL, the value in CURRVAL is changed to which in the following ways or to which of the following values?**

   A. Is incremented by one

   B. Is now in PREVVAL

C. Is equal to NEXTVAL

D. Is unchanged

6. **The EMP_SALARY table has two columns: EMP_USER and SALARY. EMP_USER is set to be the same as the Oracle username. To support user MARTHA, the salary administrator, you create a view with the following statement:**

```
CREATE VIEW EMP_SAL_VW
AS SELECT EMP_USER, SALARY
FROM EMP_SALARY
WHERE EMP_USER <> 'MARTHA';
```

MARTHA is supposed to be able to view and update anyone's salary in the company except her own through this view. Which of the following clauses do you need to add to your view-creation statement in order to implement this functionality?

A. with admin option

B. with grant option

C. with security option

D. with check option

7. **The INVENTORY table has three columns: UPC_CODE, UNITS, and DELIV_DATE. The primary key is UPC_CODE. New records are added daily through a view. The view was created using the following code:**

```
CREATE VIEW DAY_INVENTORY_VW
AS SELECT UPC_CODE, UNITS, DELIV_DATE
FROM INVENTORY
WHERE DELIV_DATE = SYSDATE
WITH CHECK OPTION;
```

What happens when you try to insert a record with duplicate UPC_CODE?

A. The statement fails due to the with check option clause.

B. The statement will succeed.

C. The statement fails due to the primary key constraint.

D. The statement will insert everything except the date.

8. You are cleaning information out of an Oracle database. Which of the following statements will get rid of all views that use a table at the same time you eliminate the table from the database?

   A. `drop view`

   B. `alter table`

   C. `drop index`

   D. `alter table drop` constraint

9. You create a view with the following statement:

   ```
   CREATE VIEW BASEBALL_TEAM_VW
   AS SELECT B.JERSEY_NUM, B.POSITION, B.NAME
   FROM BASEBALL_TEAM B
   WHERE B.NAME = USER;
   ```

   What will happen when user JONES attempts to select a listing for user SMITH?

   A. The `select` statement will receive an error.

   B. The `select` statement will succeed.

   C. The `select` statement will receive the NO ROWS SELECTED message from Oracle.

   D. The `select` statement will add data only to BASEBALL_TEAM.

Fill-in-the-Blank Answers

1. Synonym

2. CURRVAL

3. Updatable join view

4. Function-based index

5. Primary key (unique constraint also acceptable)

6. with check option

7. NEXTVAL

Answers to Chapter Questions

1. B. The index will be dropped.

Explanation Like automatically generated indexes associated with a table's primary key, the indexes created manually on a table to improve performance will be dropped if the table is dropped. Choices A, C, and D are therefore invalid because the effects listed in those choices do not take place in this context.

2. C. Columns with high cardinality are handled well by B-tree indexes.

Explanation Columns with low cardinality are the bane of B-tree indexes, thus eliminating choice A. Furthermore, bitmap indexes are primarily used for performance gains on columns with low cardinality, thus eliminating choice B. The correct answer is choice C. Review the discussion of how B-tree indexes work for more information.

3. D. Drop and re-create the view with references to select more columns.

Explanation Choice A is incorrect because adding columns to the underlying table will not add columns to the view; instead, it will likely invalidate the view. Choice B is incorrect because the alter view statement simply recompiles an existing view definition, whereas the real solution in this example is to change the existing view definition by dropping and recreating the view. Choice C is incorrect because a correlated subquery will likely worsen performance. This underscores the real problem—a column must be added to the view. Review the discussion of altering the definition of a view.

4. C. `maxvalue`

Explanation   The `maxvalue` option is a valid option for sequence creation. Choices A and B are both part of the `create user` statement, whereas choice D is a part of a constraint declaration in an `alter table` or `create table` statement. Review the discussion on creating sequences.

5. F. This statement contains no errors.

Explanation   Even though the reference to `with check option` is inappropriate, considering that `insert` operations into complex views are not possible, the statement will not actually produce an error when compiled. Therefore, no errors occur in the view. This is not something that can be learned. It requires hands-on experience with Oracle.

6. C. Is equal to NEXTVAL

Explanation   Once NEXTVAL is referenced, the sequence increments the integer and changes the value of CURRVAL to be equal to NEXTVAL. Refer to the discussion of sequences for more information.

7. D. `with check option`

Explanation   The appropriate clause is `with check option`. You can add this clause to a `create view` statement so that the view will not let you add rows to the underlying table that cannot then be selected in the view. The `with {admin|grant} option` clauses are used to assign administrative ability to users, along with granting them privileges. Therefore, choices A and B are incorrect. The `with security option` is fictitious—it does not exist in Oracle. Therefore, choice C is incorrect.

8. C. The statement fails due to the primary key constraint.

Explanation   It should be obvious that the statement fails—the real question here is why. The reason is because of the primary key constraint on UPC_CODE. As soon as you try to add a duplicate record, the table will reject the addition. Although the view has `with check option` specified, this is not the reason the addition fails. It would be the reason an `insert` fails if you attempt to add a record for a day other than today, however.

9. A. `drop view`

Explanation   When a table is dropped, Oracle eliminates all related database objects, such as triggers, constraints, and indexes—except for views. Views are actually considered separate objects, and although the view will not function properly after you drop the underlying table, Oracle will keep the view around after the table is dropped.

10. C. The `select` will receive the NO ROWS SELECTED message from Oracle

Explanation Although the query will succeed (translation: you won't receive an error), you must beware of the distracter in choice B. In reality, choice C is the better answer because it more accurately identifies what really will occur when you issue this statement. Oracle will behave as it would for any `select` statement you issue when you list criteria in the `where` clause that no data satisfies—by returning the NO ROWS SELECTED message. This is not an error condition, but you wouldn't call it a successful search for data either, making choices A and B incorrect. Finally, `select` statements never add data to a table. Therefore, choice D is incorrect.

CHAPTER
8

User Access Control in Oracle

n this chapter, you will learn about and demonstrate knowledge in the following areas of user access and privileges in the Oracle database:

- Creating users
- Granting and revoking object privileges
- Using roles to manage database access

The most secure database is one with no users, but take away the users of a database and the whole point of having a database is lost. In order to address the issues of security within Oracle, a careful balance must be maintained between providing access to necessary data and functions and preventing unnecessary access. Oracle provides a means of doing this with its security model, which consists of several options for limiting connect access to the database and for controlling what a user can and cannot see once a connection is established. Database security includes system security and data security. System security specifies using the database at the system level (includes username, password, and diskspace allocated to users). Database security specifies the use of database objects and the actions that the users can perform on the database objects. This section will focus on security on the Oracle database—from creating users, to administering passwords, to administering security on individual objects in the database. This chapter covers 7 percent of the material tested on OCP Exam 1.

Creating Users

The basic Oracle database security model consists of two parts. The first part consists of password authentication for all users of the Oracle database. Password authentication is available either directly from the Oracle server or from the operating system supporting the Oracle database. When Oracle's own authentication system is used, password information is stored in Oracle in an encrypted format. For the purposes of OCP Exam 1, we'll focus exclusively on Oracle's own authentication mechanism. The second part of the Oracle security model consists of controlling which database objects a user may access, the level of access a user may have to these objects, and whether a user has the authority to place new objects into the Oracle database. At a high level, these controls are referred to as *privileges*. We'll talk about privileges and database access later in this section.

TIP

In Oracle, the Oracle security model has additional components, including such features as fine-grained access control, certificate-based authentication, and advanced password-management functions such as

*password rotation expiry and complexity
verification. These features are tested extensively in
OCP Exam 2, but not on OCP Exam 1. Oracle9i
promises to offer even more security features, such
as Oracle Label Security.*

How to Create Users

Let's start our discussion of creating users with an example. We referred to user
TURNER in an earlier example. He's a divorced salesman working for our company
who used to have ties to Hollywood. Only privileged users such as the DBA can
create other users in Oracle. For now, we'll pretend that user SCOTT is the DBA.
SCOTT creates TURNER's user ID in Oracle with the `create user` command. You
must have CREATE USER system privilege to be able to create users. The most basic
version of the command for creating users defines only the user we want to create,
along with a password, as seen in the following example:

```
SQL> connect scott/tiger
Connected.
SQL> create user turner identified by ike;
User created.
```

TIP

*The user does not have privileges at this point. The
DBA can then grant privileges to the user. The
privileges determine the actions that the user can do
with the objects in the database. Also, usernames
can be up to 30 characters in length and can
contain alphanumeric characters as well as the $, #,
and _ characters.*

Creating a User Authenticated by the Host

Host authentication isn't used by Oracle databases too often, but it can be. Host
authentication means that you create a user in Oracle whose password is validated
by the underlying host system. When the user logs onto the host with a correct
password, Oracle then trusts the host's authentication and gives the user access to
Oracle without providing another password. The username identifying the user in
Oracle must match that used on the host system, prefixed by OPS$, as shown in the
following example:

```
SQL> create user OPS$harvey identified externally;
User created.
```

Later, when HARVEY wants to connect to Oracle from a host system command prompt, he can specify the following to do so and does not need to provide a password:

```
C:\windows> c:\oracle\ora81\bin\sqlplus /
```

TIP
You must first be connected directly to the host system (via Telnet on UNIX or at a DOS prompt) in order for host authentication to work.

Finding Information about Users

Once users are created in Oracle, you can look in the dictionary view ALL_USERS to gain some basic information about them, including the username and the day each user was created. Take a look at the following code block:

```
SQL> select * from all_users;
USERNAME                        USER_ID CREATED
------------------------------ --------- ---------
SYS                                   0 23-JUN-99
SYSTEM                                5 23-JUN-99
OUTLN                                11 23-JUN-99
DBSNMP                               18 23-JUN-99
PO8                                  26 17-JUL-00
AURORA$ORB$UNAUTHENTICATED           23 23-JUN-99
JASON                                27 18-JUL-00
STUDENT2                             46 30-OCT-00
STUDENT1                             45 30-OCT-00
SPANKY                               43 30-OCT-00
JASON2                               48 31-OCT-00
SCOTT                                52 19-MAR-01
JASON3                               49 16-NOV-00
JASON10                              50 18-NOV-00
GIANT                                51 08-DEC-00
TURNER                               53 21-MAR-01
```

TIP
The USER_USERS dictionary view also gives important information about your own user ID, related to the advanced password-management features available in Oracle (not tested on OCP

Exam 1). Take a look at this view and try to figure out what it contains before moving onto the exercises at the end of this discussion.

Getting Users Started with System Privileges

Now that SCOTT has created user TURNER, let's have SCOTT help TURNER get started by having SCOTT grant TURNER some privileges. Remember, privileges are the second part of the basic Oracle security model. Privileges are the right to execute particular SQL statements. The database administrator is a high-level user with the ability to grant users access to the database and its objects.

Everything you can possibly do in an Oracle database is regulated by privileges. Two types of privileges exist in Oracle: object privileges and system privileges. *Object privileges* regulate access to database objects in Oracle, such as querying or changing data in tables and views, creating foreign key constraints and indexes on tables, executing PL/SQL programs, and a handful of other activities. Fewer than ten object privileges can be granted in Oracle, so they are easy to memorize. You'll learn more about object privileges in the next discussion. *System privileges* govern every other type of activity in Oracle, such as connecting to the database, creating tables, creating sequences, creating views, and much, much more.

TIP
All told, more than 100 separate privileges can be granted in Oracle, the vast majority of which are system privileges. We'll focus our discussion only on those system and object privileges tested on OCP Exam 1.

Privileges are given to users with the grant command, and they are taken away with the revoke command. The ability to grant privileges to other users in the database rests on users who can administer the privileges. The owner of a database object can administer object privileges related to that object, whereas the DBA administers system privileges. We'll keep pretending that SCOTT is the DBA for our system as we take a look at some grant commands that give TURNER various system privileges to work on the database:

```
SQL> connect scott/tiger
Connected.
SQL> grant create session to turner;
Grant succeeded.
SQL> grant create table to turner;
Grant succeeded.
```

```
SQL> grant create sequence to turner;
Grant succeeded.
SQL> grant create procedure to turner;
Grant succeeded.
```

Now, when TURNER attempts to connect to Oracle and do some work, he'll be able to

```
SQL> connect turner/ike
Connected.
SQL> create table my_table
  2  (my_column number);
Table created.
```

TIP
You can grant multiple privileges at the same time with the grant command, such as grant
select, update on emp to ELMO *or grant* create session, create table to ELMO.

Taking Away System Privileges

Now, let's say that management has decided that TURNER is all washed up with our company. KING hands TURNER a pink slip, and TURNER returns to his cubicle to clean out his desk. SCOTT now has to keep TURNER out of Oracle, but let's say he's too busy to do all the work today. SCOTT can simply revoke TURNER's ability to create sessions by using the following command:

```
SQL> connect scott/tiger
Connected.
SQL> revoke create session from turner;
Revoke succeeded.
```

TURNER is quite steamed about being fired, as you might imagine. He has been with the company for a long time and is going through some serious personal issues. While cleaning out his desk, TURNER decides to get even with his employer by sabotaging the data in Oracle. However, because SCOTT has revoked his ability to create database sessions, the following happens to TURNER:

```
SQL> connect turner/ike
ERROR:
ORA-01045: user TURNER lacks CREATE SESSION privilege; logon denied
```

TIP
Even though TURNER can no longer log into Oracle, he still has all the other privileges that have been granted to him.

System Privileges to Know for OCP

Several categories of system privileges relate to each object. Those categories determine the scope of ability that the privilege grantee will have. The classes or categories of system privileges are listed in this section. Note that in the following subtopics, the privilege itself gives the ability to perform the action against your own database objects, and the `any` keyword refers to the ability to perform the action against any database object of that type in Oracle.

Database Access   These privileges control who accesses the database, when he or she can access it, and what he or she can do regarding management of his or her own session. Privileges include `create session`, `alter session`, and `restricted session`.

Users   These privileges are used to manage users on the Oracle database. Typically, these privileges are reserved for DBAs or security administrators. Privileges include `create user`, `become user`, `alter user`, and `drop user`.

Tables   You already know that tables store data in the Oracle database. These privileges govern which users can create and maintain tables. The privileges include `create table`, `create any table`, `alter any table`, `backup any table`, `drop any table`, `lock any table`, `comment any table`, `select any table`, `insert any table`, `update any table`, and `delete any table`. The `create table` or `create any table` privilege also enables you to drop the table. The `create table` privilege also bestows the ability to create indexes on the table and to run the `analyze` command on the table. To be able to truncate a table, you must have the `drop any table` privilege granted to you.

Indexes   You already know that indexes are used to improve SQL statement performance on tables containing lots of row data. The privileges include `create any index`, `alter any index`, and `drop any index`. You should note that no `create index` system privilege exists. The `create table` privilege also enables you to alter and drop indexes that you own and that are associated with the table.

Synonyms   A synonym is a database object that enables you to reference another object by a different name. A public synonym means that the synonym is available to every user in the database for the same purpose. The privileges include `create synonym`, `create any synonym`, `drop any synonym`, `create public synonym`, and `drop public synonym`. The `create synonym` privilege also enables you to alter and drop synonyms that you own.

Views   You already know that a view is an object containing a SQL statement that behaves like a table in Oracle, except that it stores no data. The privileges include `create view`, `create any view`, and `drop any view`. The `create view` privilege also enables you to alter and drop views that you own.

Sequences   You already know that a sequence is an object in Oracle that generates numbers according to rules you can define. Privileges include `create sequence`, `create any sequence`, `alter any sequence`, `drop any sequence`, and `select any sequence`. The `create sequence` privilege also enables you to drop sequences that you own.

Roles   Roles are objects that can be used for simplified privilege management. You create a role, grant privileges to it, and then grant the role to users. Privileges include `create role`, `drop any role`, `grant any role`, and `alter any role`.

> **TIP**
> *We'll talk more about roles later in this chapter.*

Transactions   These privileges are for resolving in-doubt distributed transactions being processed on the Oracle database. Privileges include `force transaction` and `force any transaction`.

PL/SQL   There are many different types of PL/SQL blocks in Oracle. These privileges enable you to create, run, and manage those different types of blocks. Privileges include `create procedure`, `create any procedure`, `alter any procedure`, `drop any procedure`, and `execute any procedure`. The `create procedure` privilege also enables you to alter and drop PL/SQL blocks that you own.

Triggers   A trigger is a PL/SQL block in Oracle that executes when a specified DML activity occurs on the table to which the trigger is associated. Privileges include `create trigger`, `create any trigger`, `alter any trigger`, and `drop any trigger`. The `create trigger` privilege also enables you to alter and drop triggers that you own.

Using Dictionary Views to Display Privileges

To display privileges associated with users and roles, you can use the following views:

- **USER_SYS_PRIVS** Shows all system privileges associated with this user
- **SESSION_PRIVS** Shows all privileges available in this session

Changing Passwords

Security in the database is a serious matter, so users have to keep their passwords a secret. Most small organizations let the DBA handle database security, but larger ones use a security administrator. However, depending on the environment, developers, DBAs, or even end users may need to understand the options available in the Oracle security model for the version of Oracle the organization uses.

Toward that end of tighter security, SCOTT's new responsibilities as DBA require that he change his password to something less obvious. SCOTT must do this because he's worried that TURNER may try to log into Oracle using the SCOTT user ID and password. Like tables, passwords can contain alphanumeric characters (including $, #, and _). Let's look at what SCOTT must do with the `alter user` command in order to change his password:

```
SQL> connect scott/tiger
Connected.
SQL> alter user scott identified by 1#secure_pw;
User altered.
```

TIP
Several other options are available in both the `create user` *and* `alter user` *commands. However, basic user creation and password definition is all that's tested in OCP. If password management piques your interest, you can check out the Oracle documentation to see what other options are available. More advanced user management is tested on OCP Exam 2 in the DBA track.*

For Review

1. Be sure you can identify the two basic components of the Oracle security model: password authentication and privilege administration.

2. Know how to create a user along with his or her password using the `create user` command. Also, be sure you know how to change a password using the `alter user` command.

3. Understand where to look in the data dictionary for information about users.

4. Be sure you know what system and object privileges are and how to use `grant` and `revoke` to give out and take away privileges.

Exercises

1. User IMADBA wants to give user DAVIS, a brand-new employee who started today, the ability to create tables in the Oracle database. Which of the following choices identifies a step that doesn't need to take place before DAVIS can start creating tables?

   A. `create user davis identified by new_employee;`

   B. `grant create session to davis;`

   C. `grant create table to davis;`

   D. `grant create public synonym to davis;`

2. This is the privilege required for connecting to the Oracle database:
   _____

3. This is the privilege required for creating some public synonyms:
   _____

4. This is the clause used in the `alter user` statement for changing a password: _____

Answer Key
1. D. 2. `create session` 3. `create public synonym` 3. `identified by`

Granting and Revoking Object Privileges

As mentioned before, every possible activity in Oracle is governed by privileges. We already covered system privileges, so let's talk now about object privileges. All granting of object privileges is managed with the `grant` command. In order to grant an object privilege, the grantor must either have been granted the privilege with the `with grant option` privilege or must own the object. To grant an object privilege, the grantor of the privilege must determine the level of access a user requires on the object. Then, the privilege must be granted. An *object privilege* is a privilege or right to perform a particular action on a specific table, view, sequence, or procedure. Each object has a particular set of grantable privileges.

Available Object Privileges

The object privileges for any database object belong to the user who created that object. Object privileges can be granted to other users for the purpose of enabling them to access and manipulate the object. Object privileges include the following:

- **select** Permits the grantee of this object privilege to access the data in a table, sequence, view, or snapshot.

- **insert** Permits the grantee of this object privilege to insert data into a table or, in some cases, a view. You can also restrict this privilege to specified columns of a table.

- **update** Permits the grantee of this object privilege to update data in a table or view. You can also restrict this privilege to specified columns of a table.

- **delete** Permits the grantee of this object privilege to delete data from a table or view. You can also restrict this privilege to specified columns of a table.

- **alter** Permits the grantee of this object privilege to alter the definition of a table or sequence *only*; the `alter` privileges on all other database objects are considered system privileges.

- **index** Permits the grantee of this object privilege to create an index on a table already defined.

- **references** Permits the grantee of this object privilege to create or alter a table in order to create a foreign key constraint against data in the referenced table.

- **execute** Permits the grantee of this object privilege to run a stored procedure or function.

TIP
Oracle has less than ten object privileges. In contrast, it has dozens of system privileges. If you want an easy way to distinguish the two, try

memorizing the object privileges. Then, you can simply assume that any privilege you encounter on the OCP exam that is not an object privilege is a system privilege.

Granting Object Privileges in Oracle

The administrative abilities over an object privilege include the ability to grant the privilege or revoke it from anyone as well as the ability to grant the object privilege to another user with administrative ability over the privilege. For these examples, let's say that KING has reconsidered his haste in firing TURNER and has allowed TURNER back on a probationary basis. Now, SCOTT has to set up TURNER with access to the EMP table, as follows:

```
SQL> GRANT select, update, insert ON emp TO turner;
Grant succeeded.
SQL> GRANT references ON emp.empno TO turner;
Grant succeeded.
SQL> GRANT select, update, insert ON emp TO turner;
Grant succeeded.
```

Open to the Public

Another aspect of privileges and access to the database involves a special user on the database. This user is called PUBLIC. If a system privilege or object privilege is granted to the PUBLIC user, then every user in the database has that privilege. Typically, it is not advised that the DBA should grant many privileges or roles to PUBLIC, because if a privilege or role ever needs to be revoked, then every stored package, procedure, or function will need to be recompiled. Let's take a look:

```
SQL> GRANT select, update, insert ON emp TO public;
Grant succeeded.
```

TIP
Roles can be granted to the PUBLIC user as well. We'll talk more about roles in the next discussion.

Granting Object Privileges All at Once

The keyword all can be use as a consolidated method for granting object privileges related to a table. Note that all in this context is not a privilege; it is merely a specification for all object privileges for a database object. The following code block shows how `all` is used:

```
SQL> GRANT ALL ON emp TO turner;
Grant succeeded.
```

Giving Administrative Ability along with Privileges

When another user grants you a privilege, you then have the ability to perform whatever task the privilege enables you to do. However, you usually can't grant the privilege to others, nor can you relinquish the privilege without help of the user who granted the privilege to you. If you want some additional power to administer the privilege granted to you, the user who gave you the privilege must also give you administrative control over that privilege. For example, let's say KING now completely trusts TURNER to manage the creation of tables (a system privilege) and wants to give him access to the EMP table (an object privilege). Therefore, KING tells SCOTT to give TURNER administrative control over both these privileges, as follows:

```
SQL> GRANT CREATE TABLE TO turner WITH ADMIN OPTION;
Grant succeeded.
SQL> GRANT SELECT, UPDATE ON turner TO SPANKY WITH GRANT OPTION;
Grant succeeded.
```

TIP
The GRANT OPTION is not valid when granting an object privilege to a role. You'll learn more about roles later in this chapter.

A system privilege or role can be granted with the ADMIN OPTION. A grantee with this option has several expanded capabilities. The grantee can grant or revoke the system privilege or role to or from any user or other role in the database. However, a user cannot revoke a role from himself. The grantee can further grant the system privilege or role with the ADMIN OPTION. The grantee of a role can alter or drop the role.

The `with admin option` clause gives TURNER the ability to give or take away the `create table` *system* privilege to others. The `with grant option` clause gives TURNER that same ability for the `select` and `update` *object* privileges on table EMP. TURNER can make other users administrators of those privileges as well.

TIP
Finally, if a role is granted using the `with admin`
`option` *clause, the grantee can alter the role or*
even remove it. You'll learn more about roles in the
next discussion.

You can grant INSERT, UPDATE, or REFERENCES privileges on individual columns in a table.

Revoking Object Privileges in Oracle

Let's say that, once again, KING changed his mind and has fired TURNER. Revoking object privileges is handled with the `revoke` command. If you want to revoke system or object privileges granted with the `with admin option` clause or an object privilege granted with the `with grant option` clause, no additional syntax is required for doing so. Simply revoke the privilege, and the ability to administer that privilege gets revoked, too. You can see some examples of using this command for object privileges in the following code block:

```
SQL> revoke select, update, insert ON emp from turner;
Revoke succeeded.
SQL> revoke references ON emp.empno from turner;
Revoke succeeded.
SQL> revoke select, update, insert on emp from turner;
Revoke succeeded.
```

TIP
When the CASCADE CONSTRAINTS option is
specified, any foreign key constraints currently
defined that use the revoked REFERENCES privilege
are dropped.

Cascading Effects of Revoking System Privileges

Consider the following situation related to the cascading effects of system privileges. User SCOTT gives TURNER the ability to create tables with administrative ability, and TURNER turns around and gives the same privilege to FORD, an aging auto factory worker who switched into computer programming:

```
SQL> connect scott/tiger
Connected.
SQL> grant create table to turner with admin option;
```

```
Grant succeeded.
SQL> connect turner/ike
Connected.
SQL> create table my_table
  2  (my_column number);
Table created.
SQL> grant create table to ford;
Grant succeeded.
SQL> connect ford/henry
Connected.
SQL> create table my_table
  2  (my_column number);
Table created.
```

SCOTT finds out that TURNER gave the `create table` privilege to FORD, who is only supposed to be able to create PL/SQL programs. SCOTT gets mad at TURNER and revokes the `create table` privilege from TURNER, along with the administrative ability, as follows:

```
SQL> connect scott/tiger
Connected.
SQL> revoke create table from turner;
Revoke succeeded.
```

Will FORD continue to be able to create tables? Let's see:

```
SQL> connect ford/henry
Connected.
SQL> create table my_table_2
  2  (my_column number);
Table created.
```

As you can see, FORD still has the ability to create tables, even though TURNER (the guy who gave FORD the privilege) does not. This means that no cascading effects of revoking system privileges from users occur. FORD keeps his ability to create tables, and TURNER's table, called MY_TABLE, doesn't get dropped. If you want to take away a system privilege from a user, you have to explicitly revoke that privilege directly from the user as well as drop whatever objects that user has created while having the privilege.

Cascading Effects of Revoking Object Privileges

Now let's consider the same situation, only this time, the privilege in question is an object privilege. SCOTT grants `select` access on EMP to TURNER with administrative ability, who turns around and gives it to FORD. Check it out in the following block:

```
SQL> connect scott/tiger
Connected.
SQL> grant select on emp to turner with grant option;
Grant succeeded.
SQL> connect turner/ike
Connected.
SQL> select ename, job from scott.emp
  2  where empno =7844;
ENAME      JOB
---------- ---------
TURNER     SALESMAN
SQL> grant select on scott.emp to ford;
Grant succeeded.
SQL> connect ford/henry
Connected.
SQL> select ename, job from scott.emp
  2  where empno = 7369;
ENAME      JOB
---------- ---------
SMITH      CLERK
```

SCOTT then finds out what TURNER did and revokes the privilege from TURNER:

```
SQL> connect scott/tiger
Connected.
SQL> revoke select on emp from turner;
Revoke succeeded.
```

Will FORD still be able to access table EMP? Take a look a the following:

```
SQL> connect ford/henry
Connected.
SQL> select ename, job
  2  from scott.emp
  3  where empno = 7360;
from scott.emp
          *
ERROR at line 2:
ORA-00942: table or view does not exist
```

So, when an object privilege is revoked from a grantor of that privilege, all grantees receiving the privilege from the grantor also lose the privilege. However, in cases where the object privilege involves `update`, `insert`, or `delete`, if subsequent grantees have made changes to data using the privilege, the rows already changed don't get magically transformed back the way they were before.

Facts to Remember about Granting and Revoking Object Privileges

You should try to remember the following facts about granting and revoking object privileges before taking OCP:

- If a privilege has been granted on two individual columns, the privilege cannot be revoked on only one column—the privilege must be revoked entirely and then regranted on the individual column.

- If the user has been given the `references` privilege and has used it to create a foreign key constraint to another table, you must use the `cascade constraints` clause to revoke the `references` privilege (otherwise, the revoke will fail), as follows:

  ```
  REVOKE REFERENCES ON emp FROM spanky CASCADE CONSTRAINTS.
  ```

- The `insert`, `update`, and `references` privileges can be granted on columns within the database object. However, if a user has the `insert` privilege on several columns in a table but not all columns, the privilege administrator must ensure that no columns in the table that do not have the `insert` privilege granted are not NULL columns.

- If a user has the ability to execute a stored procedure owned by another user, and the procedure accesses some tables, the object privileges required to access those tables must be granted to the *owner* of the procedure, not the user to whom `execute` privileges were granted. What's more, the privileges must be granted directly to the user, not through a role.

- Depending upon what is granted or revoked, a grant or revoke takes effect at different times. All grants/revokes of privileges (system and schema object) to users, roles, or PUBLIC are immediately observed. All grants/revokes of roles to users, other roles, or PUBLIC are observed only when a current user session issues a SET ROLE statement to reenable the role after the grant/revoke, or when a new user session is created after the grant/revoke.

For Review

1. Be sure you can identify all the object privileges and use the grant and revoke commands to give the privileges to users and take them away.

2. Know what happens when you grant object privileges to the PUBLIC user. Know when and how to use the all keyword when granting object privileges on a table to a user.

3. Understand how to grant administrative abilities over a privilege to other users along with the privilege itself. Memorize the syntax difference between granting system privileges with the with admin option clause and granting object privileges with the with grant option clause.

4. Be sure you know the differences between system and object privileges with respect to cascading effects of revoking those privileges.

5. Make sure you understand all the points I made about special conditions with respect to granting and revoking object privileges.

Exercises

1. **You want to grant user TIMOTHY the ability to update data in the EMP table as well as the ability to administer that access for others. Which of the following commands would you issue?**

   A. grant update to timothy;

   B. grant update on emp to timothy;

   C. grant update on emp to timothy with grant option;

   D. grant update on emp to timothy with admin option;

2. **User REED can administer the create session privilege. User REED grants the same create session privilege to MANN using the with admin option clause. MANN then grants the privilege to SNOW. REED discovers MANN issued the privilege to SNOW and revokes the privilege from MANN. Who can connect to Oracle?**

   A. REED only

   B. SNOW and MANN only

   C. REED, MANN, and SNOW

   D. REED and SNOW only

3. User SNOW owns table SALES, and she grants `delete` privileges to user REED using the `with grant option` clause. REED then grants `delete` privileges on SALES to MANN. SNOW discovers MANN has the privilege and revokes it from REED. Which of the following users can delete data from the SALES table?

   A. MANN only

   B. SNOW only

   C. SNOW and MANN only

   D. REED and MANN only

4. When this user has the privilege, everyone has the privilege:
   _____

5. When revoking the references privilege after a user has built a foreign key constraint using that privilege, you must include this clause (two words):
   _____

Answer Key
1. C. 2. D. 3. B. 4. Public. 5. `cascade constraints`

Using Roles to Manage Database Access

When your databases has lots of tables, object privileges can become unwieldy and hard to manage. You can simplify the management of privileges with the use of a database object called a *role*. A role acts in two capacities in the database. First, the role can act as a focal point for grouping the privileges to execute certain tasks. Second, the role can act as a "virtual user" of a database, to which all the object privileges required to execute a certain job function can be granted, such as data entry, manager review, batch processing, and so on. Figure 8-1 illustrates how to manage privileges with roles. In order to use roles, your privilege-management process must consist of four steps:

1. You must logically group certain types of users together according to the privileges they need to do their jobs.

2. You must define a role (or roles) for each user type.

3. You must grant the appropriate privileges to each of the roles.

4. You can then grant the roles to specific users of each type.

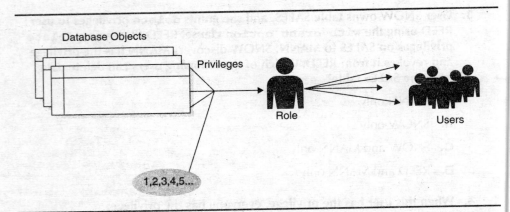

FIGURE 8-1. *Managing privileges with roles*

Creating Roles to Correspond to User Types

Step 1 is a process that can happen outside the database. A role mechanism can be used to provide authorization. A single person or a group of people can be granted a role or a group of roles. One role can be granted in turn to other roles. By defining different types of roles, administrators can manage access privileges much more easily. You simply sit down and think to yourself, how many different purposes will users be accessing this application for? Once this step is complete, you can create the different roles required to manage the privileges needed for each job function. Let's say people using the EMP table have two different job roles: those who can query the table and those who can add records to the table. The next step is to create roles that correspond to each activity. This architecture of using roles as a middle layer for granting privileges greatly simplifies administration of user privileges. Let's take a look at how to create the appropriate roles:

```
SQL> connect scott/tiger
Connected.
SQL> create role rpt_writer;
Role created.
SQL> create role data_changer;
Role created.
```

TIP
You must have the CREATE ROLE system privilege to create a role.

Modifying Roles

Let's say that after we create our roles, we realize that changing records in the EMP table is serious business. To create an added safeguard against someone making a change to the EMP table in error, the DATA_CHANGER role can be altered to require a password by using the `alter role identified by` statement. Anyone wanting to modify data in EMP with the privileges given via the DATA_CHANGER role must first supply a password. Code for altering the role is shown in the following example:

```
SQL> alter role data_changer
  2  identified by highly#secure;
Role altered.
```

Granting Privileges to Roles

The next step is to grant object privileges to roles. You can accomplish this task using the same command as you would use to grant privileges directly to users—the `grant` command. The following code block demonstrates how to grant privileges to both our roles:

```
SQL> grant select on emp to rpt_writer;
Grant succeeded.
SQL> grant update, delete, insert on emp to data_changer;
Grant succeeded.
```

TIP
Revoking privileges from roles works the same way as it does for users. System privileges are granted and revoked with roles in the exact same way they are with users as well.

Granting Roles to Users

Once a role is created and privileges are granted to it, the role can then be granted to users. This step is accomplished with the `grant` command. Let's see an example of how this is done:

```
SQL> grant rpt_writer to turner;
Grant succeeded.
SQL> grant data_changer to ford;
Grant succeeded.
```

TIP
*If a role already granted to a user is later granted
another privilege, that additional privilege is
available to the user immediately. The same
statement can be made for privileges revoked from
roles already granted to users, too.*

Defining User Default Roles

Now user TURNER can execute all the privileges given to him via the RPT_WRITER
role, and user FORD can do the same with the privileges given from
DATA_CHANGER. Or can he? Recall that we specified that DATA_CHANGER
requires a password in order for the grantee to utilize its privileges. Let's make a
little change to FORD's user ID so that this status will take effect:

```
SQL> alter user ford default role none;
User altered.
```

TIP
You can use the following keywords in the `alter`
`user default role` *command to define default
roles for users:* `all, all except rolename,` *and*
`none.` *Note that users usually cannot issue* `alter`
`user default role` *themselves to change their
default roles—only a privileged user such as the
DBA can do it for them.*

By default, when a role is granted to a user, that role becomes a default role for
the user. We changed FORD's default role with the preceding code so that FORD
has no role. Let's see how this factor affects things when FORD tries to modify the
contents of the EMP table:

```
SQL> connect ford/henry
Connected.
SQL> insert into scott.emp (empno, ename, job)
  2  values (1234, 'SMITHERS','MANAGER');
insert into scott.emp (empno, ename, job)
            *
ERROR at line 1:
ORA-00942: table or view does not exist
```

TIP
Roles can be granted to other roles!

Enabling the Current Role

FORD knows he is supposed to be able to accomplish this task because he has the DATA_CHANGER role. Then he remembers that this role has a password on it. FORD can use the `set role` command to enable the DATA_CHANGER role in the following way:

```
SQL> set role data_changer identified by highly#secure;
Role set.
```

Now FORD can make the change he needs to make:

```
SQL> insert into scott.emp (empno, ename, job)
  2  values (1234, 'SMITHERS','MANAGER');
1 row created.
```

TIP
You must already have been granted the roles that you name in the SET ROLE statement. Also, you can disable all roles with the SET ROLE NONE statement.

Revoking and Dropping Roles

Finally, a role can be revoked by the role's owner or by a privileged administrative user using the `revoke` statement, much like revoking privileges:

```
SQL> connect scott/tiger
Connected.
SQL> revoke rpt_writer from turner;
Revoke succeeded.
SQL> revoke data_changer from ford;
Revoke succeeded.
```

Roles can be deleted from the database using the `drop role` statement. When a role is dropped, the associated privileges are revoked from the users granted the role. The following code block shows how to eliminate roles from Oracle:

```
SQL> connect scott/tiger
Connected.
SQL> drop role rpt_writer;
Role dropped.
SQL> drop role data_changer;
Role dropped.
```

Some Predefined Roles Available in Oracle

Some special roles are available to the users of a database. The roles available at database creation from Oracle7 onward include the CONNECT, RESOURCE, DBA, EXP_FULL_DATABASE, and IMP_FULL_DATABASE roles. Additionally, Oracle adds the roles DELETE_CATALOG_ROLE, EXECUTE_CATALOG_ROLE, and SELECT_CATALOG_ROLE to the mix, and much more. The predefined roles you might need to know about for OCP Exam 1 include the following:

- **CONNECT** Enables the user extensive development ability within his or her own user schema, including the ability to perform `create table`, `create cluster`, `create session`, `create view`, `create sequence`, and more. The privileges associated with this role are platform specific; therefore, the role can contain a different number of privileges, but typically the role never enables the creation of stored procedures.

- **RESOURCE** Enables the user moderate development ability within his or her own user schema, such as the ability to execute `create table`, `create cluster`, `create trigger`, and `create procedure`. The privileges associated with this role are platform specific; therefore, the role can contain a different number of privileges.

- **DBA** Enables the user to administer and use all system privileges.

Dictionary Views for Roles

The following views are available in the Oracle data dictionary pertaining to role information:

- **USER_ROLE_PRIVS** Identifies the roles granted to you

- **ROLE_ROLE_PRIVS** Identifies the roles granted to other roles in the database

- **ROLE_TAB_PRIVS** Identifies object privileges granted to roles

- ■ **ROLE_SYS_PRIVS** Identifies system privileges granted to roles
- ■ **SESSION_ROLES** Identifies roles available to the current session

For Review

1. Know what a role is and how it can assist you in managing privileges in Oracle. Understand the four steps required for managing privileges when you want to do so with roles.

2. Know how to use the `create role`, `alter role identified by`, `alter user default role`, `set role`, and `drop role` commands. Also, understand how to use the `grant` and `revoke` commands with respect to roles.

3. When a role has an associated password, you shouldn't grant it to users as a default role. By granting a role to a user as a non-default role, you force the grantee to enable the role using the `set role identified by` command. This extra step enforces a higher level of security on that user when the user wants to employ the privileges granted by the role.

4. Know the available dictionary views that contain information about roles.

Exercises

1. **User THOMAS has been granted the role SALES_ANALYZER, which gives her to access the SALES table for writing reports. However, when she tries to do so, she gets the following error:**

```
ORA-00942: table or view does not exist.
```

   Which of the following statements can she issue in order to resolve the problem?

   A. `alter user thomas default role sales_analyzer;`

   B. `set role sales_analyzer;`

   C. `grant select on sales to sales_analyzer;`

   D. `grant sales_analyzer to thomas;`

2. **User FRANKLIN owns the PROFITS table and the SALES_ANALYZER role, which has already been granted to DAVIS. FRANKLIN grants `select` privileges on PROFITS to the SALES_ANALYZER role. At what point will that privilege be made available to DAVIS?**

   A. The next time DAVIS logs into Oracle

   B. The next time FRANKLIN grants the SALES_ANALYZER role to DAVIS

    C. The next time FRANKLIN grants the privilege to SALES_ANALYZER

    D. Immediately after the privilege is granted to SALES_ANALYZER

3. **You are defining default roles for a user. Under which of the following circumstances should a role not be made a default role for a user?**

    A. When the role has object privileges granted to it

    B. When the role has system privileges granted to it

    C. When the role has a password assigned to it

    D. When the role has other roles assigned to it

4. **This dictionary view can identify the roles available to you in your current connection to Oracle:** _____

Answer Key
1. B. 2. D. 3. C. 4. SESSION_ROLES.

Chapter Summary

This chapter has covered a great deal of information you need to know about user access control in the Oracle database. We started the chapter by covering how to create users in Oracle. We then discussed privileges, covering what they are and how to use them to control access to information in the Oracle database. You learned that access to everything in the database is controlled by a privilege. We also discussed how to use roles to manage privileges more efficiently.

Two-Minute Drill

■ The Oracle database security model consists of two parts: limiting user access with password authentication and controlling object use with privileges.

■ Available privileges in Oracle include system privileges, for maintaining database objects, and object privileges, for accessing and manipulating data in database objects.

- Changing a password can be performed by a user with the `alter user identified by` statement.

- Granting system and object privileges is accomplished with the `grant` command.

- Taking away system and object privileges is accomplished with the `revoke` command.

- Creating a synonym is accomplished with the `create public synonym` command.

Fill-in-the-Blank Questions

1. This type of database object can act as an intermediary for consolidating privileges granted to users around job functions:
   _____

2. This command is used for enabling a default role in Oracle:
   _____

3. This clause is used for defining a password for a user:
   _____

4. This command is used for giving privileges to users:
   _____

5. This command is used for taking privileges away from users:
   _____

Chapter Questions

1. You are granting privileges on your table to another user. Which object privilege enables the user to create his or her own table with a foreign key on a column in your table?

   A. references

   B. index

   C. select

   D. delete

2. Which of the following statements are true about roles? (Choose three.)

   A. Roles can be granted to other roles.

   B. Privileges can be granted to roles.

   C. Roles can be granted to users.

   D. Roles can be granted to synonyms.

3. **You want to connect to the Oracle database. Which of the following choices identifies a method that will _not_ be required in order for you to connect?**

   A. Granting `create session` privilege

   B. Granting the CONNECT role

   C. Issuing the `create user` statement

   D. Granting the `create table` privilege

4. **A user named JACOB is configured in Oracle so that he can create some tables. Then user ESAU is configured to insert some data into JACOB's tables with administrative ability. JACOB then revokes all insert privileges from ESAU. Which of the following choices identifies an event that will happen when the DBA revokes ESAU's `insert` privilege?**

   A. ESAU will be able to insert data into JACOB's tables.

   B. ESAU's records added to JACOB's tables will be removed

   C. Any users ESAU granted insert access to JACOB's tables will no longer have those privileges.

   D. Any users ESAU granted insert access to JACOB's tables will continue to have those privileges.

5. **You are attempting to grant the `create table` privilege to user TABLEMAKER with administrative ability. Which of the following choices identifies the proper `with` clause you will use for this purpose?**

   A. `with admin option`

   B. `with grant option`

   C. `with check option`

   D. `with summary as`

Fill-in-the-Blank Answers

1. Role

2. `set role`

3. `identified by`

4. `grant`

5. `revoke`

Answers to Chapter Questions

1. A. `references`

Explanation   The `references` privilege gives the user the ability to refer back to your table in order to link to it via a foreign key from his or her table to yours. Choice B is incorrect because the `index` privilege enables the user to create an index on a table, whereas choice C is incorrect because the `select` privilege enables the user to query data in your table. Finally, choice D is incorrect because the `insert` privilege is only required for enabling the user to insert data into your table.

2. A, B, and C.

Explanation   Choice D is the only option not available to managing roles. Roles cannot be granted to synonyms. Refer to the discussion of roles and privileges in this chapter.

3. D. Granting the `create table` privilege

Explanation   You do not need the `create table` privilege in order to connect to the Oracle database. Choice A is incorrect because the `create session` privilege is required for connecting to Oracle. Choice B is incorrect because the CONNECT role has the `create session` privilege granted to it to enable users to connect to Oracle. Choice C is incorrect because you have to create the user first before that user can connect to Oracle.

4. C. Any users ESAU granted insert access to JACOB's tables will no longer have those privileges.

Explanation   Cascading effects for revoking object privileges occur in Oracle. If a user who was granted administrative abilities over an object privilege grants that privileges to others, and that user then has the object privilege revoked, then all users to whom that user granted the object privilege will also lose the privilege. Choice A is incorrect because ESAU will no longer have insert access to JACOB's tables. Choice B is incorrect because any records ESAU added to JACOB's tables will be removed. Choice D is incorrect because it is the logical opposite of the correct answer, choice C.

5. A. `with admin option`

Explanation   The `with admin option` clause is used for granting system privileges like create table with administrative ability. The `with grant option` clause is used for granting object privileges like `insert` with administrative ability, making choice B incorrect. Choice C is incorrect because the `with check option` is used for enforcing heightened security on changing data in tables via views on those tables. Finally, choice D is incorrect because the `with summary as` clause is used for eliminating redundancy in subqueries.

PART
II

OCP Oracle9i DBA
Practice Exams

CHAPTER
9

OCP Exam 1:
Introduction to SQL

CP Exam 1 in the Oracle DBA track covers concepts and practices involving the use of SQL commands. To pass this exam, you need to demonstrate an understanding of the basic SQL constructs available in Oracle, including built-in functions. You should also understand the basic concepts of an Oracle relational database management system (RDBMS). In more recent editions of OCP Exam 1, the focus has shifted to a complete understanding of use of the SQL programming language. In addition, new features introduced in Oracle9i are tested, so you should also be sure you understand these new features.

Practice Exam 1

1. **You are formulating a SQL statement to retrieve data from Oracle. Which of the following SQL statements is invalid?**

   A. `select NAME, JERSEY_NO where Jersey_No = 6;`

   B. `select NAME, JERSEY_NO from PLAYERS;`

   C. `select * from PLAYERS where JERSEY_NO = 6;`

   D. `select JERSEY_NO from PLAYERS;`

2. **You are processing some data changes in your SQL*Plus session as part of one transaction. Which of the following choices does not typically indicate the end of a transaction?**

   A. Issuing an `update` statement

   B. Issuing a `commit` statement

   C. Issuing a `rollback` statement

   D. Ending your session

3. **You have just removed 1,700 rows from a table. In order to save the changes you've made to the database, which of the following statements is used?**

   A. `savepoint`

   B. `commit`

   C. `rollback`

   D. `set transaction`

4. **To identify the columns that are indexed exclusively as the result of their inclusion in a constraint, which of the following dictionary views is appropriate?**

   A. USER_INDEXES

   B. USER_TAB_COLUMNS

   C. USER_COLUMNS

   D. USER_CONS_COLUMNS

5. **You are creating some tables in your database as part of the logical data model. Which of the following constraints can only be created as a column constraint (that is, not as a table constraint) either when you create or alter the table?**

   A. Unique

   B. Foreign key

   C. Check

   D. Not NULL

6. **You have a table with three associated indexes, two triggers, two references to that table from other tables, and a view. You issue the `drop table cascade constraints` statement. Which of the following objects will still remain after the statement is issued?**

   A. The triggers

   B. The indexes

   C. The foreign keys in the other tables

   D. The view

7. **You are using SQL operations in Oracle. All of the following DATE functions return a DATE datatype except one. Which one is it?**

   A. NEW_TIME

   B. LAST_DAY

   C. ADD_MONTHS

   D. MONTHS_BETWEEN

8. You issue a `select` statement on the BANK_ACCT table containing the `order by` clause. Which of the following uses of the `order by` clause would produce an error?

   A. `order by acctno DESC;`

   B. `order by 1;`

   C. `order by sqrt(1);`

   D. `order by acctno ASC;`

9. You execute the query `select 5 + 4 from DUAL`. You have never inserted data into the DUAL table before. Which of the following statements best describes the DUAL table?

   A. Dictionary view containing two schema names

   B. Table with one column and one row used in various operations

   C. Dictionary view containing two index names

   D. Table with two columns and no rows used in various operations

10. You issue the following statement:

    ```
    SELECT DECODE(ACCTNO, 123456, 'CLOSED', 654321, 'SEIZED',
    590395, 'TRANSFER','ACTIVE') FROM BANK_ACCT;
    ```

    If the value for ACCTNO is 503952, what information will this statement display?

    A. ACTIVE

    B. TRANSFER

    C. SEIZED

    D. CLOSED

11. You are entering several dozen rows of data into the BANK_ACCT table. Which of the following statements enables you to execute the same statement again and again, entering different values for variables at statement runtime?

    A. `insert into BANK_ACCT (ACCTNO, NAME) VALUES (123456,'SMITH');`

    B. `insert into BANK_ACCT (ACCTNO, NAME) VALUES (VAR1, VAR2);`

    C. insert into BANK_ACCT (ACCTNO, NAME) VALUES (&VAR1, '&VAR2');

    D. insert into BANK_ACCT (select ACCTNO, NAME from EMP_BANK_ACCTS);

12. **You execute the following SQL statement: select ADD_MONTHS ('28-APR-97',120) from DUAL. What will Oracle return?**

    A. 28-APR-03

    B. 28-APR-07

    C. 28-APR-13

    D. 28-APR-17

13. **On Monday, June 26, 2037, at 10:30 P.M., you issue the following statement against an Oracle database:**

```
ALTER SESSION SET NLS_DATE_FORMAT =
'DAY MONTH DD, YYYY: HH:MIAM';
```

    Then you issue the following statement:

```
SELECT SYSDATE FROM DUAL;
```

    What will Oracle return?

    A. 26-JUN-37

    B. June 26, 2037, 22:30

    C. 26-JUN-2037

    D. MONDAY JUNE 26, 2037: 10:30PM

14. **You want to join the data from two tables, A and B, into one result set and display that set in your session. Tables A and B have a common column, called C in both tables. Which of the following choices correctly displays the where clause you should use if you want to see the data in table A where the value in column C equals 5, even when no corresponding value appears in table B?**

    A. where A.C = 5 AND A.C = B.C;

    B. where A.C = 5 AND A.C = B.C (+);

    C. where A.C = 5 AND A.C (+) = B.C(+);

    D. where A.C = 5;

15. **Each of the following statements is true about associated columns and datatypes except one. Which of the following statements is not true?**

    A. A column designed to hold data in a table must be declared with a datatype large enough to hold values for that column.

    B. When creating composite primary keys, the datatypes in all columns within the primary key must be the same datatype.

    C. When creating referential integrity constraints between two tables, the datatype of the referenced column in the parent table must be identical to the referencing column in the child.

    D. When creating record variables designed to hold a row's worth of data, each element's datatype in the record must be large enough to hold the associated column from the table.

16. **You have a group of values from a column in a table, and you would like to perform a group operation on them. Each of the following functions operates on data from all rows as a group except for which of the following choices?**

    A. avg ( )

    B. sqrt ( )

    C. count ( )

    D. stddev ( )

17. **You have a situation where you need to use the nvl ( ) function. All the following statements about the nvl ( ) function are true except one. Which is it?**

    A. nvl ( ) returns the second value passed if the first value is NULL.

    B. nvl ( ) handles values of many different datatypes.

    C. nvl ( ) returns NULL if the first value is not equal to the second.

    D. Both the values passed for nvl ( ) must be the same datatype.

18. **You create a sequence with the following statement:**

```
CREATE SEQUENCE MY_SEQ
START WITH 394
INCREMENT BY 12
NOMINVALUE
NOMAXVALUE
NOCACHE
NOCYCLE;
```

A user issues SQL statements to obtain NEXTVAL three times, and then issues SQL statements to obtain CURRVAL four times. What is the current value of the sequence?

- **A.** 406
- **B.** 418
- **C.** 430
- **D.** 442

19. Table EMP has 17,394,430 rows in it. You issue a delete from EMP statement, followed by a commit. Then you issue a select count(*) to find out how many rows are in the table. Several minutes later, Oracle returns zero. Why did it take so long for Oracle to obtain this information?

- **A.** The table was not empty.
- **B.** The high-water mark was not reset.
- **C.** Oracle always performs slowly after a commit is issued.
- **D.** The table data did not exist to be counted anymore.

20. After creating a view, you realize that several columns were left out. Which of the following statements should you issue in order to add some columns to your view?

- **A.** alter view
- **B.** create or replace view
- **C.** insert into view
- **D.** create view

21. You are testing several SQL statements for accuracy and usefulness. A SQL statement will result in a Cartesian product as the result of which of the following items?

- **A.** A join statement without a where clause
- **B.** The result of the sum ( ) operation
- **C.** select * from DUAL
- **D.** The result of the avg ( ) operation

22. **In order to set your SQL*Plus session so that your NLS_DATE_FORMAT information is altered in a specific way every time you log into Oracle, what method should you use?**

    A. Setting preferences in the appropriate menu option

    B. Creating an appropriate `login.sql` file

    C. Issuing the `alter user` statement

    D. Issuing the `alter table` statement

23. **The EMP_SALARY table has two columns: EMP_USER and SALARY. EMP_USER is set to be the same as the Oracle username. To allow user MARTHA, the salary administrator, to see her own salary only, you create a view with the following statement:**

    ```
    CREATE VIEW EMP_SAL_VW
    AS SELECT EMP_USER, SALARY
    FROM EMP_SALARY
    WHERE EMP_USER = 'MARTHA';
    ```

    Later, you decide to deploy this view to other users. Which of the following choices identifies a revision of this view that would prevent users from seeing any salary information other than their own?

    A. ```
    create or replace view emp_sal_vw as select
    emp_user,_salary from emp_salary where emp_user <>
    user;
    ```

    B. ```
    create or replace view emp_sal_vw as select
    emp_user,_salary from emp_salary where emp_user =
    user;
    ```

    C. ```
    create or replace view emp_sal_vw as select
    emp_user,_salary from emp_salary where emp_user <>
    'MARTHA';
    ```

    D. ```
    create or replace view emp_sal_vw as select
    emp_user,_salary from emp_salary where emp_user in
    (select emp_user from emp_salary where emp_user <>
    'MARTHA');
    ```

24. **You are trying to store data in an Oracle table. All of the following scalar datatypes can be stored in an Oracle database except one. Which is it?**

    A. CHAR

    B. RAW

    C. DATE

    D. INTEGER

25. **You are performing some conversion operations in your SQL*Plus session. To convert a date value into a text string, you should use which of the following conversion functions?**

    A. CONVERT

    B. TO_CHAR

    C. TO_NUMBER

    D. TO_DATE

26. **Your attempt to read the trigger code stored in the Oracle data dictionary view ALL_TRIGGERS has encountered a problem. The contents of the TRIGGER_BODY column appear to be getting cut off at the end. In order to resolve this problem, which of the following measures is appropriate?**

    A. Grant appropriate `select` privileges on ALL_TRIGGERS to yourself.

    B. Increase your memory allocation limit with the `alter user` statement.

    C. Use the `set` command to allow for larger LONG column values.

    D. Drop and recreate the ALL_TRIGGERS view.

27. **You issue the following `update` statement against the Oracle database:**

```
UPDATE BANK_ACCT SET NAME = 'SHAW';
```

    Which records will be updated in that table?

    A. The first record only

    B. All records

    C. The last record only

    D. None of the records

28. **You create a table but then subsequently realize you need a few new columns. To add those columns later, you should issue which of the following statements?**

    A. `create or replace table`

    B. `alter table`

    C. `create table`

    D. `truncate table`

29. You are busy creating your tables based on a logical data model. Which of the following constraints requires the `references` privilege in order to be created?

    A. `unique`

    B. `foreign key`

    C. `check`

    D. `not NULL`

30. The INVENTORY table has three columns: UPC_CODE, UNITS, and DELIV_DATE. The primary key is UPC_CODE. You want to add new records daily through a view. The view will be created using the following code:

    ```
    CREATE VIEW DAY_INVENTORY_VW
    AS SELECT UPC_CODE, UNITS, DELIV_DATE
    FROM INVENTORY
    WHERE DELIV_DATE = SYSDATE
    ORDER BY UPC_CODE;
    ```

    What happens when you try to create the previous view?

    A. Oracle returns an error stating that the `order by` clause is not permitted on views.

    B. Oracle returns an error stating that the `with check option` clause is required for creating this view.

    C. Oracle returns an error stating that the `select` statement must be enclosed in parentheses.

    D. Oracle creates the view successfully.

31. You need to search for text data in a column, but you only remember part of the string. Which of the following SQL operations enables the use of wildcard comparisons?

    A. `in`

    B. `exists`

    C. `between`

    D. `like`

32. You have a script you plan to run using SQL*Plus that contains one SQL statement that inserts data into one table. Which of the following options is the easiest way for this script to enable you to specify values for

variables once in the script in a way where no user interaction is required at the SQL*Plus prompt?

A. Use define to capture values.

B. Use accept to capture values for each run.

C. Use & to specify values at runtime for the statement.

D. Use hard-coded values in the statement.

33. You join data from two tables, EXPNS and EMP, into one result set and display that set in your session. The tables have a common column called EMPID. Which of the following choices correctly displays the where clause you would use if you wanted to see the data in table EMP where the value in column EMPID equals 39284, but only when a corresponding value appears in table EXPNS?

A. where EMP.EMPID = 39284 AND EMP.EMPID = EXPNS.EMPID;

B. where EMP.EMPID = 39284 (+) AND EMP.EMPID = EXPNS.EMPID;

C. where EMP.EMPID = EXPNS.EMPID;

D. where EMP.EMPID = 39284 AND EMP.EMPID = EXPNS.EMPID (+);

34. Review the following transcript of a SQL*Plus session:

```
INSERT INTO INVENTORY (UPC_CODE, PRODUCT )
VALUES (503949353,'HAZELNUT COFFEE');
INSERT INTO INVENTORY (UPC_CODE, PRODUCT)
VALUES (593923506,'SKIM MILK');
INSERT INTO INVENTORY (UPC_CODE, PRODUCT)
VALUES (402392340,'CANDY BAR');
SAVEPOINT INV1;
UPDATE INVENTORY SET UPC_CODE = 50393950
WHERE UPC_CODE = 402392340;
UPDATE INVENTORY SET UPC_CODE = 4104930504
WHERE UPC_CODE = 402392340;
COMMIT;
UPDATE INVENTORY SET PRODUCT = (
SELECT PRODUCT FROM INVENTORY
WHERE UPC_CODE = 50393950)
WHERE UPC_CODE = 593923506;
ROLLBACK;
```

Which of the following UPC codes will not have records in the INVENTORY table as a result of this series of operations?

A. 593923506

B. 503949353

C. 4104930504

D. 50393950

35. You are removing a table from the Oracle database. When you issue the `drop table` command to remove the table, what happens to any of the views that may have an object dependency on that table?

    A. The views are dropped automatically along with the table.

    B. Views in the same schema as the table are dropped automatically, but views outside that schema are not dropped.

    C. Views in the same database as the table are dropped automatically, but views that access the table via database link are not dropped.

    D. Views with object dependencies on the table being dropped are rendered invalid automatically, but are not dropped.

36. You want to join data from four tables into one result set and display that set in your session. Table A has a column in common with table B, table B with table C, and table C with table D. You want to further restrict data returned from the tables by only returning data where values in the common column shared by A and B equal 5. How many conditions should you have in the `where` clause of your `select` statement?

    A. Two

    B. Three

    C. Four

    D. Five

37. You are attempting to explain the Oracle security model for an Oracle database to the new security administrator. What are two components of the Oracle database security model?

    A. Password authentication and granting privileges

    B. Password authentication and creating database objects

    C. Creating database objects and creating users

    D. Creating users and password authentication

38. You have a script you plan to run using SQL*Plus that contains several SQL statements that manage milk inventory in several different tables based on various bits of information. You want the output to go into a file for review later. Which command should you use?

    A. `prompt`

    B. `echo`

    C. `spool`

    D. `define`

39. You have a table called TEST_SCORE that stores test results by student personal ID number, test location, and date the test was taken. Tests given in various locations throughout the country are stored in this table. A student is not allowed to take a test for 30 days after failing it the first time, and a check in the application prevents the student from taking a test twice in 30 days at the same location. Recently, it has come to everyone's attention that students are able to circumvent the 30-day rule by taking a test in a different location. Which of the following SQL statements would be useful for identifying the students who have done so?

    A. `select A.STUDENT_ID, A.LOCATION, B.LOCATION from TEST_SCORE A, TEST_SCORE B where A.STUDENT_ID = B.STUDENT_ID AND A.LOCATION = B.LOCATION AND trunc(A.TEST_DATE)+30 <= trunc(B.TEST_DATE) AND trunc(A.TEST_DATE)-30 >= trunc(B.TEST_DATE);`

    B. `select A.STUDENT_ID, A.LOCATION, B.LOCATION from TEST_SCORE A, TEST_SCORE B where A.STUDENT_ID = B.STUDENT_ID AND A.LOCATION <> B.LOCATION AND trunc(A.TEST_DATE)+30 >= trunc(B.TEST_DATE) AND trunc(A.TEST_DATE)-30 <= trunc(B.TEST_DATE);`

    C. `select A.STUDENT_ID, A.LOCATION, B.LOCATION from TEST_SCORE A, TEST_SCORE B where A.STUDENT_ID = B.STUDENT_ID AND A.LOCATION = B.LOCATION AND trunc(A.TEST_DATE)+30 >= trunc(B.TEST_DATE) AND trunc(A.TEST_DATE)-30 <= trunc(B.TEST_DATE);`

    D. `select A.STUDENT_ID, A.LOCATION, B.LOCATION from TEST_SCORE A, TEST_SCORE B where A.STUDENT_ID = B.STUDENT_ID AND A.LOCATION <> B.LOCATION AND trunc(A.TEST_DATE)+30 <= trunc(B.TEST_DATE) AND trunc(A.TEST_DATE)-30 >= trunc(B.TEST_DATE);`

40. In an expense application, you are searching for employee information in the EMPLOYEE table corresponding to an invoice number you have. The INVOICE table contains EMPID, the primary key for EMPLOYEE. Which of the following options is appropriate for obtaining data from EMPLOYEE using your invoice number?

    A. `select * from EMPLOYEE where empid = &empid;`

    B. `select * from EMPLOYEE where empid = 69494;`

    C. `select * from EMPLOYEE where empid = (select empid from invoice where invoice_no = 4399485);`

    D. `select * from EMPLOYEE;`

41. Which of the following uses does not describe an appropriate use of the having clause?

    A. To put returned data into sorted order

    B. To exclude certain data groups based on known criteria

    C. To include certain data groups based on unknown criteria

    D. To include certain data groups based on known criteria

42. You are managing data access for an application with 163 tables and 10,000 users. Which of the following objects would assist in managing access in this application by grouping privileges into an object that can be granted to users at once?

    A. Sequences

    B. Tables

    C. Indexes

    D. Roles

43. After logging onto Oracle the first time to access table EMP, user SNOW is told to change his password. Which of the following statements enables him to do so?

    A. `alter user`

    B. `alter table`

    C. `alter role`

    D. `alter index`

44. User SNOW executes the following statement: `select * from EMP`. This statement executes successfully, and SNOW can see the output. User REED owns table EMP. What object is required in order for this scenario to happen?

A. User SNOW needs the role to view table EMP.

B. User SNOW needs the privileges to view table EMP.

C. User SNOW needs a synonym for table EMP.

D. User SNOW needs the password for table EMP.

45. You issue the following statement in Oracle:

```
SELECT * FROM EMP WHERE DEPT IN
(SELECT DEPT FROM VALID_DEPTS
WHERE DEPT_HEAD = 'SALLY'
ORDER BY DEPT);
```

Which of the following choices best indicates how Oracle will respond to this SQL statement?

A. Oracle returns the data selected.

B. Oracle returns data from EMP but not VALID_DEPTS.

C. Oracle returns data from VALID_DEPTS but not EMP.

D. Oracle returns an error.

46. You are coding SQL statements in SQL*Plus. Which of the following is a valid SQL statement?

A. `select nvl(sqrt(59483)) from dual;`

B. `select to_char(nvl(sqrt(59483), 0)) from dual;`

C. `select to_char(nvl(sqrt(59483), 'VALID')) from dual;`

D. `select (to_char(nvl(sqrt(59483), '0')) from dual;`

47. The following output is from a SQL*Plus session:

```
select PLAY_NAME||', ' || AUTHOR play_table from PLAYS;
My Plays and Authors
-----------------------------------
Midsummer Night's Dream, SHAKESPEARE
Waiting For Godot, BECKETT
The Glass Menagerie, WILLIAMS
```

Which of the following SQL*Plus commands produced it?

A. `column PLAY_TABLE alias "My Plays and Authors"`

B. `column PLAY_TABLE format a12`

C. `column PLAY_TABLE heading "My Plays and Authors"`

D. `column PLAY_TABLE as "My Plays and Authors"`

48. **You create a view with the following statement:**

```
CREATE VIEW BASEBALL_TEAM_VW
AS SELECT B.JERSEY_NUM, B.POSITION, B.NAME
FROM BASEBALL_TEAM B
WHERE B.NAME = (SELECT UNAME FROM MY_USERS);
```

The contents of the MY_USERS table are listed as follows:

```
UNAME
-----
JONES
SMITH
FRANK
JENNY
```

Which of the following players will not be listed when user JONES attempts to query the view?

A. JONES

B. SMITH

C. BABS

D. JENNY

49. **Your attempt to read the view-creation code stored in the Oracle data dictionary has encountered a problem. The view code appears to be getting cut off at the end. In order to resolve this problem, which of the following measures is appropriate?**

A. Increase the size of the dictionary view.

B. Increase your user view allotment with the `alter user` statement.

C. Use the `set long` statement.

D. Use the `set NLS_DATE_FORMAT` statement.

50. Inspect the following SQL statement:

```
SELECT FARM_NAME, COW_NAME,
COUNT(CARTON) AS NUMBER_OF_CARTONS
FROM COW_MILK
GROUP BY COW_NAME;
```

Which of the following choices contains the line with the error?

A. select FARM_NAME, COW_NAME,

B. count(CARTON) as NUMBER_OF_CARTONS

C. from COW_MILK

D. group by COW_NAME;

E. This statement has no errors.

51. Inspect the following SQL statement:

```
SELECT COW_NAME,
  MOD(CARTON, FILL_STATUS)
FROM COW_MILK
GROUP BY COW_NAME;
```

Which of the following lines contains an error?

A. select COW_NAME,

B. mod(CARTON, FILL_STATUS)

C. from COW_MILK

D. group by COW_NAME;

E. This statement has no errors.

52. You are writing queries against an Oracle database. Which of the following queries takes advantage of an inline view?

A. select * from EMP_VW where EMPID = (select EMPID from INVOICE where INV_NUM = 5506934);

B. select A.LASTNAME, B.DEPT_NO from EMP A, (select EMPID, DEPT_NO from DEPT) B where A.EMPID = B.EMPID;

C. select * from EMP where EMPID IN (select EMPID from INVOICE where INV_NUM > 23);

D. select 'select * from EMP_VW where EMPID is not NULL;' from USER_TABLES;

53. You have several indexes on a table that you want to remove. You want to avoid removing the indexes associated with constraints, however. Each of the following statements will remove the index associated with a constraint except one. Which choice will not remove the index associated with a constraint?

    A. `drop index`

    B. `alter table drop primary key cascade`

    C. `alter table drop constraint`

    D. `drop table`

54. You are managing constraints on a table in Oracle. Which of the following choices correctly identifies the limitations on primary key constraints?

    A. Every primary key column value must be unique.

    B. No primary key column value can be NULL.

    C. Every primary key column value must be unique and none can be NULL.

    D. Every primary key column must be the same datatype as other columns in the table.

55. Review the following statement:

    ```
    CREATE TABLE FOOBAR
    ( MOO VARCHAR2(3),
      BOO NUMBER);
    ```

    This table contains 60,000,000 rows. You issue the following statement:

    ```
    SELECT MOO, BOO FROM FOOBAR WHERE MOO = 'ABC'
    ```

    This value is unique in column MOO, yet the query takes several minutes to resolve. Which of the following explanations is the best reason why?

    A. Oracle didn't use the existing primary key index.

    B. `select` statements that do not use views take longer to resolve.

    C. Table FOOBAR has no primary key, and therefore has no index on MOO.

    D. The table had been dropped and recreated.

56. You have created a table called EMP with a primary key called EMP_PK_01. In order to identify any objects that may be associated with

that table and primary key, what dictionary views and characteristics would you look for?

A. USER_SEQUENCES, sequences created at the same time

B. USER_TABLES, tables with the same number of columns

C. USER_IND_COLUMNS, constraints with the same name as the table

D. USER_INDEXES, indexes with the same name as the constraint

57. You are designing your database and attempting to determine the best method for indexing your tables. Which of the following is a main advantage of using bitmap indexes on a database?

A. To improve performance on columns with many unique values

B. To improve performance on columns with few unique values

C. To improve performance on columns with all unique values

D. To improve performance on sequences with all unique values

58. User HARRIS would like to change a row into the EMPLOYEE table that has three columns: EMPID, LASTNAME, and SALARY. The user would like to update salary data for employee number 59694. Which statement would work best?

A. `update employee set salary = 5000 where empid = 59694;`

B. `update employee set empid = 45939 where empid = 59694;`

C. `update employee set lastname = 'HARRIS' where empid = 59694;`

D. `update employee set salary = 5000 where lastname = 'HARRIS';`

59. You want to grant user TIMOTHY the ability to update data in the EMP table as well as the ability to administer that access for others. Which of the following commands would you issue?

A. `grant update to timothy;`

B. `grant update on emp to timothy;`

C. `grant update on emp to timothy with grant option;`

D. `grant update on emp to timothy with admin option;`

60. User REED can administer the `create session` privilege. User REED grants the same `create session` privilege to MANN using the appropriate clause. MANN then grants the privilege to SNOW. REED discovers MANN issued the privilege to SNOW and revokes the privilege from MANN. Who can connect to Oracle?

    A. REED only

    B. SNOW and MANN only

    C. REED, MANN, and SNOW

    D. REED and SNOW only

Practice Exam 2

1. You join data from two tables, COW_MILK (C) and CARTON_CRATE (C1), into one result set and display that set in your session. The tables have a common column, called CARTON_NUM in both tables. You want to see the data in table COW_MILK for BESS the cow and all corresponding information in CARTON_CRATE, but if no data is in CARTON_NUM, you don't want to see the data in COW_MILK. Which of the following choices correctly displays the `where` clause you should use?

   A. `where C.COW_NAME <> 'BESS' AND C.CARTON_NUM = C1.CARTON_NUM;`

   B. `where C.CARTON_NUM = C1.CARTON_NUM;`

   C. `where C.COW_NAME = 'BESS';`

   D. `where C.COW_NAME = 'BESS' AND C.CARTON_NUM = C1.CARTON_NUM;`

   E. `where C.COW_NAME = 'BESS' AND C.CARTON_NUM = C1.CARTON_NUM (+);`

2. You create a table with a primary key that is populated on `insert` with a value from a sequence, and then you add several hundred rows to the table. You then drop and recreate the sequence with the original sequence code. Suddenly, your users are getting constraint violations. Which of the following explanations is most likely the cause?

   A. Dropping a sequence also removes any associated primary keys.

   B. Any cached sequence values before the sequence was dropped are unusable.

   C. The table is read-only.

   D. The `insert` statements contain duplicate data due to the reset sequence.

3. You are developing SQL statements for the application. Which of the following SQL operations requires the use of a subquery?

   A. `in`

   B. `exists`

   C. `between`

   D. `like`

4. **Review the following transcript from a SQL*Plus session:**

```
SELECT CEIL(4093.505) FROM DUAL;
CEIL(4093.505)
--------------
          4094
```

   Which single-row function could not be used to produce 4093 from the number passed to the `ceil( )` function?

   A. `round( )`

   B. `trunc( )`

   C. `floor( )`

   D. `abs( )`

5. **You have a script you plan to run using SQL*Plus that contains several SQL statements that update banking information for one person in several different tables based on name. Because the script only changes information for one person, you want the ability to enter the name only once and have that information reused throughout the script. Which of the following options is the best way to accomplish this goal in such a way that you don't need to modify the script each time you want to run it?**

   A. Use `define` to capture the name value for each run.

   B. Use `accept` to capture the name value for each run.

   C. Use the & character to specify lexical substitution for names at runtime.

   D. Hard-code names in all SQL statements, and change the value for each run.

6. **You need to undo some data changes. Which of the following data changes cannot be undone using the `rollback` command?**

   A. `update`

   B. `truncate`

   C. `delete`

   D. `insert`

7. **You are developing some code to handle transaction processing. Each of the following items signifies the beginning of a new transaction except one. Which is it?**

   A. `savepoint`

   B. `set transaction`

C. Opening a new session

D. commit

8. **The following SQL statement is invalid:**

```
SELECT  PRODUCT, BRAND
WHERE UPC_CODE = '650-35365656-34453453454-45';
```

Which of the following choices indicates an area of change that would make this statement valid?

A. A select clause

B. A from clause

C. A where clause

D. An order by clause

9. **You are at the beginning of your current transaction and want to prevent your transaction from being able to change data in the database. To prevent any statements in the current transaction from altering database tables, which statement is used?**

A. set transaction

B. rollback

C. commit

D. savepoint

10. **Your application searches for data in the EMP table on the database on a nullable column indicating whether a person is male or female. To improve performance, you decide to index the table. The table contains more than 2,000,000 rows, and the column contains few NULL values. Which of the following indexes would be most appropriate?**

A. Nonunique B-tree index

B. Unique B-tree index

C. Bitmap index

D. Primary key index

11. **Your employee expense application stores information for invoices in one table. Each invoice can have several items, which are stored in another table. Each invoice may have one or more items, or none at all, but every item must correspond to one invoice. The relationship between the INVOICE table and INVOICE_ITEM table is best described as which of the following?**

A. Parent to child

B. Detail to master

C. Primary key to foreign key

D. Foreign key to primary key

12. **You issue the following statement:**

```
SELECT DECODE(UPC_CODE, 40390, 'DISCONTINUED', 65421, 'STALE',
90395, 'BROKEN', 'ACTIVE') FROM INVENTORY;
```

If the value for UPC_CODE is 20395, what information will this statement display?

A. DISCONTINUED

B. STALE

C. BROKEN

D. ACTIVE

13. **You are developing advanced queries for an Oracle database. Which of the following where clauses makes use of Oracle's capability to logically test values against a set of results returned without explicitly knowing what the set is before executing the query?**

A. where COL_A = 6

B. where COL_A in (6,7,8,9,10)

C. where COL_A between 6 AND 10

D. where COL_A in (select NUM from TAB_OF_NUMS)

14. **You are developing a multiple-row query to handle a complex and dynamic comparison operation in the Olympics. Two tables are involved. CONTESTANT lists all contestants from every country, and MEDALS lists every country and the number of gold, silver, and bronze medals they have. If a country has not received one of the three types of medals, a zero appears in the column. Thus, a query will always return data, even for countries that haven't won a medal. Which of the following queries shows only the contestants from countries with more than ten medalists of any type?**

A. select NAME from CONTESTANT C, MEDALS M where
   C.COUNTRY = M.COUNTRY;

B. select NAME from CONTESTANT where COUNTRY C in
(select COUNTRY from MEDALS M where C.COUNTRY =
M.COUNTY)

C. select NAME from CONTESTANT where COUNTRY C =
(select COUNTRY from MEDALS M where C.COUNTRY =
M.COUNTY)

D. select NAME from CONTESTANT where COUNTRY in
(select COUNTRY from MEDALS where NUM_GOLD +
NUM_SILVER + NUM_BRONZE > 10)

15. You issue the following query in a SQL*Plus session:

```
SELECT NAME, AGE, COUNTRY FROM CONTESTANT
WHERE (COUNTRY, AGE) IN ( SELECT COUNTRY, MIN(AGE)
FROM CONTESTANT GROUP BY COUNTRY);
```

Which of the following choices identifies both the type of query and the expected result from the Oracle database?

A. Single-row subquery, the youngest contestant from one country

B. Multiple-row subquery, the youngest contestant from all countries

C. Multiple-column subquery, the youngest contestant from all countries

D. Multiple-column subquery; Oracle will return an error because = should replace in

16. The contents of the CONTESTANTS table are listed as follows:

```
NAME                     AGE COUNTRY
----------------    -------------- ---------------
BERTRAND                 24 FRANCE
GONZALEZ                 29 SPAIN
HEINRICH                 22 GERMANY
TAN                      39 CHINA
SVENSKY                  30 RUSSIA
SOO                      21
```

You issue the following query against this table:

```
SELECT NAME FROM CONTESTANT
WHERE (COUNTRY, AGE) IN ( SELECT COUNTRY, MIN(AGE)
FROM CONTESTANT GROUP BY COUNTRY);
```

Which of the following contestants will not be listed among the output?

A. SOO

B. HEINRICH

C. BERTRAND

D. GONZALEZ

17. An object in Oracle contains many columns that are functionally dependent on the key column for that object. The object requires segments to be stored in areas of the database other than the data dictionary. The object in question is correctly referred to as which of the following objects?

A. Synonym

B. Table

C. Sequence

D. View

18. You need to compute an *N*-dimensional cross-tabulation in your SQL statement output for reporting purposes. Which of the following clauses can be used for this purpose?

A. having

B. cube

C. rollup

D. trim()

19. You are indexing Oracle data in an application. The index will be on a column containing sequential numbers with at least seven significant digits. Most, if not all, entries will start with the digit 1. Which of the following indexes is best suited for the task?

A. B-tree indexes

B. Reverse-key indexes

C. Bitmap indexes

D. Descending indexes

20. You need to store a large block of text data in Oracle. These text blocks will be around 3,500 characters in length. Which datatype should you use for storing these large objects?

A. VARCHAR2

B. CLOB

C. BLOB

D. BFILE

21. **Dropping a table has which of the following effects on a non-unique index created for the table?**

  A. It has no effect.

  B. The index is dropped.

  C. The index is rendered invalid.

  D. The index contains NULL values.

22. **Which of the following statements about indexes is true?**

  A. Columns with low cardinality are handled well by B-tree indexes.

  B. Columns with low cardinality are handled poorly by bitmap indexes.

  C. Columns with high cardinality are handled well by B-tree indexes.

23. **Which of the following methods should you use to add to the number of columns selected by a view?**

  A. Add more columns to the underlying table.

  B. Issue the `alter view` statement.

  C. Use a correlated subquery in conjunction with the view.

  D. Drop and recreate the view with references to select more columns.

24. **Which of the following choices is a valid parameter for sequence creation?**

  A. `identified by`

  B. `using temporary tablespace`

  C. `maxvalue`

  D. `on delete cascade`

25. **The following options each show a line in a statement issued against the Oracle database. Which line will produce an error?**

  A. `create view EMP_VIEW_01`

  B. `as select E.EMPID, E.LASTNAME, E.FIRSTNAME,`
  `A.ADDRESS`

  C. `from EMPLOYEE E, EMPL_ADDRESS A`

  D. `where E.EMPID = A.EMPID`

  E. `with check option;`

  F. This statement contains no errors.

26. You are granting privileges on your table to another user. Which object privilege enables the user to create his or her own table with a foreign key on a column in your table?

    A. references

    B. index

    C. select

    D. delete

27. Which of the following statements about roles are true? (Choose three.)

    A. Roles can be granted to other roles.

    B. Privileges can be granted to roles.

    C. Roles can be granted to users.

    D. Roles can be granted to synonyms.

28. After referencing NEXTVAL, what happens to the value in CURRVAL?

    A. It is incremented by one.

    B. It is now in PREVVAL.

    C. It is equal to NEXTVAL.

    D. It is unchanged.

29. The EMP_SALARY table has two columns: EMP_USER and SALARY. EMP_USER is set to be the same as the Oracle username. To support user MARTHA, the salary administrator, you create a view with the following statement:

```
CREATE VIEW EMP_SAL_VW
AS SELECT EMP_USER, SALARY
FROM EMP_SALARY
WHERE EMP_USER <> 'MARTHA';
```

    MARTHA is supposed to be able to view and update anyone's salary in the company except her own through this view. Which of the following clauses do you need to add to your view-creation statement in order to implement this functionality?

    A. with admin option

    B. with grant option

C. with security option

D. with check option

30. The INVENTORY table has three columns: UPC_CODE, UNITS, and DELIV_DATE. The primary key is UPC_CODE. New records are added daily through a view. The view was created using the following code:

```
CREATE VIEW DAY_INVENTORY_VW
AS SELECT UPC_CODE, UNITS, DELIV_DATE
FROM INVENTORY
WHERE DELIV_DATE = SYSDATE
WITH check OPTION;
```

What happens when a user tries to insert a record with duplicate UPC_CODE?

A. The statement fails due to the with check option clause.

B. The statement succeeds.

C. The statement fails due to the primary key constraint.

D. The statement inserts everything except the date.

31. You are cleaning information out of the Oracle database. Which of the following statements gets rid of all views that use a table at the same time you eliminate the table from the database?

A. drop view

B. alter table

C. drop index

D. alter table drop constraint

32. You create a view with the following statement:

```
CREATE VIEW BASEBALL_TEAM_VW
AS SELECT B.JERSEY_NUM, B.POSITION, B.NAME
FROM BASEBALL_TEAM B
WHERE B.NAME = USER;
```

What will happen when user JONES attempts to select a listing for user SMITH?

A. The select receives an error.

B. The select succeeds.

C. The select receives NO ROWS SELECTED.

D. The select adds data only to BASEBALL_TEAM.

33. Which of the following integrity constraints automatically create an index when defined? (Choose two.)

    A. Foreign keys

    B. unique constraints

    C. not NULL constraints

    D. Primary keys

34. Which of the following dictionary views gives information about the position of a column in a primary key?

    A. ALL_PRIMARY_KEYS

    B. USER_CONSTRAINTS

    C. ALL_IND_COLUMNS

    D. ALL_TABLES

35. Developer ANJU executes the following statement: `create table ANIMALS as select * from MASTER.ANIMALS;`. What is the effect of this statement?

    A. A table named ANIMALS is created in the MASTER schema with the same data as the ANIMALS table owned by ANJU.

    B. A table named ANJU is created in the ANIMALS schema with the same data as the ANIMALS table owned by MASTER.

    C. A table named ANIMALS is created in the ANJU schema with the same data as the ANIMALS table owned by MASTER.

    D. A table named MASTER is created in the ANIMALS schema with the same data as the ANJU table owned by ANIMALS.

36. User JANKO would like to insert a row into the EMPLOYEE table that has three columns: EMPID, LASTNAME, and SALARY. The user would like to enter data for EMPID 59694 and LASTNAME Harris, but no salary. Which statement would work best?

    A. `insert into EMPLOYEE values (59694,'HARRIS', NULL);`

    B. `insert into EMPLOYEE values (59694,'HARRIS');`

    C. `insert into EMPLOYEE (EMPID, LASTNAME, SALARY) values (59694,'HARRIS');`

    D. `insert into EMPLOYEE (select 59694 from 'HARRIS');`

37. No relationship officially exists between two tables. Which of the following choices is the strongest indicator of a parent-child relationship?

    A. Two tables in the database are named VOUCHER and VOUCHER_ITEM, respectively.

    B. Two tables in the database are named EMPLOYEE and PRODUCTS, respectively.

    C. Two tables in the database were created on the same day.

    D. Two tables in the database contain none of the same columns.

38. Which of the following are valid database table datatypes in Oracle? (Choose three.)

    A. CHAR

    B. VARCHAR2

    C. BOOLEAN

    D. NUMBER

39. Omitting the where clause from a delete statement has which of the following effects?

    A. The delete statement fails because no records are present to delete.

    B. The delete statement prompts the user to enter criteria for the deletion.

    C. The delete statement fails because of syntax error.

    D. The delete statement removes all records from the table.

40. The following options each show a line in a statement. Which line will produce an error?

    A. `create table GOODS`

    B. `(GOODNO NUMBER,`

    C. `GOOD_NAME VARCHAR2(20) check(GOOD_NAME in (select NAME from AVAIL_GOODS)),`

    D. `constraint PK_GOODS_01`

    E. `primary key (GOODNO));`

    F. This statement has no errors.

41. **Which of the following is the transaction control that prevents more than one user from updating data in a table?**

    A. Locks

    B. Commits

    C. Rollbacks

    D. Savepoints

42. **Which of the following methods should you use to increase the number of nullable columns for a table?**

    A. Use the `alter table` statement.

    B. Ensure that all column values are NULL for all rows.

    C. First, increase the size of adjacent column datatypes, and then add the column.

    D. Add the column, populate the column, and then add the `not NULL` constraint.

43. **A user issues the statement `select count(*) from EMPLOYEE`. The query takes an inordinately long time and returns a count of zero. Which of the following is the most cost-effective solution?**

    A. Upgrade the hardware.

    B. Truncate the table.

    C. Upgrade the version of Oracle.

    D. Delete the high-water mark.

44. **You are creating some tables in your database as part of the logical data model. Which of the following constraints have an index associated with them that is generated automatically by Oracle?**

    A. `unique`

    B. `foreign key`

    C. `check`

    D. `not NULL`

45. **Each of the following statements is true about referential integrity except one. Which is it?**

    A. The referencing column in the child table must correspond with a primary key in the parent.

B. All values in the referenced column in the parent table must be present in the referencing column in the child.

C. The datatype of the referenced column in the parent table must be identical to the referencing column in the child.

D. All values in the referencing column in the child table must be in present in the referenced column in the parent.

46. You are managing constraints on a table in Oracle. Which of the following choices correctly identifies the limitations on `check` constraints?

A. Values must be obtained from a lookup table.

B. Values must be part of a fixed set defined by `create` or `alter table`.

C. Values must include reserved words like `sysdate` and `user`.

D. Column cannot contain a NULL value.

47. Which of the following is not a group function?

A. `avg( )`

B. `sqrt( )`

C. `sum( )`

D. `max( )`

48. In order to perform an inner join, which criteria must be true?

A. The common columns in the join do not need to have shared values.

B. The tables in the join need to have common columns.

C. The common columns in the join may or may not have shared values.

D. The common columns in the join must have shared values.

49. Once defined, how long will a variable remain defined in SQL*Plus?

A. Until the database is shut down

B. Until the instance is shut down

C. Until the statement completes

D. Until the session completes

50. You want to change the prompt Oracle uses to obtain input from a user. Which of the following choices are used for this purpose? (Choose two.)

   A. Change the prompt in the `config.ora` file.

   B. Alter the prompt clause of the `accept` command.

   C. Enter a new prompt in the `login.sql` file.

   D. A prompt in Oracle cannot be changed.

51. No search criteria for the EMPLOYEE table are known. Which of the following options is appropriate for use when search criteria are unknown for comparison operations in a `select` statement? (Choose two.)

   A. `select * from EMPLOYEE where EMPID = &empid;`

   B. `select * from EMPLOYEE where EMPID = 69494;`

   C. `select * from EMPLOYEE where EMPID = (select empid from invoice where INVOICE_NO = 4399485);`

   D. `select * from EMPLOYEE;`

52. Which of the following is the default character for specifying substitution variables in `select` statements?

   A. Ampersand

   B. Ellipses

   C. Quotation marks

   D. Asterisk

53. A user is setting up a join operation between tables EMPLOYEE and DEPT. The user wants the query to return some of the employees in the EMPLOYEE table, but the employees are not assigned to department heads yet. Which `select` statement is most appropriate for this user?

   A. `select e.empid, d.head from EMPLOYEE e, dept d;`

   B. `select e.empid, d.head from EMPLOYEE e, dept d where e.dept# = d.dept#;`

   C. `select e.empid, d.head from EMPLOYEE e, dept d where e.dept# = d.dept# (+);`

   D. `select e.empid, d.head from EMPLOYEE e, dept d where e.dept# (+) = d.dept#;`

54. **Which of the following uses of the having clause are appropriate? (Choose three.)**

    A. To put returned data into sorted order

    B. To exclude certain data groups based on known criteria

    C. To include certain data groups based on unknown criteria

    D. To include certain data groups based on known criteria

55. **Which of the following best describes a Cartesian product?**

    A. A group function

    B. Produced as a result of a join `select` statement with no `where` clause

    C. The result of fuzzy logic

    D. A special feature of Oracle server

56. **Which of the following methods is used to change the default character that identifies runtime variables?**

    A. Modifying the `init.ora` file

    B. Modifying the `login.sql` file

    C. Issuing the `define` *variablename* command

    D. Issuing the `set define` command

57. **User THOMAS has been granted the role SALES_ANALYZER, which gives her access the SALES table for writing reports. However, when she tries to do so, she gets this error: `ORA-00942: table or view does not exist`. Which of the following statements can she issue in order to resolve the problem?**

    A. `alter user thomas default role sales_analyzer;`

    B. `set role sales_analyzer;`

    C. `grant select on sales to sales_analyzer;`

    D. `grant sales_analyzer to thomas;`

58. **User FRANKLIN owns the PROFITS table and the SALES_ANALYZER role, which has already been granted to DAVIS. FRANKLIN grants `select` privileges on PROFITS to the SALES_ANALYZER role. At what point will that privilege be made available to DAVIS?**

    A. The next time DAVIS logs into Oracle

    B. The next time FRANKLIN grants the SALES_ANALYZER role to DAVIS

C. The next time FRANKLIN grants the privilege to SALES ANALYZER

D. Immediately after the privilege is granted to SALES_ANALYZER

59. **User IMADBA wants to give user DAVIS, a brand-new employee who started today, the ability to create tables in the Oracle database. Which of the following choices identifies a step that doesn't need to take place before DAVIS can start creating tables?**

    A. `create user davis identified by new_employee;`

    B. `grant create session to davis;`

    C. `grant create table to davis;`

    D. `grant create public synonym to davis;`

60. **You are granting privileges on the Oracle database. Which of the following choices identifies a system privilege enabling you to connect to the database?**

    A. CONNECT

    B. RESOURCE

    C. `create session`

    D. `references`

Practice Exam 3

1. You issue the following `select` statement in Oracle:

```
SQL> select e.empno, e.ename, d.loc
from emp e, dept d
  3  where e.deptno = d.deptno
  4  and substr(e.ename,1,1) = 'S';
```

   Which of the following statements identifies an ANSI-compliant equivalent statement usable on the Oracle database?

   A. `select empno, ename, loc from emp join dept on emp.deptno = dept.deptno where substr(emp.ename,1,1) = 'S';`

   B. `select empno, ename, loc from emp, dept on emp.deptno = dept.deptno where substr(emp.ename,1,1) = 'S';`

   C. `select empno, ename, loc from emp join dept where emp.deptno = dept.deptno and substr(emp.ename,1,1) = 'S';`

   D. `select empno, ename, loc from emp join dept on emp.deptno = dept.deptno and substr(emp.ename,1,1) = 'S';`

2. You are trying to manipulate data on the Oracle database. Which of the following choices identifies a capacity of `select` statements in Oracle and does not require the use of a subquery?

   A. You can change data in Oracle using `select` statements.

   B. You can remove data from Oracle using `select` statements.

   C. You can create a table with the contents of another using `select` statements.

   D. You can truncate tables using `select` statements.

3. You issue a query in the Oracle database. Which of the following choices does not identify a component of your query if you want the query to execute a mathematical operation on user-defined static expressions?

   A. Column clause

   B. Table clause

   C. The DUAL table

   D. The where clause

4. **You are manipulating data in Oracle. Which of the following is not a SQL command?**

   A. `select * from dual;`

   B. `set define ?`

   C. `update emp set empno = 6543 where ename = 'SMITHERS';`

   D. `create table employees (empid varchar2(10) primary key);`

5. **You are defining SQL queries in Oracle. Which of the following database objects cannot be referenced directly from a `select` statement?**

   A. Tables

   B. Sequences

   C. Indexes

   D. Views

6. **You need to filter return data from your query on the PROFITS table according to the PRODUCT_NAME column. Which of the following clauses in your SQL query will contain reference to the appropriate filter criteria?**

   A. `select`

   B. `from`

   C. `where`

   D. `having`

7. **A partial listing of output from the PROFITS table is shown in the following code block:**

```
PRODUCT_NAME  PRODUCT_TYPE  QTR_END_DATE        PROFIT
------------  ------------  ------------   ------------
BARNEY DOLL   TOY           31-MAR-2001     6575430.30
GAS GRILL     APPLIANCE     31-MAR-2001     1234023.88
PENCIL        OFFICE        30-JUN-2001       34039.99
```

   Which of the following choices identifies the proper setup of a where clause for a query that calculates the total profits for all appliances sold in the six-month period from January 1 to June 30, 2001?

   A. `where product_name = 'GAS GRILL' and qtr_end_date between '01-JAN-2001' and '01-JUL-2001';`

B. where product_type = 'APPLIANCE' and product_name = 'GAS GRILL' and qtr_end_date = '31-JAN-2001' or '30-JUN-2001';

C. where product_type = 'APPLIANCE' and qtr_end_date between '01-JAN-2001' and '01-JUL-2001';

D. where product_name = 'GAS GRILL' and qtr_end_date = '01-JAN-2001' or '30-JUN-2001';

Use the contents of the EMP table shown in the following code block to answer the next eight questions:

```
EMPNO ENAME      JOB        MGR HIREDATE   SAL COMM DEPTNO
--------- -------- --------- --------- ---------- ---- ---- ------
 7369 SMITH    CLERK     7902 17-DEC-80  800        20
 7499 ALLEN    SALESMAN  7698 20-FEB-81 1600  300   30
 7521 WARD     SALESMAN  7698 22-FEB-81 1250  500   30
 7566 JONES    MANAGER   7839 02-APR-81 2975        20
 7654 MARTIN   SALESMAN  7698 28-SEP-81 1250 1400   30
 7698 BLAKE    MANAGER   7839 01-MAY-81 2850        30
 7782 CLARK    MANAGER   7839 09-JUN-81 2450        10
 7788 SCOTT    ANALYST   7566 19-APR-87 3000        20
 7839 KING     PRESIDENT      17-NOV-81 5000        10
 7844 TURNER   SALESMAN  7698 08-SEP-81 1500    0   30
 7876 ADAMS    CLERK     7788 23-MAY-87 1100        20
 7900 JAMES    CLERK     7698 03-DEC-81  950        30
 7902 FORD     ANALYST   7566 03-DEC-81 3000        20
 7934 MILLER   CLERK     7782 23-JAN-82 1300        10
```

8. Which of the following choices identifies the value that would be returned from the following query: select sum(sal) + sum(comm) from emp where job = 'ANALYST' or ename like 'J%'?

A. 6000

B. 9925

C. 9975

D. NULL

9. Which of the following choices identifies the value that would be returned from the following query: select count(mgr) from emp where deptno = 10?

A. One

B. Two

C. Three

D. NULL

10. Which of the following choices identifies the value returned if you issued the following query: `select count(*) from emp where mgr = 7700-2`?

   A. Five

   B. Six

   C. Seven

   D. NULL

11. Which of the following choices identifies the third employee listed from the top of the output from the following SQL command: `select ename, sal from emp where job = 'SALESMAN' order by empno desc`?

   A. ALLEN

   B. MARTIN

   C. TURNER

   D. WARD

12. Which of the following choices identifies the third employee listed from the top in the output generated from the following SQL command: `select ename, job from emp where job = 'SALESMAN' order by 1 desc`?

   A. ALLEN

   B. MARTIN

   C. TURNER

   D. WARD

13. Which of the following choices identifies the value returned by Oracle when you issue the following query: `select substr(job, 1,3) from emp where ename like upper('_ _ar%')`?

   A. ANA

   B. CLE

   C. MAN

   D. SAL

14. Which of the following choices identifies the value returned by Oracle
    when you issue: `select trunc(months_between(min(hiredate),`
    `max(hiredate)))` `from emp`?

    A. 24

    B. 25

    C. −24

    D. −25

15. Which of the following choices identify the value returned by Oracle when
    you issue the following query: `select * from emp where`
    `hiredate > '23-JAN-82'`? (Choose two.)

    A. ADAMS

    B. MILLER

    C. SCOTT

    D. SMITH

16. A table called TEST contains two columns: TESTCOL, defined as a
    NUMBER(10) datatype; and TESTCOL_2, defined as a VARCHAR2(10)
    datatype. You issue the following statement on Oracle: `insert into`
    `test (testcol, testcol_2) values (null, 'FRANCIS')`. You
    then issue the following query against that table: `select`
    `nvl(testcol,'EMPTY') as testcol from test where`
    `testcol_2 = 'FRANCIS'`. Which of the following choices correctly
    identifies the result?

    A. Oracle returns zero as the result.

    B. Oracle returns EMPTY as the result.

    C. Oracle returns NULL as the result.

    D. Oracle returns an error as the result.

17. You want to obtain data from the ORDERS table, which contains three
    columns: CUSTOMER, ORDER_DATE, and ORDER_AMT. Which of the
    following choices identifies how you would formulate the where clause in
    a query against the ORDERS table when you want to see orders for
    customer LESLIE that exceed 2700?

    A. `where customer = 'LESLIE';`

    B. `where customer = 'LESLIE' and order_amt < 2700;`

    C. `where customer = 'LESLIE' or order_amt > 2700;`

    D. `where customer = 'LESLIE' and order_amt > 2700;`

18. **Use the following output to answer the question (assume that the information shown comes from the EMP table we've been using in the chapter):**

```
ENAME
----------
SMITH-dog-
ALLEN-dog-
WARD-dog-d
JONES-dog-
MARTIN-dog
BLAKE-dog-
CLARK-dog-
SCOTT-dog-
KING-dog-d
TURNER-dog
ADAMS-dog-
JAMES-dog-
FORD-dog-d
MILLER-dog
```

    Which of the following choices identifies the SQL statement that produced this output?

    A. `select trim(trailing '-dog' from ename) as ename from emp;`

    B. `select rpad(ename, 10, '-dog') as ename from emp;`

    C. `select substr(ename, 1, 10) as ename from emp;`

    D. `select lpad(ename, 10, '-dog') as ename from emp;`

19. **Use the following code block to answer the question:**

```
SQL> select _____ (-45) as output from dual;
OUTPUT
------
   -45
```

    Which of the following choices identifies a single-row function that could not have produced this output?

    A. `abs( )`

    B. `ceil( )`

C. floor( )

D. round( )

20. For a certain row in a table, a VARCHAR2 column contains the value SMITHY, padded to the right with seven spaces by the application. When the `length( )` function processes that column value, what will be the value returned?

   A. 6

   B. 13

   C. 30

   D. 60

21. You issue the following statement in SQL*Plus:

```
SQL> select ceil(-97.342),
  2    floor(-97.342),
  3    round(-97.342,0),
  4    trunc(-97.342)
  5  from dual;
```

   Which of the following choices identifies the function that will not return –97 as the result?

   A. ceil( )

   B. floor( )

   C. round( )

   D. trunc( )

22. You issue the following statement in SQL*Plus:

```
SQL> select ceil(256.342),
  2    floor(256.342),
  3    round(256.342,0),
  4    trunc(256.342)
  5  from dual;
```

   Which of the following choices identifies the function that will not return 256 as the result?

   A. ceil( )

   B. floor( )

   C. round( )

   D. trunc( )

23. You issue the following query in Oracle:

```
SQL> select months_between('15-MAR-83', '15-MAR-97') from dual;
```

What will Oracle return?

A. 14

B. −14

C. 168

D. −168

24. You want to use a format mask for date information in Oracle. In which of the following situations is this format mask not appropriate?

A. `to_date( )`

B. `to_char( )`

C. `alter session set nls_date_format`

D. `to_number( )`

25. Two tables, PRODUCT and STORAGE_BOX, exist in a database. Individual products are listed in the table by unique ID number, product name, and the box a particular product is stored in. Individual storage boxes (identified by number) listed in the other table can contain many products, but each box can be found in only one location. Which of the following statements will correctly display the product ID, name, and box location of all widgets in this database?

A. `select p.prod_id, p.prod_name, b.box_loc from product p, storage_box b where p.prod_id = b.prod_id and prod_name = 'WIDGET';`

B. `select p.prod_id, p.prod_name, b.box_loc from product p, storage_box b where prod_name = 'WIDGET';`

C. `select p.prod_id, p.prod_name, b.box_loc from product p, storage_box b where p.stor_box_num = b.stor_box_num and p.prod_name = 'WIDGET';`

D. `select prod_id, prod_name, box_loc from product, storage_box where stor_box_num = stor_box_num and prod_name = 'WIDGET';`

26. You want to join information from three tables as part of developing a report. The tables are EMP, DEPT, and SALGRADE. Only records corresponding to employee, department location, and salary range are required for employees in grades ten and higher for the organization. How many comparison operations are required for this query?

A. Two

B. Three

C. Four

D. Five

27. You want to join the contents of two tables, PRODUCT and STORAGE, to list the location of all boxes containing widgets. PRODUCT has three columns: ID, NAME, and BOX#. STORAGE has two columns: BOX# and LOC. Which of the following choices will not give the desired result?

A.
```
select product.id, product.name, storage.loc from
product, storage where product.box# = storage.box#;
```

B.
```
select product.id, product.name, storage.loc from
product join storage on product.box# =
storage.box#;
```

C.
```
select product.id, product.name, storage.loc from
product natural join storage on product.box# =
storage.box#;
```

D.
```
select product.id, product.name, storage.loc from
product natural join storage;
```

28. You are defining an outer join statement. Which of the following choices is true concerning outer join statements?

A. Because outer join operations permit NULL values from one of the tables, you do not have to specify equality comparisons to join those tables.

B. In outer join statements on tables A and B, you specify the right outer join when you want all of table A's rows, even when no corresponding record exists in table B.

C. In outer join statements on tables A and B, you specify the left outer join when you want all of table B's rows, even when no corresponding record exists in table A.

D. Even though outer join operations permit NULL values from one of the tables, you still need to specify equality comparisons to join those tables.

29. Two tables, PRODUCT and STORAGE_BOX, exist in a database. Individual products are listed in the table by unique ID number, product name, and the box a particular product is stored in. Individual storage boxes (identified by number) listed in the other table can contain many products, but the box can be found in only one location. Which of the following statements will correctly display the product ID, name, and box location of all widgets in this database that have or have not been assigned to a storage box?

   A. ```
   select p.prod_id, p.prod_name, b.box_loc from
   product p left outer join storage_box b on
   p.stor_box_num = b.stor_box_num where p.prod_name =
   'WIDGET'(+);
   ```

   B. ```
   select p.prod_id, p.prod_name, b.box_loc from
   product p left outer join storage_box b on
   p.stor_box_num = b.stor_box_num where p.prod_name =
   'WIDGET';
   ```

   C. ```
   select p.prod_id, p.prod_name, b.box_loc from
   product p right outer join storage_box b where
   b.stor_box_num = p.stor_box_num (+) and p.prod_name
   = 'WIDGET';
   ```

   D. ```
   select p.prod_id, p.prod_name, b.box_loc from
   product p full outer join storage_box b on
   p.stor_box_num = b.stor_box_num where
   b.stor_box_num is NULL;
   ```

30. You issue the following command in Oracle:

   ```
   SQL> select e.ename, a.street_address, a.city, a.state, a.post_code
   from emp e, addr a
     3   where e.empno = a.empno (+)
     4   and a.state = 'TEXAS';
   ```

   Which of the following choices shows the ANSI/ISO equivalent statement?

   A. ```
   select e.ename, a.street_address, a.city, a.state,
   a.post_code from emp e outer join addr a on e.empno
   = a.empno where a.state = 'TEXAS';
   ```

   B. ```
   select e.ename, a.street_address, a.city, a.state,
   a.post_code from emp e left outer join addr a on
   e.empno = a.empno where a.state = 'TEXAS';
   ```

   C. ```
   select e.ename, a.street_address, a.city, a.state,
   a.post_code from emp e right outer join addr a on
   e.empno = a.empno where a.state = 'TEXAS';
   ```
   ```

D. `select e.ename, a.street_address, a.city, a.state,`
`a.post_code from emp e right outer join addr a`
`where e.empno = a.empno (+) and a.state = 'TEXAS';`

31. **Examine the following output from SQL*Plus:**

```
PRODUCT.ID PRODUCT.NAME BOX_LOCATION
---------- ------------ ------------
578-X      WIDGET       IDAHO
                        TENNESSEE
456-Y      WIDGET
```

Which of the following choices identifies the type of query that likely produced this result?

A. Full outer join

B. Left outer join

C. Right outer join

D. Equijoin

32. **You are developing a query on the PROFITS table, which stores profit information by company region, product type, and quarterly time period. Which of the following SQL statements will display a cross-tabulation of output showing profits by region, product type, and time period?**

A. `select region, prod_type, time, sum(profit) from`
`profits group by region, prod_type, time;`

B. `select region, prod_type, time from profits group`
`by rollup (region, prod_type, time);`

C. `select region, prod_type, time from profits group`
`by cube (region, prod_type, time);`

D. `select region, prod_type, time, sum(profit) from`
`profits group by cube (region, prod_type, time);`

33. **Which of the following choices identifies a group by query that will not result in an error from Oracle when run against the database?**

A. `select deptno, job, sum(sal) from emp group by job,`
`deptno;`

B. `select sum(sal), deptno, job from emp group by job,`
`deptno;`

C. `select deptno, job, sum(sal) from emp;`

D. `select deptno, sum(sal), job from emp group by job,`
`deptno;`

34. Review the following SQL statement:

```
SQL> select a.deptno, a.job, b.loc, sum(a.sal)
  2  from emp a, dept b
  3  where a.deptno = b.deptno
  4  group by a.deptno, a.job, b.loc
  5  order by sum(a.sal);
```

   Which of the following choices identifies the column upon which the order of output from this query will be returned?

   A. A.DEPTNO

   B. A.JOB

   C. B.LOC

   D. sum(A.SAL)

35. You are developing a query on the PROFITS table, which stores profit information by company region, product type, and quarterly time period. Which of the following choices identifies a query that will obtain the average profits greater than $100,000 by product type, region, and time period?

   A. select region, prod_type, period, avg(profit) from profits where avg(profit) > 100000 group by region, prod_type, period;

   B. select region, prod_type, period, avg(profit) from profits where avg(profit) > 100000 order by region, prod_type, period;

   C. select region, prod_type, period, avg(profit) from profits group by region, prod_type, period having avg(profit) > 100000;

   D. select region, prod_type, period, avg(profit) from profits group by region, prod_type, period having avg(profit) < 100000;

36. The company has an employee expense application with two tables. One table, called EMP, contains all employee data. The other, called EXPENSE, contains expense vouchers submitted by every employee in the company. Which of the following queries will obtain the employee ID and name for those employees who have submitted expenses whose total value exceeds their salary?

   A. select e.empno, e.ename from emp e where e.sal < (select sum(x.vouch_amt) from expense x) and x.empno = e.empno;

B. select e.empno, e.ename from emp e where e.sal <
(select x.vouch_amt from expense x where x.empno =
e.empno);

C. select e.empno, e.ename from emp e where sal <
(select sum(x.vouch_amt) from expense x where
x.empno = e.empno);

D. select e.empno, e.ename from emp e where exists
(select sum(x.vouch_amt) from expense x where
x.empno = e.empno);

37. Take a look at the following statement:

```
SQL>  select ename
2     from emp
3     where empno in
4       ( select empno
5         from expense
6         where vouch_amt > 10000 );
```

Which of the following choices identifies a SQL statement that will
produce the same output as the preceding statement, rewritten to use
the exists operator?

A. select e.ename from emp e where exists (select
x.empno from expense x where x.vouch_amt > 10000)
and x.empno = e.empno;

B. select e.ename from emp e where exists (select
x.empno from expense x where x.vouch_amt > 10000
and x.empno = e.empno);

C. select e.ename from emp e where x.empno = e.empno
and exists (select x.empno from expense x where
x.vouch_amt > 10000);

D. select e.ename from emp e, expense x where x.empno
= e.empno and x.vouch_amt > 10000 and exists
(select x.empno from expense x where x.vouch_amt >
10000);

38. Use the following code block to answer the question:

```
SQL> select deptno, job, avg(sal)
2    from emp
3    group by deptno, job
4    having avg(sal) >
```

```
5    ( select sal
6      from emp
7      where ename = 'MARTIN');
```

Which of the following choices identifies the type of subquery used in the preceding statement?

A. A single-row subquery

B. A multirow subquery

C. A from clause subquery

D. A multicolumn subquery

39. **The company's sales database has two tables. The first, PROFITS, stores the amount of profit made on products sold by the different corporate regions in different quarters. The second, REGIONS, stores the name of each departmental region, the headquarter location for that region, and the name of the region's vice president. Which of the following queries will obtain total profits on toys for regions headed by SMITHERS, FUJIMORI, and LAKKARAJU?**

A.
```
select sum(profit) from profits where region in (
   select region from regions where reg_head in
   ('SMITHERS', 'FUJIMORI', 'LAKKARAJU')) and product
   = 'TOYS';
```

B.
```
select sum(profit) from profits where region in (
   select region from regions where reg_head in
   ('SMITHERS', 'FUJIMORI', 'LAKKARAJU') and product =
   'TOYS');
```

C.
```
select sum(profit) from profits where region = (
   select region from regions where reg_head in
   ('SMITHERS', 'FUJIMORI', 'LAKKARAJU')) and product
   = 'TOYS';
```

D.
```
select sum(profit) from profits where region in (
   select region from regions where reg_head in
   ('SMITHERS', 'FUJIMORI', 'LAKKARAJU') and product =
   'TOYS';
```

40. **The following code block shows a query containing a subquery:**

```
SQL> select dname, avg(sal) as dept_avg
  2  from emp, dept
  3  where emp.deptno = dept.deptno
  4  group by dname having avg(sal) >
```

```
5  (select avg(sal) * 1/4
6   from emp, dept
7   where emp.deptno = dept.deptno)
8  order by avg(sal);
```

Which of the following choices identifies a clause you might use to redefine this query to remove redundancy of group function execution in the subquery and in the main query?

A. group by

B. order by

C. with

D. having

41. **Use the output in the code block to answer the following question:**

```
SQL> select e.deptno, e.ename, e.job, e.sal
  2  from emp e
  3  where e.sal =
  4  (select max(e2.sal)
  5   from emp e2
  6* where nvl(e.deptno,99) = nvl(e2.deptno,99));
DEPTNO ENAME       JOB          SAL
--------- ----------- --------- ---------
       30 BLAKE       MANAGER      2850
       10 CLARK       MANAGER      2450
       20 SCOTT       ANALYST      3000
          KING        PRESIDENT    5000
       20 FORD        ANALYST      3000
```

In order to display a value of 99 in the DEPTNO column in the preceding return set, which of the following SQL statements might be appropriate?

A. select nvl(e.deptno,99), e.ename, e.job, e.sal from emp e where (e.deptno, e.sal) =(select max(e2.sal) from emp e2 where nvl(e.deptno,99) = nvl(e2.deptno,99));

B. select nvl(e.deptno,99), e.ename, e.job, e.sal from emp e where e.sal =(select max(e2.sal) from emp e2 where nvl(e.deptno,99) = nvl(e2.deptno,99));

C. select nvl(e.deptno,99), e.ename, e.job, e.sal from emp e where (e.deptno, e.sal) =(select e2.deptno, max(e2.sal) from emp e2 where nvl(e.deptno,99) = nvl(e2.deptno,99));

D.
```
select nvl(e.deptno,99), e.ename, e.job, e.sal from
emp e where (e.deptno, e.sal) =(select e2.deptno,
max(e2.sal) from emp e2 where nvl(e.deptno,99) =
nvl(e2.deptno,99) group by e2.deptno);
```

42. **Your company's sales database contains one table, PROFITS, which stores profits listed by product name, sales region, and quarterly time period. If you wanted to obtain a listing of the five best-selling products in company history, which of the following SQL statements would you use?**

A.
```
select p.prod_name, p.profit from (select
prod_name, profit from profits order by profit
desc) where rownum <= 5;
```

B.
```
select p.prod_name, p.profit from (select
prod_name, sum(profit) from profits group by
prod_name order by sum(profit) desc) subq where
p.prod_name = subq.prod_name;
```

C.
```
select prod_name, profit from (select prod_name,
sum(profit) from profits group by prod_name order
by sum(profit) desc) where rownum <=5;
```

D.
```
select prod_name, profit from (select prod_name,
sum(profit) from profits order by sum(profit) desc)
where rownum <=5;
```

43. **Your sales database consists of one table, PROFITS, which lists profits for every product type the company sells listed by quarter and by sales region. You need to develop a report that users can run interactively to show them the profits on toys for a given quarter. You have concerns about the users of this report because they have frequently complained about the readability and usability of your reports. Which of the following choices shows the contents of the script you should use for your report?**

A.
```
select profit from profits where prod_type = 'TOYS'
and time_period = '&v_period';
```

B.
```
define v_periodselect profit from profits where
prod_type = 'TOYS' and time_period = '&v_period';
```

C.
```
accept v_period prompt 'Enter the time period =>
'select profit from profits where prod_type =
'TOYS' and time_period = '&v_period';
```

D.
```
accept v_periodselect profit from profits where
prod_type = 'TOYS' and time_period = '&v_period';
```

44. Review the following code block containing the contents of a script called `dates.sql`:

```
accept v_hiredate prompt 'enter hire date => '
select empno, ename, job
from emp
where trunc(hiredate) = trunc('&v_hiredate');
```

Which of the following aspects of the script must be changed in order for the script to function properly?

A. Variable `v_hiredate` must be changed to accept DATE information.

B. The `trunc( )` function in the query should be eliminated.

C. The `prompt` clause in the `accept` command is unnecessary.

D. Nothing; the script will work fine as is.

45. You are creating tables in the Oracle database. Which of the following statements identifies a table-creation statement that is not valid?

A. `create table cats (c_name varchar2(10), c_weight number, c_owner varchar2(10));`

B. `create table my_cats as select * from cats where owner = 'ME';`

C. `create global temporary table temp_cats (c_name varchar2(10), c_weight number, c_owner varchar2(10));`

D. `create table cats-over-5-lbs as select c_name, c_weight from cats where c_weight > 5;`

46. Your attempt to create a table in Oracle results in the following error: `ORA-00955 - name is already used by existing object.` Which of the following choices does not identify an appropriate correction for this situation?

A. Create the object as a different user.

B. Drop the existing object with the same name.

C. Change the column names in the object being created.

D. Rename the existing object.

47. The PROFITS column inside the SALES table is declared as NUMBER(10,2). Which of the following values cannot be stored in that column?

A. 5392845.324

    B. 871039453.1

    C. 75439289.34

    D. 60079829.25

48. **Employee KING was hired on November 17, 1981. You issue the following query on your Oracle database: `select vsize(hiredate) from emp where ename = 'KING;`. Which of the following choices identifies the value returned?**

    A. 4

    B. 7

    C. 9

    D. 17

49. **You define the PRODUCT_NAME column in your SALES table to be CHAR(40). Later, you add one row to this table with the value CAT_TOYS for PRODUCT_NAME. You then issue the following command: `select vsize(product_name) from sales`. Which of the following choices best identifies the value returned?**

    A. 8

    B. 12

    C. 40

    D. 4000

50. **The JOB table contains three columns: JOB_NAME, JOB_DESC, and JOB_WAGE. You insert a new row into the JOB_DESC table using the following command:**

```
SQL> insert into job (job_name, job_desc)
  2  values ('LACKEY','MAKES COFFEE');
```

Later, you query the table, and receive the following result:

```
SQL> select * from job where job_name = 'LACKEY';
JOB_NAME  JOB_DESC      JOB_WAGE
--------- ------------- --------
LACKEY    MAKES COFFEE       35
```

Which of the following choices identifies how JOB_WAGE was populated with data?

A. The row for LACKEY in the JOB table already existed with JOB_WAGE set to 35.

B. A `default` clause on the JOB_WAGE column defined when the table was created specified the value when the row was inserted.

C. The `values` clause in the `insert` statement contained a hidden value that was added when the row was added.

D. The only possible explanation is that a later `update` statement issued against the JOB table added the JOB_WAGE value.

51. **You want to reduce the size of a non-NULL NUMBER(10) column to NUMBER(6). Which of the following steps must be completed after the appropriate `alter table` command is issued?**

A. Copy column records to a temporary storage location.

B. Set the NUMBER column to NULL for all rows.

C. Create a temporary location for NUMBER data.

D. Copy column records from the temporary location back to the main table.

52. **You just issued the following statement: `alter table sales drop column profit;`. Which of the following choices identifies when the column will actually be removed from Oracle?**

A. Immediately following statement execution

B. After the `alter table drop unused columns` command is issued

C. After the `alter table set unused column` command is issued

D. After the `alter table modify` command is issued

53. **You want to increase the size of a non-NULL VARCHAR2(5) column to VARCHAR2(10). Which of the following steps must be accomplished after executing the appropriate `alter table` command?**

A. Set the VARCHAR2 column to NULL for all rows.

B. Create a temporary location for VARCHAR2 data.

C. Copy the column records from the temporary location back to the main table.

D. Nothing; the statement is executed automatically.

54. You want to increase the size of the PRODUCT_TYPE column, declared as a VARCHAR(5) column, to VARCHAR2(10) in the SALES table. Which of the following commands is useful for this purpose?

A. `alter table sales add (product_type varchar2(10));`

B. `alter table sales modify product_type varchar2(10));`

C. `alter table sales set unused column product_type varchar2(10));`

D. `alter table sales drop column product_type;`

55. You drop a table in an Oracle database that is the parent table in a parent-child data relationship. Which of the following objects will not be dropped when you drop the parent table?

A. Associated constraints

B. The child column

C. Associated triggers

D. Associated indexes

56. The PROFITS table in your database has a primary key on the PRODUCT_NAME and SALE_PERIOD columns. Which of the following statements could *not* have been used to define this primary key?

A. `create table profits ( product_name varchar2(10), sale_period varchar2(10), profit number, constraint pk_profits_01 primary key (product_name, sale_period));`

B. `alter table profits add constraint pk_profits_01 primary key (product_name, sale_period) deferrable initially immediate;`

C. `alter table profits add (constraint pk_profits_01 primary key (product_name, sale_period));`

D. `create table profits ( product_name varchar2(10) primary key, sale_period varchar2(10) primary key, profit number);`

57. You are defining check constraints on your SALES table, which contains two columns: PRODUCT_TYPE and UNIT_SALES. Which of the following choices identify a properly defined check constraint? (Choose two.)

A. alter table sales add constraint ck_sales_01 check
(product_type in ('TOYS', 'HOT DOGS', 'PALM
PILOTS'));

B. alter table sales add constraint ck_sales_01 check
(product_type in (select product_type from
valid_products));

C. alter table sales modify (product_type varchar2(30)
check (product_type in ('TOYS', 'HOT DOGS', 'PALM
PILOTS')));

D. alter table sales add (product_name varchar2(30)
check (product_name <> 'AK-47'));

58. **Use the following code block to answer the question:**

```
SQL> create table prices
  2  ( product_name varchar2(30),
  3    price number(10,4));
Table created.
SQL> alter table prices add constraint pk_prices_01
  2  primary key (product_name);
Table altered.
SQL> insert into prices values ('DOGGY', 499.99);
1 row created.
SQL> alter table prices disable constraint pk_prices_01;
Table altered.
SQL> insert into prices values ('DOGGY', 449.99);
1 row created.
SQL> alter table prices enable novalidate constraint pk_prices_01;
```

What happens next?

A. Existing entries are checked for violations, PK_PRICES_01 is enabled, and Oracle checks subsequent entries for violations immediately.

B. Existing entries are checked for violations, PK_PRICES_01 is not enabled, and Oracle does not check subsequent entries for violations immediately.

C. Existing entries are not checked for violations, PK_PRICES_01 is enabled, and Oracle checks subsequent entries for violations immediately.

D. Existing entries are checked for violations, PK_PRICES_01 is not enabled, Oracle checks subsequent entries for violations immediately.

59. Your attempt to disable a constraint yields the following error: ORA-02297: cannot disable constraint-dependencies exist. Which of the following types of constraints is likely causing interference with your disablement of this one?

    A. Check constraint

    B. Not NULL constraint

    C. Foreign key constraint

    D. Unique constraint

60. You are disabling a not NULL constraint on the UNIT_PRICE column in the SALES table. Which of the following choices identifies the correct statement for performing this action?

    A. `alter table sales modify (unit_prices null);`

    B. `alter table sales modify (unit_prices not null);`

    C. `alter table sales add (unit_prices null);`

    D. `alter table sales add (unit_prices not null);`

Answers to Practice Exam I

I. A. `select NAME, JERSEY_NO where JERSEY_NO = 6;`

Explanation   SQL statements in Oracle must have a `from` clause. A SQL statement can lack a `where` clause, in which case, all of the data in the table will be returned. However, if the statement does not have a `from` clause, Oracle will not know what table to retrieve data from. Recall that a special table called DUAL assists in situations where you don't want to retrieve data from a table, but instead only want to manipulate expressions. **(Topic 2.1)**

2. A. Issuing an `update` statement

Explanation   The only choice that does not end a transaction is the one that continues the transaction, namely issuing another `update` statement. A `commit` tells Oracle to save your data changes and end the transaction. A `rollback` tells Oracle to discard your data changes and end the transaction. Closing SQL*Plus or otherwise ending the session is usually treated as an implicit `commit` and ends your transaction as well. **(Topic 8.3)**

3. B. `commit`

Explanation   In order to save any change you make in Oracle, you use the `commit` command. The `savepoint` command merely identifies a logical breakpoint in your transaction that you can use to break up complex units of work. The `rollback` command discards every change you made since the last `commit`. Finally, the `set transaction` command sets up the transaction to be read-only against the Oracle database. **(Topic 8.6)**

4. D. USER_CONS_COLUMNS

Explanation   The USER_CONS_COLUMNS dictionary view shows you all of the columns in tables belonging to that user that are part of indexes used to enforce constraints. USER_INDEXES is incorrect because that view only displays information about the index itself, not the columns in the index. USER_TAB_COLUMNS displays all the columns in all tables owned by the user. Finally, USER_COLUMNS is not an actual view in the Oracle database. **(Topic 12.2)**

5. D. Not NULL

Explanation   Not NULL integrity constraints can only be declared as column constraints, meaning that the actual syntax for defining the constraint will appear next to the constrained column, as opposed to at the end of the column listing. Choices A, B, and C all identify constraints that can be defined as table constraints or as column constraints. **(Topic 10.2)**

6. D. The view

Explanation When you drop a table with the `cascade constraints` option, Oracle removes from other tables all associated indexes, triggers, and constraints that reference that table. Oracle does not remove the views that use that table, however. You must remove a view manually with the `drop view` statement. **(Topic 11.2)**

7. D. MONTHS_BETWEEN

Explanation Each of the choices accepts a DATE datatype as input and returns a DATE datatype, with one exception. The MONTHS_BETWEEN function returns a number indicating how many months there are between the two dates you give it. This number will be displayed with numbers to the right of the decimal point, which you can round off if you like. **(Topic 3.2)**

8. C. `order by sqrt(1);`

Explanation The `order by` clause in the `select` clause of the `select` statement enables you to refer to the column you want the table order determined by, either by the column name or by the number representing the column order. However, you cannot perform any sort of numeric function on that column-order number. Both the `asc` and `desc` keywords are valid for the `order by` clause, indicating ascending order (default) and descending order, respectively. **(Topic 2.2)**

9. B. Table with one column and one row used in various operations

Explanation The DUAL table is a special table in Oracle used to satisfy the requirement of a `from` clause in your SQL statements. It contains one column and one row of data. It is not a dictionary view; rather, it is an actual table. You could use the DUAL table in arithmetic expressions and not actually pull real data from the database. You should never insert data into the DUAL table under any circumstances. **(Topic 3.2)**

10. A. ACTIVE

Explanation The `decode( )` function is used as a case statement, where Oracle will review the value in the column identified in the first parameter (in this case, ACCTNO). If that value equals the second parameter, the third parameter is returned. If that value equals the fourth parameter, the fifth parameter is returned, and so on. If the value equals no parameter, the default value provided in the last parameter (in this case, ACTIVE) is returned. TRANSFER would be returned if ACCTNO equaled 590395, SEIZED would be returned if ACCTNO equaled 654321, and CLOSED would be returned if ACCTNO equaled 123456. **(Topic 3.2)**

11. C. `insert into BANK_ACCT (ACCTNO, NAME) VALUES (&VAR1, '&VAR2');`

Explanation   In order to have statement reusability where you can enter a value on-the-fly, you must use lexical references as runtime variables. These references are preceded with an ampersand (&) character, as in the correct answer. Although you can use nested subqueries in your `insert` statements, this has the effect of inserting multiple rows at once without requiring input from the user. **(Topic 7.1)**

12. B. 28-APR-07

Explanation   For this question, you really need to put on your thinking cap. ADD_MONTHS adds a specified number of months, indicated by the second parameter to the value in the first parameter. The parameter 120 months is ten years, so if you add ten to the year in the date given, you should come up with 28-APR-07, which is the correct answer. When you are taking the exam, beware of having too much of your time sucked up by this sort of brainteaser question. **(Topic 3.2)**

13. D. MONDAY JUNE 26, 2037: 10:30PM

Explanation   The first statement in this question alters the date format shown in your SQL*Plus session. The second statement returns the current date and time in that specific format. In this case, your format is the day of the week, followed by the month of the year, the date, the year, and the time in A.M./P.M. format. This being the case, the correct answer is MONDAY JUNE 26, 2037: 10:30PM. **(Topic 3.2)**

14. B. `where A.C = 5 AND A.C = B.C (+);`

Explanation   The correct choice illustrates the use of Oracle's outer join function. The question indicates that you want to see data in table A, whether or not corresponding data exists in table B. Thus, you place the outer join operation (it looks like a (+)) next to the reference to the C column in table B. If the outer join operation is removed, Oracle will only return data from table A for which corresponding data exists in table B. If the outer join operator is used for both tables, you will get a syntax error. If you omit the join operator comparing values from table A to table B, Oracle will return a Cartesian product of the data you requested from A with all the data from table B. **(Topic 4.2)**

15. B. When creating composite primary keys, the datatypes in all columns within the primary key must be the same datatype.

Explanation   No restriction exists on column datatypes for composite primary keys requiring that all columns in the primary key have the same datatype. Choice A is incorrect because you must ensure that the variables designed to hold data from table columns are large enough for the values in those columns. Choice D is incorrect for largely the same reason. Finally, choice C is incorrect because Oracle forces you to declare the column in a child table with the exact same datatype as it has in the parent table. **(Topic 10.2)**

16. B. sqrt ( )

Explanation   All the choices indicate `group by` functions except for the `sqrt ( )` function. `sqrt ( )` is a single-row function acting on each value in each column row, one at a time or individually. `avg ( )` processes data from multiple rows in a column and produces one result: the average value for all of them. `count ( )` processes all values in a column or columns and counts the number of row values in that column or columns. The `stddev ( )` function takes all values in a column of rows and determines the standard deviation for that set of values. **(Topic 5.1)**

17. C. nvl ( ) returns NULL if the first value is not equal to the second.

Explanation   The only statement that is not true is `nvl ( )` returns NULL if the first value is not equal to the second. `nvl ( )` is specifically designed to avoid returning NULL for a column by substituting another value that you pass as the second parameter. `nvl ( )` handles many different datatypes, and both values passed must be the same datatype. **(Topic 3.3)**

18. B. 418

Explanation   Regardless of what you think you know about Oracle, the only true way to know what Oracle does is to experience it. Three requests for NEXTVAL from MY_SEQ does not mean that each request increments the sequence because the first request for NEXTVAL returns the initial value. Take a look:

```
SQL> create sequence my_seq
  2   start with 394
  3   increment by 12
  4   nominvalue
  5   nomaxvalue
  6   nocycle
  7   nocache;
Sequence created.
SQL> select my_seq.nextval from dual;
  NEXTVAL
---------
      394
SQL> /
  NEXTVAL
---------
      406
```

```
SQL> /
  NEXTVAL
---------
      418
SQL> select my_seq.currval from dual;
  CURRVAL
---------
      418
SQL> /
  CURRVAL
---------
      418
SQL> /
  CURRVAL
---------
      418
SQL> /
  CURRVAL

------
      418
```

Thus, the sequence has only been incremented twice, so the answer is 418.
(Topic 12.1)

19. B. The high-water mark was not reset.

Explanation The `select count(*)` statement takes a long time because Oracle
needed to inspect the table in its entirety in order to derive the row count, even
though the table was empty. To avoid this situation on large tables, use the
`truncate` statement rather than `delete`. `truncate` resets the high-water mark
on your table, thus reducing the time it takes Oracle to perform `select
count(*)` operations. **(Topic 9.5)**

20. B. `create or replace view`

Explanation The column definitions for a view can be changed only by recreating
the view with the `create or replace view` statement. The `alter view`
command is used only to recompile a view. `insert into view` is not a valid
SQL statement. Although `create view` will technically work, you must first drop
the view you want to recreate, which requires two statements, not one. `create or
replace view` is the most accurate choice offered. **(Topic 11.2)**

21. A. A join statement without a where clause

Explanation Cartesian products are the result of select statements that contain malformed where clauses. sum( ) and avg( ) operations are group functions and do not produce Cartesian products. Selecting data from the DUAL table will not produce a Cartesian product because only one table is involved—and a table with only one row at that! **(Topic 4.1)**

22. B. Creating an appropriate login.sql file

Explanation SQL*Plus shows its roots in UNIX systems through the login.sql file. This file is used to specify settings used in your session. login.sql runs automatically after you log into Oracle. SQL*Plus in Windows environments does not have a Preferences menu, eliminating that choice. You shouldn't attempt to use the alter table or alter user statements for this purpose either. **(Topic 7.3)**

23. B. create or replace view emp_sal_vw as select emp_user, salary from emp_salary where emp_user = user;

Explanation The command in choice B is correctly defined for creating a view that will only enable users to see their own salary information from the underlying table. Choice A is incorrect because the view defined will show all salary information except for salary data for the user issuing the query. Choices C and D are incorrect because the view will show only salary data for users other than MARTHA. **(Topic 11.2)**

24. D. INTEGER

Explanation Although you can declare variables in PL/SQL blocks using the INTEGER datatype, you cannot store INTEGER datatype data in Oracle tables. All other datatypes shown—CHAR, RAW, and DATE—can be stored in the Oracle database. **(Topic 9.3)**

25. B. TO_CHAR

Explanation TO_CHAR is used to convert DATE values, numbers, and other things into text strings. The CONVERT operation is used to convert a text string from one character set to another. The TO_NUMBER operation converts numeric text to true numbers. The TO_DATE function is used to convert a properly formatted text string into a DATE value. **(Topic 3.3)**

26. C. Use the set command to allow for larger LONG column values.

Explanation The TRIGGER_BODY column in the ALL_TRIGGERS view is declared as a LONG datatype column, and SQL*Plus is most likely cutting off data from the output. Choice A is incorrect because the question says you are able to see some of the data in the view, just not all the data. Choice B is incorrect because memory allocation has nothing to do with the problem identified in the question. Finally, choice D is incorrect because nothing is wrong with the ALL_TRIGGERS view. The problem lies instead with how SQL*Plus is currently configured to display LONG column data. **(Topic 7.2)**

27. B. All records

Explanation Because the update statement does not contain a where clause, the change will be made to every record in the table. It is not possible to accurately update only the first or last record in the table. None of the records will be updated only if something is wrong with the update statement, such as a column being referenced incorrectly. **(Topic 8.3)**

28. B. alter table

Explanation The alter table statement enables you to easily add columns after the table is created, with minimal impact to your system. Unlike when you want to change views, you do not use the or replace keyword for this effort, thus creating a powerful distraction for the user who is more familiar with views than with underlying tables. The create table statement could be used for the task, but you would first need to issue the drop table statement to get rid of the initial table. **(Topic 9.4)**

29. B. foreign key

Explanation Foreign key relationships require that you grant references privileges on a table to the user who is creating the foreign key relationship from his or her table to yours. No particular special privilege must be granted to create unique, check, or not NULL constraints other than create table. **(Topic 10.2)**

30. D. Oracle creates the view successfully.

Explanation When you issue the create view command shown in the question, Oracle creates the view successfully. A view can be created with the order by clause, making choice A incorrect. You do not need to enclose the select statement in your create view command in parentheses, as choice C suggests. Finally, Choice B is incorrect because you do not need to use the with check option clause for creating a view. **(Topic 11.2)**

31. D. like

Explanation In the situation where you want to use wildcards, Oracle offers the like comparison operator. This operator enables you to search for text strings like the one you're looking for. The `in` operator specifies a set of values to which the comparison value can be equal to one of. `exists` enables you to use a subquery as a lookup validity test for some piece of information. `between` specifies a range comparison, such as `between 1 AND 5`. **(Topic 2.1)**

32. A. Use `define` to capture values.

Explanation The `define` command can be used to identify a variable and assign it a value for use throughout a script running in SQL*Plus. This is useful when you are executing a number of SQL statements in batch. Although the `accept` command can perform the same function, the key factor that makes this the wrong answer is the mention of no user interaction in the question. Hard-coded values will work, but they make the script almost completely not reusable. Finally, although lexical references using an ampersand (&) followed by a label will provide statement reusability, your users will need to keep entering values every time a statement containing the lexical reference is processed. **(Topic 7.1)**

33. A. `where EMP.EMPID = 39284 AND EMP.EMPID = EXPNS.EMPID;`

Explanation Because you only want data from each table where a match appears in the other, you are performing a regular join or equijoin operation. In Oracle, you would not use the outer join `(+)` operator for this purpose. This eliminates both of the answer choices that contain an outer join operator. **(Topic 4.1)**

34. C. 4104930504

Explanation The only record that will not be present from the choices given is 4104930504, because UPC code 402392340 does not exist at the time this statement is issued. It was already changed to 50393950, and thus the 4104930504 `update` statement fails when you issue it. In order to get the answer correct, you need to read the question for a long time, and that wastes time when you're taking the OCP exams. Be aware that this question can take up an enormous amount of time if you're not careful. **(Topic 8.2)**

35. D. Views with object dependencies on the table being dropped will be rendered invalid automatically, but will not be dropped.

Explanation Oracle does not remove views when you drop underlying tables. Instead, Oracle merely marks the view as invalid. Thus, because choices A, B, and C all indicate in various different ways that the view will be dropped, all those choices are incorrect. **(Topic 11.3)**

36. C. Four

Explanation The general rule of thumb here is that if you have *n* tables you want to join—four in this case—you will generally need *n* - 1 comparison operations in your where clause joined together by AND—three in this case. In addition, the question states that you want to further restrict return data based on values in the first table. Thus, your where clause would have four conditions, and may look something like the following block:

```
WHERE
A.COLUMN1 = 5           AND
A.COLUMN1 = B.COLUMN1   AND
B.COLUMN2 = C.COLUMN2   AND
C.COLUMN3 = D.COLUMN3
```

(Topic 4.1)

37. A. Password authentication and granting privileges

Explanation   Although in order to get database access you need to create user privileges, the two real components of the Oracle security model are password authentication and granting privileges. When users are created, they will still not be able to connect to Oracle unless they are granted a privilege (create session), and even when they connect, they still cannot see anything unless someone gives them permission via the grant command. **(Topic 13.1)**

38. C. spool

Explanation   The spool command makes SQL*Plus write an output file containing all information transacted in the session, from the time you turn spooling on and identify the output file to the time you either turn spooling off or end the session. prompt causes SQL*Plus to prompt you to enter data using a custom request message. echo causes an error because it is not a valid command in SQL*Plus. Finally, the define command is used for variable definition and variable assignment in SQL*Plus scripts. **(Topic 1.3)**

39. B. select A.STUDENT_ID, A.LOCATION, B.LOCATION from TEST_SCORE A, TEST_SCORE B where A.STUDENT_ID = B.STUDENT_ID AND A.LOCATION <> B.LOCATION AND trunc(A.TEST_DATE)+30 >= trunc(B.TEST_DATE) AND trunc(A.TEST_DATE)-30 <= trunc(B.TEST_DATE);

Explanation   Because it ensures that the student is the same, that the date the test was taken violated the 30-day rule, and that the test location is not the same, choice B is the correct answer. This question is probably the hardest on the exam. Even if you have a bit of SQL experience, this question will take you a while. When taking the OCP exam, the last thing you need is time-waster questions to throw you off. A good technique to avoid having questions like this one consume all your time is to skip it if you cannot answer it within 30 seconds. You'll most likely have some time at the end of the exam to review the questions you skipped. **(Topic 4.3)**

40. C. `select * from EMPLOYEE where empid = (select empid from invoice where invoice_no = 4399485);`

Explanation If you can use a subquery, you should do so. Only one choice displays a subquery, so that one must be the correct answer. All the other choices depend on the EMPID being provided, not using the invoice number. **(Topic 6.2)**

41. A. To put returned data into sorted order

Explanation The `having` clause is best used to include or exclude certain data groups, not to return data in sort order. The `order by` clause handles that task. **(Topic 2.2)**

42. D. Roles

Explanation Roles enable you to group privileges together into one object and grant the privileges to the user at one time. No privileges are related to indexes other than the privilege to access the associated table. Tables and sequences both require privileges to be granted to a user or role; they do not simplify the act of privilege management in any way. **(Topic 13.2)**

43. A. `alter user`

Explanation The `alter user` statement with the `identified by` clause is used to change a user's password. `alter role` is used for modifying the actual role object, and affects users insofar as the user has been granted the role. Of the remaining choices, although user SNOW may be able to execute those statements depending on what privileges he is granted, none of these privileges will handle what the question requires. **(Topic 13.1)**

44. C. User SNOW needs a synonym for table EMP.

Explanation User SNOW needs a synonym in order to refer to a table he doesn't own without prefixing that reference with a schema owner. Without privileges, SNOW would not see the data, but even with the appropriate privileges granted, SNOW still needs to prefix the table name with the schema information if no synonym exists for the table in that schema. If no synonym exists, SNOW still must prefix references to EMP with REED, as in REED.EMP. Tables don't have passwords like databases do, so that choice is patently incorrect. **(Topic 12.3)**

45. D. Oracle returns an error.

Explanation In this situation, you cannot use the `order by` clause in a subquery. Oracle will return an error. Thus, no data will be returned from any table, so all of the other choices are wrong. **(Topic 6.4)**

46. B. `select to_char(nvl(sqrt(59483), 0)) from dual;`

Explanation The `select to_char(nvl(sqrt(59483), 0)) from dual;` statement is a valid statement. The `select nvl(sqrt(59483)) from dual;` statement does not pass enough parameters to the `nvl( )` function. The `select TO_CHAR(nvl(sqrt(59483), 'VALID')) from dual;` statement breaks the rule in `nvl( )` that states that both parameters passed into the function must be the same datatype. The `select (to_char(nvl(sqrt(59483), '0')) from dual;` statement is missing a matching closing parenthesis after `'0'`. **(Topic 1.2)**

47. C. `column PLAY_TABLE heading "My Plays and Authors"`

Explanation The `heading` clause to the `column` command in SQL*Plus acts in the same way as a `column` alias does in SQL—it modifies the output of the query to use a heading of your design. Despite its similarity, however, the `heading` clause is not the same as an alias in SQL. Thus, both the choice identifying the `alias` clause and the choice using the `as` keyword are incorrect. The choice containing the `format` clause should be easy to eliminate. **(Topic 1.3)**

48. C. BABS

Explanation Because BABS is not listed in the contents of the MY_USERS table, JONES will not see BABS when he queries the view. Choices A, B, and D all identify users who are listed in the MY_USERS view, and thus will be seen by JONES when he queries BASEBALL_TEAM_VW. **(Topic 11.3)**

49. C. Use the `set long` command

Explanation The `set long` command is used for adjusting the SQL*Plus output produced from data dictionary views with long columns. The view containing view creation code contains a long column, so adjusting how SQL*Plus displays that information will solve the issue. Choice A is incorrect because you cannot change the size of a dictionary view. Choice D is incorrect because the `alter user` statement does not somehow adjust view alottments. Finally, the NLS_DATE_FORMAT controls date formatting, not long columns. **(Topic 1.3)**

50. D. `group by COW_NAME;`

Explanation When the column clause contains a mix of group and non-group expressions, all non-group expressions must be listed to the left of the group expression, and all non-group expressions listed in the column clause must also be listed in the `group by` clause. Otherwise, Oracle returns an error indicating a problem with the `group by` expression, making choice D the correct answer. **(Topic 5.3)**

51. D. `group by COW_NAME;`

Explanation The `mod( )` function is not a group function, so no `group by` clause is necessary in this query. Thus, choice D is the correct answer. **(Topic 5.3)**

52. B. `select A.LASTNAME, B.DEPT_NO from EMP A, (select EMPID, DEPT_NO from DEPT) B where A.EMPID = B.EMPID;`

Explanation An inline view is a subquery appearing in the table clause of your SQL query. Thus, because choice B is the only query showing a subquery in the `from` clause, it is the only query that uses an inline view and therefore is the correct answer. Choices A and C are incorrect because the subqueries are used in the `where` clause. Choice D is incorrect because the subquery in the column clause is really a static text string that will be listed once for as many rows as there are in the USER_TABLES view. **(Topic 11.5)**

53. A. `drop index`

Explanation An index associated with a constraint cannot be dropped using the `drop index` command, making choice A the correct answer. The other statements all indicate methods that can be used for removing indexes associated with constraints. Constraints will be removed when the table is removed or whenever you drop the constraint. **(Topic 12.2)**

54. C. Every primary key column value must be unique and none can be NULL.

Explanation Choice C is the only answer that encapsulates all the restrictions on data in primary key columns, so it is therefore the correct answer. Although choices A and B each identify some of the restrictions on primary key constraints, neither choice alone is the correct answer. Choice D does not identify a restriction on data in primary key columns so you can discard that choice immediately. **(Topic 10.1)**

55. C. Table FOOBAR has no primary key, and therefore no index on MOO.

Explanation Because no primary key was defined when you created the FOOBAR table, the later query on that table cannot use any unique index on the MOO column to speed access to data in your FOOBAR table. Thus, choice C is the correct answer. Choice A is incorrect because you have no information indicating a primary key index is present, whereas choice B is incorrect because nothing states that a query takes longer to resolve when operating on a table rather than a view—if anything, the opposite is true. Finally, choice D is incorrect because again, you have no information indicating that the table was dropped and recreated. **(Topic 10.1)**

56. D. USER_INDEXES, indexes with the same name as the constraint

Explanation   The object associated with the table and the primary key is an index, and the USER_INDEXES dictionary view contains a listing of all indexes owned by the current user. You can query this dictionary view to find indexes with the same name as the constraint identified in the question text, making choice D the correct answer. Choice A is incorrect because USER_SEQUENCES contains information about sequences, which wasn't a topic for the question. USER_TABLES contains information about tables, which also wasn't a topic for the question, making choice B incorrect as well. Finally, USER_IND_COLUMNS contains information about indexed columns, which aren't objects separate from the table or constraint, making choice C incorrect as well. Oracle has been de-emphasizing dictionary view questions on this exam of late, so consider it a bonus if you knew the correct answer. **(Topic 12.2)**

57. B. To improve performance on columns with few unique values

Explanation   Bitmap indexes are designed to improve performance on columns with few unique values. Traditional or B-tree indexes are designed for indexes with many or all unique values, making choices A and C incorrect. Sequences do not need an index, making choice D incorrect. A question about bitmap indexes may or may not be on the OCP exam, so consider it a bonus if you knew the correct answer. **(Topic 12.2)**

58. A. `update employee set salary = 5000 where empid = 59694;`

Explanation   Choice A correctly identifies a statement that will correspond to the requirements of the statement, whereby the salary information for employee 59694 is changed. Choice B is incorrect because the `update` statement changes EMPID column information, not SALARY. Choice C is incorrect because the statement changes LASTNAME column information, not SALARY. Finally, choice D is incorrect because although SALARY information is being changed, it is being done based on LASTNAME information, not EMPID information. **(Topic 8.3)**

59. C. `grant update on emp to timothy with grant option;`

Explanation   The statement offered by choice C is used for giving object privileges to other users along with the ability to grant that privilege to others. Choice D is incorrect because `with admin option` is used for giving administrative ability over system privileges with respect to other users. Choice A is not a properly formulated grant command for object privileges, making it an incorrect answer. Choice B is incorrect because although the privilege itself was given to TIMOTHY, administrative ability was not. **(Topic 13.3)**

60. D. REED and SNOW only

Explanation SNOW does not lose the ability to create sessions with Oracle just because REED revoked the privilege from MANN because Oracle does not cascade revocation of system privileges. Thus, REED still has the privilege because no one revoked it from her, and SNOW still has the privilege because Oracle didn't cascade the revocation. **(Topic 13.1)**

Answers to Practice Exam 2

1. D. where C.COW_NAME = 'BESS' AND C.CARTON_NUM = C1.CARTON_NUM;

Explanation Two components are required in your where clause—you need a join clause and something that only pulls records from COW_MILK for BESS. The right answer is where C.COW_NAME = 'BESS' AND C.CARTON_NUM = C1.CARTON_NUM;. Another choice is similar to this one, but because it uses the not equal (<>) clause for getting information only for BESS, it is not the choice you want. The other two choices are incomplete, and therefore wrong. **(Topic 2.1)**

2. D. The insert statements contain duplicate data due to the reset sequence.

Explanation The correct answer is that the insert statements contain duplicate data due to the reset sequence. When you drop and re-create the sequence from its original code, you reset the start value for that sequence. Subsequent insert statements will then attempt to add rows where the value in the primary key is duplicated information. The question has no information about read-only status, so you should assume that the answer concerning the table being read-only is not correct. Dropping a sequence does nothing to a table's primary key—no relationship exists between the two. Finally, although it is true that any cached sequence values that existed when the sequence was dropped are now unusable, this point has little relevance to the question at hand. **(Topic 12.1)**

3. B. exists

Explanation Only when using the exists statement must you use a correlated subquery. Although you can use a subquery with your use of in, you are not required to do so because you can specify a set of values instead. The between keyword indicates a range of values and does not permit the use of a subquery. The like keyword is used for wildcard comparisons and also does not permit the use of a subquery. **(Topic 2.1)**

4. D. abs ( )

Explanation   All of the functions except for abs ( ) will give you a result of 4093 when you pass them 4093.505. abs ( ) returns the absolute value of the number you pass into the function. round ( ) can give you a result of 4093 if you also pass in a second parameter defining the precision to which you want to round the function, whereas trunc ( ) will give you a result of 4093 with only 4093.505 as input. floor ( ) gives you a result of 4093, because it is the logical opposite of the ceil ( ) function. **(Topic 3.2)**

5. B. Use accept to capture the name value for each run.

Explanation   The accept command is the best way to handle the situation. Although you could use define to assign a value to a variable used throughout the script, only accept enables you to dynamically enter a value for that variable. Lexical substitutions identified with the & character will only work for the current statement, meaning that the same value assigned in one statement will not be used in the next statement unless you reenter it. **(Topic 7.3)**

6. B. truncate

Explanation   Once a truncate operation is complete, that's it—the change is made and saved. This is because truncate is not a DML operation that can be performed as part of a transaction. The truncate command is a DDL operation, and as such, it has an implied commit at the end of its execution. If you want to get the data back after truncating, you need to recover it. For the other operations listed as choices in this question—insert, update, and delete statements—Oracle enables you to discard the changes using the rollback command. **(Topic 9.5)**

7. A. savepoint

Explanation   savepoint operations simply act as logical breakpoints in a transaction. They do not cause Oracle to save or discard data, but merely act as a breakpoint with which you can perform partial transaction rollbacks later. The set transaction and commit commands indicate the beginning of a new transaction. Creating a new session with Oracle implicitly begins a transaction as well. **(Topic 8.6)**

8. B. A from clause

Explanation   No SQL statement can survive without a from clause. For this reason, Oracle provides you with the DUAL table, so that you can perform arithmetic operations on expressions and not on table data while still satisfying this syntactic construct. Because this statement already has a select clause, you don't need to add another. The `where` clause is optional, but because the statement already has one, you don't need to add another. Finally, your SQL statement does not require an `order by` clause. **(Topic 1.2)**

9. A. `set transaction`

Explanation The `set transaction` command is used to define the transaction state to be read-only. `rollback` and `commit` statements are used to end the transaction. The `savepoint` command denotes logical breakpoints for the transaction. **(Topic 8.6)**

10. C. Bitmap index

Explanation Bitmap indexes work well in situations where the data in the column is static. In this case, the column contains gender information, which rarely changes. The number of distinct possible values is limited to only two as well. Thus, this column is a bad candidate for B-tree indexes of any sort, but perfect for bitmap indexes. Remember that B-tree indexes work well for columns with high cardinality or number of distinct values corresponding to the overall number of entries in the column. **(Topic 12.2)**

11. A. Parent to child

Explanation This question describes the relationship between the INVOICE and INVOICE_ITEM table, and the appropriate answer is parent to child. This is because the relationship described between invoices and invoice items is optional, given that invoices may have no invoice items, but that all invoice items must have a corresponding invoice. **(Topic 10.2)**

12. D. ACTIVE

Explanation The `decode( )` function acts as a case statement. The first parameter indicates the column whose values you want decoded. If the value in the column equals parameter 2, then `decode( )` returns parameter 3. If the value in the column equals parameter 4, `decode( )` returns parameter 5, and so on. If the value in the column doesn't equal any of the other parameters specified, then `decode( )` returns the default value specified as the last parameter. Thus, because the column value is not specified for any of the parameters, the returned value is the default, ACTIVE. **(Topic 3.2)**

13. D. `where COL_A in (select NUM from TAB_OF_NUMS)`

Explanation The `where` clause in choice D is an excellent example of the definition of a subquery, which is the example being asked for in the question. Choice A is not a comparison operation between a column and a set of values, because only one value is being compared. Choice B is a comparison of a column to a set of values, but the set is static and defined at the time the query is issued. Choice C is a range-comparison operation, a variant on choice B, and therefore also wrong. Only choice D enables Oracle to dynamically generate the list of values to which COL_A will be compared. **(Topic 6.2)**

14. D. `select NAME from CONTESTANT where COUNTRY in (select COUNTRY from MEDALS where NUM_GOLD + NUM_SILVER + NUM_BRONZE > 10)`

Explanation   The query in choice D is correct because it contains the subquery that correctly returns a subset of countries that have contestants who won ten or more medals of any type. Choice A is incorrect because it contains a join operation, not a subquery. Choice B is simply a rewrite of choice A to use a multiple-row subquery, but does not go far enough to restrict return data. Choice C is a single-row subquery that does essentially the same thing as choice B. **(Topic 6.4)**

15. C. Multiple-column subquery, the youngest contestant from all countries

Explanation   Because the main query compares against the results of two columns returned in the subquery, this is a multiple-column subquery that will return the youngest contestant from every country in the table. This multiple-column subquery is also a multiple-row subquery, but because the defining factor is that two columns are present, you should focus more on that fact than on the rows being returned. This fact eliminates choices A and B. The subquery does return multiple rows, however. You should also be sensitive to the fact that the main query must use an `in` clause, not the equal sign (=), making choice D incorrect as well. **(Topic 6.3)**

16. A. SOO

Explanation   The correct answer is SOO because the subquery operation specified by the `in` clause ignores NULL values implicitly. Thus, because SOO has no country defined, that row is not selected as part of the subquery. As a result, SOO won't show up as having the youngest age in the results of this query. **(Topic 6.4)**

17. B. Table

Explanation   The object being referred to is a table. A table has many columns, each of which is functionally dependent on the key column. Choice A is incorrect because a synonym is simply another name you can use to reference a table, not an actual table itself. A sequence is a number generator in Oracle that, again, does not require storage in a segment other than a dictionary segment, making choice C incorrect. Finally, a view is similar to a table in that it contains many columns, each of which is functionally dependent on the key. However, views contain no data needing to be stored in a segment, so choice D is wrong as well. **(Topic 9.1)**

18. B. cube

Explanation The cube keyword included in a group by clause of a SQL statement in Oracle8i enables you to perform *N*-dimensional cross-tabulations within the Oracle database, returning the result set directly to the client. This keyword is useful in queries within data warehouses. Choice C is incorrect because even though the rollup keyword was also added to SQL queries in Oracle8i, this keyword supports subtotal and grand total calculations of grouped data. Although the having expression is also available in group operations, choice A is incorrect because you do not need to define a having clause in order to use either cube or rollup. Finally, choice D is incorrect because the trim( ) function combines the capabilities of ltrim( ) and rtrim( ). **(Topic 5.3)**

19. B. Reverse-key indexes

Explanation A reverse-key index is one where the contents of the indexed column are reversed. This gives a higher amount of lead-in selectivity than a straight B-tree index would, because the cardinality of the root node in the B-tree would be low. This is based on the fact that most records would begin with the digit 1 (recall the question content if you don't understand why), whereas the reverse of that key would have greater cardinality. Be careful of choice A because although cardinality is high, choice B gives a better option for performance. Choice C is incorrect because bitmap indexes are designed for low-cardinality records like status or gender. Finally, choice D indicates an index type that wouldn't suit this situation. **(Topic 12.2)**

20. A. VARCHAR2

Explanation Because the text blocks are within the size limits imposed in Oracle8i for the VARCHAR2 datatype, it is best to use the scalar type rather than a large object for simplicity sake. If the block were larger than 4,000 bytes, you would most likely use a CLOB, but because the size requirement is less than 4,000 bytes, choice C is incorrect. You would use a BLOB to store binary large objects, making choice B incorrect. Finally, the text block is not stored as an external file (you would not use the BFILE type), making choice D incorrect. **(Topic 9.3)**

21. B. The index is dropped.

Explanation Like automatically generated indexes associated with a table's primary key, the indexes created manually on a table to improve performance will be dropped if the table is dropped. Choices A, C, and D are therefore invalid. **(Topic 12.2)**

22. C. Columns with high cardinality are handled well by B-tree indexes.

Explanation   Columns with low cardinality are the bane of B-tree indexes, eliminating choice A. Furthermore, bitmap indexes are primarily used for performance gains on columns with low cardinality, eliminating choice B. **(Topic 12.2)**

23. D. Drop and recreate the view with references to select more columns.

Explanation   Choice A is incorrect because adding columns to the underlying table will not add columns to the view, but will likely invalidate the view. Choice B is incorrect because the `alter view` statement simply recompiles an existing view definition, whereas the real solution here is to change the existing view definition by dropping and recreating the view. Choice C is incorrect because a correlated subquery will likely worsen performance, and underscores the real problem—a column must be added to the view. **(Topic 11.2)**

24. C. `maxvalue`

Explanation   The `maxvalue` option is a valid option for sequence creation. Choices A and B are both part of the `create user` statement, whereas choice D is a part of a constraint declaration in an `alter table` or `create table` statement. **(Topic 12.1)**

25. F. This statement contains no errors.

Explanation   Even though the reference to `with check option` is inappropriate, considering that inserts into complex views are not possible, the statement will not actually produce an error when compiled. Therefore, the view has no errors. This is not something that can be learned. It requires hands-on experience with Oracle. **(Topic 11.4)**

26. A. `references`

Explanation   The `references` privilege gives the user the ability to refer back to your table in order to link to it via a foreign key from his or her table to yours. Choice B is incorrect because the `index` privilege enables the user to create an index on a table, whereas choice C is incorrect because the `select` privilege enables users to query data in your table. Finally, choice D is incorrect because the `delete` privilege is only required for enabling the other user to delete data into your table. **(Topic 13.3)**

27. A, B, and C. Roles can be granted to other roles, privileges can be granted to roles, and roles can be granted to users.

Explanation Choice D is the only option not available to managing roles. Roles cannot be granted to synonyms. **(Topic 13.2)**

28. C. It is equal to NEXTVAL.

Explanation Once NEXTVAL is referenced, the sequence increments the integer and changes the value of CURRVAL to be equal to NEXTVAL. **(Topic 12.1)**

29. D. with check option

Explanation The appropriate clause is with check option. You can add this clause to a create view statement so that the view will not let you to add rows to the underlying table that cannot then be selected in the view. The with admin option and with grant option clauses are used to assign administrative ability to users along with granting them a privilege. The with security option is a work of fiction—it does not exist in Oracle. **(Topic 11.4)**

30. C. The statement fails due to the primary key constraint.

Explanation It should be obvious that the statement fails—the real question here is why. The reason is because of the primary key constraint on UPC_CODE. As soon as you try to add a duplicate record, the table will reject the addition. Although the view has with check option specified, this is not the reason the addition fails. It would be the reason an insert fails if you attempt to add a record for a day other than today, however. **(Topic 10.2)**

31. A. drop view

Explanation When a table is dropped, Oracle eliminates all related database objects, such as triggers, constraints, and indexes. However, Oracle does not remove views. Views are actually considered separate objects, and although the view will not function properly after you drop the underlying table, Oracle will keep the view around after the table is dropped. **(Topic 11.2)**

32. C. The select receives NO ROWS SELECTED.

Explanation Although the query will succeed (translation: you won't receive an error), you must beware of the distracter in choice B. In reality, choice C is the better answer because it more accurately identifies what really will occur when you issue this statement. This view will behave as any select statement would when you list criteria in the where clause that no data satisfies—by returning NO ROWS SELECTED. This is not an error condition, but you wouldn't call it a successful search for data either, making both those choices incorrect. Finally, `select` statements never add data to a table. **(Topic 1.2)**

33. B and D. `unique` constraints and primary keys

Explanation Every constraint that enforces uniqueness creates an index to assist in the process. The two integrity constraints that enforce uniqueness are unique constraints and primary keys. **(Topic 10.2)**

34. C. ALL_IND_COLUMNS

Explanation This view is the only one listed that provides column positions in an index. Because primary keys create an index, the index created by the primary key will be listed with all the other indexed data. Choice A is incorrect because no view exists in Oracle called ALL_PRIMARY_KEYS. Choice B is incorrect because, although USER_CONSTRAINTS lists information about the constraints in a database, it does not contain information about the index created by the primary key. Choice D is incorrect because ALL_TABLES contains no information related to the position of a column in an index. **(Topic 12.2)**

35. C. A table named ANIMALS is created in the ANJU schema with the same data as the ANIMALS table owned by MASTER.

Explanation This question requires you to look carefully at the `create table` statement in the question and to know some things about table creation. First, a table is always created in the schema of the user who created it. Second, because the `create table as select` clause was used, choices B and D are both incorrect because they identify the table being created as something other than ANIMALS, among other things. Choice A identifies the schema into which the ANIMALS table will be created as MASTER, which is incorrect for the reasons just stated. **(Topic 9.2)**

36. A. `insert into EMPLOYEE values (59694,'HARRIS', NULL);`

Explanation This choice is acceptable because the positional criteria for not specifying column order are met by the data in the `values` clause. When you would like to specify that no data be inserted into a particular column, one method of doing so is to insert a NULL. Choice B is incorrect because not all columns in the table have values identified. When using positional references to populate column data, values must be present for every column in the table. Otherwise, the columns that will be populated should be named explicitly. Choice C is incorrect because when a column is named for data insert in the `insert into` clause, a value must definitely be specified in the `values` clause. Choice D is incorrect because using the multiple row `insert` option with a `select` statement is not appropriate in this situation. **(Topic 8.2)**

37. A. Two tables in the database are named VOUCHER and VOUCHER_ITEM, respectively.

Explanation This choice implies the use of a naming convention similar to the one we discussed earlier, where the two tables with a foreign key relationship are given similar names. Although it is not guaranteed that these two tables are related, the possibility is strongest in this case. Choice B implies the same naming convention, and because the two tables' names are dissimilar, it is unlikely that the tables are related in any way. Choice C is incorrect because the date a table is created has absolutely no bearing on what function the table serves in the database. Choice D is incorrect because two tables *cannot* be related if no common columns exist between them. **(Topic 10.1)**

38. A, B, and D. CHAR, VARCHAR2, and NUMBER

Explanation BOOLEAN is the only invalid datatype in this listing. Although BOOLEAN is a valid datatype in PL/SQL, it is not a datatype available in the Oracle database, meaning that you cannot create a column in a table that uses the BOOLEAN datatype. **(Topic 9.3)**

39. D. The `delete` statement removes all records from the table.

Explanation Only one effect is produced by leaving off the `where` clause from any statement that permits one: The requested operation is performed on all records in the table. **(Topic 8.4)**

40. C. `GOOD_NAME VARCHAR2(20) check(GOOD_NAME in (select NAME from AVAIL_GOODS)),`

Explanation A `check` constraint cannot contain a reference to another table, nor can it reference a virtual column, such as ROWID or SYSDATE. The other lines of the `create table` statement contain correct syntax. **(Topic 10.2)**

41. A. Locks

Explanation Locks are the mechanisms that prevent more than one user at a time from making changes to the database. All other options refer to the commands that are issued to mark the beginning, middle, and end of a transaction. Remember, the `commit` and `rollback` keywords end the current transaction and begin a new one, whereas the `savepoint` keyword marks a logical breakpoint within the transaction. **(Topic 8.6)**

42. A. Use the `alter table` statement.

Explanation The `alter table` statement is the only choice offered that enables the developer to increase the number of columns per table. Choice B is incorrect because setting a column to all NULL values for all rows does simply that. Choice C is incorrect because increasing the adjacent column sizes simply increases the sizes of the columns. Choice D is incorrect because the listed steps outline how to add a column with a not NULL constraint, something not specified by the question. **(Topic 9.4)**

43. B. Truncate the table.

Explanation Choices A and C may work, but an upgrade of hardware and software will cost far more than truncating the table (choice B). Choice D is partly correct, as some change will be required to the high-water mark, but the change is to reset, not eliminate entirely. **(Topic 9.5)**

44. A. unique

Explanation Only unique and primary key constraints require Oracle to generate an index that supports or enforces the uniqueness of the column values. foreign key, check, and not NULL constraints do not require an index. **(Topic 10.1)**

45. B. All values in the referenced column in the parent table must be present in the referencing column in the child.

Explanation Referential integrity is from child to parent, not vice versa. The parent table can have many values that are not present in child records, but the child record must correspond to something in the parent. Thus, the correct answer is all values in the referenced column in the parent table must be present in the referencing column in the child. **(Topic 10.1)**

46. B. Values must be part of a fixed set defined by create or alter table.

Explanation A check constraint may only use fixed expressions defined when you create or alter the table with the constraint definition. The reserved words like sysdate and user, or values from a lookup table, are not permitted, making those answers incorrect. Finally, NULL values in a column are constrained by not NULL constraints, a relatively unsophisticated form of check constraints. **(Topic 10.1)**

47. B. sqrt ( )

Explanation Square root operations are performed on one column value. **(Topic 3.2)**

48. B. The tables in the join need to have common columns.

Explanation It is possible that a join operation will produce no return data, just as it is possible for any select statement not to return any data. Choices A, C, and D represent the spectrum of possibilities for shared values that may or may not be present in common columns. However, joins themselves are not possible without two tables having common columns. **(Topic 4.1)**

49. D. Until the session completes

Explanation A variable defined by the user during a session with SQL*Plus will remain defined until the session ends or until the user explicitly undefines the variable. **(Topic 1.3)**

50. B and C. Alter the `prompt` clause of the `accept` command and enter a new prompt in the `login.sql` file.

Explanation Choice D should be eliminated immediately, leaving the user to select between choices A, B, and C. Choice A is incorrect because `config.ora` is a feature associated with Oracle's client/server network communications product. Choice C is correct because you can use the `set sqlprompt` command within your `login.sql` file. This is a special Oracle file that will automatically configure aspects of the SQL*Plus session, such as the default text editor, column and NLS data formats, and other items. **(Topic 7.1)**

51. A and C. `select * from EMPLOYEE where EMPID = &empid;` and `select * from EMPLOYEE where EMPID = (select empid from invoice where INVOICE_NO = 4399485);`

Explanation Choice A details the use of a runtime variable that can be used to have the user input appropriate search criteria after the statement has begun processing. Choice C details the use of a subquery that enables the user to select unknown search criteria from the database using known methods for obtaining the data. Choice B is incorrect because the statement simply provides a known search criterion; choice D is incorrect because it provides no search criteria at all. **(Topic 7.1)**

52. A. Ampersand

Explanation The ampersand (&) character is used by default to define runtime variables in SQL*Plus. **(Topic 7.1)**

53. C. `select e.empid, d.head from EMPLOYEE e, dept d where e.dept# = d.dept# (+);`

Explanation Choice C details the outer join operation most appropriate to this user's needs. The outer table in this join is the DEPT table, as identified by the (+) marker next to the DEPT# column in the comparison operation that defines the join. **(Topic 4.2)**

54. B, C, and D. To exclude certain data groups based on known criteria, to include certain data groups based on unknown criteria, and to include certain data groups based on known criteria

Explanation   All exclusion or inclusion of grouped rows is handled by the `having` clause of a `select` statement. Choice A is not an appropriate answer because sort order is given in a `select` statement by the `order by` clause. **(Topic 5.4)**

55. B. Produced as a result of a join `select` statement with no `where` clause

Explanation   A Cartesian product is the result dataset from a `select` statement where all data from both tables is returned. A potential cause of a Cartesian product is not specifying a `where` clause for the join `select` statement. **(Topic 4.1)**

56. D. Issuing the `set define` command

Explanation   Choice A is incorrect because a change to the `init.ora` file alters the parameters Oracle uses to start the database instance. Choice B is incorrect because, although the `login.sql` file can define many properties in a SQL*Plus session, the character that denotes runtime variables is not one of them. Choice C is incorrect because the `define` command is used to define variables used in a session, not an individual statement. **(Topic 1.3)**

57. B. `set role sales_analyzer;`

Explanation   The problem likely occurs because SALES_ANALYZER was not the default role assigned to THOMAS. She can enable this role using the `set role` command, making choice B the correct answer. Because the appropriate privileges are already granted to THOMAS via the role, the `grant` command needn't be issued, making choices C and D incorrect. Finally, choice A is incorrect because a user cannot alter his or her own user settings using the `alter user` statement to change role information; he or she can only use the `alter user` statement to change his or her own password. **(Topic 13.2)**

58. D. Immediately after the privilege is granted to SALES_ANALYZER

Explanation   Access to objects granted by giving the appropriate privilege to the appropriate role takes effect immediately. DAVIS does not need to log into Oracle again, making choice A incorrect. Choice B is incorrect because the SALES_ANALYZER role needn't be granted to DAVIS again. Finally, choice C is incorrect because the privilege needn't be granted to SALES_ANALYZER again. **(Topic 13.3)**

59. D. `grant create public synonym to davis;`

Explanation DAVIS doesn't need the ability to create public synonyms in order to create tables. Thus, choice D is correct. However, DAVIS will need a user ID setup on Oracle by IMADBA, making choice A incorrect. DAVIS will also need the ability to log into Oracle using the privilege identified in choice B and the ability to create tables given by the privilege in choice C. Thus, those other answers are incorrect. **(Topic 12.3)**

60. C. `create session`

Explanation The `create session` privilege enables you to connect to the Oracle database, making C the correct answer. Choices A and B both identify Oracle-created roles that already have the appropriate privileges for logging into Oracle granted to them, but remember—these are roles, not privileges themselves. Finally, choice D is incorrect because the `references` privilege is an object privilege that does not give you the ability to connect to Oracle. **(Topic 13.3)**

Answers to Practice Exam 3

1. A. `select empno, ename, loc from emp join dept on emp.deptno = dept.deptno where substr(emp.ename,1,1) = 'S';`

Explanation Choice A identifies the correct ANSI-compliant syntax for setup of table joins in Oracle9i. Choice B is incorrect because the `on` keyword is used only in the presence of the `join` keyword, which is not present in the syntax of that choice. Choice C is incorrect because the join condition must be identified as part of the `on` clause when the `join` keyword is present. Finally, choice D is incorrect because determining whether the first character in the ENAME column is S is not a join condition—it is a filtering condition. Thus, that condition should not be included in the `on` clause, but rather in a `where` clause. **(Topic 4.1)**

2. C. You can create a table with the CONTENTS of another using `select` statements.

Explanation Choice C is correct because the `create table as select` command involves a `select` statement that is not used as a subquery. Choices A and B are incorrect because the `update` and `delete` commands must include a subquery in order for you to change or remove data with the use of a `select` command. Finally, it is not possible to include a subquery in a `truncate` command. **(Topic 6.1)**

3. D. The where clause

Explanation If you are using a `select` statement to perform a mathematical operation on static expressions, you do not need to use the `where` clause. Choice A is incorrect because your query must include the static expressions and the math operation in the column clause. Choice B is incorrect because all SQL statements need to include a `from` clause. Finally, choice C is incorrect because your `from` clause in this scenario will reference the DUAL table. **(Topic 2.1)**

4. B. `set define ?`

Explanation The `set` command is not a SQL command in Oracle. Rather, it is an Oracle tool command that operates in a tool-specific way. For SQL*Plus, the `set` command enables you to define aspects of your SQL operating environment. Choices A and C are incorrect because the `select` and `update` commands are part of SQL data manipulation language. Choice D is incorrect because the `create table` command is part of SQL data definition language. **(Topic 1.3)**

5. C. Indexes

Explanation You cannot reference an index directly from a SQL command, but Oracle may use one behind the scenes to improve performance under certain conditions. Choice A is incorrect because the `select` command enables you to query Oracle for the contents of a table. You can also reference sequences directly in `select` commands, making choice B incorrect as well. Finally, choice D is incorrect because you can also reference views directly using SQL `select` commands. **(Topic 12.2)**

6. C. `where`

Explanation Filter conditions are always properly placed in the `where` clause of your SQL query. Choice A is incorrect because the columns you want to see in the output are listed in the `select` clause. Choice B is incorrect because the tables you want to query are listed in the `from` clause. Finally, choice D is incorrect because the `having` clause acts as an additional filter usually when you want to see only the output that conforms to filter conditions when a `group by` clause is used. **(Topic 2.1)**

7. C. `where product_type = 'APPLIANCE' and qtr_end_date between '01-JAN-2001' and '01-JUL-2001';`

Explanation Because you want to get the total profits for all appliances for the first six months of 2001, choice C is your best answer because it filters based on that criteria in the columns PRODUCT_TYPE and QTR_END_DATE. Choice A is incorrect because that `where` clause filters on the PRODUCT_NAME column, and although gas grills are certainly appliances, other appliances could be listed in the PROFITS table that are not gas grills that we would want to include in the total profits calculation. Choice B is incorrect because again, not all appliances are gas grills. Furthermore, the filter condition on the QTR_END_DATE column is malformed. Finally, choice D is incorrect because no filter condition appears on the PRODUCT_TYPE column and the filter condition on the QTR_END_DATE column is malformed. **(Topic 2.1)**

8. D. NULL

Explanation   This is a difficult question that tests your knowledge of how group functions react when NULL information is given. Take another look at the contents of the COMM column in the EMP table. Many rows in that table contain NULL values for the COMM column. When NULL data is fed into group functions, the result is always NULL. Thus, although the sum of salaries and commissions for analysts or employees whose names begin with the letter J is 9925, Oracle returns NULL as the answer. **(Topic 5.2)**

9. B. Two

Explanation   Again, this difficult question tests your knowledge on how group functions react when NULL information is given. Although three employees have a value of ten in the DEPTNO column, Oracle does not count KING's record because the MGR column for KING's record contains a NULL value. Thus, choice C is incorrect. **(Topic 5.2)**

10. A. Five

Explanation   7700 minus 2 equals 7698. Five employees have a value in the MGR column of 7698, so the answer is choice A. All other choices are incorrect. Be sure you understand that you can include math operations on static expressions in the filter comparisons of your SQL queries. **(Topic 1.3)**

11. D. WARD

Explanation   Take a moment to reread the question text, and attempt to rephrase what the question is asking for in your own words. First, this question asks you to identify the employees who are salesmen. Second, it asks you to list the output in descending order based on EMPNO, meaning that the employee with the highest value for EMPNO gets listed first, followed by the second highest, and so on. The listed output will be TURNER, MARTIN, WARD, and ALLEN, in that order. Finally, the question asks you to identify the employee listed third from the top of that list. Thus, choice D is the correct answer. **(Topic 2.2)**

12. B. MARTIN

Explanation   Take a moment to reread the question text, and try to rephrase the question in your own words. First, this question asks you to figure out which employees are salesmen. Second, the question asks you to list the output in descending order based on the values in the first column in the output: the ENAME column. The listed output will be WARD, TURNER, MARTIN, and ALLEN, in that order. Finally, the question asks you to identify the employee listed third from the top of that list. Thus, choice B is the correct answer. **(Topic 2.2)**

13. C. MAN

Explanation   Recall that when the `like` keyword is used, Oracle will use the wildcard characters _ and % to identify data via pattern matching. The _ character indicates that this single letter in the text string can be anything, whereas the % character indicates that the prior or subsequent text in the string can be anything. In this case, we are looking for the row whose value for ENAME can contain any letter for the first two characters, followed by AR, followed by anything. Only one name in the list matches this criteria—CLARK. The value in the JOB column for CLARK is MANAGER, and the first three characters of that text string are MAN. Thus, choice C is correct. **(Topic 3.2)**

14. C. –24

Explanation   The result Oracle produces when the query in this question is issued is –24, so choice C is correct. The result will be negative because Oracle subtracts the greater, or more recent hire date from the lesser, more distant hire date. Thus, choices A and B are incorrect. Choice D is incorrect because the `trunc( )` function truncates the value to the right of the decimal point and returns the value –24, not –25. **(Topic 3.2)**

15. A and C. ADAMS and SCOTT

Explanation   Oracle will only return rows where the value in the HIREDATE column is greater or more recent than January 23, 1982. Only two rows contain values meeting this criterion. They are shown in choices A and C. Choices B and D are both incorrect because the hire dates shown in the HIREDATE column for those two rows are both less recent than January 23, 1982. **(Topic 1.2)**

16. D. Oracle returns an error as the result.

Explanation   Any substitution value specified using the `nvl( )` function must be the same datatype as the column specified in the call to that function. Thus, because the TESTCOL column is of NUMBER datatype and 'EMPTY' is a text string, Oracle returns an error. Had we specified the TESTCOL_2 column instead of TESTCOL in our call to `nvl( )`, then choice B would have been the correct answer. **(Topic 3.2)**

17. D. `where customer = 'LESLIE' and order_amt > 2700;`

Explanation   To see order information for LESLIE where the total order exceeds $2,700, you must use the `where` clause identified in choice D. Choice A is incorrect because Oracle will indiscriminately return every order LESLIE has placed. Choice B is incorrect because Oracle will return orders LESLIE placed whose total is less than $2,700. Finally, choice C is incorrect because Oracle will return all orders that LESLIE placed and all orders for more than $2,700, even if LESLIE didn't place the order—this is too much information. **(Topic 2.1)**

18. B. `select rpad(ename, 10, '-dog') as ename from emp;`

Explanation   Each employee name is padded to the right with the text -dog repeated over and over to fill up to ten places. Thus, we have to use the `rpad( )` function. Choice A is incorrect because the `trim( )` function removes text specified from the string you pass to the function. Choice C is incorrect because the `substr( )` function returns a subset of text from a string you pass to the function. Finally, choice D is incorrect because the `lpad( )` function pads to the left with the text you specify in order to fill up to a specific number of spaces. **(Topic 3.2)**

19. A. `abs( )`

Explanation   The `abs( )` function returns the absolute value of a number, defined as the distance from zero of that number. Absolute values are always positive, so this function could not have produced the output identified in the question. Choices B, C, and D are all incorrect because the `ceil( )`, `floor( )`, and `round( )` functions all could have produced the amount given. **(Topic 3.2)**

20. B. 13

Explanation   Blank spaces are still counted as part of the overall length of a text string. Because SMITHY has six characters and seven blank spaces, the `length( )` function returns 13 for the length of this string. Choice A is incorrect because the value given doesn't take into account the blank spaces padded into the value stored in the column. Choice D would have been correct if the column had been declared as a CHAR(60) column rather than a VARCHAR2(60) column. Finally, you have no logical basis for arriving at 30 as the answer, so choice C can be eliminated immediately. **(Topic 3.2)**

21. B. `floor( )`

Explanation   The `floor( )` function always rounds to the lower integer value when given a decimal to work with, and because –98 is smaller than –97.342, that is the result `floor( )` returns. Choices A, C, and D are all incorrect because `ceil( )`, `round( )`, and `trunc( )` all return –97 as the result of this query. **(Topic 3.2)**

 22. A. `ceil( )`

Explanation   The `ceil( )` function always rounds up to the next highest integer value when presented with a decimal, and because 257 is the next highest integer, that is what `ceil( )` returns. Choices B, C, and D are all incorrect because those functions round down to the next lowest integer when given the decimal value in this question. **(Topic 3.2)**

 23. D. –168

Explanation   Oracle returns –168 as the result of this query because 168 months are between March 15, 1983, and March 15, 1997. The result is negative because 1983 is a lesser value than 1997, and because Oracle subtracts the second value from the first, the result is negative. Had the dates passed into `months_between ( )` been reversed, choice C would have been the correct answer. Choices A and B are obviously incorrect. **(Topic 3.2)**

 24. D. `to_number( )`

Explanation   Although date information is stored internally within Oracle as a number, you cannot use the `to_number( )` function to convert the date to an actual number, thus making it unnecessary and wrong to use a date format mask with the `to_number( )` function. Choices A, B, and C all indicate functions or situations where it is appropriate to use a date format mask. **(Topic 3.3)**

 25. C. `select p.prod_d, p.prod_name, b.box_loc from product p, storage_box b where p.stor_box_num = b.stor_box_num and p.prod_name = 'WIDGET';`

Explanation   The join and filter conditions required for this query are represented correctly in choice C because the common column in both tables is joined and the filtering condition on PROD_NAME for all widgets is represented correctly. Choice A is incorrect because the PRODUCT and STORAGE_BOX tables do not share the PROD_ID column in common—they share the STOR_BOX_NUM column in common. Choice B is incorrect because no joining condition exists between the two tables, which will cause the output to form a Cartesian product. Finally, choice D is incorrect because the join condition refers to the STOR_BOX_NUM columns ambiguously in both tables. **(Topic 4.1)**

26. B. Three

Explanation You will need *n* - 1 join conditions, where *n* is the number of tables, plus a filter comparison, to obtain the result requested in this question. Because three tables are present, you will need two join conditions, plus the filter condition, for a total of three comparison operations. **(Topic 4.1)**

27. C. select product.id, product.name, storage.loc from product natural join storage on product.box# = storage.box#;

Explanation Natural joins do not require you to identify a join condition because Oracle assumes the join will be executed on the common columns in both tables. Thus, the on clause in choice C is unnecessary, and will result in an error. Choice A identifies the traditional way to define a join in Oracle, whereas choice B identifies the ANSI/ISO-compliant way to define a join in Oracle. Finally, choice D is incorrect because it properly defines how to specify a natural join in Oracle. **(Topic 4.1)**

28. D. Even though outer join operations permit NULL values from one of the tables, you still need to specify equality comparisons to join those tables.

Explanation Choice D is the logical opposite of choice A, and therefore is the correct answer. For this reason, choice A is also incorrect. Choice B is incorrect because you specify a left join in order to see all of table A's rows, even when no corresponding record exists in table B. Finally, choice C is incorrect because you specify a right join in order to see all of table B's rows, even when no corresponding record exists in table A. **(Topic 4.2)**

29. B. select p.prod_id, p.prod_name, b.box_loc from product p left outer jon storage_box b on p.stor_box_num = b.stor_box_num where p.prod_name = 'WIDGET';

Explanation Choice B is the only statement that properly defines an outer join meeting the criteria specified by the question. Choices A and C are easy targets to eliminate because they combine the ANSI/ISO outer join syntax with the traditional Oracle syntax—this is not permitted in the Oracle database, and Oracle will return an error if you attempt to do so. Choice D is incorrect because it specifies a full outer join of all rows in both tables that would otherwise not have been returned if an equijoin was executed. **(Topic 4.2)**

30. C. select e.ename, a.street_address, a.city, a.state, a.post_code from emp e right outer join addr a on e.empno = a.empno where a.state = 'TEXAS';

Explanation   Choice C is correct because the Oracle outer join operator is on the right side of the join comparison operation. This signifies that you must execute a right outer join using the ANSI/ISO syntax. Choice A is incorrect because the left or right keyword is missing from the statement. Choice B is incorrect because a left outer join will return records from EMP even where no corresponding record exists in ADDR. Choice D is incorrect because the traditional Oracle syntax for outer joins is incorrectly used in the same statement as the ANSI/ISO syntax. **(Topic 4.2)**

31.   A. Full outer join

Explanation   The output in this question clearly shows a situation where records from both PRODUCT and BOX are returned even when no corresponding record exists in either table. This is precisely the functionality provided by full outer joins. Choices B and C are incorrect because full outer joins return both the records from left and right outer joins. Finally, choice D is incorrect because an equijoin operation would not have returned the second or the third records listed in the output of the query. **(Topic 4.2)**

32.   D. `select region, prod_type, time, sum(profit) from profits group by cube (region, prod_type, time);`

Explanation   When you see a question indicating that the output of a query should produce a cross-tabulation of information, you should automatically know that the result requested is produced by the cube keyword. Choice A identifies a properly formed column clause containing a group function needed by the `group by` clause, but does not contain the needed cube keyword, so it is therefore incorrect. Choice B is incorrect because the column clause contains no group function. Choice C is incorrect for the same reason. **(Topic 5.2)**

33.   A. `select deptno, job, sum(sal) from emp group by job, deptno;`

Explanation   The statement in choice A is correct because it contains reference to a group function. The `group by` clause is correct even though the columns referenced are in a different order than they appear in the column clause of the query, which is acceptable so long as all non-group columns are listed before the group expression. Choice B is incorrect because the group expression is listed before the non-group expressions, which results in an error. Choice C is incorrect because no `group by` clause appears in the query, resulting in an error. Finally, choice D is incorrect for the same reason that choice B is incorrect—the group expression is listed to the left of a non-group expression, resulting in an error. **(Topic 5.2)**

34. D. sum(A.SAL)

Explanation When an order by clause is present, then Oracle lists output of the query according to the expression included in the order by clause. Otherwise, Oracle sorts the output by columns listed in the group by clause. Thus, choices A, B, and C are all incorrect. **(Topic 5.1)**

35. C. select region, prod_type, period, avg(profit) from profits group by region, prod_type, period having avg(profit) > 100000;

Explanation Choice C contains a well-formed column clause and group by clause, and uses the having clause to filter the results according to the criteria identified in the question. A careful read of choice D enables you to discard it, because the having clause in that choice filters results where average profits are less than $100,000, not greater than that amount. Choices A and B inappropriately attempt to use the where clause in order to filter unwanted data. **(Topic 5.4)**

36. C. select e.empno, e.ename from emp e where sal < (select sum(x.vouch_amt) from expense x where x.empno = e.empno);

Explanation To obtain the correct result, you will need to have Oracle calculate the total amount for all vouchers submitted by each employee listed in the EMP table, and only choice C correctly shows the correlated subquery required for the task. Choice A shows the sum of all vouchers in the EXPENSE table, an amount that will surely be greater than everyone's salary. Choice B is incorrect because it likely results in an error where a single-row subquery expected by the parent query returns more than one row. Choice D is incorrect because the exists operator is an inappropriate comparison between parent and subquery, given the need for a listing of employees whose expense vouchers total more than the employee's salary. **(Topic 6.4)**

37. B. select e.ename from emp e where exists (select x.empno from expense x where x.vouch_amt > 10000 and x.empno = e.empno);

Explanation The statement in choice B is correct because it properly uses the exists operator and forms the correlated subquery required to obtain the same result as the query shown in the question. Choice A is incorrect because the reference to the EXPENSE table in the parent query is out of scope. Choice C is incorrect for the same reason. Finally, the where clause forming a join and using the exists operation in choice D is redundant and therefore incorrect. **(Topic 6.2)**

38. A. A single-row subquery

Explanation   The way to determine what kind of subquery is shown in this question is to determine how much output is produced by the query. Because only one record in the EMP table contains the value 'MARTIN' for ENAME, this subquery returns only one row and is therefore a single-row subquery. Choice B is incorrect for this reason. Choice C is incorrect because a `from` clause subquery is the same as an inline view, and no subquery is shown in the `from` clause of the query in this question. Finally, choice D is incorrect because the subquery does not contain reference to multiple columns. **(Topic 6.3)**

39. A. `select sum(profit) from profits where region in` `(select region from regions where reg_head in` `('SMITHERS', 'FUJIMORI', 'LAKKARAJU')) and product =` `'TOYS';`

Explanation   To obtain the correct result, you need a multiple-row subquery listing the regions headed by the region heads identified in the question. You also want a filtering condition on the PRODUCT column so only toys are returned. Choice A gives you all these things. Choice B is incorrect because the subquery incorrectly includes filter conditions operating on the REGIONS table that are meant to operate on the PROFITS table. Choice C is incorrect because the equality comparison between the REGION column and the values returned from the subquery will result in an error because the single-row subquery the parent query expects will in fact return more than one row. Finally, choice D is incorrect for the same reason as choice B, and because of a missing parenthesis at the end of the query. **(Topic 6.1)**

40. C. `with`

Explanation   The `with` clause can be used to define a summary dataset to avoid redundancy in both the parent query and the subquery in Oracle. You would not use the `group by` clause for this purpose, eliminating choice A, nor would you use the `order by` clause for this purpose, eliminating choice B. Finally, you would not use the `having` clause for this purpose, eliminating choice D. **(Topic 6.1)**

41. B. `select nvl(e.deptno,99), e.ename, e.job, e.sal from` `emp e where e.sal = (select max(e2.sal) from emp e2` `where nvl(e.deptno,99) = nvl(e2.deptno, 99));`

Explanation   Even SQL experts should find this question challenging. You are asked to determine which of these statements will return 99 in the DEPTNO column where the DEPTNO column is currently NULL in the dataset shown in the question. The most obvious answer is to find the query where the column clause contains a `nvl( )` function on the DEPTNO column in the column clause. The problem is that all the choices contain references to the nvl ( ) function in the column clause. Thus, you have to look beyond that factor for other clues, and your best bet is to try to find reasons to eliminate wrong answers rather than clues to find the right answer. Your first clue comes in choice A, where the parent query where clause tips you off that the multiple-column subquery is expected by the parent query but not provided, making that choice incorrect. Second, you should notice that in choice C, the group expression in the subquery necessitates a group by clause that is not provided in the subquery, making that choice incorrect as well. If you noticed these important clues, you've narrowed down your odds of guessing the right answer to 50/50. If you recall that 99 is not a value actually stored in the DEPTNO column and that group by clauses ignore NULL values by default, you should be able to eliminate choice D therefore leaving you with the correct answer, choice B. **(Topic 6.1)**

> **42.** C. select prod_name, profit from (select prod_name, sum(profit) from profits group by prod_name order by sum(profit) desc) where rownum <=5;

Explanation   Choice C correctly indicates the query containing an inline view that will produce a listing of the five best-selling products in the company's history. Choice A is incorrect because profits are not grouped by product name over the entire company's history in the inline view, but rather broken out by quarter, which will produce the wrong result. Choice B is incorrect because you do not need to join the contents of the PROFITS table with the inline view. Moreover, choice B does nothing to filter out the five top-selling products in company history. Finally, the inline view in choice D does not contain a group by clause, which will result in an error due to the presence of the group function in the inline view's column clause, making that choice incorrect. **(Topic 6.3)**

> **43.** C. accept v_period prompt 'Enter the time period => 'select profit from profits where prod_type = 'TOYS' and time_period = '&v_period';

Explanation   Because the users have complained about readability and interaction according to the text of the question, you should base your answer on the choice that provides interactive definition of the time period and does so with a readable prompt. Choice C provides for these conditions. Choice D is close but does not provide for a readable prompt, so that choice is incorrect. Choice A is incorrect because the prompt Oracle will use does not address the readability requirement. Choice B is incorrect because the use of the define command limits interaction between SQL*Plus and the user. **(Topic 7.1)**

44. A. Variable `v_hiredate` must be changed to accept DATE information.

Explanation When variables are defined using the `accept` command in SQL*Plus, Oracle implicitly defines the datatype as CHAR. You must therefore specify the datatype when the variable is meant to accept non-CHAR information. Thus, choice A is the answer. Choice B is incorrect because the `trunc( )` function is acceptable in this query. Choice C is incorrect because you needn't eliminate the `prompt` clause. Finally, the script does not work fine as is, so choice D is incorrect. **(Topic 7.1)**

45. D. `create table cats-over-5-lbs as select c_name, c_weight from cats where c_weight > 5;`

Explanation You cannot include hyphens or dashes as part of the name of any table in Oracle, thus making choice D the correct answer. Choice A is incorrect because that choice identifies a proper `create table` command. Choice B is incorrect because that choice identifies a proper `create table as select` command. Choice C is incorrect because that choice identifies a proper `create global temporary table` command. **(Topic 9.2)**

46. C. Change the column names in the object being created.

Explanation Changing the column names in a table when an object with that table's name already exists in Oracle will not prevent the same error from happening again. Instead, you should create the table as a different user, drop the existing object with the same name, or rename the existing object. Thus, choice C is correct, and all other choices are incorrect. **(Topic 9.4)**

47. B. 871039453.1

Explanation Because the column was defined as datatype NUMBER(10,2), Oracle only permits numbers with up to eight places to the left of the decimal point to be placed into the column on this table. Thus, choice B is correct because that number has nine digits to the left of the decimal point. Choices C and D both identify proper numbers for this column. The number in choice A can also be stored in this column, but Oracle implicitly rounds off to the hundredths place to the right of the decimal point. **(Topic 9.3)**

48. B. 7

Explanation The `vsize( )` function returns a value of 7 for all columns of DATE datatype, no matter what the actual date appears to be. The information about KING's specific value for HIREDATE is only there to distract you. **(Topic 3.3)**

49. C. 40

Explanation The vsize( ) function always returns a value equivalent to the size of the CHAR column regardless of the actual value stored in that column. This is because Oracle pads whatever value you specify for storage in a CHAR column with blanks up to the width of the CHAR column. Had the column been defined as a VARCHAR2 column, choice A would have been correct. All other choices should be easy to eliminate once you understand Oracle datatypes. **(Topic 3.3)**

50. B. A default clause on the JOB_WAGE column defined when the table was created specified the value when the row was inserted.

Explanation The purpose of a default clause is to specify a default value for a column whenever users don't explicitly identify the value to populate in the column for a row being added to the table. Choice A is incorrect because an insert statement will not populate column values for existing rows in the table. Choice C is incorrect because you cannot hide values in a values clause of an insert statement. Finally, choice D is incorrect because changing the JOB_WAGE column via a later update statement isn't the only way this value could have been added to the table. **(Topic 9.3)**

51. D. Copy column records from the temporary location back to the main table.

Explanation If you review all choices carefully before selecting an answer, you should notice that several steps of the process required to perform the task identified by the question are listed as choices. Its up to you to put those steps in order. The correct order is: C, A, B, D. The question then states that you have just completed the step identified in choice B. Thus, the only step left to perform is the one identified in choice D, the correct answer. **(Topic 9.4)**

52. A. Immediately following statement execution

Explanation Oracle drops the PROFIT column as soon as the statement identified in the answer choice is executed. Choices B and C identify the other way to remove columns from Oracle using the set unused column and drop unused columns clauses. However, we didn't see that option being used in the question, so those choices are incorrect. Finally, you cannot remove a column using the alter table modify command. **(Topic 9.4)**

53. D. Nothing; the statement is executed automatically.

Explanation Once you've issued the appropriate alter table statement to increase the size of a column, you are done with this task. Oracle will then automatically increase the size of the column. Choices A, B, and C identify steps appropriate for either decreasing the size of a column or altering that column's datatype, and therefore are incorrect. **(Topic 9.4)**

54. B. `alter table sales modify product_type varchar2(10);`

Explanation To increase the size of a column, you use the `alter table modify` command shown in choice B. Choice A is incorrect because that choice adds an extra column to the table unnecessarily. Choices C and D are incorrect because they identify steps in a process for removing a column from the table, which is not required by the question. **(Topic 9.4)**

55. B. The child column

Explanation Dropping a parent table will not remove the common column from the child table, making choice B the correct answer. Choice A is incorrect because associated constraints on the parent table are most certainly removed when you drop the parent table. Triggers and indexes on the parent table are dropped when the parent table is dropped as well, making choices C and D incorrect. **(Topic 9.5)**

56. D. `create table profits (product_name varchar2(10) primary key, sale_period varchar2(10) primary key, profit number);`

Explanation The primary key clause used for defining a primary key as a column constraint for both the PRODUCT_NAME and SALE_PERIOD columns as shown in choice D is not permitted in the Oracle database. Other choices show composite primary keys defined properly. **(Topic 10.2)**

57. B. `alter table sales add constraint ck_sales_01 check (product_type in (select product_type from valid_products));`

Explanation You cannot use subqueries when defining valid values for check constraints—all values must be static. Choices A, C, and D all identify check constraints defined with static valid values and are permitted within the Oracle database. **(Topic 10.2)**

58. B. Existing entries are checked for violations, PK_PRICES_01 is not enabled, and Oracle does not check subsequent entries for violations immediately.

Explanation Oracle ignores the `novalidate` keyword because the constraint wasn't defined as deferrable in the question. Oracle thus checks existing entries for violations, and finds violations. PK_PRICES_01 will not be enabled, and Oracle does not check for future violations because the constraint isn't enabled. Choices A, C, and D are all incorrect for this reason. **(Topic 10.2)**

59. C. Foreign key constraint

Explanation Foreign key constraints in child tables create dependencies that later make it difficult to disable primary key constraints on parent tables. Choice A is incorrect because check constraints cannot create relationships between tables. Choice B is incorrect for the same reason. Finally, unique constraints also cannot create relationships between tables and is incorrect as well. **(Topic 10.1)**

60. A. `alter table sales modify (unit_prices null);`

Explanation The syntax for removing a not NULL constraint from a table is shown correctly in choice A. Choice B is incorrect because it defines a not NULL constraint. Choices C and D identify improper syntax for defining nullabililty in Oracle columns. **(Topic 10.2)**

Index

About the BeachFrontQuizzer™ CD-ROM

BeachFrontQuizzer provides interactive certification exams to help you prepare for certification. With the enclosed CD, you can test your knowledge of the topics covered in this book with more than 300 multiple choice questions.

Installation

To install BeachFrontQuizzer:

1. **Insert the CD-ROM in your CD-ROM drive.**

2. **Follow the Setup steps in the displayed Installation Wizard. (When the Setup is finished, you may immediately begin using BeachFrontQuizzer.)**

3. **To begin using BeachFrontQuizzer, enter the 12-digit license key number of the exam you want to take:**

    Building Internet Applications I   380429273697

    Building Internet Applications II   389528292736

Study Sessions

BeachFrontQuizzer tests your knowledge as you learn about new subjects through interactive quiz sessions. Study Session Questions are selected from a single database for each session, dependent on the subcategory selected and the number of times each question has been previously answered correctly. In this way, questions you have answered correctly are not repeated until you have answered all the new questions. Questions that you have missed previously will reappear in later sessions and keep coming back to haunt you until you get the question correct. In addition, you can track your progress by displaying the number of questions you have answered with the Historical Analysis option. You can reset the progress tracking by clicking on the Clear History button. Each time a question is presented the answers are randomized so you will memorize a pattern or letter that goes with the question. You will start to memorize the correct answer that goes with the question concept.

Practice Exams

For advanced users, BeachFrontQuizzer also provides Simulated and Adaptive certification exams. Questions are chosen at random from the database. The Simulated Exam presents a specific number of questions directly related to the real exam. After you finish the exam, BeachFrontQuizzer displays your score and the passing score required for the test. You may display the exam results of this specific exam from this menu. You may review each question and display the correct answer.

NOTE
For further details of the feature functionality of this BeachFrontQuizzer software, consult the online instructions by choosing Contents from the BeachFrontQuizzer Help menu.

Technical Support

If you experience technical difficulties please call (888) 992-3131. Outside the U.S. call (281) 992-3131. Or, you may e-mail **bfquiz@swbell.net**.